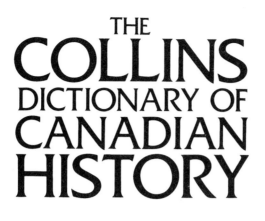

THE
COLLINS
DICTIONARY OF
CANADIAN
HISTORY

THE
COLLINS
DICTIONARY OF
CANADIAN
HISTORY

1867 to the Present

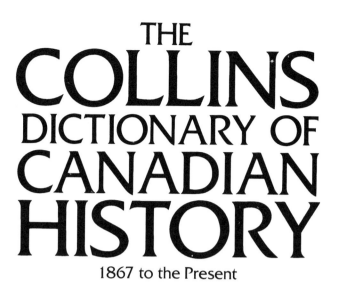

David J. Bercuson
AND
J.L. Granatstein

COLLINS
TORONTO

First published 1988
by Collins Publishers
100 Lesmill Road, Don Mills, Ontario

Every effort has been made to search for and acquire the necessary permission to reproduce the photographs contained in this book. We would welcome notice of any omission or error.

Production Editor: Kathryn Schroeder
Designer: Scott Richardson
Appendices: Pages Design

Canadian Cataloguing in Publication Data

Granatstein, J. L., 1939-
  The Collins guide to Canadian history

ISBN 0-00-217758-7

1. Canada – Dictionaries and encyclopedias.
2. Canada – History – Dictionaries.
I. Bercuson, David Jay, 1945-   . II. Title.

FC23.G73 1988
971'.003
C88-094493-5
F1006.G73 1988

Printed and bound in Canada

Table of Contents

For Elaine
and
Barrie

Preface

The Collins Dictionary of Canadian History: From 1867 to the Present is a ready reference book. It aims to provide readers, journalists, students, and browsers with an easy-to-use and easy-to-read reliable guide to the people, institutions, and events that shaped this country in the years since Confederation. Within the limitations of one volume, we have tried to provide sufficient detail to define key terms and to answer the most commonly asked queries about our collective past. A simplified time-line chart begins the dictionary and allows events in politics, for example, to be seen in context with happenings in sport and culture. Photographs of important figures and events are found throughout. Charts in the appendix lay out sometimes complicated statistical data as clearly as possible, and five maps give the evolving shape of the country.

Quite deliberately, we have kept the alphabet soup of abbreviations to a minimum, feeling strongly that the savings in space that abbreviations provide are more than outweighed by the frustration readers feel in trying to determine what, for example, something such as UNMOGIP might mean. (That abbreviation stands for the United Nations Military Observer Group in India and Pakistan, a PEACEKEEPING operation in which Canada participated.) In addition, we have used small capitals, as in peacekeeping above, to indicate cross-references. Thus if, in the entry on the Canadian army, PEACEKEEPING appears in capitals, a reader interested in the subject will know that more information can be found under that entry.

We have tried to get things right in fact and in interpretation, but we are conscious of the limitations that brevity imposes (to say nothing of disputes over interpretation). Brevity has also obliged us to leave out hundreds of entries that might have been included if space were unlimited. And readers will undoubtedly observe that in some areas our coverage is more complete than in others. Inevitably, and despite every effort to prevent this, our own research interests kept intruding.

Although we are both political historians in the broad sense, one of us is fascinated by labour unions and strikes, especially in the West; the other is attracted to art and wartime events. If our own interests have unduly shaped the book, so be it! Our idiosyncracies should not, however, interfere with the reader's ability to find what is sought and to be able to use this book as a guide to what is most important in post-Confederation Canadian history.

DJB/JLG

A number of people helped us to put this book together. In Toronto, Greg Johnson did a large part of the research and drafting, while Penny Bryden helped greatly at the end; in Calgary, Darlene Zounick and then Donna Zwicker helped generate initial subject lists and early drafts.

We are most indebted to John Saywell of York University, Norman Hillmer of the Directorate of History, National Defence Headquarters, and Brian Henderson of Copp Clark Publishing Co. for assistance in providing photographs. And, as so often in the past, we have thrown ourselves on the mercy of editors. Rosemary Shipton and Mary McDougall Maude, two uncommonly fine editors, tried manfully (and that is not a sexist term) to save us from ourselves.

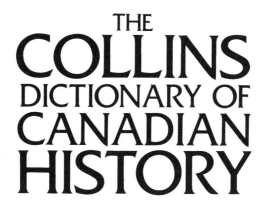

THE
COLLINS
DICTIONARY OF
CANADIAN
HISTORY

Time Line: 1867 - 1902

	Major Political Events	Major Social, Economic, & Industrial Events
	1867 Confederation Macdonald becomes prime minister	
	1869 Red River Rebellion	**1869** T. Eaton opens first store
1870	**1870** Manitoba enters Confederation	
	1871 British Columbia enters Confederation Treaty # 1 Treaty of Washington	**1872** Trade Unions Act Dominion Lands Act
	1873 Prince Edward Island enters Confederation Pacific Scandal Macdonald resigns, succeeded by Mackenzie	
	1874 Mackenzie retains prime ministership Secret ballot	
	1875 Supreme Court of Canada established	**1876** Intercolonial Railway competed
	1877 Treaty # 7	
1880	**1878** Macdonald elected National Policy introduced	**1880** CPR contract signed
	1882 Macdonald re-elected	
	1883 First Canadian high commissioner to Britain Founding of Toronto Women's Suffrage Assn.	**1885** CPR completed
	1885 North-West Rebellion Louis Riel hanged	**1886** Ontario introduces workers' compensation
	1887 Macdonald re-elected	**1887** Royal Commission on the Relations of Capital and Labour
1890	**1890** Manitoba Schools Question	
	1891 Macdonald re-elected Macdonald dies, succeeded by Abbott	**1891** First harvest excursion
		1894 Labour day established
	1896 Laurier becomes prime minister	**1896** Sifton immigration begins
	1899 Alaska boundary dispute Canadian troops to Boer War	**1897** Imperial preferences Crow's Nest Pass Agreement
		1898 Klondike gold rush National prohibition referendum
1900	**1900** Laurier re-elected	**1900** First caisse populaire opens
		1901 Territorial Grain Growers' Association
		1902 International Nickel Company (INCO) formed Berlin convention of the Trades and Labour Congress

Scientific and Technical Events

Artistic and Cultural Events

Major Sporting Events

1867
H. J. Morgan produces first scholarly guide to Canadian writers

1867
Canadians win world rowing championship in Paris

1868
Toronto YMCA established
Royal Canadian Yacht Club
Montreal Football Club

1869
Atlantic Cable

1868
Canada First movement

1871
National Meteorological Service established

1872
Public Archives of Canada opened

1873
Royal Montreal Golf Club

1874
McGill vs Harvard in first football game

1876
First long distance telephone call in Canada

1876
Ontario School of Art

1877
Electric lights

1877
W. Kirby publishes *The Golden Dog*

1878
Hamilton telephone exchange opens

1878
Edward Hanlan wins U.S. singles rowing championship

1879
Sir Sandford Fleming proposes time zones

1880
Calixa Lavalée composes O' Canada
Charles G. D. Roberts publishes *Orion*

1880
Hanlan wins world singles rowing championship

1881
Royal Society of Canada formed

1882
Canadian Rugby Union

1883
Standard time
First Canadian woman medical school graduate

1885
CPR telegraph completed from Montreal to Vancouver
Montreal smallpox epidemic

1887
Saturday Night Magazine founded

1890
George Dixon wins world bantam boxing championship
Louis Rubenstein wins world figure skating championship

1887
First electric streetcar in Canada

1888
Archibald Lampman publishes *Among the Millet*

1891
J. A. Naismith invents basketball

1888
First hydroelectricity generation in Canada

1889
W.W. Campbell publishes *Lake Lyrics and Other Poems*

1892
Osgoode Hall wins first Canadian football championship

1896
First motion pictures in Canada

1890
Sara Jeannette Duncan publishes *A Social Departure*

1893
Stanley Cup awarded for first time

1897
First gasoline car built in Canada

1893
Bliss Carman publishes *Low Tide on Grand Pré*

1896
First Canadian skiing championships

1898
First Canadian woman dentistry graduate

1897
J. J. McCulloch wins world speedskating championship

1901
Marconi receives first transatlantic wireless signal atop Signal Hill in Newfoundland

1899
H. Gibson wins world cycling championship

1902
Canada's first symphony orchestra

Time Line: 1903 - 1930

Major Political Events	Major Social, Economic, & Industrial Events
	1903 Laurier announces building of Grand Trunk Pacific and National Transcontinental Railway
1904 Laurier re-elected	
1905 Alberta and Saskatchewan enter Confederation	**1906** Ontario Hydro established
1908 Laurier re-elected	**1907** Industrial Disputes Investigation Act passed
1909 International Joint Commission established Founding of the Department of External Affairs	**1910** Combines Investigation Act passed
1910 Naval Service Act	**1911** Reciprocity defeated Canadian Northern Railway completed from Montreal to the west coast
1911 Borden becomes prime minister	
1913 Ontario issues Regulation 17	**1913** Nanaimo coal strike
1914 Canada enters World War I	**1914** Oil discovered in Turner Valley Hillcrest mine explosion, 189 killed
	1915 Canada's first war loan
1917 Conscription Borden forms Union Government Borden re-elected	**1917** Income tax imposed Canadian Northern Railway nationalized Halifax explosion
1918 World War I ends Universal female suffrage in federal elections	**1918** Farmers' platform
1919 Canada signs Versailles Treaty Canada sends troops to Siberia	**1919** Winnipeg General Strike United Farmers government in Ontario
1920 Borden resigns, succeeded by Meighen	**1920** Canadian Catholic Confederation of Labour formed
1921 King becomes prime minister	**1921** United Farmers government in Alberta
	1922 Cape Breton coal strikes
1923 Halibut Treaty	**1923** Collapse of the Home Bank of Canada
1925 King re-elected	**1925** Cape Breton coal strikes *Toronto Electric Commissioners v. Snider* decided
1926 King-Byng Affair King re-elected Balfour Declaration	**1927** Old Age Pensions established
1927 First British high commissioner to Canada	**1928** Irving Oil formed
	1929 Great Depression begins
1930 Bennett becomes prime minister Cairine Wilson first woman appointed to the Senate	**1930** Ottawa hands natural resources to Prairie provinces

1910

1920

1930

Scientific and Technical Events

Artistic and Cultural Events

Major Sporting Efvents

1903
Canada wins Strathcona Cup in curling

1904
Canada's first Olympic gold medals at the St Louis Olympics

1907
Transatlantic wireless service begins
Marquis wheat

1907
Robert Service publishes *Songs of a Sourdough*

1907
Tom Longboat wins Boston Marathon

1908
First service station in Canada

1908
Lucy Maud Montgomery publishes *Anne of Green Gables*

1909
J.A.D. McCurdy pilots the *Silver Dart* to the first powered flight in the British Empire

1909
Grey Cup donated by Governor General Lord Grey

1910
Stephen Leacock publishes *Literary Lapses*

1912
First automobile drive across Canada

1911
Pauline Johnson publishes *Legends of Vancouver*

1913
Alys Bryant first woman to make a solo flight in Canada

1912
Leacock publishes *Sunshine Sketches of a Little Town*

1914
International Ice Patrol

1916
National Research Council formed

1915
John McCrae writes *In Flanders Fields*

1917
Tom Thomson drowns

1917
National Hockey League formed

1918
Daylight Saving Time

1919
First commercial radio station in Canada

1920
First exhibition of the Group of Seven
Canadian Forum magazine

1920
Canada wins hockey championship at first winter Olympics

1922
Insulin discovered by F.G. Banting and C. H. Best
W.R. Turnbull invents variable pitch propeller
Joseph-Armand Bombardier invents the snowmobile

1921
Canadian Authors Association

1923
Banting and J.J.R. Macleod win Nobel Prize

1923
Foster Hewitt begins to broadcast "Hockey Night in Canada"

1925
Lela Brooks breaks six world speedskating records

1927
E.S. Rogers invents Batteryless Radio
Transatlantic telephone service

1927
Mazo de la Roche publishes *Jalna*

1928
Morley Callaghan publishes *Strange Fugitive*

1928
Canada wins three gold medals at Amsterdam summer Olympics

1930
Uranium discovered at Great Bear Lake

1930
H. A. Innis publishes *The Fur Trade in Canada*

Time Line: 1931 - 1957

Major Political Events	Major Social, Economic, & Industrial Events
1931 Statute of Westminster	
1932 Formation of the CCF	**1932** Imperial Economic Conference held
1934 Bank of Canada created Commission of Government in Newfoundland	Relief camps established
1935 Bennett New Deal King re-elected Aberhart elected in Alberta	**1935** On-to-Ottawa trek Canadian Wheat Board formed Canada-U.S. trade agreement signed
1936 Duplessis elected in Quebec	
1937 Royal Commission on Dominion-Provincial Relations	**1937** Trans-Canada Airlines formed Oshawa strike
1939 Canada enters World War II	**1938** Canada-U.S. trade agreement signed

1940

1940 Ogdensburg Agreement King re-elected	**1940** Formation of Canadian Congress of Labour
1941 Hyde Park Declaration	**1941** Unemployment insurance begins Wage and price freeze imposed
1942 Conscription plebiscite	**1944** P.C. 1003
1944 CCF elected in Saskatchewan Conscription crisis	
1945 World War II ends King re-elected Gouzenko Affair	**1945** Federal-provincial economic conference Family allowances begin
1947 Canadian Citizenship Act becomes law	**1946** Saskatchewan hospital insurance Rand Formula
1948 King resigns, succeeded by St Laurent	**1947** End to wartime rationing Oil discovered at Leduc Dollar crisis
1949 Newfoundland joins Confederation St Laurent retains prime ministership North Atlantic Treaty signed by Canada	**1948** Industrial Relations and Disputes Investigation Act passed Asbestos strike begins

1950

1950 Canada send troops to Korean War	**1950** Red River flood National rail strike
1951 Canada sends NATO contingent to Europe	
1952 Massey appointed first Canadian governor-general	**1952** Atomic Energy of Canada Ltd. established
1953 Korean War ends St Laurent re-elected	
1956 Pipeline Debate Canada sends troops to UNEF	**1956** Formation of Canadian Labour Congress
1957 Diefenbaker becomes prime minister Pearson wins Nobel Peace Prize Canada signs NORAD agreement	**1957** Murdochville strike

Scientific and Technical Events

1932
Trans-Canada Telephone System

1935
Norseman bush plane

1937
Transtlantic air service

1938
Electron microscope invented at University of Toronto

1945
First nuclear reactor in Canada goes active

1946
First drive-in movie in Canada

1949
First flight c-102 Avro Jetliner
First flight CF-100 Avro fighter

1951
Cobalt bomb

1952
Television transmission begins in Canada

1957
DEW line operational

Artistic and Cultural Events

1932
Canadian Radio Broadcasting Commission
Dominion Drama Festival

1936
Canadian Broadcasting Corporation

1937
"The Happy Gang" goes on the air
Donald Creighton publishes *The Commercial Empire of the St. Lawrence*

1938
Royal Winnipeg Ballet formed

1939
National Film Board organized

1941
Hugh MacLennan publishes *Barometer Rising*

1942
Earle Birney publishes *David and Other Poems*
Bruce Hutchison publishes *The Unknown Country*

1945
MacLennan publishes *Two Solitudes*
Irving Layton publishes *Here and Now*

1947
Northrop Frye publishes *Fearful Symmetry*
W. O. Mitchell publishes *Who Has Seen the Wind?*
Gabrielle Roy publishes *The Tin Flute*

1948
"Spring Thaw" begins its run
Paul-Émile Borduas publishes *Refus global*

1949
Massey Royal Commission established

1950
Cité Libre established

1951
Massey commission reports
Marshall McLuhan publishes *The Mechanical Bride*

1952
Stratford Festival opens

1953
National Library opens

1956
Glenn Gould tours the U.S.S.R.
Canada Council established

Major Sporting Events

1931
First British Empire Games
Maple Leaf Gardens opens

1944
Maurice Richard scores fifty goals in fifty games

1948
Barbara Ann Scott wins gold medal in figure skating at winter Olympics

1954
Marilyn Bell swims Lake Ontario

1955
Richard hockey riot in Montreal

1956
Canada wins two gold medals at summer Olympics

Time Line: 1958 - 1985

	Major Political Events	Major Social, Economic, & Industrial Events
	1958 Diefenbaker re-elected	**1958** Springhill mine explosion, 74 killed
1960	**1959** St Lawrence Seaway opened **1960** Quiet Revolution begins	**1959** National hospital insurance passed CLC suspends Seafarers' International Union Avro Arrow cancelled **1961** First wheat sales to China Coyne Affair Formation of the Canadian Imperial Bank of Commerce
	1962 Diefenbaker re-elected **1963** Bomarc missile crisis Pearson becomes prime minister **1964** Flag Debate **1965** Pearson re-elected **1967** Centennial Expo 67 **1968** Armed forces unification Pearson resigns, succeeded by Trudeau Trudeau wins election Formation of the Parti Québécois **1969** Official Languages Act	**1962** Canadian dollar pegged at 92.5 cents U.S. **1963** Private power companies nationalized in Quebec **1964** Canada Pension Plan passed **1965** Auto Pact signed **1966** Churchill Falls agreement **1968** Medicare begins
1970	**1970** October (FLQ) Crisis **1971** Canada recognizes Communist China **1972** Trudeau re-elected	**1971** James Bay project announced **1972** Quebec public service strike Air traffic controllers' strike **1973** Petro-Canada formed **1975** Foreign Investment Review Agency set up
	1976 Parti Québécois forms government in Quebec **1977** Quebec introduces Bill 101 **1979** Clark becomes prime minister	**1976** Canadian Labour Congress "Day of Protest" Drilling begins in Beaufort Sea **1977** Via Rail established **1980** National Energy Program
1980	**1980** Trudeau elected Quebec referendum on sovereignty-association **1982** Constitution Act proclaimed **1984** Trudeau resigns, succeeded by Turner Mulroney becomes prime minister	**1981** Petro-Canada buys Petro Fina **1982** Worst recession since 1930s **1985** Free trade talks with U.S. sought

Scientific and Technical Events

1958
First flight CF-105 Avro Arrow
Trans-Canada microwave
  system
1959
Bombardier invents the Ski-Doo

1966
Colour television transmission
  begins in Canada
Montreal subway completed
1968
First heart transplant in Canada

1970
Metrification announced
First liver transplant in Canada
1971
Gerhard Herzberg wins Nobel
  Prize
1972
Anik A-1
First Arctic oil discovery in
  Canada

1979
Mississauga train derailment

1980
L'Anse aux Meadows becomes
  world UNESCO site

1984
First Canadian in space

Artistic and Cultural Events

1959
Hugh MacLennan publishes
  *The Watch That Ends the
  Night*
Mordecai Richler publishes *The
  Apprenticeship of Duddy
  Kravitz*
1960
Jean-Paul Desbiens publishes
  Les Insolences de Frère Untel
1962
Shaw Festival

1965
Fowler Report on Broadcasting
John Porter publishes *The
  Vertical Mosaic*

1971
Banff Festival of the Arts

1972
National Ballet of Canada tours
  Europe
Margaret Atwood publishes
  Survival
1973
Karen Kain, Frank Augustyn win
  first prize at International
  Ballet Competition in U.S.S.R.
1975
Ottawa ends tax concessions for
  Time, Reader's Digest
1976
*The Man Who Skied Down
  Everest* wins Academy Award

1982
Glenn Gould dies

Major Sporting Events

1959
Harry Jerome breaks world
  record for 100 metre dash
1960
Maurice Richard retires
5BX Exercise Plan published
1961
Hockey Hall of Fame opened
1964
Canada wins one gold medal at
  winter Olympics
Canada wins one gold medal at
  summer Olympics
1967
First Canadian Winter Games
Last Stanley Cup of six-team NHL
Winnipeg hosts Pan-American
  Games
1968
Nancy Greene wins gold medal
  at winter Olympics
Canadian equestrians win gold
  medal at summer Olympics
Al Balding and George Knudson
  win world cup of golf
1969
Montreal Expos play first Nat-
  ional League baseball game
First Canada Summer Games
1972
Chinese ping-pong team tours
  Canada
Canada wins first Canada-Soviet
  Hockey series
1976
Montreal hosts summer Olympics
Canada wins first Canada Cup
  hockey series
1977
Toronto Blue Jays play first Amer-
  ican League baseball game
1980
Canada wins silver and bronze
  medals at winter Olympics
Terry Fox attempts cross-
  Canada "Marathon of Hope"
1981
Wayne Gretzky scores fifty goals
  in thirty-nine games
1982
Steve Podborski wins World Cup
  in downhill skiing
Canadian team scales Mt Everest
1983
Edmonton hosts World
  University Games
1984
Gaetan Boucher wins two gold,
  one bronze medal at winter
  Olympics, Brian Orser wins
  silver
Canada wins forty four medals
  at summer Olympics
1987
Ben Johnson breaks world
  record for 100 metre dash
1988
Canada wins five medals at
  Calgary winter Olympics

Douglas C. Abbott

ABBOTT, DOUGLAS CHARLES (1899-1986), politician, jurist. Abbott studied law after serving in World War I. Elected to Parliament as a Liberal in 1940, he went into MACKENZIE KING'S cabinet in 1945 as defence minister, took the finance portfolio the next year, and handled it with great success for eight years. Appointed to the Supreme Court of Canada in 1954, he remained on the bench until 1973.

ABBOTT, SIR JOHN JOSEPH CALDWELL (1821-93), Canada's third prime minister. Abbott was educated at the Univ. of McGill College and called to the bar in 1847. An authority in commercial law, Abbott was dean of the Faculty of Law at McGill from 1855 to 1880 and counsel to the CANADIAN PACIFIC RAILWAY from 1880 to 1887. He signed the 1849 Annexation Manifesto but later disavowed it. As HUGH ALLEN's legal adviser, he was implicated in the 1873 PACIFIC SCANDAL. Abbott entered politics as a Conservative in 1857 as a member of the Legislative Assembly of the Province of Canada and after 1867, the House of Commons. Defeated in 1874, he was returned in 1881 (his 1880 win was declared void), was elevated to the Senate in 1887, where he became government leader (1887-93) and minister without portfolio (1887-91). He was also mayor of

Montreal in 1887-9. Abbott succeeded SIR JOHN A. MACDONALD as prime minister in 1891 and governed ineffectually until ill-health forced him to hand over to SIR JOHN THOMPSON in 1892.

ABERDEEN AND TEMAIR, ISHBEL MARIA GORDON, MARCHIONESS OF, NÉE MARJORIBANKS (1857-1939), wife of the governor general and feminist. She accompanied her husband, the Earl of Aberdeen, to Canada in 1893 when he became governor general, and played a key role in the establishment of the NATIONAL COUNCIL OF WOMEN (1893) and the Victorian Order of Nurses (1897). Lady Aberdeen had a strong social conscience and her attempts to lower social barriers did not always make her popular with the Ottawa establishment.

ABERDEEN AND TEMAIR, JOHN CAMPBELL GORDON, 1ST MARQUESS OF (1847-1934), governor general. He sat as a Liberal in the House of Lords and served as lord lieutenant of Ireland (1886) before becoming governor general of Canada in 1893. He and his wife LADY ABERDEEN were devoted social reformers. The death of Prime Minister SIR JOHN THOMPSON in 1894 and the subsequent revolt in SIR MACKENZIE BOWELL's cabinet over the MANITOBA SCHOOLS QUESTION in 1896, followed by SIR CHARLES TUPPER's problems in forming a government, made his term difficult. He left Canada in 1898 and from 1905 to 1915 was again lord lieutenant of Ireland.

William A. Aberhart

ABERHART, WILLIAM (1878-1943), premier of Alberta. Educated at Queen's Univ., he was a Brantford, Ont., school principal before moving to Alberta in 1910. In 1915 he became a Baptist minister and high school principal in Calgary. He began broadcasting his famed Radio Sunday School in 1925, opened the Calgary Prophetic Bible Institute in 1927, and in 1929 founded his own fundamentalist sect, the Bible Institute Baptist Church. Converted to SOCIAL CREDIT in 1932 after reading a book by Major C.H. DOUGLAS, "Bible Bill" Aberhart preached the doctrine on his radio show as a way to end the Depression. He created the Social Credit League, promised each citizen a monthly $25 "basic dividend" and in a landslide victory took 56 of 63 seats in the 1935 provincial election, to form the first Social Credit government in Alberta. Aberhart held power until his death and the party governed Alberta until 1971.

ABORIGINAL RIGHTS, *see* INDIAN TREATIES

ABORIGINAL TITLE, *see* INDIAN TREATIES

ACTION LIBÉRALE NATIONALE, Quebec reform party. The ALN was formed in 1934 by young Quebec Liberals led by PAUL GOUIN in an effort to defeat the provincial Liberal government of LOUIS-ALEXANDRE TASCHEREAU, accused of selling out Quebec's resources to English Canadian and American capitalists. Realizing it could not defeat the government alone, the ALN joined with MAURICE DUPLESSIS and his Conservative party to create the UNION NATIONALE which took 42 of the 90 seats in the 1935 election. In 1936 the UN won power with 76 seats. Once elected, Duplessis had no intention of adopting the ALN's program and many members left it; the party soon withered into obscurity.

ADAMS, THOMAS (1871-1940), city planner. Adams was one of the fathers of the Canadian planning movement. He was born near Edinburgh, Scotland, and became planning adviser to the Canadian COMMISSION OF CONSERVATION in 1914. He planned the town of Témiscaming, Que., and worked with the National Parks Division from 1921 to 1923. From 1923 to 1930 he was director of the regional plan for New York City.

ADASKIN FAMILY, musicians. Harry (born at Riga, Latvia, in 1904), Murray (born at Toronto 1906) and John (born at Toronto 1908) rank as Canada's first family of music. Harry, a violinist, toured widely and founded the Univ. of British Columbia's music program. Murray, also a performer, turned to composition and then headed the music program at the Univ. of Saskatchewan. John worked for the CANADIAN BROADCASTING CORP. and in 1961 became executive secretary of the Canadian Music Centre.

AERIAL EXPERIMENT ASSN, association founded by ALEXANDER GRAHAM BELL at Baddeck. N.S., in 1907 to conduct experiments with heavier-than-air powered aircraft. The association's first success was J.A.D. MCCURDY's 1909 flight of the SILVER DART.

AGRICULTURAL REHABILITATION AND DEVELOPMENT ACT, 1961, regional development scheme begun by the DIEFENBAKER government to ease rural poverty and to keep small farmers on the land. ARDA's programs ended in March 1979.

AID TO THE CIVIL POWER, legal process initiated by the Militia Act of 1904 by which municipal authorities called upon the federal government to provide troops to maintain order. The process normally involved the mayor of a municipality making formal application to a local magistrate to order out troops to keep the peace. This was done several times, such as during the WINNIPEG GENERAL STRIKE. In 1924 this authority was removed from the local magistrates and given to the attorneys general of the provinces.

AIR CANADA, crown corporation formed in 1937 as Trans Canada Airlines. It was a subsidiary of the CANADIAN NATIONAL RAILWAY and had a mandate to provide public air transportation to the nation. Controversy surrounded its formation because it was a government-backed rival to the privately owned CANADIAN AIRWAYS, based in Winnipeg. In late 1937 TCA initiated Montreal-to-Vancouver service and during World War II it began operating a regular transatlantic service. After the war, TCA purchased Canadian-built NORTH STAR aircraft and expanded its operations to Britain, the Caribbean, and the southern United States. In 1950 the airline was again embroiled in controversy when it refused to purchase the AVRO JETLINER. In the early 1960s TCA entered the jet-age with the purchase of Viscount and Vanguard aircraft and DC-8 jetliners. After 1965 when it became Air Canada, it expanded its international service while losing its monopoly on domestic transcontinental operations.

AIRD, SIR JOHN (1855-1938), banker, royal commissioner. Born at Longueuil, Canada East, he joined the Bank of Commerce in 1878 and became president in 1924. In 1928, MACKENZIE KING named him to chair a royal commission on broadcasting, and his report led to the establishment in 1932 of the Canadian Radio Broadcasting Commission, ancestor of the CANADIAN BROADCAST-

courtesy of The New Brunswick Museum/W2630

Lord Beaverbrook (William Maxwell Aitken)

AITKEN, WILLIAM MAXWELL, 1ST BARON BEAVERBROOK (1879-1964), financier, publisher. Born at Maple, Ont., but raised in New Brunswick, Aitken began his career selling bonds, established Royal Securities in 1903, and became a millionaire before age 30. He created the Steel Co. of Canada (STELCO) and Canada Cement before moving to London, Eng., in 1910. There he entered politics, winning a seat in the House of Commons, and established a chain of newspapers. During World War I he served as the Canadian government's eyewitness at the front and then as minister of information in the British government. Aitken was a personal friend and confidant of Winston Churchill and was minister of aircraft production in Churchill's cabinet during World War II.

ALABAMA AFFAIR, diplomatic dispute between the United States and Britain. The *Alabama*, a Confederate commerce raider, was built in a British shipyard during the American

Civil War. The ship was sunk in 1864, but after the war ended, the United States claimed compensation from Britain for the losses it caused. Some American congressmen wanted a large part of Canada to settle the claims! The U.S. claims were submitted to international arbitration in 1871. Canada remained intact, but the United States received $15.5 million in 1872.

ALASKA BOUNDARY DISPUTE, territorial dispute between Canada and the United States over the location of the boundary along the Alaskan Panhandle. The dispute was settled when a tribunal composed of three Americans, two Canadians, and one Englishman, Lord Alverstone, voted on the issue in 1903. Alverstone cast his vote with the Americans who largely won the day. The ensuing uproar in Canada again forced Canadians to consider whether their interests were served by an imperial foreign policy that sacrificed Canadian interests to a British desire for good relations with Washington.

ALASKA HIGHWAY, highway built in 1942-3 from Dawson Creek, B.C., to Fairbanks, Alaska. U.S. President Franklin Roosevelt and British Columbia Premier DUFF PATTULLO had long called for a land route to Alaska. The Japanese threat to the West Coast during World War II provided the impetus, and the road, sometimes called the Alcan Highway, was bulldozed over 2451 km of mountain and muskeg in only eight months by U.S. Army engineers at a cost of just under $150 million. It allowed the United States to reinforce its troops in Alaska by road. In 1946 the Canadian Army took over maintenance of the 1954 km portion of the route on Canadian territory, a responsibility it yielded in 1964 to the Department of Public Works.

ALBANI, DAME EMMA (1847-1930), soprano. Born at Chambly, Canada East, Marie-Louise-Cécile-Emma Lajeunesse was trained by her parents and became, as Mme Albani, the first Canadian to win international renown in opera. She attracted attention in Italy in 1869, and then had major triumphs in London, Paris, and New York. She retired from the opera stage in 1896 but continued touring until 1906.

ALBERTA ENERGY CO., a crown corporation established by the Alberta government in 1974.

It was given most of the government's holdings in energy. In 1975 it made a public share offering in which the people of Alberta were allowed to buy shares two weeks before everyone else. The Alberta government holds a substantial portion of AEC shares in 1988, but private shareholders have the majority. *See also* PETER LOUGHEED.

ALBERTA HERITAGE SAVINGS TRUST FUND, a provincial trust established by the government of Alberta in 1976. It was set up to oversee, invest, and spend surplus moneys earned from the windfall oil royalties that flowed into the Alberta treasury following rapid increases in world oil prices in the early 1970s. By 1985 the fund controlled approximately $15 billion. *See also* PETER LOUGHEED.

ALBERTA PRESS ACT REFERENCE, a 1938 legal case involving freedom of the press. The Alberta government of WILLIAM ABERHART, facing hostile press coverage, passed legislation forcing all newspapers in the province to print the government's side of a story whenever the government did not like a newspaper's criticism. The Supreme Court of Canada overturned the law on the grounds that the provincial government had exceeded its power.

ALBERTA PROSPERITY CERTIFICATES, $25 certificates issued by the Social Credit government of Premier WILLIAM ABERHART in 1937. The certificates were dubbed "funny money" by the press. The courts eventually declared them illegal on the grounds that only the federal government had the power to issue currency. *See also* ALBERTA SOCIAL CREDIT LEAGUE.

courtesy Glenbow Archives, Calgary/NA-2590-1

Members of the Alberta Social Credit League on parade, 1935

ALBERTA SOCIAL CREDIT LEAGUE, political party, founded by WILLIAM ABERHART in 1934.

Aberhart discovered the theory of SOCIAL CREDIT in 1932 and attempted to convince the government of Alberta to adopt it. The theory, developed by C.H. DOUGLAS in England, postulated that the economic woes of capitalism could be solved if the government paid its citizens a national dividend to replace the interest money that Douglas claimed the banks were removing from the economy. When the province refused, Aberhart founded the Social Credit League which won the 1935 provincial election and formed the government. At first Aberhart refused to implement Social Credit measures, but popular pressure and a backbenchers' revolt in 1937 forced him to act. He introduced a number of bills that would have given the province partial control over banking and the money supply in Alberta and issued ALBERTA PROSPERITY CERTIFICATES. All these measures were struck down by the courts as unconstitutional. Thereafter his government restricted itself to improving working and living conditions for the depression-wracked province. The Social Credit League governed Alberta under Aberhart, ERNEST MANNING, and HARRY STROM until 1971. It spawned a number of imitators, the most successful of which was the Social Credit Party of British Columbia which gained office under W.A.C. BENNETT in 1952.

ALCAN ALUMINIUM LTD, aluminum company. A Montreal-based multinational corporation, it was founded as Northern Aluminium Ltd in 1902 by the Aluminum Co. of America (ALCOA) and was renamed Aluminium Co. of Canada Ltd in 1925. In 1928 it severed its connections with ALCOA and in 1966 it became Alcan Aluminium Ltd. Alcan is 51 per cent Canadian owned.

ALEXANDER, HAROLD RUPERT LEOFRIC GEORGE, 1ST EARL ALEXANDER OF TUNIS (1891-1969), governor general. The last British governor general of Canada, Alexander was born into the Irish aristocracy and wanted to be an artist before his service in World War I intervened. A skilful officer, he became the youngest major-general in the British army by 1937 and during World War II led divisions in France, Burma, and Italy, where he commanded Canadian troops. Governor general 1946-52, he returned to Britain to be minister of defence in Churchill's government.

ALGOMA STEEL CORP. LTD, steel company founded by American-born entrepreneur FRANCIS CLERGUE in 1902. Algoma began manufacturing steel rails at Sault Ste Marie, Ont., and quickly developed a reputation for technological innovation and tough, anti-union labour policies. Under SIR JAMES DUNN after 1935, the company eventually developed into Canada's second largest steel company.

ALIEN LABOUR ACT, labour law passed by the federal Parliament in 1897 to prohibit the importation into Canada of foreign workers under contract. It was specifically intended to stop foreign strike-breakers from entering Canada and was prompted by a similar American law aimed at Canadians.

ALLAN, ANDREW EDWARD FAIRBAIRN (1907-74), radio producer. Born in Scotland, Andrew Allan emigrated to Canada when he was 17 and attended the Univ. of Toronto. He joined the CANADIAN BROADCASTING CORP. in 1942 and became its major drama producer, noted for giving Canadian writers and actors their chance. He retired in 1962, becoming the first artistic director of the Shaw Festival at Niagara-on-the-Lake, 1963-5.

ALLAN, SIR HUGH (1810-82), businessman. Allan came to Canada from Scotland in 1826 and entered the general merchandising trade. After ten years, he had raised enough capital to join his father's transatlantic shipping business — the ALLAN LINE — by opening a Montreal office. In 1856 Allan won the exclusive contract to carry mail between Canada and Britain. He then expanded into passenger services and railway investments. Allan was well connected with the Conservative Party in Montreal. In 1872, however, he was embroiled in what became known as the PACIFIC SCANDAL when he agreed to act as a conduit for American financiers attempting to bribe Conservative Prime Minister JOHN A. MACDONALD to obtain the contract to build a railway from central Canada to the Pacific coast. Allan had hoped to be president of that company.

ALLAN LINE, steamship company, established in Scotland by Alexander Allan in the early nineteenth century. The company was a major carrier of transatlantic mail and passengers. In 1909, it was sold to the CANADIAN PACIFIC STEAM-SHIP CO. after it experienced difficulties raising capital for the purchase of new ships. The operations of the two companies were gradually merged so that the Allan Line ceased to exist by 1931.

ALLARD, JEAN-VICTOR (1913–), soldier. Allard was educated in Montreal and Kitchener, Ont., and joined the militia during the Depression. He served overseas in WORLD WAR II with the Royal 22e Régiment, ending the war as a much decorated brigadier. He then was military attaché in the U.S.S.R., and commanded the Canadian brigade in the KOREAN WAR and a British division in NATO. He became commander of Mobile Command and in July 1966, as a general, became chief of the defence staff, responsible for implementing UNIFICATION of the armed forces in 1968. He was successful in making the armed forces more receptive to francophones.

ALL-CANADIAN CONGRESS OF LABOUR, a labour federation formed in 1926 under A.R. MOSHER, president of the CANADIAN BROTHERHOOD OF RAILWAY EMPLOYEES. The ACCL was initially composed of the CBRE and 14 other small unions opposed to the American-dominated TRADES AND LABOUR CONGRESS. At its peak it contained about 50,000 members. In 1940 the ACCL merged with Canadian affiliates of the Congress of Industrial Organizations to form the CANADIAN CONGRESS OF LABOUR.

ALLEN, RALPH (1913-66), editor. Born at Winnipeg and raised in Oxbow, Sask., Allen achieved distinction as a war correspondent. He became editor of MACLEAN's in 1946 and won great affection from his writers. In 1964 he went to the *Toronto Star*. He wrote several novels and a popular history of 20th-century Canada.

ALL RED ROUTE, proposed mail service linking the colonies and dominions of the British Empire by sea and rail. The idea was discussed as early as 1894 and was on the agenda of the 1907 Colonial Conference but, because of its cost, never became a reality.

ALOUETTE I, the first Canadian-designed and built artificial earth satellite. It was designed to conduct a variety of scientific experiments and was launched by an American rocket from Vandenberg Air Force Base in California on 29 Sept. 1962.

ALTHOUSE, JOHN GEORGE (1889-1956), educator. Educated at the Univ. of Toronto, Althouse was headmaster of the Univ. of Toronto Schools, dean at the Ontario College of Education, and director of education for Ontario from 1944. He implemented Premier GEORGE DREW's conservative educational policies.

AMALGAMATED MINE WORKERS OF NOVA SCOTIA, labour union formed in 1917 by the merger of the PROVINCIAL WORKMEN'S ASSN and the United Mine Workers of America in Nova Scotia. The AMWA was transformed into District 26, United Mine Workers of America, in 1919. *See also* J.B. MCLACHLAN.

AMES, SIR HERBERT BROWN (1863-1954), businessman, politician. Born in Montreal, Ames was a successful engineer and businessman who was interested in alleviating the living conditions of Montreal's poor. In 1897 he published *The City Below the Hill*, which described the Saint-Henri area. Ames advocated a philosophy of "philanthropy plus five percent," believing that he could convince the business community to invest in good quality housing for the working class and still turn a profit. He was elected to the Montreal city council in 1898 and won a seat in the House of Commons for the Conservative party in 1904.

courtesy National Archives of Canada/PA-2853

Canadian soldiers and POWs, Amiens, 1918

AMIENS, BATTLE OF, 1918, a battle 8-11 Aug. spearheaded by the CANADIAN CORPS. Described by the Germans as "the black day of the German army" and featuring a coordinated as-

sault with tanks, artillery, infantry, aircraft, and cavalry, the battle saw the four Canadian divisions destroy all or part of 15 enemy divisions. The Amiens battle initiated "the hundred days" that saw the Corps score some of its most famous victories and greatest gains.

ANDRÉ, BROTHER, NÉ ALFRED BESSETTE (1845-1937), religious leader. Born at St-Grégoire-d'Iberville, he was one of Quebec's most popular religious figures. Although illiterate, he had thousands of followers who believed in his powers as a faith healer, and who contributed to his efforts to build St. Joseph's Oratory in Montreal.

ANGERS, FÉLICITÉ (pseudonym LAURE CONAN) (1845-1924), writer. The first French Canadian female novelist, Laure Conan wrote of *famille, patrie, et foi*. Her most notable work was *Angéline de Montbrun*, but her corpus was substantial.

ANIK A-1, a Canadian-designed and built communications satellite. Anik A-1 was launched aboard a United States rocket from Cape Canaveral, Fla, on 9 Nov. 1972. Anik was the world's first geostationary domestic communications satellite. It was placed at a point high enough above the equator so as to be at the same spot over the earth at all times. It was the first of a series of Anik satellites owned and operated by TELESAT CANADA.

ANKA, PAUL ALBERT (1941–), singer, songwriter. Born at Ottawa, Anka became famous in the 1950s with his hit song "Diana," which he followed with other hits. He has continued through the 1960s, 1970s, and 1980s as an entertainer and successful composer of pop songs.

ANNAND, WILLIAM (1808-87), publisher, politician, premier of Nova Scotia. Annand founded the Halifax *Chronicle* in 1844 after he had begun his political career as a Reform member of the legislature. He could not decide whether or not to support CONFEDERATION, and saw leadership of the anti-confederates pass to JOSEPH HOWE. Nonetheless, he became premier in 1867, serving until 1875 when he became first Canada's and then Nova Scotia's agent-general in London.

ANTIGONISH MOVEMENT, a social movement originating in the late 1920s with the Department of Extension of St Francis Xavier Univ. in Antigonish, N.S. Its objective was to bring social and economic improvement to the Atlantic region through adult education and the establishment of cooperatives, particularly credit unions.

ANTI-INFLATION BOARD, *see* WAGE AND PRICE CONTROLS

ANTI-LOAFING LAW, a federal law passed under the authority of the WAR MEASURES ACT in 1918 to force able-bodied males between the ages of 16 and 60 to find work or join the army. Organized labour viewed the law as a blow against union members' freedom to change jobs or to go on strike and strongly opposed it. It lapsed with the expiration of the WMA.

APPLEBAUM, LOUIS (1918–), composer. Born at Toronto, Applebaum studied at the Toronto Conservatory, the Univ. of Toronto and in New York. He has composed for films, theatre, and radio, emphasized music at the Stratford Festival, and served as a consultant to arts agencies in Canada. He was executive director of the Ontario Arts Council, 1970-9, and served as co-chair of the Federal Cultural Policy Review Committee.

APPS, CHARLES JOSEPH SYLVANUS, "SYL" (1915–), hockey player. A gifted athlete, Apps also played football and represented Canada at the 1936 Berlin Olympics in pole vaulting. He is best remembered for his play with the Toronto Maple Leafs hockey team from 1936 to 1943 and from 1945 to 1948. He was later elected to the Ontario legislature.

AQUIN, HUBERT (1929-77), novelist, politician. Aquin studied at the Univ. de Montréal and in Paris and worked at Radio-Canada and the NATIONAL FILM BOARD. An INDÉPENDANTISTE, he was charged with terrorism and put in a mental asylum in 1964 where he wrote *Prochain épisode*, his first novel. In 1969 he refused a Governor General's Award, resigned from the RASSEMBLEMENT POUR L'INDÉPENDANCE NATIONALE, and published *L'Antiphonaire*. His last novel, *Neige noire*, appeared in 1974, three years before his death by his own hand.

ARCAND, ADRIEN (1900-67), Quebec fascist. Arcand led the Parti de l'unité nationale in the 1930s, an anti-Semitic party that was, for a time in the early 1930s, partly funded by the federal Conservatives. Interned 1940-5, he continued to promote anti-Semitism until his death.

courtesy Manitoba Archives

Sir Adams G. Archibald

ARCHIBALD, SIR ADAMS GEORGE (1814-92), politician. Archibald studied law and sat in the Nova Scotia Assembly from 1851 to 1867. He attended the CHARLOTTETOWN CONFERENCE and the QUEBEC CONFERENCE and became secretary of state in SIR JOHN A. MACDONALD's first government. In May 1870 he was named first lieutenant governor of Manitoba and the North-West Territories. He was lieutenant governor of Nova Scotia from 1873 to 1883.

ARCHIBALD, EDGAR SPINNEY (1885-1968), agricultural scientist. Born in Yarmouth, N.S., Archibald was director of the Experimental Farms Service in Ottawa from 1919 to 1951. Although he took no part in drafting the act which established the PRAIRIE FARM REHABILITATION ADMINISTRATION in 1935, he was an active PFRA supporter with a talent for translating the work of agricultural scientists into language prairie farmers could understand.

ARCTIC ARCHIPELAGO, islands north of the Canadian mainland. The islands were claimed by Britain by virtue of the explorations of Martin Frobisher in 1576-8, John Davis in 1585-7, and William Baffin in 1615-16 in search of the NORTHWEST PASSAGE. Although Canadian ownership of the archipelago (transferred from Britain in 1880) is recognized internationally, the waters of the archipelago are considered international by the United States.

ARGUE, HAZEN ROBERT (1921–), politician. Born at Moose Jaw, Sask., Argue graduated from the Univ. of Saskatchewan and was first elected to Parliament in 1945 for the CO-OPERATIVE COMMONWEALTH FEDERATION. He became house leader in 1958 and was elected leader of the party in 1960. After losing the leadership of the NEW DEMOCRATIC PARTY to T.C. DOUGLAS in 1961, Argue joined the Liberals. He was named to the Senate in 1966 and became a minister in the TRUDEAU government in 1980.

ARVIDA STRIKE, strike at Arvida, Que., by 4500 unorganized workers against the Aluminum Co. of Canada, 24-28 July 1941. Since the strike was considered a threat to an essential war industry, Ottawa sent troops to Arvida to keep the peace. The workers later won a slight wage increase through conciliation.

ASBESTOS STRIKE, a four-month strike at Asbestos, Que., in 1949 seen as pivotal in Quebec's social history. The strike began illegally in Feb. when 5000 asbestos workers walked off the job, paralysing Quebec's asbestos mines. The strike marked the beginning of a period of labour conflict in Quebec and embittered relations between the Roman Catholic Church (some of the bishops supported the workers) and the government of MAURICE DUPLESSIS. Intellectuals, such as PIERRE TRUDEAU, actively supported the strikers.

ASSELIN,   JOSEPH-FRANÇOIS-OLIVAR (1874-1937), journalist, nationalist. Never a typical Quebec nationalist, Asselin worked with HENRI BOURASSA in the pre-World War I politics of Quebec but surprised his political colleagues by joining the CANADIAN EXPEDITIONARY FORCE and serving overseas. He later served with the Canadian delegation to the Paris Peace Conference in 1919. After his return to Canada, Asselin worked in business and journalism.

ASSEMBLY OF FIRST NATIONS, founded in 1980 by a meeting of native chiefs, the assembly is the national political voice of treaty Indians across Canada. These are the status Indians who live on reserves and who have been recognized by the federal government as being entitled to all the benefits and rights conferred by the INDIAN TREATIES.

ASSINIBOIA, administrative district in the North-West Territories prior to 1905 encompassing the southern part of southeastern Alberta. It was created in 1882 and disappeared in 1905 when the provinces of Saskatchewan and Alberta were established.

ATHABASCA TAR SANDS, oil sands, located along the Athabasca River near Fort McMurray, Alta. The oil-bearing nature of the sands had been known to traders and geologists for 200 years, but a commercially practical method of extraction was not discovered until the 1950s. Great Canadian Oil Sands Ltd, a subsidiary of Sun Oil Co., first began extraction on a major scale in 1969. A larger company, Syncrude, followed later.

ATHLONE,   ALEXANDER   AUGUSTUS FREDERICK WILLIAM ALFRED GEORGE CAMBRIDGE, EARL OF (1874-1957), governor general of Canada, 1940-6. A member of the royal family, Athlone was commissioned in the Life Guards, fought in the BOER WAR, and married Princess Alice, a granddaughter of Queen Victoria, in 1904. He served as governor general of South Africa (1923-30).

ATKINSON, JOSEPH (1865-1946), newspaper publisher. "Holy Joe" Atkinson built the *Toronto Star*, which he took over in 1899, into a great newspaper. Strongly interested in social causes, Atkinson made the paper popular, aggressively pursued stories, and hired able reporters. He left much of his $8.7 million estate to a charitable foundation.

ATLANTIC, BATTLE OF THE, the war against German U-boats in WORLD WAR II. After the fall of France in June 1940, Britain's survival hinged on the fragile supply links from North America to the British Isles, supply lines challenged by the wolfpacks of Nazi submarines. In early 1941, in particular, the battle hung in the balance with Allied shipping suffering terrible losses. But the British success in cracking the German naval code, the arrival of continuous convoy protection, and gradual enhancement of air cover began to turn the tide. By 1943, the North Atlantic was an Allied lake. In this struggle, the fledgling ROYAL CANADIAN NAVY played a major role, providing half the escort force in the Newfoundland and Western Atlantic zones, while the ROYAL CANADIAN AIR FORCE gave much of the air cover. In all, 49 Axis submarines were sunk by Canadian action.

ATLANTIC CABLE, the first submarine cable to link North America to Great Britain by telegraph in 1858. The cable connected Trinity Bay, Nfld, with Valentia, Ireland, and was laid from the iron-hulled steamship *Great Eastern*. The first message was sent on 5 Aug. 1858 but, shortly after, the cable suddenly stopped functioning. It was successfully relaid in 1866.

ATLANTIC DEVELOPMENT BOARD, created in 1962 to advise the federal government on ways to accelerate growth in the Atlantic provinces. In 1969, it was replaced by the Atlantic Development Council.

ATOMIC ENERGY OF CANADA LTD, crown corporation incorporated under the Atomic Energy Control Act in 1952. It was given responsibility for operating the NATIONAL RESEARCH COUNCIL's nuclear research facilities at Chalk River, Ont. The company engages in a wide variety of atomic research activities and developed the COBALT BOMB and the CANDU (Canadian Deuterium Uranium) reactor used to produce electricity.

ATWOOD, MARGARET ELEANOR (1939–), writer. Atwood is one of Canada's best-known writers. *The Circle Game*, for which she received the 1966 Governor General's Award, established her reputation as a poet. This was followed by a number of works, including the popular novels *The Edible Woman* (1969), *Surfacing* (1972), *Life Before Man* (1979), and *The Handmaid's Tale* (1985). *Survival* (1972), her most important nationalist work, is a guide to Canadian literature, arguing that survival is the distinctive theme of Canadian writers.

AUSTERITY PROGRAM, program implemented by the government in mid-1962 to stop a run on the dollar. Departments cut back on expenditures wherever possible, temporary surcharges were placed on tariffs, and the dollar was devalued to 92.5 cents U.S. As this took place during and immediately following the 1962 election, the political embarrassment was substantial.

AUTONOMY BILLS, acts passed by the federal government in 1905 to create the provinces of Alberta and Saskatchewan from the North-West Territories. The bills laid out the geographical boundaries of the provinces, specified that they were to have tax-supported SEPARATE SCHOOLS, and reserved ownership over lands and resources for the federal government, to ensure federal direction of settlement. The bills caused great political embarrassment for the Liberal government of SIR WILFRID LAURIER, whose minister of colonization, CLIFFORD SIFTON, resigned to protest the establishment of separate schools in the two new provinces.

AUTO PACT, *see* CANADA-UNITED STATES AUTO PACT

courtesy DND/DL-07372

Artist's concept of the CF-105 Arrow

AVRO ARROW (CF-105), interceptor jet aircraft developed by A.V. ROE CANADA LTD in the early 1950s. The supersonic, twin-engine, all-weather interceptor, with its great speed and advanced technology, was intended to counter the threat of Soviet bombers over Canada's north. In 1959 the Conservative government of Prime Minister JOHN DIEFENBAKER cancelled production of the aircraft, citing mounting costs, disappointing performance of the aircraft, and diminished threat of manned bombers. The cancellation resulted in the loss of thousands of jobs.

A.V. ROE CANADA LTD (AVRO), aircraft company established in Toronto in 1945 as a subsidiary of Hawker Siddeley Aviation of Great

Britain. Avro used facilities and loans advanced by Victory Aircraft, a wartime crown corporation, and was a company with great engineering talent but little business acumen. It produced a number of advanced designs such as the AVRO ARROW, the AVRO JETLINER, and the CF-100. The company ceased operations shortly after the cancellation of the Arrow in 1959.

AVRO JETLINER (C-102), North America's first jetliner. An experimental aircraft produced by A.V. ROE CANADA LTD, it had its first flight on 10 Aug. 1949. In spite of outstanding aeronautical achievements, the aircraft was never produced commercially, principally because of TRANS-CANADA AIRLINES' refusal to purchase any. After Avro failed to interest United States buyers, the single aircraft built was sold for scrap in 1956.

BABY BONUS, *see* FAMILY ALLOWANCES

BABY BOOM, popular term for the increase in the birth rate from the end of World War II to approximately 1959. The phenomenon was primarily caused by people postponing having children during the GREAT DEPRESSION (1929-39) and World War II. The babies born in this period of post-war prosperity are referred to as "baby boomers" and are part of a massive population bulge that affects all aspects of organized life including educational, medical and social services, and the job market.

BAGSHAW, ELIZABETH CATHERINE (1881-1982), birth control advocate. Bagshaw graduated in medicine from the Univ. of Toronto. For three decades from 1932 she directed a birth control clinic in Hamilton, Ont., despite opposition from religious organizations and elements of the medical profession.

BAIE DES CHALEURS SCANDAL, political scandal that caused the downfall of the Liberal government of Quebec Premier HONORÉ MERCIER in 1891. Disclosure that contractors building the

Baie des Chaleurs railway had paid bribes to the provincial government was first made during a Senate inquiry ordered by the federal Conservative government of Prime Minister J.J.C. ABBOTT. The disclosures were confirmed by a subsequent Quebec royal commission. Mercier was dismissed by the lieutenant governor of Quebec in Dec. 1891 but was acquitted of malfeasance in Nov. 1892.

BALFOUR DECLARATION, report issued by Arthur, Lord Balfour, chairman of the 1926 Imperial Conference, on its discussions of the status of self-governing dominions in the British Empire. The report described the dominions to be "equal in status" to each other and "freely associated" within the British Commonwealth. This report signalled the transformation of the dominions into autonomous nations later embodied in the 1931 STATUTE OF WESTMINSTER.

BANFF NATIONAL PARK, Canada's first National Park, located 125 km west of Calgary, Alta. It is one of a grouping of mountain national parks which includes Jasper, Kootenay, Yoho, Glacier, and Mount Revelstoke. The park was created by the Conservative Government of Prime Minister JOHN A. MACDONALD in 1885 at the behest of the CANADIAN PACIFIC RAILWAY which saw a potentially lucrative tourist attraction in the sulphur hot springs there and wished them preserved.

BANK ACT, legislation by which the federal government controls and regulates banking in Canada. The first Bank Act was passed in 1871; revisions have customarily occurred every 10 years.

BANK OF BRITISH COLUMBIA, one of the first regional banks chartered by the federal government in the modern era, established with its head office in Vancouver in 1966. The founding of the bank was largely due to political pressures on Ottawa from regional entrepreneurs who claimed that the Canadian chartered banks discriminated against the hinterland regions of Canada. The Bank of British Columbia was followed by a number of other regional chartered banks, most in western Canada. The majority of these disappeared in the mid-1980s because of insufficient capital to meet the demands of a fluctuating resource-based economy of western Canada. *See also* ROYAL COMMISSION ON BANKING AND FINANCE.

BANK OF CANADA, a central bank established by the Bank of Canada Act of 1934, following the recommendations of the 1933 Royal Commission on Banking and Currency. The bank opened for business as a privately owned institution on 11 Mar. 1935 but was nationalized in 1938. The bank holds the main accounts of the Canadian government, issues Canada's paper currency, and sets the bank discount rate (the benchmark by which the chartered banks and other financial institutions establish the rates they charge customers for loans). The governor, deputy governor, and the 12 directors of the bank are appointed by the federal government. Governors have been GRAHAM TOWERS (1935-54), J.E. COYNE (1955-61), LOUIS RASMINSKY (1961-73), G.K. BOUEY (1973-86), and John Crow (1986–).

BANK OF COMMERCE, *see* CANADIAN IMPERIAL BANK OF COMMERCE

BANK OF MONTREAL, established in 1817 as a commercial bank to channel investments from the Montreal business community into transportation improvements such as canals and railways. The bank served as the general banker and holder of the accounts of the Canadian government from before Confederation until the BANK OF CANADA opened in 1935. One of Canada's five largest chartered banks, the Bank of Montreal was an important participant in Canadian development, providing investment capital for projects such as the CANADIAN PACIFIC RAILWAY.

BANK OF NOVA SCOTIA, a commercial bank founded in Halifax in 1832. It expanded to western Canada, the United States, and the Caribbean by the late 19th century and in 1900 moved its head office to Toronto. It is one of Canada's five largest chartered banks.

BANK OF TORONTO, *see* TORONTO-DOMINION BANK

BANKS, HAROLD (HAL) CHAMBERLAIN (1909-85), head of the Seafarers International Union of Canada, 1949-63. Born at Waterloo, Iowa, Banks was invited to Canada by anti-Com-

munist labour leaders and shipping companies to counter the Communist-led CANADIAN SEAMEN'S UNION. Using a combination of secret agreements with shipping companies, intimidation, and blackmail, he quickly destroyed the CSU. By 1959 his tactics had turned former labour allies against him, and his union was suspended from the CANADIAN LABOUR CONGRESS. In 1962-3 a government-appointed commission of inquiry under Justice T.G. Norris uncovered more than a decade of union gangsterism in the SIU. Following the commission's recommendation, Ottawa placed the SIU and four other maritime unions under trusteeship. Banks was convicted of conspiracy but fled Canada in July 1964 while on bail. *See also* NORRIS INQUIRY.

BANTING, SIR FREDERICK GRANT (1891-1941), medical researcher. Born at Alliston, Ont., Banting became famous for his role in the discovery of insulin, a drug used to control diabetes, in 1921-2. Although his idea launched the research project, he was part of a team that included C.H. BEST, J.J.R. MACLEOD and J.B. COLLIP. Banting shared the 1923 Nobel Prize for physiology with Macleod, but he gave half of his prize money to Best. Banting, also a gifted amateur artist, died in a World War II air crash in Newfoundland.

BARBEAU, CHARLES MARIUS (1883-1969), folklorist. He studied law at Univ. Laval and became fascinated with ethnology as a Rhodes Scholar at Oxford. He worked at the National Museum in Ottawa, collecting folklore material in Quebec and among the native peoples of British Columbia.

BARKER, WILLIAM GEORGE, "BILLY" (1894-1930), pilot. Born at Dauphin, Man., Barker served in the Royal Flying Corps during WORLD WAR I, where he scored 53 "kills," winning the Victoria Cross.

BARR COLONY, agricultural settlement established in May 1903 on a tract that straddles the present Alberta-Saskatchewan border. Its founder, the Reverend Isaac Barr, brought approximately 2000 colonists from England to settle on it. He eventually resigned from the leadership of the colony and moved to Toronto because of the colonists' discontent. He was succeeded by the Reverend George Lloyd for whom the colony's first town, Lloydminster, was named.

BARRETT, DAVID (1930–), premier of British Columbia. Born at Vancouver, Barrett entered politics as a CO-OPERATIVE COMMONWEALTH FEDERATION candidate in the 1960 B.C. provincial election. In 1969 he became leader of the provincial NEW DEMOCRATIC PARTY and formed the first NDP government in British Columbia in 1972. The NDP was defeated in 1975 by SOCIAL CREDIT and Barrett resigned the party leadership in 1983.

BARRETTE, ANTONIO (1899-1968), premier of Quebec. First elected for the UNION NATIONALE in 1936, Barrette was labour minister from 1944 to 1960, implementing MAURICE DUPLESSIS's anti-union policies. After PAUL SAUVÉ's death in Jan. 1960, he became premier until defeated by JEAN LESAGE in June 1960. He was ambassador to Greece, 1963-6.

BATA, THOMAS JOHN (1914–), shoe manufacturer. Born in Prague, Czech., Bata entered his father's shoe company, already the world's largest. Bata came to Canada just prior to World War II to build a shoe factory at Batawa, Ont. It became the centre of Bata's world-wide operations after the war.

BATOCHE, BATTLE OF, battle for the capital of LOUIS RIEL's provisional government during the NORTH-WEST REBELLION of 1885. On 9 May General FRED MIDDLETON and 800 men of the North-West Field Force attacked the Métis positions surrounding Batoche, located 44 km southwest of Prince Albert. The Métis, led by GABRIEL DUMONT, successfully resisted the Canadians until 12 May when they were overrun. The Métis defeat effectively ended the rebellion; Riel surrendered several days later and Dumont fled to the United States. *See also* JOHN A. MACDONALD.

BAXTER, JOHN BABINGTON MACAULAY (1868-1946), premier of New Brunswick. Baxter was attorney-general of New Brunswick, 1915-17, then served in ARTHUR MEIGHEN's Conservative cabinet in 1921. In 1925-31 he was premier of New Brunswick and played a major role in the MARITIME RIGHTS movement. He was chief justice of the province from 1935 until his death.

BAY STREET, a street in the heart of the Toronto financial district. "Bay Street" or "The Street" is a term often used to refer to the leaders of Canadian capitalism. The Street was often used in association with St James Street, the heart of the Montreal financial district.

BEATTY, SIR EDWARD WENTWORTH (1877-1943), businessman. Beatty acted as general counsel for the CANADIAN PACIFIC RAILWAY before becoming its first Canadian-born president in 1918. In 1942 he established CANADIAN PACIFIC AIRLINES.

BEAUHARNOIS SCANDAL, a 1931 political scandal. The scandal broke when a House of Commons committee investigating the profits of the Beauharnois Power Corporation, authorized by MACKENZIE KING's government to divert water on the St Lawrence River for a hydroelectric project, discovered that King and two political friends received gifts from the corporation and that both the Liberal and Conservative parties received huge donations. For King, this was the "valley of humiliation."

BEAVER (DHC-2), bush plane. Built by DE HAVILLAND AIRCRAFT OF CANADA LTD, it succeeded the NOORDUYN NORSEMAN as Canada's principal all-purpose bush plane. It is noted for its short take-off and landing (STOL) capabilities and its capacity for heavy loads. By the mid-1960s, there were approximately 1600 Beaver aircraft operating in 63 countries.

BEAVERBROOK, LORD, *see* AITKEN, WILLIAM MAXWELL

BECK, SIR ADAM (1857-1925), businessman. Born at Baden, Canada West, Beck pursued a career as a manufacturer and municipal politician before becoming involved in the movement for a publicly owned electric power system in Ontario. When the Hydro-Electric Power Commission of Ontario (ONTARIO HYDRO) was formed as a crown corporation in 1906, Beck was named head. He spearheaded the expansion of the HEPC into the world's largest publicly owned power authority. When the UNITED FARMERS OF ONTARIO took power following the 1919 provincial election, they offered the premiership to Beck but he refused.

courtesy PABC #HP2322

Sir Matthew B. Begbie

BEGBIE, SIR MATTHEW BAILLIE (1819-94), jurist. Begbie came from England in 1858 to be the first judge in British Columbia. Fair but firm, he helped keep the scattered colony British during the turbulent gold rush days. When B.C. entered CONFEDERATION in 1871, Begbie became the province's chief justice, a post he held until his death.

BEGG, ALEXANDER (1839-97), author. Born at Quebec City, Begg was a businessman who moved to Winnipeg in 1867. His career included stints as deputy treasurer of Manitoba, as the CANADIAN PACIFIC RAILWAY's immigration agent in London, Eng., and latterly as a journalist in Seattle, Wash., and Victoria, B.C. His historical writing on Manitoba and the North-West Territories are of interest.

courtesy Glenbow Archives, Calgary/NA-3680-3

Grey Owl (Archibald Belaney)

BELANEY, ARCHIBALD STANSFELD (GREY OWL) (1888-1938), writer. Born at Hastings, Eng., Belaney became fascinated by North American Indians as a child and moved to northern Canada at age 17. Assimilating into Indian life and claiming to be half-Indian, he took the name Grey Owl and published widely, stressing the necessity of conservation. After his death, his English birth was revealed, largely destroying his reputation until recent years.

BELIVEAU, JEAN (1931-), hockey player. Jean Beliveau joined the Montreal Canadiens in 1953 and for the next 18 seasons played the game with grace and style. In 1125 games he scored 507 goals and 1219 points, including a record 176 points in 162 playoff games. He became a vice-president of the Canadiens organization in 1971.

BELL, ALEXANDER GRAHAM (1847-1922), inventor. Born in Edinburgh, Scot., Bell immigrated to Canada with his parents in 1870. His work in developing devices to help the deaf led him to move to the United States where he invented and perfected the telephone. He founded the Bell Telephone Co. in 1876 and successfully fought a number of patent-infringement suits in U.S. courts. After achieving fame and fortune, Bell purchased a property in Baddeck, N.S. in 1890 and spent much time there organizing scientific experiments with devices such as the hydrofoil and heavier-than-air aircraft. Bell helped found the AERIAL EXPERIMENT ASSN in 1907 which built a number of successful aircraft including the SILVER DART, which made the first powered and manned flight in the British Empire in 1909. Bell also worked on the photoelectric cell, the phonograph, the iron lung and other inventions. *See also* J.A.D. MCCURDY.

BELL, MARILYN (1937-), long-distance swimmer. Born at Toronto, Bell swam across Lake Ontario in 1954, became the youngest person to swim the English Channel, and also conquered the Straits of Juan de Fuca.

BENGOUGH, JOHN WILSON (1851-1923), political cartoonist. Bengough began working at GEORGE BROWN's *Globe* in 1871 but left in 1873 to create the weekly *Grip*. Until 1894 Bengough caricatured many political figures of the time. He also lectured as a social critic and wrote books until his death.

BENGOUGH, PERCY (1883-1972), labour leader. Born in London, Eng., Bengough became a machinist and joined the union movement after settling in Canada in 1905. As president of the TRADES AND LABOUR CONGRESS OF CANADA (1943-54), he strongly supported the Liberal government during World War II. He later worked for a merger of the TLC and the CANADIAN CONGRESS OF LABOUR.

courtesy PABC #HP63208

R.B. Bennett and his sister, Mrs. Mildred Herridge

BENNETT, RICHARD BEDFORD, VISCOUNT (1870-1947), prime minister of Canada. Born at Hopewell Hill, N.B., Bennett graduated from Dalhousie Univ. in 1893 and taught school before moving to Calgary in 1897 to start a successful law partnership with JAMES LOUGHEED. He was elected to the assembly of the North-West Territories in 1898 but resigned to run unsuccessfully in the 1900 federal election. After again failing in the 1905 Alberta provincial election, he finally won a provincial seat in 1909. First elected to the House of Commons as a Conservative in 1911, Bennett, by then wealthy, was passed over for a cabinet position and did not run in the 1917 federal election. He returned to the House in 1925 and was briefly minister of finance. Bennett succeeded ARTHUR MEIGHEN as Conservative leader in 1927 and took the party to victory in the 1930 federal election. Despite spending large sums on relief during the GREAT DEPRESSION, his government was perceived as reactionary to the core – both unaware of and unconcerned with the dreadful plight of so many at the time. On the eve of the 1935 election Bennett announced his BENNETT "NEW DEAL," an ambitious reform platform the voters rejected. He continued as opposition leader until 1938, when he left Canada and moved to England.

BENNETT, WILLIAM ANDREW CECIL, "WACKY" (1900-79), premier of British Columbia. Born at Hastings, N.B., he purchased a hardware store in Kelowna, B.C., in 1930. He entered the B.C. legislature as a Conservative in 1941 and sat as an Independent in 1951 before running as a SOCIAL CREDIT candidate in the 1952 provincial election. Chosen leader and asked to form a government that year, he led B.C. through an era of enormous growth in hydroelectric power, roads, and education, while tightly controlling labour and cutting welfare spending. He was defeated by the NEW DEMOCRATIC PARTY in 1972 and was succeeded as party leader by his son, BILL BENNETT, in 1973.

BENNETT, WILLIAM (BILL) RICHARDS (1932–), premier of British Columbia. Son of W.A.C. BENNETT, he worked in his father's hardware store before he and his brother moved into real estate and other business ventures. He was elected to the B.C. legislature as a SOCIAL CREDIT member in 1973, succeeded his father as leader, and guided the party to victory in the 1975 provincial election. Re-elected twice, he introduced a controversial restraint program, fought viciously with the trade unions, cut back on government spending, and readied the province for the 1986 Vancouver World Exposition. He resigned as party leader in May 1986.

courtesy Manitoba Archives

A Bennett buggy of the Great Depression

BENNETT BUGGY, term used during the GREAT DEPRESSION in western Canada for a horse-drawn car with the motor removed. The owner would thus not have the expense of buying gasoline. It was named after Prime Minister R.B. BENNETT.

BENNETT NEW DEAL, the series of legislative measures introduced by Conservative Prime Minister R.B. BENNETT in 1935 to fight the GREAT DEPRESSION and restore Conservative party fortunes. At the urging of W.D. HERRIDGE, Bennett's brother-in-law and the Canadian minister in Washington, Bennett decided to try to emulate U.S. President Franklin D. Roosevelt's "New Deal." In Jan. 1935, Bennett began a series of radio speeches announcing measures such as unemployment insurance, a federal minimum wage, a federal maximum hours of work law, health and accident insurance, and improved pensions. Eventually, most of these measures were declared ULTRA VIRES by the JUDICIAL COMMITTEE OF THE PRIVY COUNCIL.

BENTLEY, MAXWELL HERBERT LLOYD (1920-84), hockey player. Max Bentley played hockey with the Chicago Black Hawks until he was traded to the Toronto Maple Leafs in 1947. A superb stickhandler and skater, Bentley was able to score goals consistently. After six years in Toronto, he was traded to New York and retired in 1954.

BENY, ROLOFF (1924-84), photographer. Born at Medicine Hat, Alta., Beny studied at the univs. of Toronto and Iowa. His first photography show was held in London in 1955, and he began to specialize in books of photographs, including lavish studies of Iran, Japan, India, and Canada.

BERGER, THOMAS RODNEY (1933-), politician, jurist. Born at Victoria, B.C., Berger attended the Univ. of British Columbia and practised law in Vancouver. He was elected to Parliament in 1962 for the NEW DEMOCRATIC PARTY and was B.C. provincial leader, 1966-9. In 1971 he was named to the province's supreme court, but he is best known for his role as commissioner of the MACKENZIE VALLEY PIPELINE Inquiry. His report argued for a 10-year moratorium on pipeline construction to allow settlement of native LAND CLAIMS. In 1981 he attacked the federal-provincial constitutional accord for its removal of ABORIGINAL RIGHTS from the constitution. He resigned from the bench in 1983.

BERLIN CONVENTION, convention of the TRADES AND LABOUR CONGRESS, held in Berlin (Kitchener), Ont. in 1902, that adopted resolutions making the Trades and Labour Congress subordinate to the American Federation of Labor. This subordination meant that no Canadian union could retain membership in the TLC while a similar AFL union was also a TLC member.

BERNIER, JOSEPH-ELZÉAR (1852-1934), Arctic navigator. Born at L'Islet, Canada East, Bernier was at sea from the age of 14. In 1904 his ship was drafted into government service patrolling the eastern Arctic, and he undertook annual voyages for some years thereafter, collecting information and asserting Canada's claims to the ARCTIC ARCHIPELAGO. He retired in 1925.

BERTON, PIERRE (1920-), writer, broadcaster. Born at Whitehorse, Y.T., he moved to Vancouver to work on the *News-Herald* in 1942. He joined the staff of MACLEAN's in Toronto in 1947 and moved to the *Toronto Star* in 1958. With the 1958 publication of *Klondike*, a history of the 1898 KLONDIKE GOLD RUSH, he established his reputation as a popular historian. The work was followed by *The National Dream* (1970), *The Last Spike* (1971), *The Dionne Years* (1977), *The Invasion of Canada* (1980), *Flames across the Border* (1981), *The Promised Land* (1984), and *Vimy* (1986). Berton has also achieved great success as a television personality.

BESSBOROUGH, VERE BRABAZON PONSONBY, 1ST EARL OF (1880-1956), governor general of Canada, 1931-5. Born at London, Eng., Bessborough sat as a Conservative in the House of Commons and the Lords before coming to Canada. Supporters of the dramatic arts and amateur actors, he and his wife initiated the Dominion Drama Festival in 1932. Although Bessborough looked the aristocrat he was, he asked for and received a symbolic 10 per cent cut in pay to show concern for those suffering during the GREAT DEPRESSION.

BEST, CHARLES HERBERT (1899-1978), physiologist, co-discoverer of insulin. Born in West Pembroke, Me, Best was educated at the Univ. of Toronto. In the summer of 1921 he was hired as researcher-assistant by F.G. BANTING for work Banting intended to do leading towards a cure for diabetes. Banting and Best worked in facilities provided by J.J.R. MACLEOD and were aided by Macleod and J.B. COLLIP. Although Best was not a co-recipient of the Nobel Prize awarded to Banting and Macleod for the discovery of insulin, Banting shared his prize money with Best.

BETHUNE, HENRY NORMAN (1890-1939), physician. Norman Bethune is, even 47 years after his death from septicemia at Huang Shiko in North China, an internationally recognized figure. He was born at Gravenhurst, Ont., and pursued a career in thoracic surgery after he discovered he had contracted pulmonary tuberculosis. Although his medical innovations were important, he became disillusioned with aspects of medical practice. In 1935 he joined the COMMUNIST PARTY and devoted the rest of his life to the anti-fascist cause, first in the Spanish Civil War, where he organized a blood-transfusion unit, and then as a surgeon in China, where the Communists were battling the Japanese. Mao Zedong's tribute, "In Memory of Norman Bethune," became required reading during China's Cultural Revolution and he is a genuinely revered figure there, the archetypal "good friend" of China.

BEYNON, FRANCIS MARION (1884-1951), journalist, feminist. Born at Streetsville, Ont., Beynon accompanied her family to Winnipeg where she found work as a journalist, notably on the GRAIN GROWERS' GUIDE. In a column on women's questions, she pressed for WOMEN'S SUFFRAGE and took a pacifist position during World War I. She left the paper in 1917 and moved to the United States.

BICKELL, JOHN PARIS (1884-1951), businessman. He made his fortune through investments in Ontario gold mines in the 1930s. President and chairman of McIntyre-Porcupine Mines Ltd, Bickell was one of a coterie of mine owners who influenced Ontario premier MITCHELL HEPBURN's anti-union philosophy in the late 1930s when the U.S.-based Congress of Industrial Organizations began to move into that province. During WORLD WAR II, Bickell donated his services to the British and Canadian governments, serving as a "dollar-a-year" man.

BIENFAIT STRIKE, strike of coal miners affiliated to the MINE WORKERS UNION OF CANADA in southern Saskatchewan in 1931. The strike led to the ESTEVAN MASSACRE that Sept., when the RCMP fired on a miners' parade in Estevan after the mayor had banned demonstrations.

BIG BEAR (1825?-88), Plains Cree chief. After the federal government refused to negotiate with him, members of his band, on the verge of starvation, took part in the NORTH-WEST REBELLION of 1885, killing nine whites at Frog Lake and capturing Fort Pitt. Big Bear surrendered at Fort Carlton in 1885. Tried and convicted of treason-felony though he had always tried to restrain his people, he was released after serving a two-year sentence and died several months later at the Poundmaker Reserve.

BIG BLUE MACHINE, term describing the Conservative Party of Ontario and its effective electoral organization, 1943-85. The Big Blue Machine held power under the leadership of GEORGE DREW (1943-8), LESLIE FROST (1949-61), JOHN ROBARTS (1961-71), and WILLIAM DAVIS (1971-85). It ground to a halt under Frank Miller when the party lost the 1985 election to the Liberals and disappeared in disarray after the Liberal sweep in Sept. 1987.

BIG FOUR CATTLEMEN, ranchers who founded the CALGARY STAMPEDE in 1912. The four, Archibald McClean, PATRICK BURNS, A.E. CROSS and GEORGE LANE, were persuaded to put up $100,000 to finance the first exhibition by cowboy showman Guy Weadick.

BIGGAR, OLIVER MOWAT (1876-1948), public servant. During WORLD WAR I, he played an important role on the Military Service Council that dealt with CONSCRIPTION questions, as judge advocate general, and as an adviser at the Paris Peace Conference. He was chief electoral officer, 1920-7, and became chair of the Canadian section of the PERMANENT JOINT BOARD ON DEFENCE, 1940-5.

"BILINGUALISM AND BICULTURALISM," sometimes referred to as "B & B," the words were linked in the late 1960s during discussions of the place of French Canada in the nation. Advocates of bilingualism and biculturalism maintained that Canada was, or ought to be, a country with two recognized founding peoples – English-speaking and French-speaking – and that this should be recognized in a variety of ways. Foremost among the changes proposed were the creation of a bilingual federal civil service, the provision of French-language services by the federal government and/or its institutions wherever there was a demand for them, and the promotion of the two cultures throughout Canada. The concept was considerably advanced by the ROYAL COMMISSION ON BILINGUALISM AND BICULTURALISM. Prime Minister PIERRE TRUDEAU, who introduced the OFFICIAL LANGUAGES ACT, was a strong proponent of B & B. The emergence of the concept of MULTICULTURALISM was, in part, a reaction to bilingualism and biculturalism.

BILL OF RIGHTS, federal legislation passed in 1960 that guaranteed civil liberties (the right to life, liberty, and personal security), language, education, and enjoyment of private property. The DIEFENBAKER government never sought to entrench the bill as part of the constitution for fear of provincial dissent. The 1982 CANADIAN CHARTER OF RIGHTS AND FREEDOMS superseded the bill.

BILL 22, Quebec legislation passed in 1974, making French the official language of the Quebec civil service and limiting the teaching of English in Quebec schools. Brought in by the Liberal government of ROBERT BOURASSA, the bill was strongly opposed by Quebec's English-speaking minority. It was at the same time condemned by Quebec nationalists for being too moderate in that it did not make French the sole official language of the province.

BILL 80, a 1942 bill to amend the NATIONAL RESOURCES MOBILIZATION ACT. After the PLEBISCITE of 1942 on CONSCRIPTION, the Liberal government felt obliged to amend the NRMA to delete its ban on the use of conscripts overseas. Bill 80, the vehicle for this change, provoked a serious split in the MACKENZIE KING cabinet and almost led to the resignation of defence minister J.L. RALSTON.

BILL 101, Quebec legislation passed in 1977 and designed to ensure the primacy of the French language in Quebec. Entitled *Charte de la langue française* ("Charter of the French language"), Bill 101 was introduced by the PARTI QUÉBÉCOIS government of RENÉ LÉVESQUE. It made French the official language of the courts and the provincial government and restricted the use of English on signs, in commerce, and in education. Part of the law was struck down by the SUPREME COURT OF CANADA in 1980.

BILLION DOLLAR GIFT, Canadian donation to the British war effort announced in Jan. 1942. By that time, Britain had been purchasing an increasing amount of war supplies from Canada on credit and the billion dollar gift was, in fact, mostly a cancellation of existing debts. The gift was announced amid great fanfare to publicize the government's war policies, especially its support for Britain in WORLD WAR II.

BIRD, FLORENCE BAYARD (ANNE FRANCIS) (1908–), journalist. Born at Philadelphia, Pa, Florence Rhein came to Canada in 1931, finding work as a journalist and broadcaster. In 1967, she was named to head the ROYAL COMMISSION ON THE STATUS OF WOMEN IN CANADA. She became a senator in 1978.

BIRKS, HENRY (1840-1928), retailer. Born in Montreal, Birks opened a watchmaking and jewellery establishment in that city in 1879. This was the basis for Henry Birks & Sons. The company has since expanded across Canada to become a large chain-style jewellery establishment. Birks also helped found the Royal Automobile Club of Canada in Montreal.

BIRNEY, ALFRED EARLE (1904–), writer. Birney, born in Calgary, was educated at the univs. of British Columbia, Toronto, California, and London. Best known for his many volumes of poetry, Birney is also a novelist of distinction, his World War II story, *Turvey*, ranking as a Canadian classic. He established the creative writing department at the Univ. of British Columbia.

BISHOP, WILLIAM AVERY, "BILLY" (1894-1956), fighter pilot. Born at Owen Sound, Ont., he entered WORLD WAR I with the Canadian cavalry and finished as one of the most successful flying aces of the war with 72 victories. He won a Victoria Cross, the first Canadian airman to do so, for a 1917 attack on a German airfield. In 1918 he was promoted lieutenant-colonel and sent to England. He was promoted honorary air

courtesy DND/AH-4704

William "Billy" Bishop

vice-marshal of the ROYAL CANADIAN AIR FORCE in 1936 and during WORLD WAR II he served as honorary air-marshal. He wrote *Winged Warfare* (1918) and *Winged Peace* (1944). In 1985 the NATIONAL FILM BOARD produced a controversial portrayal of Bishop, which was widely denounced for calling the number of his victories into question.

BLACK, MARTHA LOUISE (1866-1957), naturalist, politician. Born at Chicago, Ill., Martha Munger joined the KLONDIKE GOLD RUSH, opened a mill to support her three children from her first marriage, and in 1904 married George Black. Her husband became commissioner of the Yukon under the BORDEN government and was a Conservative MP, 1921-35. In 1935, her husband ill, Black held his seat for him, becoming the second woman MP.

BLADEN, VINCENT WHEELER (1900-81), economist. Born at Stoke-on-Trent, Eng., he was educated at Oxford, coming to the Univ. of Toronto in 1921, where he established the *Canadian Journal of Economics and Political Science*. He served government as a royal commissioner to investigate the Canadian auto industry, 1960, and as chair of the Adjustment Assistance Board, 1965-71. He also led the Assn of Universities and Colleges of Canada study of university financing, 1964.

BLAIR, ANDREW GEORGE (1844-1907), premier of New Brunswick. Born and educated at Fredericton, N.B., Blair taught and practised law before entering politics in 1878. He became leader of the opposition in the N.B. legislature in 1879 and premier in 1883, subsequently forming his coalition government into the provincial Lib-

eral party. In 1896 he left the premiership to become minister of railways and canals in WILFRID LAURIER's Liberal cabinet, but resigned in 1903 to protest Laurier's railway policy. He served briefly as chief commissioner of the BOARD OF RAILWAY COMMISSIONERS in 1904.

BLAIS, MARIE-CLAIRE (1939-), author. Born at Quebec City, Blais published her first novel, *La Belle Bête*, in 1959, soon translated as *Mad Shadows*. Other novels and plays followed, as did fellowships and prizes. Her best-known work is *Une Saison dans la vie d'Emmanuel* (1965).

courtesy National Archives of Canada/PA-13010

Edward Blake

BLAKE, DOMINICK EDWARD (1833-1912), politician, premier of Ontario. One of the most powerful figures in 19th-century Canadian politics, he was born in Adelaide Township, Upper Canada, and educated at the Univ. of Toronto. He became a prominent lawyer and entered politics in 1867, sitting in both the Ontario legislature and the House of Commons. In 1868 he became leader of the Ontario Liberal party and in 1871 premier of the province, after defeating JOHN SANDFIELD MACDONALD. He left Ontario politics in 1872 when dual representation was abolished and served as minister without portfolio (1873-4), minister of justice (1875-7), and president of the Privy Council (1877-8) in ALEXANDER

MACKENZIE's Liberal government. In 1880 he succeeded Mackenzie as party leader, but the public did not warm to his cerebral style, and he remained in opposition until his resignation as leader in 1887. Blake moved to Ireland in 1892 and sat in the British House of Commons as an Irish Nationalist MP until 1907, when he returned to Canada.

BLAKE, HECTOR, "TOE" (1912–), hockey player. Toe Blake joined the Montreal Canadiens in the 1936 season and played with them until 1948. He was National Hockey League scoring champion in 1939. Blake became the coach of the Canadiens in 1955 and his team won the STANLEY CUP eight times in 13 seasons.

BLAKENEY, ALLAN EMRYS (1925–), premier of Saskatchewan. Born and raised in Nova Scotia, he moved to Saskatchewan and entered the civil service in 1950, becoming a legal adviser to T.C. DOUGLAS's CO-OPERATIVE COMMONWEALTH FEDERATION government. He was first elected in the 1960 provincial election and served as minister of education, minister of finance, and minister of health before succeeding WOODROW LLOYD as NEW DEMOCRATIC PARTY leader in 1971. An able, cautious man, in 1971 he led the party to victory over ROSS THATCHER's Liberals and was premier until his party lost to the Conservatives in 1982. He resigned the party leadership in 1987.

BLAND, SALEM GOLDWORTH (1859-1950), leader of the Social Gospel movement. Born at Lachute, Canada East, and educated at McGill Univ., he was ordained as a Methodist minister in 1884. He was a popular leader of the SOCIAL GOSPEL movement, which sought in the late 19th and early 20th century to eradicate the evils of industrialism with Christian social reform. In 1927 he started writing for the *Toronto Star*, though his lasting contribution is his book, *The New Christianity* (1920). Bland was one of many who mixed Christian doctrine with moderate socialism, and he played a part in the creation of the CO-OPERATIVE COMMONWEALTH FEDERATION. In 1934 he helped found the FELLOWSHIP FOR A CHRISTIAN SOCIAL ORDER.

BLOC POPULAIRE CANADIEN, a Quebec-based political movement formed in 1942, largely

in response to MACKENZIE KING's CONSCRIPTION policy. Led federally by MAXIME RAYMOND and provincially by ANDRÉ LAURENDEAU, the Bloc opposed English-Canadian domination and advocated FAMILY ALLOWANCES and health insurance, nationalization of hydroelectric power companies, improved labour laws, and Canadian neutrality. The Bloc did not achieve much electoral success and quietly passed away in 1949.

"BLOODY SATURDAY," labour disturbance in Winnipeg on 21 June 1919. Returned soldiers organized a parade on that day in support of the general strike that had gripped the city since 15 May, despite bans on demonstrations issued by the mayor. Before the parade began, the mayor called for help from the Royal North-West Mounted Police and the militia. The Mounties charged the crowd and opened fire after rocks and sticks were thrown at them; two men were killed and many others wounded. After the crowds panicked and ran, the militia occupied downtown Winnipeg. As a result of Bloody Saturday, the general strike collapsed. *See also* WINNIPEG GENERAL STRIKE.

BLUENOSE, THE, fishing schooner launched at Lunenburg, N.S., in 1921. It was famed for its racing ability, taking the International Fisherman's Trophy in 1921, 1922, 1923, 1931, and 1938. Sold to a West Indies trading company in 1943, it was wrecked in 1946. A portrayal of *The Bluenose* has appeared on the Canadian dime since 1937.

BOARD OF BROADCAST GOVERNORS, federal agency established by the Conservative government of Prime Minister JOHN DIEFENBAKER in 1958 to assume responsibility for broadcast regulation and licensing. From 1936 to 1958 that responsibility had been lodged with the CANADIAN BROADCASTING CORP., to the chagrin of private broadcasters who complained that the CBC should not regulate its privately owned rivals. The BBG was replaced by the CANADIAN RADIO AND TELEVISION COMMISSION in 1967.

BOARD OF GRAIN COMMISSIONERS, federal agency created under the Canada Grain Act passed in 1912 in response to western complaints about abuses in the grain-marketing system. The board was placed under the Department of Trade and Commerce and was charged with supervising and regulating the Canadian grain trade, although it had no power to set prices or establish selling quotas.

BOARD OF GRAIN SUPERVISORS, federal marketing board appointed in 1917 to market grain during wartime. It was given broad powers to regulate prices and to control the grain trade generally. Its creation marked a temporary end to the free market in grain in Canada. In 1919 the government disbanded the board but the following year, it created a Wheat Board with similar powers in response to farm complaints about the drastic post-war fall in wheat prices. That board was also disbanded after one year because of the government's determination to restore the free market in grain. *See also* CANADIAN WHEAT BOARD.

BOARD OF RAILWAY COMMISSIONERS, federal regulating agency that took over in 1903 from the Railway Committee of the Privy Council (established 1868). The board was eventually given jurisdiction over telegraph, telephone, and express companies, government-owned railways, international bridges and tunnels, abandonment of railway lines, and the Hudson Bay and Newfoundland railways. As a result of the Transportation Act of 1938, the name of the board was changed to the Board of Transport Commissioners for Canada.

courtesy National Archives of Canada/C-15300

Canadians seizing a *kopje* during the Boer War

BOER WAR, the South African War, 1899-1902, between Britain and the Boer republics of the Transvaal and the Orange Free State. War broke out on 11 Oct. 1899. Public opinion in Canada was already sharply divided on the question of Canadian participation. French Canadians, led by HENRI BOURASSA, and some farm groups thought that Britain should handle this war on its own lest participation set a precedent obliging Canada to join in every British conflict; many English Canadians saw the war as a struggle for the freedom of the *uitlanders*, or foreigners, in the Boer republics and demanded that Canada participate in a major way in this great adventure. In the middle was the prime minister, SIR WILFRID LAURIER, and his Liberal government. A compromise that pleased no one was reached: Canada would recruit a force of a thousand infantry but Britain would be responsible for their pay and costs. Commanded by Colonel W.D. OTTER, the 2nd (Special Service) Battalion of the Royal Canadian Regiment (RCR), raised from regulars and the MILITIA, sailed from Quebec before the end of October. As critics had feared, the calls for more men mounted; a second contingent, 1320 strong and consisting of Canadian Mounted Rifles and three batteries of artillery, reached South Africa in March 1900. Other units were raised by individuals – Lord Strathcona's Horse being the most notable example – and the government helped to raise, but paid none of the costs for, further units of Mounted Rifles and a field hospital.

The RCR played a distinguished part in the Battle of PAARDEBERG in late Feb. 1900. Before their return home in Oct., the RCR participated in a number of additional skirmishes as the war changed character and became a prolonged guerilla campaign; casualties were more frequently the result of disease than illness. The later contingents also distinguished themselves in this war, notable engagements being fought at Boschbult and Leliefontein. In all, 7368 Canadians served in South Africa and casualties were 89 killed in action, 252 wounded, and 135 dead by disease and accident. *See also* DONALD ALEXANDER SMITH.

BOIS-BRÛLÉS, *see* MÉTIS

BOMARC MISSILE CRISIS, 1963, political crisis over the Bomarc anti-aircraft missiles that destroyed the Diefenbaker government. The government of JOHN DIEFENBAKER in Sept. 1958 decided to acquire Bomarc missiles from the United

States and to locate the weapons, effective only with nuclear warheads, at North Bay, Ont., and La Macaza, Que. But by 1960, secretary of state for external affairs HOWARD GREEN and defence minister DOUGLAS HARKNESS had become locked in controversy over the acquisition of nuclear weapons, and Diefenbaker dithered. Fanciful schemes to fly the warheads in from the United States in the event of crisis could not be worked out, and when Diefenbaker made an equivocal speech in Parliament on 25 Jan. 1963 that revealed secret details of the negotiations, President John F. Kennedy's administration issued a scathing press release denouncing the prime minister. Within days, Harkness resigned, the government lost a vote of confidence in its defence policy, and the Diefenbaker government's days were numbered. The Liberal government of LESTER PEARSON accepted the nuclear warheads soon after it took power in April. PIERRE TRUDEAU's government phased out the missiles in 1971.

BOMBARDIER, JOSEPH-ARMAND (1908-64), inventor. Born at Valcourt, Que., Bombardier invented an operational snowmobile in 1922 combining skis for steering and tracks for propulsion. In 1959 he invented the SKI-DOO, a motorcycle-sized, one-track snowmobile. It spawned many imitators, became a popular winter-sports vehicle, and is used extensively in the north for transportation.

BONAVENTURE, **HMCS**, aircraft carrier. *Bonaventure* was purchased in 1952 and used primarily as a training vessel and for coastal and anti-submarine patrol. The government sold it for scrap in 1970 following a controversy over its expensive refitting.

Sir Frederick W. Borden

BORDEN, SIR FREDERICK WILLIAM (1847-1917), politician. Borden entered politics as a Liberal in the 1870s and served in the House of Commons for 32 years. He was named minister of militia in the government of WILFRID LAURIER and presided over the dispatch of volunteers to South Africa during the BOER WAR. Borden instituted reforms to modernize the MILITIA, including one which, for the first time, allowed a Canadian to serve as militia commander.

courtesy PABC #HP2297

Sir Robert Borden

BORDEN, SIR ROBERT LAIRD (1854-1937), prime minister of Canada. Born at Grand Pré, N.S., Borden taught school in New Jersey, before returning to Nova Scotia to study law. He was called to the bar in 1878 and became head of his own firm in 1889. Elected to the House of Commons in 1896, to his own and other's surprise he succeeded Sir CHARLES TUPPER as Conservative leader in 1901. He spent the next 10 years rebuilding the party and, with the financial help of the TORONTO EIGHTEEN, opposed the Laurier government's RECIPROCITY policy, won the 1911 federal election and took Canada into WORLD WAR I. Not brilliant but a determined man, Borden's wartime government introduced some difficult special measures, including income tax, nationalization of the CANADIAN NORTHERN RAILWAY, the MILITARY SERVICE ACT (which provoked the CONSCRIPTION CRISIS of 1917), and the MILITARY VOTERS ACT. He created the 1917 UNION GOVERNMENT and led it to electoral victory. In 1919 he attended the Paris Peace Conference and fought for Canada's right to sign the peace treaty as an au-

courtesy National Archives of Canada/C-14416

tonomous nation. Borden quit politics in 1920 but remained respected as an international statesman, representing Canada at the 1921 Washington Conference and the LEAGUE OF NATIONS in 1930.

BORDUAS, PAUL-ÉMILE (1905-60), artist, leader of a group of Canadian painters known as the Automatistes. He studied at Montreal and Paris, and took a teaching position at the École du Meuble in Montreal in 1937. In 1948 Borduas wrote REFUS GLOBAL, a tract that attacked the establishment and advocated total freedom of expression. He was dismissed from the École and, after an attempt to defend himself failed to win him another position, moved to New York and then to Paris in 1955, where he died five years later.

BOUCHARD, TÉLESPHORE-DAMIEN (1881-1962), politician. Bouchard worked as a journalist before being elected to the Quebec legislature as a Liberal in 1912 and becoming mayor of his home town in 1917. He held both posts until 1944. He was speaker of the legislature, a minister under L.A. TASCHEREAU and ADÉLARD GODBOUT, and was appointed a senator in 1944. He caused a furor in 1944 by maintaining that a secret Quebec society, the Ordre de Jacques Cartier, was a danger to democracy.

BOUEY, GERALD KEITH (1920-), central banker. Bouey served in the RCAF during World War II, attended Queen's Univ. and joined the BANK OF CANADA in 1948, succeeding LOUIS RASMINSKY as governor in 1973. During the early 1980s, Bouey sought to handle inflation with monetarist policies. He retired in 1986.

BOUNDARY WATERS TREATY, treaty negotiated between Canada and the United States in 1909 regarding the use of water resources along the border. The treaty created the INTERNATIONAL JOINT COMMISSION in 1911 to deal with disputes.

BOURASSA, HENRI (1878-1952), Quebec politician. One of Quebec's most famous nationalist figures, Bourassa was born at Montreal to a prominent family; his grandfather, Louis-Joseph Papineau, was a leader of the 1837 Rebellion. Bourassa entered politics at 22 when he was elected mayor of Montebello. In 1896 he was

elected to the House of Commons as a Liberal but resigned in 1899 over Prime Minister WILFRID LAURIER's decision to send troops to the BOER WAR. He was re-elected in 1900, resigned again in 1907 to sit in the Quebec Legislature from 1908 to 1912, and returned again to the House of Commons from 1925 to 1935. He founded *Le Devoir*, the influential nationalist newspaper, in 1910, but resigned from it in 1932. Always at the centre of the nationalist question, the high point of Bourassa's career came in 1911 when his efforts to defeat Laurier helped ROBERT BORDEN to power. In 1917, he joined with Laurier to oppose Borden's CONSCRIPTION measure. Bourassa devoted his later years to defending Catholic values against the threat posed by modern society.

BOURASSA, ROBERT (1933-), premier of Quebec. Born at Montreal, Bourassa was called to the bar in 1957 before attending Oxford Univ. He returned to Canada and between 1960 and 1966 served as fiscal adviser to the Department of National Revenue and professor at the univs. of Ottawa, Laval, and Montréal. He entered Quebec politics in 1966, succeeding JEAN LESAGE as Liberal leader in 1970. He formed his first government that year and won the 1973 election, taking 102 of 110 seats. Defeated by the PARTI QUÉBÉCOIS in 1976, Bourassa resigned and went abroad. He returned to Quebec in 1980 to oppose SOVEREIGNTY-ASSOCIATION and was re-elected Liberal leader in 1983, taking the party to victory over the Parti Québécois in 1985.

BOURGAULT, PIERRE (1934-), separatist leader. Bourgault worked in radio and television; he joined the RASSEMBLEMENT POUR L'INDÉPENDANCE NATIONALE, becoming leader in 1964. After the party did better than expected in the 1966 provincial election, he united it with the PARTI QUÉBÉCOIS in 1968.

BOURGET, IGNACE (1799-1885), Roman Catholic bishop of Montreal. Born at Point-Lévis, Lower Canada, Bourget was educated at the Séminaire de Québec and Collège de Nicolet, and ordained in 1822. By 1840 he was bishop of Montreal and he worked with great energy to expand and consolidate the church's hold on his large flock. Leading the ultramontane faction, Bourget clashed with PARTI ROUGE elements and the INSTITUT CANADIEN DE QUÉBEC, which looked to see clerical influence diminished. Bourget fought without quarter and, if only for planting the seeds of political strife, was unquestionably the most influential cleric of his day. *See also* ULTRAMONTANISM.

BOURINOT, SIR JOHN GEORGE (1837-1902), parliamentarian. He founded and edited the Halifax *Herald*. He joined the staff of HANSARD in the House of Commons in 1868, became assistant and then chief clerk of the Commons, and the leading expert on parliamentary procedure. *Bourinot's Rules* remain the basic guide.

Sir Mackenzie Bowell

BOWELL, SIR MACKENZIE (1823-1917), prime minister of Canada. Born at Rickinghall, Eng., he apprenticed as a printer, becoming owner and editor of the Belleville *Intelligencer* and a prominent member of the ORANGE ORDER. Bowell was elected to the House of Commons as a Conservative in 1867 and served as minister of customs and minister of militia and defence before becoming a senator in 1892. He was minister of trade and commerce from 1892 until he succeeded SIR JOHN THOMPSON as prime minister in 1894. Weak and ineffectual, he was forced to resign after seven of his ministers threatened to

quit over the MANITOBA SCHOOLS QUESTION in 1896. Bowell led the opposition in the Senate between 1896 and 1906.

BOWSER, WILLIAM JOHN (1867-1933), premier of British Columbia. Born at Rexton, N.B., Bowser, a lawyer, moved to Vancouver in 1891. Elected to the legislature as a Conservative in 1903, Bowser succeeded SIR RICHARD MCBRIDE as premier in Dec. 1915. The next year he lost the election and led the opposition until 1924.

BOYLE, JOSEPH WHITESIDE (1867-1923), adventurer. He was born in Toronto and raised in Woodstock, Ont. In his teens he worked as a sailor, and then started a freighting company in New York. The KLONDIKE GOLD RUSH made his fortune, and he remained in the Yukon until the outbreak of World War I when he contributed a machine gun battery to the government. He then did intelligence work in Russia, and after the Armistice he stayed in Europe where he became a close friend and rescuer of Queen Marie of Romania.

John Bracken

BRACKEN, JOHN (1883-1969), premier of Manitoba, federal politician. Born at Ellisville, Ont., Bracken moved to the Prairies, becoming professor of field husbandry at the Univ. of Saskatchewan in 1910 and president of the Manitoba Agricultural College in 1920. He involved himself in politics and was premier of the province for twenty years as head of the UNITED FARMERS OF MANITOBA (1922-8), PROGRESSIVE PARTY (1928-31), Liberal-Progressive party (1931-40), and the coalition (1940-3). In 1942 he succeeded ARTHUR MEIGHEN as leader of the federal Conservatives after the party agreed to change its name to PROGRESSIVE CONSERVATIVE but he did not seek election to the House of Commons until 1945, a fatal error. A wooden speaker, he led the party to defeat in 1945 and sat as opposition leader until ill-health and incipient party revolt forced him to resign in 1948.

BRANCH PLANT, term used to describe business establishments in Canada, usually engaged in manufacturing, which are branches of companies based in the United States. The NATIONAL POLICY tariff of 1879, which generally blocked U.S.-produced goods from free entry into the Canadian market, encouraged the establishment of branch plants by companies wishing to avoid those tariffs. Canadians generally welcomed the jobs and investment these plants brought.

BRASCAN, holding company, founded in 1912 as Brazilian Traction, Light, Heat and Power. In that year SIR WILLIAM MACKENZIE and F.S. Pearson pulled a number of Brazilian investments into one holding company. It was enormously successful for 50 years but by the 1960s the Brazilian government's nationalization policy began undermining the corporation's profitability. After turning to North America as a field for investment, the company acquired a major share in the John Labatt brewing empire. The name of the holding company was then changed to Brascan. With profitable investments in North and South America, the company has become one of Canada's most powerful corporations.

BRAZILIAN TRACTION, LIGHT, HEAT AND POWER, *see* BRASCAN

BREBNER, JOHN BARTLET (1895-1957), historian. Trained at the univs. of Toronto, Oxford, and Columbia, Brebner taught at the Univ. of Toronto for four years, moving to Columbia Univ. in 1925. His most important work was *The*

North Atlantic Triangle (1945), a study of the interplay of Canada, the United States, and Britain.

BREN GUN SCANDAL, 1938 scandal over a contract to build Bren light machine guns awarded to the John Inglis Co. of Toronto by the Canadian and British governments. GEORGE DREW cricitized the award because Inglis was the only company approached, and a royal commission was set up to investigate the matter. The commission found no evidence of corruption but recommended that negotiation of future contracts be placed in the hands of an advisory group of "competent business men." The government subsequently set up a Defence Purchasing Board (1939) and instituted the principle of competitive bids. Inglis was allowed to keep the contract and before the end of World War II, the company produced over 200,000 Bren guns.

BRICKLIN, sports car manufactured by Bricklin (Canada) Ltd in New Brunswick. The New Brunswick provincial government provided financial assistance to Malcolm Bricklin, a millionaire from Phoenix, Ariz., who designed and developed the car. The first car was produced in 1973 but the company went into receivership in 1975.

BRITISH AMERICAN OIL CO., company founded in 1906 by Toronto's E.L. Ellesworth. By the 1930s, British American was one of Canada's largest oil companies, rivalling IMPERIAL OIL in service station sales. In 1956 Gulf Oil (Canada), a subsidiary of the Gulf Oil Co., merged with BA and the Canadian company became part of the world-wide Gulf empire.

BRITISH COLUMBIA FEDERATIONIST, Labour newspaper founded in 1912 when the British Columbia Federation of Labor purchased an interest in and renamed the *Western Wage Earner*, official organ of the Vancouver Trades and Labor Council. For more than a decade it was a prominent voice of western labour radicalism.

BRITISH COMMONWEALTH AIR TRAINING PLAN, a WORLD WAR II scheme to train air crew agreed to on 17 Dec. 1939 by Britain, Canada, Australia, and New Zealand. Canada became the hub of this extraordinary training plan. Under the agreement, Canada undertook to cover most of the costs, in substantial part because Prime Minister MACKENZIE KING assumed that air war, which he hoped could be the focus of the Canadian effort, would not produce casualties as large as those suffered in trench fighting in World War I. This, King hoped, could prevent another CONSCRIPTION crisis. The ROYAL CANADIAN AIR FORCE ran the training program which got underway in late April 1940. At its peak, the BCATP had 107 Canadian schools, a ground establishment of more than 104,000, and 10,906 aircraft. Aircrew trained numbered 131,553 pilots, bombardiers, gunners, navigators, and flight engineers of which 72,835 were Canadian. The cost to Canada was $1.6 billion, 75 per cent of the total.

The Canadian graduates did not all join RCAF squadrons. The British expected Canadian aircrew to join Royal Air Force units, and the King government had insisted only that Canada badges be worn, while relying on a vague clause in the 1939 agreement that RCAF units and formations overseas might be organized. As a result, and despite Air Minister C.G. POWER's long struggle for "Canadianization," most RCAF personnel served with RAF units, although eventually there were 45 RCAF squadrons overseas and another 40 at home.

BRITISH EMPIRE STEEL CO. (BESCO), holding company formed in 1920 which amalgamated several Cape Breton industries including NOVA SCOTIA STEEL, DOMINION COAL, DOMINION IRON AND STEEL, and Dominion Steel. Roy Wolvin of Montreal put together the syndicate that financed the formation of Besco. The syndicate hoped to modernize the existing industries and turn them into world-class operations. A postwar decline in markets and fierce labour struggles upset Wolvin's plans and in 1928, Besco went bankrupt.

BRITISH NORTH AMERICA ACT, constitution of the Dominion of Canada, passed by the British Parliament in Mar. 1867 and proclaimed 1 July 1867 (DOMINION DAY). It brought about the CONFEDERATION of the British colonies of Nova Scotia, New Brunswick, and the UNITED PROVINCE OF CANADA. The new dominion remained a colony with no control over foreign affairs although it was virtually self-governing in internal matters and trade policy. The BNA Act established four provincial governments, Ontario (formerly Canada West), Quebec (formerly Canada East), New Brunswick, and Nova Scotia, with powers over local and municipal matters, culture, education, PROPERTY AND CIVIL RIGHTS, and general welfare within the province. It also established a federal government, located at Ottawa, with wide powers of taxation, responsibility for the "PEACE, ORDER AND GOOD GOVERNMENT" of Canada, and authority over internal trade, transportation, and communications across provincial boundaries. The proclamation of the BNA Act brought the DOMINION OF CANADA into existence. Other provinces were later added beginning with Manitoba in 1870. In 1982 the British North America Act was incorporated into the CONSTITUTION ACT, and was renamed the CONSTITUTION ACT, 1867. *See also* MANITOBA ACT.

BRITISH PREFERENCE, see IMPERIAL PREFERENCES

BRITISH SUBJECT, official status of Canadians until the CANADIAN CITIZENSHIP ACT of 1947 introduced the legal concept of Canadian citizenship. Until 1947, persons born or naturalized in Canada became British citizens or subjects, while British subjects moving to Canada were automatically given the right to vote or contest elections.

BRITNELL, GEORGE EDWIN (1903-61), economist. Born at London, Eng., Britnell was educated at the univs. of Saskatchewan and Toronto and the London School of Economics. He taught at the Univ. of Saskatchewan from 1930, was an adviser to the provincial government on transportation and dominion-provincial questions, and chaired a federal royal commission on coal mining. His best-known book was *The Wheat Economy* (1939).

BRITTAIN, MILLER GORE (1912-68), artist. Born at Saint John, N.B., Brittain attended the Art Students League in New York in 1930-2. His most notable paintings were of ordinary citizens or workers, sometimes satirically drawn. After wartime service in the ROYAL CANADIAN AIR FORCE, his work became more surrealistic.

BROADBENT, JOHN EDWARD (1936–), politician. Born at Oshawa, Ont., Ed Broadbent became professor of political science at York Univ. in 1965. First elected to the House of Commons in 1968, he succeeded DAVID LEWIS as leader of the federal NEW DEMOCRATIC PARTY in 1975, and led the party to its peak of popularity in the opinion polls well into 1987. For the first time in its history, the NDP led the Liberals and Progressive Conservatives, and Broadbent himself was the preferred party leader by a wide margin.

"BROADENING OUT," concept advocated by some members of the PROGRESSIVE PARTY in the 1920s, which called for the spread of Progressive ideals to others. It looked to the creation of a broad national movement but was countered within the party by the idea of GROUP GOVERNMENT.

BROCKINGTON, LEONARD WALTER (1888-1966), broadcaster. Born at Cardiff, Wales, Brockington was called to the bar in Edmonton in 1919. He was named chairman of the CANADIAN BROADCASTING CORP. in 1936, was special assistant to MACKENZIE KING from 1939 to 1942, and an adviser to the British Ministry of Information in 1942-3. He was best known, however, as a great speaker.

BRODA, WALTER, "Turk" (1914-72), hockey player. Born at Brandon, Man., Broda was goaltender for the Toronto Maple Leafs from 1936 to 1952, and thrice winner of the VEZINA Trophy. Chubby, he was once ordered to lose weight by the team's owners, a diet that attracted front-page attention.

BRONFMAN, SAMUEL (1891-1971), manufacturer. Born in Brandon, Man., Bronfman was the son of a Russian immigrant who arrived in Canada in 1889. Samuel was instrumental in his family's domination of the Canadian liquor manufacturing and sales business which came with the takeover of the JOSEPH SEAGRAM CO. in 1928. The Bronfman-owned Distillers Corp. boomed selling liquor to American gangsters during the PROHIBITION era. After the repeal of prohibition, Bronfman engineered a world-wide expansion of Distillers Corp. providing a base for major investments by the Bronfman family in the financial industry, landholding and development, manufacturing, and food and beverages.

BROWN, ARTHUR ROY (1893-1944), WORLD WAR I pilot. Born at Carleton Place, Ont., Brown claimed 11 victories and was said to have shot down Manfred von Richtofen, the "Red Baron." After suffering a flying accident, he left the Royal Air Force.

courtesy Notman and Fraser/National Archives of Canada/C-6165

George Brown

BROWN, GEORGE (1818-80), journalist, politician, FATHER OF CONFEDERATION. Born in Alloa, Scot., he settled in Toronto in 1843 after spending a brief time in the United States. In 1844 he founded the *Globe* newspaper to support the causes of responsible government and freer trade, and in 1851 he was elected to the Legislative Assembly of the UNITED PROVINCE OF CANADA. As politician and newspaper publisher, Brown pushed the interests of Toronto as a major transportation and commercial centre, although he also reflected the concerns of the farmers of the western part of the province. The latter group wanted cheaper government, lower tariffs, more democracy – and especially representation by population (REP-BY-POP) – and no government aid to Catholic schools. Their political views were most clearly reflected by the CLEAR GRIT movement, which Brown eventually led. At one point in

1858, he shared power with A.-A. DORION, leader of the PARTI ROUGES, in the assembly. In 1864 Brown joined with JOHN A. MACDONALD and others to form the GREAT COALITION, a temporary political alliance that engineered CONFEDERATION. Brown was defeated in a bid to win a seat in the first Canadian Parliament in the 1867 election but remained a major political force through the *Globe*. He was strongly anti-union and led Toronto publishers in the TORONTO PRINTERS' STRIKE of 1872. He died in 1880 after being shot by a disgruntled former employee.

BROWN, JAMES SUTHERLAND (1881-1951), soldier. Born at Simcoe, Ont., "Buster" Brown joined the militia in 1896, the regular army in 1906, and served overseas in WORLD WAR I. In the 1920s as director of Military Operations and Intelligence at army headquarters, he drafted a defence scheme against the United States that saw Canadian mobile columns striking southward. He retired in 1933.

BROWNLEE, JOHN EDWARD (1883-1961), premier of Alberta. Born at Port Ryerse, Ont., Brownlee attended the Univ. of Toronto before venturing to Alberta in 1909. He joined the Alberta bar and became a legal adviser for the UNITED FARMERS OF ALBERTA, serving as attorney general in its first government from 1921 to 1924. He took over as premier in 1925 after HERBERT GREENFIELD resigned, and he won control for Alberta over its natural resources. Unable to pull the province out of the Depression and involved in a paternity suit, he passed the leadership to R.G. Reid shortly before a 1935 election disaster for him and his party. He was president of the UNITED GRAIN GROWERS before his death at Calgary.

BRUCE, HERBERT ALEXANDER (1868-1963), physician, politician. Born at Blackstock, Ont., Bruce studied at the Univ. of Toronto and at leading hospitals elsewhere. He founded Wellesley Hospital in Toronto, and then became inspector-general of the Canadian Army Medical Corps in 1916, a post that involved him in massive controversy over his charges of patronage and poor care of the wounded. Named lieutenant-governor of Ontario in 1932 by the BENNETT government, he played a more active political role than was the norm. In 1940 he was elected to

Parliament as a Conservative, called for CONSCRIPTION, and was ejected from the House in 1944 for his denunciations of Quebec during the debate on FAMILY ALLOWANCES.

BRUCHÉSI, JEAN (1901-79), diplomat, historian. Born at Montreal, Bruchési, a lawyer, taught international politics at the Univ. de Montréal from 1929 to 1952 and Canadian history at the Collège Marguerite Bourgeoys from 1932 to 1959. He produced a number of books on Canadian history and international relations. In 1959 he became ambassador to Spain, and then served in Morocco, Argentina, and other South American countries.

BRUNET, MICHEL (1917-85), historian. Born at Montreal, Brunet taught at the Univ. de Montréal from 1949. His major work, *Le Présence anglaise et les Canadiens* (1958), along with his other writings, helped prepare the intellectual climate of SEPARATISM.

BRYCE, ROBERT B. (1910–), public servant. Born at Toronto, Bryce was educated at the Univ. of Toronto, Cambridge (under J.M. Keynes), and Harvard. He returned to Canada and entered the Department of Finance in 1938. An early advocate of Keynesian economic theory, he played a key role in the development of economic policy for 30 years. He served as clerk of the Privy Council and secretary to the cabinet during the DIEFENBAKER government, became deputy minister of finance in 1963, and Canadian executive director to the INTERNATIONAL MONETARY FUND in 1971. In 1975 he was appointed to head the Royal Commission on Corporate Concentration.

BUCHAN, JOHN, 1st BARON TWEEDS-MUIR (1875-1940), governor general of Canada. Buchan had a varied career which included a stint in South Africa, literary adviser and later director of Thomas Nelson and Sons (1906-29), and member of the British House of Commons (1927-35). An intelligence officer during World War I, he developed a deep commitment to peace, something he shared with Prime Minister MACKENZIE KING who was in power during his Canadian term, 1935-40. He was a prolific writer of history, biography, and thrillers, notably *Sir Walter Raleigh* (1911), *Lord Minto* (1924), *The*

courtesy National Archives of Canada/C-8057

John Buchan, 1st Baron Tweedsmuir

Thirty-Nine Steps (1915), and his autobiography, *Memory Hold-the-door*, completed shortly before his death at Montreal. In 1937 he initiated the Governor General's Literary Awards.

BUCHANAN, JOHN MACLENNAN (1931–), premier of Nova Scotia. Born at Sydney, N.S., Buchanan, a lawyer, was elected to the provincial legislature in 1967 and became leader of the N.S. Progressive Conservative party in 1971. He led his party to victory in 1978 and won elections in 1981 and 1984.

BUCK, TIM (1891-1973), leader of the COMMUNIST PARTY OF CANADA from 1929 to 1961. He came to Canada from England in 1910 and became active in the machinists' union. In 1921 he helped found the CPC. During the worldwide Communist split between the followers of Leon Trotsky and Joseph Stalin in the late 1920s, Buck followed the Stalinists and, as a result, he was named party leader in 1929. He spent 1932-4 in jail during the GREAT DEPRESSION when the CPC was outlawed. He was also forced "underground" during World War II when the government again outlawed the CPC, this time because of its opposition to the war. When the CPC re-emerged as the legal LABOUR PROGRESSIVE PARTY in 1943, Buck was once again leader.

BUHAY, REBECCA, "BECKY" (1896-1953), Communist activist. Born in London, Eng., Buhay came to Montreal in 1912 and became a labour activist during and after World War I, organizing in the garment districts. She joined the COMMUNIST PARTY OF CANADA in 1922, served on its national executive, and continued her proselytizing until her death.

BUNKHOUSE MEN, workers who laboured in the bush in the late 19th and early 20th century, usually for the railways in northern areas of Canada. Bunkhouse men repaired track and rights of way and often lived in freight cars adapted for sleeping. The name was used by Edmund Bradwin in *The Bunkhouse Men*, published in 1928, a study of the lives of these men.

BURNS, EEDSON LOUIS MILLARD (1897-1986), soldier. Born at Westmount, Que., Burns graduated from the ROYAL MILITARY COLLEGE in 1915, fought in World War I, and pursued studies in England and India before returning to Canada to head the geographical section of the General Staff, 1931-6. He held a number posts during WORLD WAR II in England and Italy, where he commanded the 5th Canadian Armoured Division and 1st Canadian Corps. He was relieved in 1944, retired from the army in 1947, and became a public servant. In 1955 Burns joined the Department of External Affairs and was commander of the UNITED NATIONS EMERGENCY FORCE from 1956 to 1959. Between 1960 and 1969 he was chief adviser to the Canadian government on disarmament. He was professor of strategic studies at Carleton Univ. from 1972 to 1975.

BURNS, PATRICK (1856-1937), rancher, meat packer. Born in Oshawa, Canada West, Burns began homesteading in Manitoba in the 1880s and earned extra cash by selling beef to CPR construction gangs. He later moved to southern Alberta, where he ranched and entered the meat-packing business in BURNS MEATS LTD. He was a founder of the CALGARY STAMPEDE. Burns was appointed to the Senate in 1931. *See also* BIG FOUR CATTLEMEN.

BURNS, TOMMY (1881-1955), boxer. Born at Hanover, Ont., as Noah Brusso, he trained as a welterweight before taking the heavyweight title away from Marvin Hart in 1906. The only Canadian world heavyweight boxing champion, he defended his title 10 times before losing to the famed Jack Johnson in Dec. 1908.

BURNS MEATS LTD, Calgary meat-packing company founded by PATRICK BURNS in 1890 as P. Burns and Co. Burns sold his interest in the company in 1928. Burns Meats introduced canned meats into the Canadian market in 1928. It eventually diversified into many different areas of food merchandising, acquiring dairies and other subsidiary companies.

BUSH, JOHN HAMILTON (1909-77), painter. Jack Bush was born at Toronto and trained there and in Montreal. He worked in advertising as an illustrator and began painting representational landscapes. By the 1960s he was hailed as Canada's leading abstract artist, notable for his boldly coloured canvases.

Viscount Byng of Vimy

BYNG, JULIAN HEDWORTH GEORGE, VISCOUNT BYNG OF VIMY (1862-1935), soldier, governor general of Canada. Born at Wrotham Park, Eng., he entered the British army in 1883 and served in the Sudan and South Africa before entering WORLD WAR I as a calvary officer. In May 1916 he took command of the CANADIAN CORPS and directed the attack on VIMY RIDGE in April 1917. Appointed governor general in 1921, he was involved in the controversial KING-BYNG AFFAIR after refusing Prime Minister MACKENZIE KING's request for a dissolution of Parliament in

1926. He later was chief commissioner of the London Metropolitan police (1928-31).

CABBAGETOWN, nickname for the area in Toronto bounded by Parliament Street on the west, the Don Valley on the east, St James Cemetery on the north, and Gerrard Street on the south. The area was originally settled by Irish peasants fleeing the Irish potato famine in the 19th century. It became known as an area of poor and unemployed people, especially during the GREAT DEPRESSION. HUGH GARNER's novel, *Cabbagetown*, made it into a national institution.

CABINET WAR COMMITTEE, senior ministerial committee formed to deal with problems arising from Canada's participation in WORLD WAR II. Initially called the "Emergency Council," it assumed its title on 5 Dec. 1939. The committee included the ministers who directed Canada's war effort.

Léo Cadieux

CADIEUX, LÉO (1908–), politician. A journalist, Cadieux worked for *L'Avenir du Nord* until joining the Canadian army's directorate of public relations in 1940. In 1944 he was a war correspondent overseas for *La Presse*, and on his return to Canada he became involved in municipal politics in Quebec. He won election to Parliament as a Liberal in 1962, then became associate defence minister in 1965 and defence minister two years later with the task of implementing UNIFICATION. In that post under PIERRE TRUDEAU, he fought vigorously – and successfully – to maintain the Canadian military commitment to NATO but was unable to prevent troop cuts. From 1970 to 1975 he was ambassador in Paris, charged with blocking French attempts to meddle in Quebec.

CAISSES POPULAIRES, savings and loan cooperatives found largely in Quebec but occasionally also in other francophone areas of Canada. The first caisse was established by ALPHONSE DESJARDINS in 1900 in Lévis, Que., primarily in an effort to keep the savings of francophones in Quebec. Many caisses were religiously or locally based, accounting for their great popularity in rural areas and in small towns where great distrust existed for the large anglophone banks. The caisses are now among the most popular deposit-taking institutions in Quebec and are a major factor in the financial life of that province.

CALGARY STAMPEDE, annual agricultural fair and rodeo held at Calgary. The first stampede, organized by Guy Weadick and financed by the BIG FOUR CATTLEMEN, was held in 1912.

CAMP, DALTON KINGSLEY (1920–), writer, politician, bureaucrat. Born in Woodstock, N.B., Camp was educated at the Univ. of New Brunswick, Columbia Univ. and the London School of Economics. Initially a Liberal, he switched to the Conservatives and, as an advertising specialist, helped organize ROBERT STANFIELD's first election victory in Nova Scotia in 1956. He worked for the federal party in the elections of 1957 and 1958 and became the PROGRESSIVE CONSERVATIVE PARTY national president in 1964. Disillusioned with JOHN DIEFENBAKER, Camp played a critical role in organizing the Chief's ouster in 1967 and Stanfield's selection as national leader. Camp then became a newspaper columnist, published several books, and, during the government of BRIAN MULRONEY, joined the Privy Council Office as a senior adviser to the prime minister.

CAMP X, spy training camp near Whitby, Ont., 1941-6. Special Training School No. 103 was run by British Security Coordination, the British agency operating from New York and run by SIR WILLIAM STEPHENSON, to train agents in techniques of secret warfare. The camp was also the site of Hydra, a communications network linking Canada, the United States, and Britain.

CAMPBELL, ALEXANDER BRADSHAW (1933–), premier of Prince Edward Island. Born at Summerside, P.E.I., and a lawyer, he became premier in 1966. His Liberal government introduced progressive legislation and negotiated with Ottawa the Comprehensive Development Plan to encourage economic growth. He left politics in 1978 and was appointed to the P.E.I. Supreme Court.

CAMPBELL, DOUGLAS LLOYD (1895–), premier of Manitoba. Born at High Bluff, Man., he won election to the legislature in 1922 as a farmer's candidate. Fourteen years later he became agriculture minister in JOHN BRACKEN's government, and in 1948 he became Liberal premier of a coalition government. He won the 1949 and 1953 elections but lost in 1958 to the Conservatives – who were if anything more liberal than he.

CAMPBELL, THANE ALEXANDER (1895-1978), premier of Prince Edward Island. A Rhodes Scholar and a lawyer, Campbell was born at Summerside, P.E.I. In 1930 he was named attorney general in a Liberal administration that lost power in 1931. In 1935 he returned to the same office and in 1936 became premier, a post he held until 1943 when he was named the Island's chief justice. He filled that office until 1970.

CAMSELL, CHARLES (1876-1958), mining engineer. Born in Fort Liard, NWT, Camsell joined the GEOLOGICAL SURVEY OF CANADA in 1904. He was named deputy minister of mines in 1920. During his time as deputy minister he modernized the department's approach to surveying, mapping, and laboratory work.

CANADA AND ITS PROVINCES, major historical series published in Toronto between 1917 and 1923. Edited by ADAM SHORTT and ARTHUR

DOUGHTY, it covered Canada's historical, political, and economic development in 23 volumes. The sections on the economy retain their usefulness 70 years later.

CANADA ASSISTANCE PLAN, federal program, established 1966, to pay 50 per cent of the costs of provincial-municipal social assistance programs, including health care of welfare recipients, assistance to needy mothers, job training, etc. It remains in effect.

CANADA COUNCIL, cultural agency established by the federal government in 1957 following recommendations contained in the report of the ROYAL COMMISSION ON THE NATIONAL DEVELOPMENT OF THE ARTS, LETTERS AND SCIENCES, headed by VINCENT MASSEY. The council was set up with funds drawn from federal taxes levied on the estates of IZAAK KILLAM and SIR JAMES DUNN. It was designed to stimulate artistic and cultural activity, as well as post-graduate education, through grants to individuals and institutions. Many of its granting functions to scholars were assumed by the Social Sciences and Humanities Research Council after the latter began operations in 1978.

CANADA CYCLE AND MOTOR CO. LTD, manufacturing company formed in 1899 when the GEORGE COX financial group amalgamated five small bicycle companies into one large manufacturer. At one time CCM branched out of bicycle manufacturing to produce and sell automobiles; it sold the first Ford in Canada and manufactured the Ivanhoe electric car and the Russell, a popular car named after CCM's general manager. Although CCM still markets bicycles, it is now better known as a producer of sports equipment.

CANADA DEVELOPMENT CORP., investment company created by the federal government in 1971 to stimulate Canadian investment in the economy. A number of CROWN CORPORATIONS were given to the CDC by the federal government including Canterra Energy Ltd, Polysar Ltd, and Connaught Laboratories. It is 48 per cent owned by the federal government, the rest by private shareholders, and its headquarters are in Vancouver.

CANADA EAST, the eastern administrative district of the UNITED PROVINCE OF CANADA. It was referred to as LOWER CANADA prior to the Constitution Act of 1840 which united Upper and Lower Canada. Canada East became the Province of Quebec at CONFEDERATION.

CANADA FIRST, Ontario-based nationalist movement formed in 1868. Led by GEORGE DENISON, CHARLES MAIR and others, Canada First was committed to fostering Canadian nationalism through the imperial tie with Britain. It was supposed to stimulate national feeling in the new dominion, but became a stridently anglophone nationalistic movement which alienated French Canada and roused prejudices in Ontario against the MÉTIS and their leader, LOUIS RIEL. It effectively disappeared before 1900.

CANADA HOUSE, office of the Canadian HIGH COMMISSIONER in the United Kingdom. Canada House stands on Trafalgar Square in London and was opened in 1925.

CANADA LABOUR RELATIONS BOARD, federal labour agency established by the INDUSTRIAL RELATIONS AND DISPUTES INVESTIGATION ACT of 1948. The board had jurisdiction over all federal employees, employees of crown corporations, and employees engaged directly in interprovincial trade and commerce. It is a quasi-judicial board with power to certify and decertify unions, conduct certification votes, decide the size and composition of bargaining units, and enforce unfair labour practices legislation.

CANADA MORTGAGE AND HOUSING CORP., CROWN CORPORATION established in 1945 to administer the NATIONAL HOUSING ACT. CMHC insures mortgage loans, funds construction of socially useful housing, and does research on building technology.

CANADA PACKERS INC., food products company established in 1927. It amalgamated a number of packing houses including the WILLIAM DAVIES CO. which had once been headed by J.W. FLAVELLE. *See also* J.S. MCLEAN.

CANADA PENSION PLAN, a universal, publicly operated pension plan funded by employers and employees, introduced by the Liberal government of Prime Minister LESTER PEARSON in 1966. The pension payable to eligible persons is dependent on earnings, unlike the OLD AGE PENSION which is a standard, lump sum paid to all Canadians over 65 years of age. SOCIAL INSURANCE NUMBERS for all employed Canadians were introduced along with the Canada Pension Plan to enable the federal government to keep track of pensionable earnings.

CANADA-SOVIET HOCKEY SERIES, a series of eight games pitting a team of Canadian professional all-stars from the National Hockey League against the national team of the Soviet Union in Sept. 1972. This was the first occasion in which Canadian professionals played in international competition. After losing the first game in Montreal, Canada won the series four games to three with one game tied. Paul Henderson scored the winning goal for Canada in the final game.

CANADA STEAMSHIP LINES INC., transportation company incorporated in 1913 following the merger of several shipping lines. Its parent company was the Richelieu Steamboat Co., formed in 1845 by a group of farmers from the St-Charles-sur-Richelieu area of Quebec. The company provided both freight and passenger service on the Great Lakes and the St Lawrence River until 1965 when the passenger operations were discontinued. After 1965 the company's freight business expanded with the introduction of container services.

CANADA STUDIES FOUNDATION, organization founded in 1970 to promote the study of Canada. Originally financed by Trinity College School in Port Hope, Ont., provincial and federal support has kept it going since 1978.

CANADA TEMPERANCE ACT, see PROHIBITION

CANADA-UNITED KINGDOM LOAN AGREEMENT, 1946, loan granted to Britain by the government of Prime Minister MACKENZIE KING. The loan was an attempt to keep up Canada's exports to Britain in the postwar years and also to help the British. London secured $1.25 billion from Canada and another $3.75 billion from the United States.

CANADA-UNITED STATES AUTO PACT, signed in Jan. 1965 to provide a large measure of free trade in motor vehicles and motor vehicle parts between Canada and the United States. For all intents and purposes, the Auto Pact created a North American free trade automotive market and ended Canada's isolation from basic automotive manufacturing. There has always been disagreement over whether the Auto Pact most benefited Canada or the United States but there can be no doubt that the Canadian automotive industry has thrived as a result of the treaty.

CANADA WEST, the western administrative district of the UNITED PROVINCE OF CANADA. It was referred to as UPPER CANADA prior to the Constitution Act of 1840 which united Upper and Lower Canada. Canada West became the Province of Ontario at CONFEDERATION.

CANADAIR LTD, aircraft manufacturer founded during World War II as a CROWN CORPORATION based on the Vickers Aircraft Co. of Montreal. From 1944 to 1947 it produced the PBY-5 aircraft used by a variety of Allied sea and air forces. In 1947 Canadair was purchased by the Electric Boat Co. of the United States to become part of the General Dynamics Corp. Canadair produced a variety of civilian and military aircraft in the 1940s, 1950s, and 1960s including the Canadair Sabre and the NORTH STAR transport. Canadair was purchased by the federal government in 1976 and sold to a Quebec consortium headed by Bombardier Ltd in 1986.

CANADARM, a complex crane used aboard the U.S. Space Shuttle to load cargo and launch satellites in space. Designed and built in Canada, it won high marks when first used in 1981 on the second Space Shuttle flight. The National Aeronautics and Space Administration has since purchased three Canadarms.

CANADIAN AIRWAYS, air transportation company formed in 1930 when JAMES RICHARDSON's Western Canadian Airways amalgamated with several other transportation companies. Richardson's hopes to win federal airmail contracts were squashed by a government economy drive and, throughout the 1930s, Canadian Airways was forced to rely on northern bush service to keep itself in operation. In 1937 the federal Liberal government created a major rival to Canadian Airways when it established Trans-Canada Airlines (AIR CANADA). Richardson realized that Canadian Airways would not be able to compete with TCA and sold the airline to Canadian Pacific during World War II. In 1942 Canadian Pacific amalgamated Canadian Airways and several other small companies to form CANADIAN PACIFIC AIRLINES.

CANADIAN ARMED FORCES, name of the Canadian military established by the Canadian Forces Reorganization Act. When the act came into force on 1 Feb. 1968, the CANADIAN ARMY, the ROYAL CANADIAN NAVY, and the ROYAL CANADIAN AIR FORCE ceased to exist. In their place was a single service with officers and men wearing a new dark green uniform. In April 1969 Prime Minister PIERRE TRUDEAU announced Canada's new defence priorities, putting the protection of sovereignty at the top of the list and peacekeeping at the bottom. In that same year, Canada's NATO contingent was halved to 5000 and the overall strength of the forces was cut by 20,000 to approximately 82,000. Canada's military was entering its long, dark night, and for the next 15 years, equipment grew older and more obsolescent. By September 1984 the Canadian Armed Forces were remarkably weak. The new Conservative government of BRIAN MULRONEY promised to remedy this and began on its task, slowly beginning to undo unification with expensive new uniforms, building new ships, buying new aircraft, bolstering the NATO commitment, and in mid-1987 producing a new White Paper that called for the purchase of nuclear submarines, an enhanced effort to protect sovereignty, and greater commitment to the NATO front.

CANADIAN ARMY, the land forces of Canada, 1946-68. Before 1946 Canada's land forces had been called by a variety of names—MILITIA, the CANADIAN EXPEDITIONARY FORCE, the NON-PERMANENT ACTIVE MILITIA, and NATIONAL RESOURCES MOBILIZATION ACT soldiers. The strength of the Canadian army regular force was fixed at 25,000 in 1946, but with rearmament, NATO membership, and the KOREAN WAR, numbers soared to 52,000 by 1952. The army in that year had a brigade in Europe and another in Korea. In 1956 the force sent a substantial contingent to the UNITED NATIONS EMERGENCY FORCE in Egypt, and in 1964 a battalion to Cyprus for UN duties. By the 1960s equipment was aging, tanks especially needing replacement, and by the time UNIFICATION came into effect in 1968, the Canadian land forces were in serious need of re-equipment and a redefinition of policy.

CANADIAN BANKERS' ASSN, organization established in 1900 by Canadian banks to lobby government for more favourable treatment in the BANK ACT. Since the first such act was passed in 1871 the government had been reviewing it approximately once every decade. Inevitably the government came to rely on the association for advice not only in the drafting of new legislation but in choosing the minister of finance. The association's influence began to wane in the 1970s with the expansion of trust companies and other "near banks" into the deposit-taking market.

CANADIAN BANK OF COMMERCE, *see* CANADIAN IMPERIAL BANK OF COMMERCE

CANADIAN BROADCASTING CORP., crown corporation created in 1936 to replace the CANADIAN RADIO BROADCASTING COMMISSION (1932) and to broadcast to all parts of Canada. Initially given wide powers to regulate private stations and disseminate Canadian culture in the face of growing American intrusion (better the state than the States, R.B. BENNETT was said to have remarked in connection with the CBC's predecessor which his government established in 1932), the CBC owns and operates radio and, since 1952, television stations across the country, operates in French and English, and has the capacity to produce drama, comedy, and news specials in both languages. It is in 1988, like other broadcasting media, under the scrutiny of the Canadian Radio-television and Telecommunications Commission.

CANADIAN BROTHERHOOD OF RAILWAY EMPLOYEES, labour union founded in 1908 at Moncton, N.B. The Union was led through most of its early history by A.R. MOSHER. One of the few large all-Canadian unions in the early 20th century, the CBRE was expelled from the TRADES AND LABOUR CONGRESS in 1921 as a "dual" union. It formed part of the ALL-CANADIAN CONGRESS OF LABOUR in 1926 and the CANADIAN

CONGRESS OF LABOUR in 1940. Its name was later changed to Canadian Brotherhood of Railway, Transport and General Workers.

CANADIAN CAMPAIGN FOR NUCLEAR DISARMAMENT, anti-nuclear war organization, founded in 1959 from the Committee for the Control of Radiation Hazards. The CCND was an active lobby group, protesting Canadian acceptance of nuclear weapons. The Canadian University Campaign for Nuclear Disarmament, a student offshoot, also began in 1959 and the journal, *Our Generation Against Nuclear War*, was begun by its Montreal branch.

CANADIAN CHARTER OF RIGHTS AND FREEDOMS, the entrenched bill of rights that came into force on 17 April 1982. The creation of Prime Minister PIERRE TRUDEAU, though modified by federal-provincial negotiation, it was designed to protect the citizen against the state and minorities against majorities. The charter covers fundamental rights, democratic rights, equality rights, equality between men and women, language rights, and legal rights.

CANADIAN CITIZENSHIP ACT, 1947, legislation creating Canadian citizenship. Pressed for by PAUL MARTIN, secretary of state in Prime Minister MACKENZIE KING's Liberal government, the act came into effect on 1 Jan. 1947. Hitherto, Canadian citizenship had not existed, and Canadian nationals were British subjects. In the debate in the House of Commons, some Conservatives suggested that the bill would destroy the Commonwealth, and Martin was obliged to agree that Canadian citizens would remain British subjects. King received the first citizenship certificate and began his remarks: "I speak as a citizen of Canada."

CANADIAN CONGRESS OF LABOUR, founded in 1940 by a merger of the ALL-CANADIAN CONGRESS OF LABOUR and the Canadian unions affiliated to the Congress of Industrial Organizations. Its first president was A.R. MOSHER. The CCL was never as large as its rival, the TRADES AND LABOUR CONGRESS. Unlike the TLC, it supported the CO-OPERATIVE COMMONWEALTH FEDERATION throughout most of its history. In 1956 the CCL merged with the TLC to form the CANADIAN LABOUR CONGRESS.

CANADIAN CO-OPERATIVE WHEAT PRODUCERS LTD, agency established in Aug. 1924 by the three prairie WHEAT POOLS to act as a central selling agency for their grain. Alberta farm leader HENRY WISE WOOD was one of the leading advocates of its establishment.

CANADIAN CORPS, the Canadian army formation that achieved renown during WORLD WAR I. Formed in late 1915 from the two Canadian divisions then in France, the corps reached its full strength of four divisions and ancillary troops in 1916. See also CANADIAN EXPEDITIONARY FORCE.

CANADIAN COUNCIL OF AGRICULTURE, farm lobby organization established in 1909 by organizations from Ontario, Manitoba, Saskatchewan, and Alberta to influence national agricultural, transportation, and tariff policies. In 1916 the council issued a FARMERS' PLATFORM, which advocated lower tariffs, reform of the tax system, and nationalization of transportation and communications companies. This was followed in 1918 by the adoption of a NEW NATIONAL POLICY which called for sweeping social, political, and economic reforms, and independent farm political action. The New National Policy became a rallying point for farmers in the post–World War I era.

CANADIAN EXPEDITIONARY FORCE, the troops raised by Canada for overseas service in WORLD WAR I. At the outbreak of war in Aug. 1914 Canada offered Britain an expeditionary force which set sail in October and numbered more than 31,000. This 1st Canadian Division went to France early in 1915 and was joined by the 2nd later that year. By late 1916 the CANADIAN CORPS had its full strength of four divisions and a growing reputation for ferocity and efficiency that was capped by the capture of VIMY RIDGE in April 1917. Its reputation ensured that the CEF became a Canadian army, no longer just a colonial levee, although the corps was not commanded by a Canadian until General SIR ARTHUR CURRIE took over on 9 June 1917. In all, 619,636 served in the CEF including 142,588 enlisted as conscripts under the MILITARY SERVICE ACT, 1917. Only 24,132 conscripts reached France. A total of 424,589 served overseas of whom 59,544 were killed and 172,950 wounded or injured.

CANADIAN FEDERATION OF LABOUR, federation founded in 1902 as the National Trades and Labour Congress. It was formed by Canadian unions expelled from the TRADES AND LABOUR CONGRESS after the BERLIN CONVENTION of 1902. Its main support came from the remnants of the KNIGHTS OF LABOR in Canada. The CFL joined the ALL-CANADIAN CONGRESS OF LABOUR in 1926.

CANADIAN FORUM, magazine founded in 1920 as a journal of artistic and political thought. The *Forum*'s political orientation was always progressive and in the 1930s it virtually became a house organ for the CO-OPERATIVE COMMONWEALTH FEDERATION under editor FRANK UNDERHILL. In the 1960s and 1970s under editor Abraham Rotstein, the *Forum* had a resurgence as a nationalist voice.

CANADIAN GOVERNMENT RAILWAYS, umbrella name used to designate railways owned by the Canadian government from the late 19th century up to 1918. It included the INTERCOLONIAL RAILWAY, which linked the Maritime provinces with Quebec and Ontario, and the NATIONAL TRANSCONTINENTAL RAILWAY, which ran from Moncton, N.B., to Winnipeg. The Canadian Government Railways was joined to CANADIAN NATIONAL RAILWAYS in 1923.

CANADIAN IMPERIAL BANK OF COMMERCE, formed in 1961 with the merger of the Canadian Bank of Commerce and the Imperial Bank of Canada. Both of these banks were established in the mid-19th century, and the Canadian Bank of Commerce was Canada's second largest bank by 1900, heavily engaged in the financing of foreign trade, particularly in American cotton. The Imperial Bank had smaller beginnings as an Ontario-based regional bank but pioneered in establishing savings departments designed to attract the small investor.

CANADIAN INSTITUTE OF INTERNATIONAL AFFAIRS, private foreign affairs body founded in 1928 by a distinguished group that included SIR ROBERT BORDEN, NEWTON ROWELL, and J.W. DAFOE. The CIIA works in a non-partisan way to increase Canadian knowledge of and interest in foreign affairs. The institute has branches across the country and from its headquarters in Toronto sponsors research and publishes books, journals, and pamphlets.

CANADIAN INTERNATIONAL DEVELOPMENT AGENCY, agency created by the Liberal government of Prime Minister PIERRE TRUDEAU in 1968 to distribute Canada's aid to developing countries. It replaced the External Aid office, established in 1960. Aid was directed both to governments and to non-governmental agencies. CIDA's first director was MAURICE STRONG.

CANADIAN INTERVENTION IN RUSSIA, 1918-19, anti-Soviet expeditions. After Lenin's revolutionary government reached a peace treaty with the Germans in early 1918, the Allies feared that the German forces would be able to concentrate on the Western Front and win the war. British and French leaders were concerned to support anti-Soviet "White" forces and also to safeguard Allied supplies sent to Russia for the Czarist army. SIR ROBERT BORDEN was asked to offer Canadian troops, and, believing that commercial advantages might follow, agreed. An estimated 6000 Canadian troops participated from spring 1918 to summer 1919, serving both in Siberia and in the Murmansk area. Their involvement was unpopular at home and in the CANADIAN EXPEDITIONARY FORCE and the operation was unsuccessful, the only result being a deep Soviet enmity to the Allies.

CANADIAN LABOUR PARTY, political party created by the TRADES AND LABOUR CONGRESS in 1917. It was supposed to be modelled after the British Labour party but was, in fact, a loose federation of federations. The national CLP was obliged to accept any labour or socialist party which had affiliated to a provincial CLP organization. These provincial CLPs were supposed to unite to form a national party but a unified national party never emerged. The CLP disappeared by the end of the 1920s.

CANADIAN LABOUR CONGRESS (1883), grandiose title for a meeting of 48 delegates from different labour unions in Ontario held in Dec. 1883. The meeting was called by the TORONTO TRADES ASSEMBLY which aimed to establish a national labour lobby organization. Only one meeting was ever held.

CANADIAN LABOUR CONGRESS (1956), federation founded in 1956 by a merger of the TRADES AND LABOUR CONGRESS of Canada and the CANADIAN CONGRESS OF LABOUR. The merger was made possible by the prior formation of the parent American Federation of Labor–Congress of Industrial Organizations in 1955. The congress contained more than one million members at its beginning and was instrumental in the founding of the NEW DEMOCRATIC PARTY in 1961.

CANADIAN LABOUR DEFENCE LEAGUE, labour organization founded by the COMMUNIST PARTY OF CANADA in 1925. Ostensibly set up to provide legal defence funds for workers, the CLDL was a Communist Party of Canada front. For much of its history it was headed by A.E. SMITH, a Methodist minister turned Communist.

CANADIAN LABOUR UNION, Canada's first attempt at a national labour organization, formed in 1873 at the initiative of the TORONTO TRADES ASSEMBLY. It was designed primarily as a lobby group. Never large, the CLU disappeared by the end of the 1870s.

CANADIAN LAKE SEAMEN'S UNION, union formed in 1947 by Pat Walsh, president of the CANADIAN SEAMEN'S UNION, after he resigned because of the strength of Communists in the CSU. In 1948 the CLSU became part of the Seafarers' International Union which was dominated in Canada by HAL BANKS.

CANADIAN LEAGUE AGAINST WAR AND FASCISM, Communist-dominated pacifist organization launched by the COMMUNIST PARTY in 1934. The league was the Canadian branch of a world-wide movement to "mobilize intellectuals prepared to combine opposition to war and fascism with support of Soviet foreign policy," or so a leading historian of the Canadian Communist party wrote. Its aim was to steer pacifists towards a "realistic understanding" of the 1930s' struggle. Its Communist backing was sufficiently hidden, despite having A.A. MacLeod, an open Communist, at its head, that even people such as T.C. DOUGLAS joined. In 1937 the league changed its name to the League for Peace and Democracy and worked to support anti-Franco Spain.

CANADIAN LEGION, see ROYAL CANADIAN LEGION

CANADIAN MANUFACTURERS' ASSN, lobby organization originally founded as the Society for the Protection of Industry but known by its present name since 1871. Its purpose was to persuade provincial and federal governments to adopt policies and programs favourable to industry. It was a strong proponent of tariffs for the protection of industry and members of the CMA helped Prime Minister JOHN A. MACDONALD and his finance minister, SAMUEL TILLEY, put together the NATIONAL POLICY tariffs of 1879. Although it generally followed conservative social and economic policies, CMA members, caught up in the progressive movement of turn-of-the-century Canada, pushed for the establishment of the BOARD OF RAILWAY COMMISSIONERS and supported the initiation of WORKERS' COMPENSATION programs in a number of provinces.

CANADIAN MEDICAL ASSN, association of medical doctors founded in Quebec City in 1867. Its first president was SIR CHARLES TUPPER. At first the association concentrated on persuading legislatures to adopt strict licensing requirements for doctors and to pass legislation allowing doctors to establish self-regulating societies. In subsequent years the CMA became involved with a broad range of social and political questions and was especially active in opposing MEDICARE.

CANADIAN NATIONAL RAILWAYS, a CROWN CORPORATION created by the Unionist government of Prime Minister ROBERT BORDEN in Dec. 1919. Between then and 1923 it acquired a number of government-owned railways including the NATIONAL TRANSCONTINENTAL RAILWAY and the INTERCOLONIAL RAILWAY, formerly part of the CANADIAN GOVERNMENT RAILWAYS system, and the railways that had been nationalized during and since World War I, the CANADIAN NORTHERN, the GRAND TRUNK, and the GRAND TRUNK PACIFIC. The organization of the company was completed in 1923 and SIR HENRY THORNTON was appointed its first president. Canadian National played a role in the earliest development of government-owned radio broadcasting in Canada and the establishment of TRANS-CANADA AIRLINES.

CANADIAN NORTHERN RAILWAY, founded as a small Manitoba railway in 1899 by WILLIAM MACKENZIE and DONALD MANN. From one line connecting Gladstone, Man., to Lake Winnipegosis, the Canadian Northern gradually expanded. It was popular with farmers, who were given good service at low rates, and western provincial governments, which granted charters in exchange for Mackenzie and Mann's assurance that the Canadian Northern would abide by provincial rate regulation. Mackenzie and Mann eventually decided to build to the west coast and to Montreal and incurred heavy construction debts just at the start of World War I. When they turned to the federal government for assistance, Ottawa agreed to help, but in 1917, when it was obvious that the railway was failing, the government nationalized the railway by forcibly buying Mackenzie and Mann out. The railway subsequently became part of CANADIAN NATIONAL RAILWAYS.

CANADIAN PACIFIC AIRLINES, airline company begun in 1942. In that year CANADIAN PACIFIC RAILWAY president SIR EDWARD BEATTY decided to enter the air passenger transportation business. Canadian Pacific then acquired Winnipeg-based CANADIAN AIRWAYS and a number of other small airlines to form Canadian Pacific Airlines. Former bush pilot and small airline operator GRANT MCCONACHIE was named president of the airline in 1947. Canadian Pacific helped organize and operate the TRANS-ATLANTIC FERRY SERVICE during World War II and, after the war, expanded its operations across the Pacific to Hawaii, China, and Australia. Canadian Pacific struggled against the monopoly in trans-Canadian operations held by TRANS-CANADA AIRLINES throughout the 1950s. It purchased up-to-date NORTH STAR, Constellation, Britannia, and jet aircraft and slowly expanded its share of Canadian passenger traffic while building up its overseas routes. By the early 1970s, when Ottawa ended all regulation favouring Trans-Canada Airlines (AIR CANADA), Canadian Pacific, operating under the name CP Air, emerged as a major rival to Air Canada at home and abroad. In 1986 the airline was purchased by the smaller PACIFIC WESTERN AIRLINES and it subsequently was consolidated into Canadian Airlines International in 1987.

CANADIAN PACIFIC RAILWAY, rail link promised to British Columbia when it entered CONFEDERATION in 1871. The railway was to be completed within ten years. The start of the project was delayed by the PACIFIC SCANDAL which broke in 1873, and an economic depression which handcuffed efforts of the Liberal government of Prime Minister ALEXANDER MACKENZIE to continue the project. When JOHN A. MACDONALD's Conservatives came back to power in 1878, however, they turned to a syndicate ready to build the railway including GEORGE STEPHEN, president of the BANK OF MONTREAL, and JAMES J. HILL a Canadian-born railroader who lived in St Paul, Minn. The government and the syndicate drew up a mutually acceptable contract in the fall of 1880 which was confirmed by Parliament in 1881. This marked the formal birth of the Canadian Pacific Railway. The CPR was given massive subsidies in cash and land, and was given ownership of all track laid for a Pacific railway up to that time. Under the direction of WILLIAM VAN HORNE, construction proceeded rapidly and, by Nov. 1885, the LAST SPIKE was driven at Craigellachie, B.C., in the EAGLE PASS. Although the period of construction was marked by constant money shortages and government bail-outs, the railway proved profitable from the day it opened and became the basis for Canadian Pacific enterprises in shipping, air transport, mining and smelting, telecommunications, land development, and other industries.

CANADIAN PACIFIC STEAMSHIP CO., shipping company organized by WILLIAM VAN HORNE in 1891 as a subsidiary of the CANADIAN PACIFIC RAILWAY. Its first ships, called the *Empresses* or *White Empresses*, in addition to winning lucrative British government mail contracts, provided luxury passenger service and transported cargo between Vancouver and the Orient. President THOMAS SHAUGHNESSY later added an Atlantic fleet. In 1909 the company acquired the ALLAN LINE.

CANADIAN RADIO AND TELEVISION COMMISSION, federal agency established in 1967 to oversee broadcasting in Canada. It was given the power to regulate overall programming content, to issue new broadcast licences, to review and renew old ones, and to oversee cable and pay television operations in Canada. It replaced the BOARD OF BROADCAST GOVERNORS established in 1958. In 1976 the CRTC was also given jurisdiction over telecommunications and became the Canadian Radio-television and Telecommunications Commission.

CANADIAN RADIO BROADCASTING COMMISSION,

a commission created by the Conservative government of Prime Minister R.B. BENNETT in 1932 to regulate Canadian broadcasting and provide programs over a government-sponsored network. The CRBC's creation followed the recommendations of the AIRD COMMISSION that the federal government take control of broadcasting in Canada and create a government-owned broadcast monopoly much like the British Broadcasting Corp. The Aird Report was strongly supported by the CANADIAN RADIO LEAGUE, a national lobby group founded and directed by ALAN PLAUNT and GRAHAM SPRY. Before the report could be implemented, the question of which level of government controlled radio had to be settled. The Radio Case, heard by the JUDICIAL COMMITTEE OF THE PRIVY COUNCIL in fall 1931, established that radio broadcasting fell within the jurisdiction of the federal government. Bennett then acted to create the CRBC. It never functioned as it was designed, to the disappointment of supporters of public broadcasting in Canada. In 1936, after the Liberals were returned to power, the CRBC was disbanded and the CANADIAN BROADCASTING CORP. established.

CANADIAN RADIO LEAGUE, group founded

in fall 1930 by ALAN PLAUNT and GRAHAM SPRY to lobby for the establishment of a federally owned radio broadcasting monopoly in Canada. The members of the league were convinced that such ownership was essential to the preservation of the national character, especially given the spread of privately owned broadcasting in the United States. The league recruited prominent supporters across Canada and supported the case for federal jurisdiction before the courts. League members continued to play a prominent role in the determination of broadcast policy in Canada in subsequent years, with Plaunt being named to the first board of governors of the CANADIAN BROADCASTING CORP.

CANADIAN RADIO-TELEVISION AND TELECOMMUNICATIONS COMMISSION,

see CANADIAN RADIO AND TELEVISION COMMISSION

CANADIAN SEAMEN'S UNION, union

founded in 1936 and headed by COMMUNIST PARTY member J.A. "PAT" SULLIVAN. It was dominated by Communists from the start. A 1946 CSU strike virtually tied up Canada's inland waterways and prompted the federal government and anti-Communist unions to destroy the CSU by bringing HAL BANKS and the Seafarers' International Union to Canada. By the early 1950s the CSU had been crushed.

CANADIAN SECURITY AND INTELLIGENCE SERVICE,

domestic counter-espionage agency. Founded in 1984 by the government of PIERRE TRUDEAU, CSIS was formed in an attempt to separate the ROYAL CANADIAN MOUNTED POLICE's policing and security functions. Although there had been complaints about the RCMP's counter-espionage activities since before World War II, the RCMP's public-relations image was so strong that government shied away from the task of separation. After revelations of RCMP wrongdoing in the 1970s, not least against legitimate INDÉPENDANTISTE movements in Quebec, the Trudeau government decided it must do so. CSIS, however, was largely formed from former RCMP officers, and the agency quickly ran into difficulties and charges of sloppy procedure.

CANADIAN SOCIALIST LEAGUE, political

organization founded in 1898. One of Canada's earliest socialist groups, it was set up by George Wrigley, an Ontario newspaper editor. It combined religious and scientific socialism.

CANADIAN TRANSPORT COMMISSION,

agency established in 1967 to regulate federally controlled transportation in Canada. It replaced agencies which had been responsible for the regulation of air, land, and maritime transportation.

CANADIAN WHEAT BOARD, government

agency, created in 1935 as a voluntary agency responsible for the orderly marketing of Canadian wheat. It succeeded the BOARD OF GRAIN SUPERVISORS. The board was established to regulate grain prices after the disastrous fall in prices of the early 1930s threatened to destroy the Canadian grain industry. In 1943 its voluntary nature was ended and grain growers were compelled by law to sell their wheat to the board. In 1949 prairie barley and oats were also placed within the board's sphere of jurisdiction.

CWAC recruits beginning training, 1943

CANADIAN WOMEN'S ARMY CORPS, established in Aug. 1941 to bring Canadian women into the armed forces in non-combat support functions. Until March 1942 the CWAC was a separate branch of the army. Close to 22,000 women eventually served in the Canadian Women's Army Corps, many in Britain; a number were dispatched to Europe in support roles after the Normandy invasion of June 1944.

CANADIAN YOUTH CONGRESS, pacifist organization formed in 1935 by representatives of the Young Men's and Young Women's Christian Assn, the Christian Cooperative Youth Movement, the Student Christian Movement, and other groups. It tried to act as a lobby group on peace questions, education, and unemployment. Representatives attended world conferences, and the CYC became involved in anti-Franco activities and called for boycotts against Japanese goods as a protest against Japan's aggression in Asia. Anti-fascism eventually moved the congress to call for a government strategy for resistance to aggression.

CANDU, the Canadian Deuterium Uranium nuclear power generating system. A unique design, Candu reactors, cooled by heavy water, arose from research at Chalk River after World War II. Efforts to sell the system abroad, made by ATOMIC ENERGY OF CANADA LTD, have had only mixed results.

CAOUETTE, Joseph-David-Réal (1917-76), politician. Born at Amos, Que., he operated an automobile business before joining the SOCIAL CREDIT movement in 1939. He was first elected to the House of Commons in a by-election in 1946

but was defeated in 1949. In 1962, however, an alliance of his RALLIEMENT DES CRÉDITISTES with ROBERT THOMPSON'S SOCIAL CREDIT PARTY took 30 seats nationally, including 26 in Quebec held by Caouette followers. In 1963 the demagogic Caouette, who was skilled at using television to appeal to poor, rural voters, split with Thompson to become leader once more of the Ralliement des créditistes, a position he held until 1976.

CARDIN, LOUIS-JOSEPH-LUCIEN, (1919–88), federal politician. Born at Providence, R.I., Cardin attended Loyola College and the Univ. de Montréal. He was elected to the House of Commons in 1952 as a Liberal, and served in the PEARSON cabinet in a number of portfolios from 1963 to 1967. A sharp opponent of JOHN DIEFENBAKER, Cardin was a major player in the "scandal" sessions of Parliament after 1963 and precipitated the MUNSINGER AFFAIR by blurting out a reference to the "Monseigneur" affair in the House of Commons.

CARDIN, PIERRE-JOSEPH-ARTHUR, (1879-1946), politician. Born at Sorel, Que., Cardin was elected to Parliament as a Liberal in 1911, and held cabinet posts in Prime Minister MACKENZIE KING's governments from 1924. Minister of public works from 1935, he resigned to protest the introduction of BILL 80 during the CONSCRIPTION CRISIS, 1942.

CARIBOU (DHC-4), twin-engine STOL aircraft, built by DE HAVILLAND AIRCRAFT OF CANADA. Designed and built in the 1950s, it first flew in a military capacity in 1958. In 1965 it was replaced by the larger DHC-5 Buffalo.

CARMAN, ALBERT (1833-1917), Methodist clergyman. Born at Iroquois, Upper Canada, he was educated at Victoria Univ. and ordained in 1859. He was headmaster of the Dundas Grammar School and then principal of Albert College (later Univ.). In 1874 he became a bishop and in 1883 he was elected general superintendent of the Methodist church, a post he held until 1915.

CARMAN, BLISS (1861-1929), poet. Born at Fredericton, N.B., and educated at the Univs. of New Brunswick, Edinburgh, and Harvard, Carman worked as a literary editor and writer in the United States from 1890, although he lectured widely in Canada. His poetry and columns were published in numerous volumes and he was called the Canadian poet laureate.

CARMICHAEL, FRANKLIN (1890-1945), painter. A founding member of the GROUP OF SEVEN, he was born at Orillia, Ont., studied at the Ontario College of Art, and apprenticed with Grip Ltd, a Toronto commercial art company where many of the group first met. He studied in Europe before returning to Canada to work as a designer. Carmichael was president of the Canadian Society of Painters in Water Colour (1932-4) and a teacher at the Ontario College of Art after 1932.

CARR, EMILY (1871-1945), painter, writer. Born at Victoria, B.C., she studied art in San Francisco and returned to Victoria in 1893 to set up a studio. Trips to Britain and France shaped her style, and by 1911 her work was beginning to take form. By the late 1920s, under the influence of the GROUP OF SEVEN, Carr's painting reached fruition, and her paintings on Indian and nature themes were popular. Her book *Klee Wyck* (1941) received the Governor General's Award and a half dozen books followed, some posthumously.

CARTIER, SIR GEORGE-ÉTIENNE (1814-73), politician. Cartier, one of the FATHERS OF CONFEDERATION, was born at St-Antoine, Lower Canada. He studied law, was called to the bar in 1835, and after returning in 1838 from exile for his part in the 1837 rebellion, began to practise. Although Cartier was active in politics long before he ran as a Liberal Reformer in 1848, he made his mark as leader of the PARTI BLEU and JOHN A. MACDONALD's right-hand man, serving as co-premier of the Province of Canada in 1857-8 and 1858-62 and as the first minister of militia and defence after Confederation from 1867 to 1873. He played a key role in negotiating the transfer of Rupert's Land to Canada, as well as the Manitoba and British Columbia acts, bringing those provinces into Confederation. Cartier was also involved in railway promotion and was implicated with Macdonald and HECTOR LANGEVIN in the PACIFIC SCANDAL, but he died before the government resigned in 1873. *See also* MANITOBA ACT.

CARTWRIGHT, SIR RICHARD JOHN (1835-1912), politician. Cartwright was born at King-

ston, Upper Canada, and educated at Trinity College, Dublin, before building his business empire. He sat in Parliament from 1863 to 1904, first as a Conservative (1863-9), then as an Independent (1869-73), and finally as a Liberal (1873-1911). He was named to the Senate in 1904. A militant free-trader, Cartwright was one of the most powerful Liberal members of the House, serving as minister of finance (1873-8) and minister of trade and commerce (1896-1911).

courtesy National Archives of Canada/PA-127290

Thérèse Casgrain

CASGRAIN, THÉRÈSE (1896-1981), feminist reformer. Thérèse Forget was born at Montreal and in 1921 started campaigning in Quebec for WOMEN'S SUFFRAGE, not won provincially until April 1940. A radio show host in the 1930s, during World War II she sat on the Women's Surveillance Committee for the WARTIME PRICES AND TRADE BOARD. In 1946 Casgrain joined the CO-OPERATIVE COMMONWEALTH FEDERATION, serving as provincial leader from 1951 to 1957. She was named to the Senate in 1970; her autobiography, *A Woman in a Man's World*, appeared two years later.

CASHIN, PETER J. (1890-1977), politician. Born at Cape Broyle, Nfld, he served overseas in World War I with the Newfoundland Regiment and joined his father's business on his return. He was elected to the Newfoundland Assembly in 1923 and served as finance minister, 1928-32. Cashin fought the COMMISSION OF GOVERNMENT, won election to the National Convention in 1946, and led the anti-Confederate responsible government forces. He was elected as an independent in the first provincial election in 1949, joined the Conservatives and became Opposition leader until retiring in 1953.

CASSON, ALFRED JOSEPH (1898–), painter. The last surviving member of the GROUP OF SEVEN, he was born in Toronto, studied in Hamilton and Toronto, worked as a commercial artist, and began to specialize in watercolours. In 1926 he joined the group, replacing FRANZ JOHNSTON, and his work began to centre on the small towns not far from Toronto. By the 1970s Casson had achieved a near-mythic status, and his substantial production of work belied his age.

CASTORS, term used to signify French-Canadian Conservatives who felt a strong allegiance to the Roman Catholic church and opposed the Quebec Conservative party under premiers J.A. CHAPLEAU and J.A. MOUSSEAU. The term was derived from the pseudonym "Castor" used by one member of the group in signing his name to a pamphlet in 1882. *See also* ULTRAMONTANISM.

CATHERWOOD, ETHEL (1909–), track and field athlete. She broke the world high jump record for women at a 1926 meet and again in 1928. At the 1928 Olympics she won the gold medal, still the solitary track and field gold won by a Canadian woman.

CAUCHON, JOSEPH-EUSÈBE-NOULAN (1872-1935), engineer. Born in Quebec City, he was one of Canada's earliest urban planners. He helped found the Town Planning Institute of Canada in 1919 and two years later became the first chairman of the Ottawa Town Planning Commission.

CCM, *see* CANADA CYCLE AND MOTOR CO. LTD

CENTENNIAL, term generally used to refer to the centennial of CONFEDERATION, celebrated 1 July 1967. An entire year of festivities was arranged across Canada by the Centennial Commission, headed by John Fisher, and thousands of communities, governments, institutions and private organizations added to the celebration. The highlight of the year was EXPO 67, a first-category world fair held in Montreal.

CF-100 (CANUCK), a two-place, all-weather aircraft designed to intercept high-altitude bombers. It was designed and built in Toronto by A.V. ROE CANADA LTD in the late 1940s and first flew in Jan. 1950. It became operational in 1953 and equipped air defence squadrons operated by the ROYAL CANADIAN AIR FORCE in Canada and Europe. The aircraft was used for 10 years by the RCAF particularly in the extreme conditions of Canada's north because of its all-weather capabilities. It was the only operational all-Canadian war plane ever built.

CHALMERS, FLOYD SHERMAN (1898–), editor. Born at Chicago, Ill., Chalmers grew up in Ontario. He served overseas during World War I, then joined the *FINANCIAL POST*, becoming its editor in 1925. He was president of the publishing company Maclean-Hunter from 1952 to 1964, a patron of the arts, and chancellor of York Univ. The Chalmers Foundation gives annual awards for playwrights and choreographers.

CHANAK CRISIS, 1922, political crisis between Britain and Canada. In Sept. 1922 Turkey attacked Greece and then threatened the British garrison at Chanak, a small town on the Straits of Dardanelles. Britain appealed to the dominions for help on 15 Sept., but the message sent to Ottawa was misplaced and Prime Minister MACKENZIE KING read about the crisis and the British request in the morning newspaper. King met with his cabinet and a message was sent to the British informing them that "PARLIAMENT WILL DECIDE" the matter of Canada's participation, a useful delaying tactic since Parliament was not in session. It was the first but not the last time King used this line to warn Britain not to expect an automatic commitment from Canada to fight in British wars.

CHAPLEAU, SIR JOSEPH-ADOLPHE (1840-98), premier of Quebec. Born in St-Thérèse-de-Blainville, Lower Canada, Chapleau was admitted to the bar in 1861. Thereafter he taught law at Univ. Laval, invested in newspapers and railway companies, and entered Quebec politics. He was first elected to the Quebec legislature in 1867 and sat as a Conservative. He later held the offices of attorney general and provincial secretary, and was named premier in 1879. In 1882 he entered federal politics, winning a seat in the

Sir Joseph-Adolphe Chapleau

House of Commons. He became secretary of state in Prime Minister JOHN A. MACDONALD'S government (1882-92) and, after agonizing, supported the execution of LOUIS RIEL in 1885. He was minister of customs in SIR JOHN ABBOTT'S short-lived administration. He served as lieutenant-governor of Quebec from 1892 until his death.

CHARLOTTETOWN CONFERENCE, conference of political leaders from the UNITED PROVINCE OF CANADA and the colonies of Newfoundland, Nova Scotia, New Brunswick, and Prince Edward Island held 1-9 Sept. 1864. The conference was originally organized to discuss union of the Atlantic colonies but, at the behest of the delegates from Canada, it shifted its attention to the union of all the British North American colonies. It was here that the broad outlines of CONFEDERATION were first laid out. *See also* FATHERS OF CONFEDERATION, BRITISH NORTH AMERICA ACT, QUEBEC CONFERENCE.

CHARPENTIER, ALFRED (1888-1982), labour leader. He was one of the founders of the Catholic union movement in Quebec. Charpentier helped draft the constitution of the CONFÉDÉRATION DES TRAVAILLEURS CATHOLIQUES DU CANADA / CANADIAN CATHOLIC CONFEDERATION OF LABOUR, founded in 1921, and was its president from 1935 to 1946.

CHAUVEAU, PIERRE-JOSEPH-OLIVIER (1820-90), premier of Quebec. Born at Charlesbourg, Lower Canada, Chauveau became a lawyer and won election to the assembly of the Province of Canada at age 24. In 1855 he became superintendent of education, and in 1867 JOHN A. MACDONALD and GEORGE-ÉTIENNE CARTIER selected him as Quebec's first premier. In 1873, after an undistinguished tenure in Quebec City, he was named to the Senate.

CHEVRIER, LIONEL (1903-87), politician. Born at Cornwall, Ont., and educated at the Univ. of Ottawa, Chevrier practised law. He was elected to the House of Commons in 1935 for Cornwall as a Liberal and joined the cabinet in 1945 as transport minister. He was placed in charge of the ST LAWRENCE SEAWAY Authority in 1954. In 1957 he was elected to Parliament in Montreal and became one of the key Liberals in opposition. Minister of justice in 1963, he went to England as high commissioner in 1964 and handled a number of diplomatic chores for the government after he returned to Canada in 1967.

CHILKOOT TRAIL, trail from Skagway, Alaska, to Whitehorse, Yukon, used by prospectors and others to reach the Yukon Gold fields during the KLONDIKE GOLD RUSH of 1898.

CHINA, RECOGNITION OF, 1970-1, agreement reached in 1970 on Canada's recognition of the People's Republic of China. Ambassadors were exchanged in 1971. Canada had exchanged diplomatic representatives with Nationalist China in 1941-2, but, with the Communist victory in 1948, relations lapsed. Efforts to renew them with the new regime were frustrated by the KOREAN WAR and U.S. hostility, and it was not until Liberal Prime Minister PIERRE TRUDEAU came to power in 1968 that Canada again sought to recognize China. The strenuous negotiations in Stockholm centred on Beijing's claims to Taiwan.

CHISHOLM, GEORGE BROCK (1896-1971), psychiatrist. Born at Oakville, Ont., and educated at the Univ. of Toronto and in the United States and England, Chisholm served with great distinction in World War I. He then practised in Toronto. During World War II he became director general of medical services in Ottawa and then deputy minister of national health and welfare in 1944. He moved to the World Health Organization in 1946 and was director general from 1948 to 1953. A controversial figure, he debunked Santa Claus and challenged conventional morality.

CHRÉTIEN,   JOSEPH-JACQUES-JEAN (1934–), politician. Chrétien was born at Shawinigan, Que., attended the Univ. Laval, and practised law from 1958 until elected to the House of Commons in 1963. He rose quickly, serving as minister of state and minister of national revenue under Prime Minister LESTER PEARSON and then in a number of portfolios under PIERRE TRUDEAU. In 1980 he led the fight against the SOVEREIGNTY-ASSOCIATION referendum. A strong candidate in the 1984 Liberal leadership race to succeed Trudeau, he came second to JOHN TURNER and was one of the few Liberals returned in the 1984 federal election. He soon resigned to practise law and write an extraordinarily popular autobiography, amid speculation about his continuing leadership ambitions.

CHURCH UNION, the union of the Methodist, Presbyterian, and Congregational churches in June 1925 to form the United Church of Canada. Although part of the Presbyterian and Congregational churches did not join the new religious organization, the United Church became Canada's largest Protestant church as a result of the union.

CHURCHILL, GORDON MINTO (1898-1985), politician. Born at Coldwater, Ont., and educated at the Univ. of Manitoba, Churchill was a machine gunner in World War I, a schoolteacher and principal between the wars, and a regimental commander during World War II. Elected to the Manitoba legislature as army representative in 1945, he failed to win a seat in the 1949 federal election and began to practise law. He entered the House of Commons as a Conservative after winning a 1951 by-election and became minister of trade and commerce in 1957 under Prime Minister JOHN DIEFENBAKER. In 1960 he was shuffled to veterans affairs and then to the defence portfolio when DOUGLAS HARKNESS resigned in 1963. Churchill remained a staunch supporter and close confidant of Diefenbaker.

CITÉ LIBRE, Quebec magazine, founded in 1950 by PIERRE TRUDEAU, and GÉRARD PELLETIER, and others. It was an uncompromising critic of the Quebec government of MAURICE DUPLESSIS, a policy that took substantial courage. The magazine was one of the forces that helped shape the QUIET REVOLUTION that burst forth after Duplessis' death.

CITIZENS' COMMITTEE OF 1000, committee of prominent Winnipeg citizens, many of whom were members of the board of trade, the chamber of commerce, and the Canadian Manufacturers' Assn, formed to oppose the WINNIPEG GENERAL STRIKE of 15 May to 26 June 1919. The Committee of 1000 helped provide strike-breakers and special police, and helped the federal government recruit MILITIA for the duration of the strike.

CIVIL SERVICE COMMISSION, federal government hiring agency created in 1908. The Civil Service Act, 1918, entrenched the principle of merit (instead of patronage), and the commission was given the responsibility for hiring, classifying, and recommending pay scales. It was renamed the Public Service Commission in 1967.

CLANCY, FRANCIS MICHAEL, "KING" (1903-86), hockey player. King Clancy played for the Ottawa Senators from 1921 to 1930. He was sold to the Toronto Maple Leafs in 1930, became a National Hockey League referee, and the Maple Leaf coach. He was later a vice-president of the Toronto club.

CLARK, CHARLES JOSEPH (1939–), prime minister of Canada. Born at High River, Alta, Joe Clark graduated from the Univ. of Alberta and was national PROGRESSIVE CONSERVATIVE PARTY student president before being elected to the House of Commons in 1972. A surprise winner at the 1976 leadership convention, Clark, despite an unfortunate television image, became the youngest and first western-born prime minister in 1979. He headed a weak minority government for nine months until defeated over Finance Minister JOHN CROSBIE's budget in a vote of non-confidence in Dec. 1979. His party lost the 1980 election and he lost the leadership to BRIAN MULRONEY in 1983. In Sept. 1984 he took over the external affairs portfolio in Mulroney's cabinet.

CLARK, SAMUEL DELBERT (1910–), sociologist. Clark was born at Lloydminster, Alta, and studied at the univs. of Saskatchewan, McGill, and Toronto and at the London School of Economics. He joined the political economy department at the Univ. of Toronto in 1938 and became the first notable sociologist in the country, his research examining Canadian social development. His studies include a book on the CANADIAN MANU-FACTURERS' ASSN, *Church and Sect in Canada*, and *Movements of Political Protest in Canada*.

CLARK, WILLIAM CLIFFORD (1889-1952), public servant. Deputy minister of finance for 20 years and one of the most powerful MANDARINS, Clark was born at Martintown, Ont. He attended Queen's and Harvard univs. and returned to teach at Queen's in 1915. In 1923 he left Canada for the United States and worked at a number of development industry jobs before the 1929 stock market crash nearly wiped him out. Recruited by former colleague O.D. SKELTON to advise Prime Minister R.B. BENNETT's government during the OTTAWA CONFERENCE in 1932, Clark went on to a distinguished career in the civil service, helping to expand the role of the state in economic planning. His efforts to mobilize Canada's financial resources during World War II and his post-war efforts to steer Canada's recovery were exemplary.

CLARKE, CHARLES KIRK (1857-1924), psychiatrist. Born at Elora, Canada West, and educated in medicine at the Univ. of Toronto, he began work at the Toronto Asylum in 1874. He then worked at other asylums in Ontario until in 1911 he became superintendent of Toronto General Hospital and dean of medicine at the Univ. of Toronto. In 1918 he was co-founder of the Canadian National Commission for Mental Hygiene.

CLAXTON, BRIAN BROOKE (1898-1960), politician. Born at Montreal, Claxton served overseas with the artillery in World War I, and then returned to Canada to study law. A strong nationalist, he was involved with the Canadian Club and the CANADIAN INSTITUTE OF INTERNATIONAL AFFAIRS in the interwar years. He won election to the House of Commons in 1940 as a Liberal, helped turn the party in a progressive direction in 1943, and, as minister of national health and welfare in 1944, was responsible for the introduction of FAMILY ALLOWANCES. Named defence minister in 1946, Claxton had to rebuild the armed forces for their NATO and KOREAN WAR roles. He retired from politics in 1954; in 1957 he became the first chairman of the CANADA COUNCIL.

CLEAR GRITS, *see* GRIT

CLERGUE, FRANCIS HECTOR (1856-1939), industrialist. Born in Bangor, Maine, Clergue became a legend in Canadian industrial development. His first enterprise was a small power plant at Sault Ste Marie, Ont. This was followed by a pulp mill, factories, foundries, and other industrial and manufacturing complexes in north central Ontario. He was perhaps best known for the development of the ALGOMA STEEL CORP. which he founded in 1902. Clergue also invested in and developed transportation companies such as the Algoma Central Railway. His vision of a consolidated network of companies led him to amalgamate many of his businesses into Lake Superior Corporation Ltd.

CLOSURE, term to describe a method by which the government can stop debate in the House of Commons and force a vote. It was devised by Solicitor-General ARTHUR MEIGHEN in 1912 and used for the first time to stop debate over ROBERT BORDEN'S NAVAL AID BILL in 1913.

COBALT BOMB, medical device used for radiation therapy in the treatment of diseases such as cancer. It was developed under the auspices of the NATIONAL RESEARCH COUNCIL and ATOMIC ENERGY OF CANADA LTD at the NRX reactor in Chalk River, Ont., in 1951.

COHEN, JACOB LAURENCE (1898-1950), labour lawyer. Born in Montreal, Que., Cohen became a champion of Canadian and left-wing causes in the labour movement. Cohen did much of his work for the ALL-CANADIAN CONGRESS OF LABOUR in the late 1920s and for Communist unions in the 1930s. He was a member of the NATIONAL WAR LABOUR BOARD and, in 1943, conducted a study for the federal government which recommended that Ottawa legislate the right of workers to form their own unions. The NATIONAL WAR LABOUR ORDER issued early in 1944 met this recommendation.

COHEN, LEONARD (1934–), poet, songwriter. Cohen was one of the most influential Canadian writers during the 1960s. Born at Montreal, he attended McGill and Columbia univs. but devoted most of his time to writing. His first book of poetry was published when he was 22. His *Selected Poems, 1956-68*, won the 1968 Governor General's Award, but Cohen declined to accept it. His novels include *The Favourite Game* (1963) and *Beautiful Losers* (1966). Cohen has recorded numerous records since "The Songs of Leonard Cohen" appeared in 1968.

COHEN, SAMUEL NATHAN (1923-71), critic. Born at Sydney, N.S., Nathan Cohen was educated at Mount Allison Univ. He worked for militant union and Communist newspapers, and then made his way to radio as a theatre critic, eventually starting and dominating the program "Fighting Words" on CBC-TV. His theatre criticism was unsparing, and as critic for the *Toronto Star* from 1959 he made his columns feared and respected.

COLDWELL, MAJOR JAMES WILLIAM (1888-1974), politician. One of the founders of the CO-OPERATIVE COMMONWEALTH FEDERATION and national leader from 1942 to 1960, Coldwell was born at Seaton, Eng., and educated at University College, Exeter, before immigrating to Canada in 1910. He was a teacher and principal at various schools in Alberta and Saskatchewan. In 1932 Coldwell became leader of the Saskatchewan Farmer-Labour Party (which merged with the CCF) and fought the 1934 provincial election. Defeated, he turned to federal politics and was elected as MP for Rosetown-Biggar in 1935, a seat he held until defeated in 1958. Coldwell succeeded J.S. WOODSWORTH as leader of the CCF in 1942.

COLLIP, JAMES BERTRAM (1892-1965), biochemist. Born in London, Ont., he studied at the Univ. of Toronto. In the summer of 1921 he was at that university on leave from the Univ. of Alberta when he joined the team working with FREDERICK G. BANTING on the discovery of insulin. Collip's special contribution to the discovery was the purification of the raw insulin isolated by Banting so that it could be used in humans. J.J.R. MACLEOD shared his half of the Nobel Prize with Collip. *See also* CHARLES HERBERT BEST.

courtesy DND/DL-998

Raymond Collishaw

COLLISHAW, RAYMOND (1893-1976), pilot. Born at Nanaimo, B.C., he was a WORLD WAR I ace with 60 victories, second only to BILLY BISHOP. He remained with the Royal Air Force, serving in Russia, Persia, and Egypt, until retiring as air vice-marshal in 1943.

COLONIAL AND IMPERIAL CONFERENCES, a series of meetings of British and dominion prime ministers between 1887 and 1937. These conferences discussed economic, military, and foreign policy matters affecting the British Empire. Until 1907 they were known as colonial conferences; from 1911 to 1937 they were referred to as imperial conferences. From 1944 to the present, the conferences have been called prime ministers' meetings or Commonwealth conferences.

COLONIST CARS, special railway cars used by the Canadian railways, especially the CANADIAN PACIFIC RAILWAY, to transport immigrants from east coast and St Lawrence ports to western

Canada. Colonist cars were uncomfortable, poorly heated and ventilated, and had roughly finished interiors with wooden seats and sleeping platforms. There was a wood-burning stove at one end of the car. The immigrants brought their own food and bedding for the trip west.

COLUMBIA RIVER TREATY, 1961, Canada-United States treaty to run for 60 years. Canada agreed to build dams in British Columbia to increase generating capacity for the United States. In return Canada was to receive 50 per cent of power generated plus payment for flood control benefits. Though signed in 1961, the treaty was not implemented until 1964, thanks to a controversy between British Columbia and the federal government over which government had the jurisdiction to sell the power.

COLVILLE, ALEXANDER (1920–), painter. Born at Toronto, Colville grew up in Nova Scotia and studied at Mount Allison Univ. During World War II he served overseas as a war artist with the Canadian army. He then taught at his alma mater until 1963, giving exhibitions of his work, notably in New York. His representational paintings have achieved extraordinary renown in Canada and abroad.

COMBINED BOARDS, bodies created by Britain and the United States in early 1942 to run their joint war effort against the Axis Powers. Developing an argument based on FUNCTIONALISM, Canada sought membership on those boards where it had world-class capability. Thus, no claim was pressed for inclusion in the Combined Chiefs of Staff, but a strong case was made for membership on the Combined Food Board on the grounds that Canada was the Allies' second largest food producer. That argument succeeded in Oct. 1943 but only after Ottawa pressed its case with Britain. Canada also became a member of the Combined Production and Resources Board, a less important body. No other Allied nation secured membership on any of the boards.

COMBINES INVESTIGATION ACT (1889), federal legislation passed at the onset of the progressive era to meet a demand for protection from combines and monopolies which were thought to be fixing prices. The Conservative government of Prime Minister JOHN A. MACDONALD was not, however, about to pass anti-business legislation on the one hand while stimulating business growth through the NATIONAL POLICY on the other. The act, therefore, lacked teeth and did nothing to restrain a growing movement towards mergers and monopolies.

COMINCO, mining and smelting company formed in 1906 as Consolidated Mining and Smelting Co. when a number of mines near Trail B.C. were amalgamated by CANADIAN PACIFIC RAILWAY. (In 1966 the name was changed to Cominco.) It also built a smelter at Trail. Cominco was the largest mining company in the B.C. interior from the start and, in subsequent years, it expanded its operations through buy-outs of mining and smelting rivals in the region. It is in 1988 virtually the only mining company in the southern interior of the province.

COMMISSION OF CONSERVATION, established in 1909 to advise the federal government on conservation of resources. It was headed by SIR CLIFFORD SIFTON until 1918 and lasted until 1921. It directed research and published papers but had little influence on public policy.

COMMISSION OF GOVERNMENT, commission established by the British government to administer Newfoundland in Feb. 1934 after that dominion had surrendered its self-governing status. Wracked by the GREAT DEPRESSION, Newfoundland was close to bankruptcy when its government in 1933 asked London to have a royal commission investigate its financial problems. The subsequent report advocated replacing responsible government with commission government. An appointed governor and six commissioners ran the colony, preparing innumerable redevelopment schemes. World War II brought the Canadian and American military and prosperity, and by 1946 there were demands for self-government and/or union with Canada. After two referenda in which the retention of the commission was soundly trounced, Newfoundland joined Canada as the tenth province on 31 March 1949. *See also* LEASED BASES AGREEMENT.

COMMISSION OF INQUIRY CONCERNING CERTAIN ACTIVITIES OF THE ROYAL CANADIAN MOUNTED POLICE, federal commission established on 6 July 1977 to investigate, among other things, the adequacy of the law as it applies to ROYAL CANADIAN MOUNTED POLICE activities in discharge of its responsibility to protect the security of Canada. The commission, under Mr Justice D.C. McDonald, reported initially in November 1979 with a small pamphlet and two years later with a three-volume report and a number of subsidiary studies. The report led directly to the creation of the CANADIAN SECURITY AND INTELLIGENCE SERVICE.

COMMITTEE FOR AN INDEPENDENT CANADA, lobby organization established in the fall of 1970 by a group of Canadians concerned with the degree of foreign, especially American ownership of the Canadian economy. The mentor of this group was WALTER GORDON, who had been minister of finance in the first government of Liberal Prime Minister LESTER PEARSON in 1963. Gordon had advocated tough measures to control foreign investment in Canada and had been eased out of office as a result. The CIC recruited many Canadian writers, publishers, and intellectuals and achieved an influence far out of proportion to its small numbers.

COMMITTEE OF INQUIRY ON WAR CRIMINALS, government inquiry into the presence of Nazi war criminals in Canada, appointed under commissioner Jules Deschênes in Feb. 1985. The commission was appointed by the government of BRIAN MULRONEY to investigate "all persons, whatever their past or present nationality, currently residing in Canada and allegedly responsible for crimes against peace, war crimes, or crimes against humanity related to the activities of Nazi Germany and committed between 1 Sept. 1939 and 9 May 1945 inclusive." The commission report, only part I of which was made public in Dec. 1986, named a number of suspected war criminals. The commission's work stirred bitterness between Jewish and Ukrainian Canadians.

COMMONWEALTH TRADE AND ECONOMIC CONFERENCE, 1958, trade meeting held in Montreal. JOHN DIEFENBAKER's government professed interest in increasing Commonwealth trade and Diefenbaker had even proposed in 1957 to divert 15 per cent of Canada's trade from the United States to Britain, something government officials pronounced impossible. But when the British offered free trade to Canada, Diefenbaker hastily backed off.

Unemployed Communist Party members on march

COMMUNIST PARTY OF CANADA, political party formed as an underground organization in Ontario in 1921. The party was officially recognized by the Communist International (Comintern) as the Comintern's representative in Canada. In 1922 the CPC, still operating "underground," established an open, "legal" party, the WORKERS' PARTY OF CANADA. In 1924 the Workers' party was disbanded and the CPC emerged to operate in public. In the late 1920s the party was split by factional fights pitting the followers of Leon Trotsky against those of Joseph Stalin. At this time TIM BUCK, a Stalinist, emerged as party leader. In late 1929 the party established the WORKERS' UNITY LEAGUE as a Communist-led labour federation. The party was outlawed from 1931 to 1936 and from 1939 to 1943. In 1943 it emerged as the LABOUR PROGRESSIVE PARTY. It resumed its official name in the late 1950s.

COMPACT THEORY OF CONFEDERATION, theory advanced by provincial governments and advocates of greater decentralization of Canada. It was first enunciated at the Interprovincial Conference of 1887 to justify provincial demands for greater power. It is based on the idea that CONFEDERATION was a compact between the British North American colonies and that the federal government was and is a creature of those colonies. The theory ignores the legal reality that the colonies were united by the British

Parliament with the passage of the BRITISH NORTH AMERICA ACT of 1867 and that the British Parliament created the federal government. The MEECH LAKE ACCORD concluded between Conservative Prime Minister BRIAN MULRONEY and the ten provincial premiers in the spring of 1987 apparently was based, in part, on this theory.

CONACHER, LIONEL PRETORIA (1900-54), athlete. "The Big Train" was Canada's greatest athlete in the first half of the 20th century. Born at Toronto, he was an outstanding football, hockey, lacrosse, and baseball player, the Ontario wrestling champion in the 125-pound class at 16 and the Canadian light-heavyweight boxing champion in 1920. In 1921 he led the Toronto Argonauts to the Grey Cup; in 1922 he helped Toronto clinch the senior Ontario Lacrosse title; and in 1934 he was the National Hockey League's first all-star. He began a second career in politics when elected as a Liberal to the Ontario legislature in 1937 and then to the House of Commons in 1949. For many years the Ontario athletic commissioner, he died while playing a charity softball game at Ottawa.

CONAN, LAURE, *see* ANGERS, FÉLICITÉ

John A. Macdonald, the Father of Confederation

CONFEDERATION, 1867, the union of the UNITED PROVINCE OF CANADA (which became Ontario and Quebec), Nova Scotia, and New Brunswick on 1 July 1867 to create the Dominion of Canada. Confederation was sanctioned by an act of the British Parliament known as the BRITISH NORTH AMERICA ACT. The idea of a federation of the British American colonies had existed for some time but was not discussed seriously until delegates met at the CHARLOTTETOWN CONFERENCE in Sept. 1864. In Oct. they met again at the QUEBEC CONFERENCE and adopted 72

RESOLUTIONS which the British government accepted with minor changes at a final conference in London two years later. Among the FATHERS OF CONFEDERATION were JOHN A. MACDONALD, GEORGE-ÉTIENNE CARTIER, and GEORGE BROWN of Canada, CHARLES TUPPER of Nova Scotia, and SAMUEL TILLEY of New Brunswick. Prime motives for the negotiations included the desire to form a stronger financial union and a free trade area within the British American colonies, the perceived need to unite for defence against the United States, the need to break an ongoing political deadlock in Canada, and the desire, on the part of some Canadians, to expand westward. There was strong opposition to British American union in the Maritime colonies, but fears of American invasion prevailed. Manitoba joined Confederation in 1870, British Columbia in 1871, Prince Edward Island in 1873, Saskatchewan and Alberta in 1905, and Newfoundland in 1949.

CONFÉDÉRATION DES SYNDICATS NATIONAUX / CONFEDERATION OF NATIONAL TRADE UNIONS, labour federation, successor to the CONFÉDÉRATION DES TRAVAILLEURS CATHOLIQUES DU CANADA / CANADIAN CATHOLIC CONFEDERATION OF LABOUR which changed its name in 1960. It is a highly centralized organization of industrial unions. In the late 1960s it became both militant and separatist in orientation, especially after leader JEAN MARCHAND joined the federal Liberal party in 1965.

CONFÉDÉRATION DES TRAVAILLEURS CATHOLIQUES DU CANADA / CANADIAN CATHOLIC CONFEDERATION OF LABOUR, federation of Quebec unions, mostly Catholic, founded in 1921. The federation began with about 18,000 workers. At first it eschewed strikes and boycotts and placed the achievement of Christian harmony above the improvement of the economic status of the working class. This began to change during World War II when the federation grew less Catholic and more militant. In 1960 it became the CONFÉDÉRATION DES SYNDICATS NATIONAUX/CONFEDERATION OF NATIONAL TRADE UNIONS.

CONFERENCE OF HISTORIC PEACE CHURCHES, organization formed in 1940 by pacifist denominations. As sentiment in favour of CONSCRIPTION grew during WORLD WAR II, the

Quakers, the Mennonites, and the Brethren in Christ (Tunker) organized to defend the interests of those with "religious or moral objections to participation in war." The conference advocated "alternative service" for CONSCIENTIOUS OBJECTORS.

CONNAUGHT AND STRATHEARN, ARTHUR WILLIAM PATRICK ALBERT, 1st DUKE OF (1850-1942), governor general of Canada. Queen Victoria's third son, the duke was born at Buckingham Palace and educated at the Royal Military Academy. He entered the British army in 1868, fought in Canada during the 1870 raid by the FENIANS, and served in Egypt, India, Ireland, and South Africa before returning to Canada as governor general from 1911 to 1916. The duke, a field marshal since 1902, at times believed himsef actual commander-in-chief and had to be reminded of constitutional reality by SIR ROBERT BORDEN.

CONNOLLY, HAROLD JOSEPH (1901-80), premier of Nova Scotia. Born at Sydney, N.S., Connolly was editor of the Halifax *Daily Star* when elected to the legislature as a Liberal in 1936. When ANGUS L. MACDONALD died in office in 1954, he became premier until a convention was held later that year to choose a successor, which he lost. He was named to the Senate in 1955.

CONNOR, RALPH, *see* GORDON, CHARLES W.

CONSCIENTIOUS OBJECTOR, term for a person who objected to service in the armed forces for religious reasons in World Wars I and II. Large numbers of conscientious objectors were found among pacifist religious groups such as the Mennonites and the DOUKHOBORS.

CONSCRIPTION, the drafting of persons for the armed forces. Canada instituted conscription in World Wars I and II. In WORLD WAR I service in the armed forces was voluntary until May 1917, when the Conservative government of Prime Minister ROBERT BORDEN introduced the MILITARY SERVICE ACT to draft eligible males for overseas military service. The bill was introduced because of an increased demand for troops at the front and a decline in the rate of voluntary enlistment. Many supporters of conscription were convinced that the measure was necessary to force French-Canadian males to assume an equal burden of

the war effort. Organized labour and many farm groups opposed the measure. In WORLD WAR II conscription was initially introduced only for domestic service with the passage of the NATIONAL RESOURCES MOBILIZATION ACT in June 1940, by the Liberal government of Prime Minister MACKENZIE KING. In Apr. 1942, following an increase in demands for conscription for overseas service, the King government conducted a national plebiscite on the question. There was tremendous opposition in Quebec but the government received a strong mandate in the rest of Canada to send men overseas. Despite the results of the vote, King refused to act, fearing damage to national unity. In Nov. 1944, however, with increased casualty rates from the intensified fighting in northwest Europe, the government dispatched a number of men overseas who had been drafted only for domestic service.

CONSCRIPTION CRISIS, 1917, 1942, 1944, political crises over methods of securing military manpower in World Wars I and II. The first crisis took place in 1917 after Prime Minister SIR ROBERT BORDEN returned from the IMPERIAL WAR CONFERENCE in London convinced that, because of the war situation, Canada had to raise more men. Borden attempted to coax SIR WILFRID LAURIER into supporting a coalition government but Laurier refused, knowing that Quebec would never support conscription. While Borden still struggled to create a coalition, his government in Aug. 1917 passed the MILITARY SERVICE ACT and the WARTIME ELECTIONS ACT, and the latter measure pushed provincial Liberals into joining Borden's UNION GOVERNMENT. Borden then won the Dec. 1917 election, fought on conscription. It was a costly victory because the Conservatives alienated Quebec and Western Canada. Militarily, conscription did not produce the men. Of 401,882 men registered, 221,949 were granted exemptions, 24,139 defaulted, 26,225 were available but not called, 96,379 were taken on strength of the CANADIAN EXPEDITIONARY FORCE, and only 24,132 joined CEF units in France.

The conscription crises which occurred during WORLD WAR II were less severe than that of WORLD WAR I and were handled much better. The crises went through two phases. Even before the outbreak of war, the Liberals had made explicit promises against conscription for overseas service, pledges that were repeated during the election of 1940 (when even Conservative leader R.J. MANION spoke against conscription). The government did pass the NATIONAL RESOURCES MOBILIZATION ACT in response to the military disasters in May-June 1940, and conscription for home defence was put in place without much opposition. Eventually 60,000 men served in the home defence force. By the beginning of 1942, however, with Japan in the war and Allied defeats continuing, the clamour for conscription for overseas service forced Prime Minister MACKENZIE KING to take action. The government called for a plebiscite on 27 April to ask the people to release it from the pledges it had made against compulsory service overseas. Quebec voted 72.9 per cent against conscription while the rest of Canada voted heavily for it. With his cabinet also sharply divided, King appeased both sides with his now famous statement: "not necessarily conscription, but conscription if necessary," an exact description of his policy to impose conscription only if the war situation demanded it. Parliament passed BILL 80, giving it the right to send conscripts overseas, but King declared that the NRMA soldiers or ZOMBIES would for the present serve only in the Western hemisphere.

The second phase took place in 1944 when Minister of National Defence J.L. RALSTON returned from a trip to the fronts in France and Italy convinced of the necessity to find more reinforcements, although victory was at hand. Taking one of the biggest risks of his career, King fired Ralston in an effort to avert conscription and replaced him with General A.G.L. MCNAUGHTON, who had been at the head of the FIRST CANADIAN ARMY in England until his removal in 1943. However, McNaughton, a supporter of voluntary enlistment, failed to produce the necessary number of infantry volunteers to bring the fighting battalions to strength, and the King government was forced in late November to agree to send up to 16,000 NRMA conscripts overseas. The decision again split the country, but King's acute sense of timing managed to soften the blow. Militarily, the results again were insignificant. By war's end, 12,908 NRMA soldiers went overseas, and 2463 reached units in Northwest Europe.

CONSERVATIVE PARTY, political party. The roots of the Canadian Conservative party lie in British Toryism and in the anti-democratic traditions of the Family Compact in Upper Canada of the 1820s and 1830s. But Conservatives have often shown more deftness than tradition implies, and the founder of the modern party in Canada, JOHN A. MACDONALD, was the most deft of all. After the 1854 election in the Province of Canada, Macdonald created the Liberal-Conservative party that fashioned CONFEDERATION and dominated it for a quarter century. The name itself was a synonym for moderation, and Macdonald found room in his party for all, French or English, Orange or Catholic, farmer or businessman. Moreover, Macdonald had a vision of Canada, and his nation-building became the central tenet of the early party. His alliance with business was cemented by the NATIONAL POLICY of tariff protection and railway construction that proved more successful electorally than in creating a vibrant economy. Macdonald's solid support in French Canada was shaken by his government's decision to hang LOUIS RIEL in 1885 and by fratricidal fights in the Quebec party. Macdonald died in 1891 and his successors proved less successful than he in balancing the competing elements in the polity. Not until ROBERT BORDEN came to power in 1911, thanks to his anti-RECIPROCITY policy and an alliance with Quebec nationalism, did Conservatives hold office again for a long stretch. But Borden was largely indifferent to party concerns and, during WORLD WAR I, he created the UNION GOVERNMENT of Conservatives and pro-CONSCRIPTION Liberals and the party machinery fell into disarray. Under his successor, ARTHUR MEIGHEN, the Conservatives ran third to the Liberals and the PROGRESSIVE PARTY in the 1921 election. With the wily Liberal MACKENZIE KING in charge, a succession of Conservative leaders came to naught, the exception being R.B. BENNETT who won the 1930 election and scarcely survived five depression years in power. The party suffered from the reputation Bennett gave it — high tariff, reactionary, anti-American — and although strenuous efforts were made to become more modern in outlook (notably at the PORT HOPE CONFERENCE in 1942 and in the party's adoption of the name PROGRESSIVE CONSERVATIVE at a convention in Dec. 1942), Conservatives did not find a leader able to capture the public mood until JOHN DIEFENBAKER in 1956. Diefenbaker won in 1957 and massively in 1958, almost lost in 1962, and was defeated in 1963, thanks to his inability to make decisions, to get on with the United States, and to hold urban Canada. Under him, the party's strongest support was in the west, hitherto poor ground for the Conservatives; under him, the party lost the urban working-class support that had often sustained it; and under him, there were persistent leadership crises. Efforts to regain support largely foundered in the 1970s, although the Conservatives under JOE CLARK took power in a minority government in 1979 only to be defeated the next year by resurgent Liberals. Clark was dumped as leader in 1983. In Sept. 1984, finally, the Conservatives won a landslide victory under the bilingual Quebecer BRIAN MULRONEY and supporters thought, just as in 1958, that they were assured of a generation in power. The new government quickly ran into problems with patronage and scandals, had difficulty sorting out its priorities, and fell disastrously in the opinion polls to third place by early 1988. Since Macdonald, the Conservative party has had persistent difficulties with leadership and with its priorities. Was it a conservative party on the right? Or was it a centrist party in the Canadian mainstream?

CONSOLIDATED MINING AND SMELTING CO., *see* COMINCO

CONSTITUTION, PATRIATION OF, 1982,
the bringing home of the constitution from Britain to Canada. Efforts to amend the BRITISH NORTH AMERICA ACT in Canada, rather than in Britain, had repeatedly foundered on provincial objections. Prime Minister PIERRE TRUDEAU, after helping to defeat the PARTI QUÉBÉCOIS in its referendum on SOVEREIGNTY-ASSOCIATION in May 1980 with his promises of constitutional reform, began yet another attempt to cut the Gordian knot. For 18 months the federal government and provinces argued over the division of powers and the entrenchment of the CANADIAN CHARTER OF RIGHTS AND FREEDOMS. In Oct. 1980, balked by the premiers, Trudeau declared his intent to make a unilateral request to Westminster to patriate the constitution, a move that the Supreme Court in Sept. 1981 upheld as constitutional, though noting that it violated convention. At a climatic federal-provincial meeting in Nov., confrontation seemed certain to produce a complete breakdown of talks when, at the last moment, a compromise was hammered out overnight that proved accept-

able to all parties except Quebec. An amending formula, a "notwithstanding" clause, and the Charter formed the package which, after some further amendment to protect native rights and women's rights, was sent to Westminster. The new Constitution Act, 1982, was proclaimed on 17 Apr. 1982. The Quebec government indicated its willingness to accept the constitution in mid-1987 after federal-provincial meetings at MEECH LAKE and Ottawa.

CONSTITUTION ACT, 1867, name since 1982
of Canada's first constitution, the BRITISH NORTH AMERICA ACT, 1867.

CONSTITUTION ACT, 1982, *see* CONSTITUTION, PATRIATION OF, 1982

CONTINENTALIST, term used to categorize
Canadians in favour of closer relations with the United States. One of the earliest continentalists was GOLDWIN SMITH.

CO-OPERATIVE COMMONWEALTH FEDERATION, political party. The CCF was
founded in Aug. 1932 when representatives from farm, labour, intellectual, and socialist groups assembled in the Labour Temple in Calgary, Alta. J.S. WOODSWORTH was elected as its first leader. The new party held its first annual convention one year later at Regina and adopted the REGINA MANIFESTO, a 14-point program which advocated social and economic reforms, such as health and welfare insurance, WORKERS' COMPENSATION, and UNEMPLOYMENT INSURANCE, which Canadians now take for granted. The CCF was branded as a dangerous bolshevik party, but in reality it was the natural coming together of Progressive elements, especially the Woodsworth-led GINGER GROUP, the LEAGUE FOR SOCIAL RECONSTRUCTION and the UNITED FARMERS OF ALBERTA, searching for a way to eradicate the effects of the GREAT DEPRESSION. Although the CCF gained in popularity at both the federal and provincial level (the party led the opinion polls briefly in 1943 and a CCF government under T.C. DOUGLAS took office in Saskatchewan in 1944), it was vulnerable to right-wing assaults and its appeal waned with the onset of the Cold War. The party attempted to moderate its image with the adoption of the Winnipeg Declaration in 1956 but its disastrous showing in the 1958 election

forced it to reorganize. In 1961 the CCF joined forces with the CANADIAN LABOUR CONGRESS to found the NEW DEMOCRATIC PARTY.

COOPERATIVE FEDERALISM, a formula of Canadian government in which institutions are less important than practices. Brought to its high point in the mid-1960s by Prime Minister LESTER PEARSON's government, the theory called for frequent consultations between various levels of government on a wide range of policy matters.

COOPERATIVE MOVEMENT, social and economic movement. Cooperative organizations appeared in British North America in the 1840s, initially to market goods. Producers' coops soon appeared as well. Although the cooperative movement was important in Atlantic and central Canada, its major impact was on the Prairies. Led by E.A. PARTRIDGE, who urged grain growers to create a company that could sell their harvest and release them from the tyranny of middlemen, western farmers formed the GRAIN GROWERS' GRAIN CO. in 1906, and, not without difficulty, it won the right to use grain exchanges. The company, and other cooperatives organized by farmers (and by the government of Saskatchewan), eventually took over some of the grain elevators so that by 1914 there were almost 400 coop elevators across the Prairies. The coop movement on the Prairies soon began "cooperative pooling" of wheat, creating huge organizations that plunged into debt with the GREAT DEPRESSION. Despite these difficulties, the very name, cooperative, was so potent that the CO-OPERATIVE COMMONWEALTH FEDERATION appropriated it to show both its roots and aims.

CORVETTES, convoy protection vessels used by the ROYAL CANADIAN NAVY in WORLD WAR II. Based on a British design, 122 corvettes were built in Canada throughout the war; 12 more were launched in Britain and operated by RCN. Small, cramped, hard-sailing, and lightly gunned, the corvettes were remarkably durable and performed with great distinction against German U-boats in the North Atlantic and to a much lesser extent on the West coast. Nine corvettes were lost to enemy action.

COSTAIN, THOMAS BERTRAM (1885-1965), writer. Born at Brantford, Ont., Costain worked as a journalist, becoming editor of MACLEAN'S from 1914 to 1920. He then worked at the *Saturday Evening Post*, at Twentieth Century Fox, and Doubleday. During World War II, he began to write historical fiction and captured an enormous North American market. Some of his novels had Canadian settings.

COTTON'S WEEKLY, radical periodical published in the early 20th century by H.F. Carter-Cotton in Cowansville. Que. Carter-Cotton became a socialist in the years just before World War I and supported the SOCIAL DEMOCRATIC PARTY OF CANADA, founded in 1911, in his periodical.

COX, GEORGE ALBERTUS (1840-1914), businessman. Born in Colborne, Upper Canada. Cox was active in municipal politics and business in Peterborough, Ont. before moving to Toronto in 1888. There he quickly rose into the upper ranks of the business and financial community. A liberal, Cox was one of Prime Minister WILFRID LAURIER's first appointments to the Senate in 1896. He was the founder, president, or vice-president of over 40 firms.

COYNE, JAMES ELLIOTT (1910-), central banker. Born at Winnipeg, Coyne joined the BANK OF CANADA in 1938, becoming governor of the bank in 1955. His warnings about the dangers of increasing foreign investment in Canada and difficulties in determining the government's monetary policy led to a dispute with Prime Minister JOHN DIEFENBAKER's administration in 1961. The government clumsily demanded Coyne's resignation. He initially refused but relented after vindication by a Senate committee.

CP AIR, *see* CANADIAN PACIFIC AIRLINES

CRAWLEY, FRANK RADFORD, "BUDGE" (1911-87), filmmaker. Crawley was born at Ottawa and began shooting films during the 1930s. His small company was hired by JOHN GRIERSON of the NATIONAL FILM BOARD to make films during World War II. With the peace, Crawley produced films for government agencies and corporations, and then moved into television and feature films. In 1976 his film *The Man Who Skied Down Everest* won an Academy Award.

CRÉDITISTES, *see* RALLIEMENT DES CRÉDITISTES

CREIGHTON, DONALD GRANT (1902-79), historian. Born at Toronto and educated at the univs. of Toronto and Oxford, he joined the Univ. of Toronto's history department in 1927. His first book, *The Commercial Empire of the St. Lawrence* (1937), written under the influence of HAROLD INNIS, had a tremendous impact on the writing of Canadian history. At the centre of Creighton's work was the LAURENTIAN THESIS, the idea of the St Lawrence River as the basis of a transcontinental economic and political system which ran on an east-west axis. Variations of the theme influenced his two-volume biography of JOHN A. MACDONALD, *The Young Politician* (1952) and *The Old Chieftain* (1955), as well as *British North America at Confederation* (1939), *Dominion of the North* (1944) and his least successful book, *The Forked Road: Canada, 1939-1957* (1976). A committed nationalist and centralist, he warned of the dangers of continentalism and regionalism.

General H.D.G. Crerar

CRERAR, HENRY DUNCAN GRAHAM (1888-1965), soldier. Born at Hamilton, Ont., he graduated from the ROYAL MILITARY COLLEGE. Com-

missioned in 1910, he attained the rank of lieutenant-colonel during WORLD WAR I and held various staff positions between the wars. In 1940 he became chief of the general staff, in 1941 commander of 1 Canadian Corps, and in 1944 he took command of the FIRST CANADIAN ARMY. Crerar led the army in the invasion of France in June 1944. Promoted general in November 1944, he commanded operations in northwest Europe until the German surrender in May 1945. Not a brilliant field commander, Crerar was cautious and careful. He retired from the army in 1946.

Thomas A. Crerar

CRERAR, THOMAS ALEXANDER (1876-1975), farm leader, politician. Although born at Molesworth, Ont., Crerar was raised and educated in Manitoba. He taught school, farmed, and from 1907 to 1929 was president of the GRAIN GROWERS' GRAIN CO. First elected to the House of Commons in 1917, he served as minister of agriculture in Prime Minister ROBERT BORDEN'S UNION GOVERNMENT until resigning over the government's tariff policy in 1919. Re-elected in 1921, he became leader of the PROGRESSIVE PARTY and, after refusing to form the opposition after the 1921 election, resigned again in 1922. In 1929 he turned up as Liberal Prime Minister MACKENZIE KING's minister of railways and canals but lost his seat in the 1930 election. He returned with the Liberals in the 1935 election, becoming minister of mines and resources for nine of the next 10 years. Called to the Senate in 1945, he resigned in 1966.

CROLL, DAVID (1900–), labour lawyer, politician. Croll was minister of labour in the Ontario Liberal government of MITCHELL HEPBURN at the time of the General Motors OSHAWA STRIKE of 1937. He objected to Hepburn's anti-union tactics and resigned from the government. He was appointed to the Senate by Prime Minister LOUIS ST LAURENT in 1955, where he was an advocate for the poor and the aged.

CROP INSURANCE ACT, federal legislation passed in 1959 to establish a cost-sharing crop insurance program. Designed to complement and coordinate existing provincial crop insurance laws, the program is intended to aid farmers who suffer heavy financial losses through natural disasters such as flooding or hail.

CROSBIE, JOHN CARNELL (1931–), politician. Born at St John's, Nfld, and educated at Queen's, Dalhousie, and London univs., Crosbie practised law in his home city. He went from municipal politics to JOSEPH SMALLWOOD's Liberal cabinet in 1966, tried for the party leadership in 1969, lost, and switched to the Conservatives. Crosbie served in FRANK MOORES's cabinet, and then won a federal seat in 1976. He was finance minister in the government of Prime Minister JOE CLARK and, his budget led to the government's defeat in the House. After losing the 1983 leadership race to BRIAN MULRONEY, he became justice minister in Mulroney's government.

CROSS, ALFRED EARNEST (1861-1932), rancher, brewer. Cross was a Calgary veterinarian before starting his own ranch in 1885. He became one of the most prominent ranchers in southern Alberta, founding the Calgary Brewing and Malting Co. and helping to finance the first CALGARY STAMPEDE. *See also* BIG FOUR CATTLEMEN.

CROTHERS, THOMAS WILSON (1850-1951), politician. Crothers served as minister of labour in Prime Minister ROBERT BORDEN's cabinet from 1911 to 1918 and was subsequently appointed to the Senate. He was one of the less able men to head the Department of Labour.

CROWFOOT (d. 1890), Blackfoot chief. Born near the Belly River (in what is now Alberta) about 1830, Crowfoot was a notable warrior. He became chief of the Big Pipes band in 1865 and five years later one of the three Blackfoot head chiefs. His policy was to maintain good relations with the Cree and the traders, and he welcomed the NORTH-WEST MOUNTED POLICE when they came west in 1874. Placed on a reserve after Treaty 7 was signed in 1877, Crowfoot had many grievances against Ottawa, but he did not join in the NORTH-WEST REBELLION in 1885, largely because he discerned that the MÉTIS and Indians had little chance to prevail.

CROWN CORPORATION, a corporation owned by either federal or provincial governments but which has its own board of governors or directors and management structure. Crown corporations are usually established to achieve government objectives in instances where the government does not wish to use its own departments or where private entrepreneurs have been unwilling to act. They are deliberately designed to keep political interference to a minimum. Crown corporations were first established in the 19th century but only came into wide use during and immediately after World War I. Some famous national crown corporations are CANADIAN NATIONAL RAILWAYS, established in 1919, and the CANADIAN BROADCASTING CORP., founded in 1936. A large number of crown corporations set up during World War II were disbanded after the war was over.

CROW'S NEST PASS AGREEMENT, agreement between the federal government and the CANADIAN PACIFIC RAILWAY signed in 1897, that established a schedule of reduced FREIGHT RATES on east-bound grain and west-bound settlers' effects. After large deposits of coal and other minerals were discovered in the Crow's Nest Pass and the Kootenay Mountains in the early 1890s, the CPR decided to build a westward extension of its main line from Medicine Hat, Alta, through the Crow's Nest Pass into the British Columbia interior. When it sought federal support, Ottawa agreed as long as the railway agreed to reduced freight rates. These Statutory Rates or Crow Rates were eventually applied to all railways linking the Prairies with the east and remained in effect until 1984.

CUBAN MISSILE CRISIS, 1962, a Cold War crisis between the Soviet Union and the United States over the installation of Soviet missiles in Cuba. When the United States detected the Soviet activities, President John Kennedy ordered a blockade of the Caribbean island on 22 Oct. Prime Minister JOHN DIEFENBAKER, informed just prior to the announcement of the blockade, refused to put Canadian forces, and especially those in NORAD, on alert until 24 Oct. Instead Diefenbaker called on the United Nations to send observers to Cuba to verify the presence of missiles. Defence minister DOUGLAS HARKNESS, on his own authority, ordered defensive precautions, but the Americans and the Canadian public, when it learned of the prime minister's delays after the USSR withdrew the weapons, were angered. Although he argued (with some reason) that Canada's NORAD membership entitled Ottawa to be consulted, not merely informed, Diefenbaker never recovered from the impression of indecision his inaction created.

CULLEN, MAURICE GALBRAITH (1866-1934), painter. Cullen studied in Montreal and Paris, his style becoming more impressionistic. Best known for his paintings of Montreal in winter, Cullen had a substantial influence on Canadian artists generally and especially the GROUP OF SEVEN.

CULTURAL DUALISM, *see* BILINGUALISM AND BICULTURALISM

CURRIE, SIR ARTHUR WILLIAM, (1875-1933), soldier. Born at Strathroy, Ont., he moved to British Columbia in 1893, taught school, and ran a successful business in Victoria until nearly wiped out in the 1913 depression. Active in the militia from 1893, Currie was given command of the 2nd Canadian Infantry Brigade when WORLD WAR I began. In Sept. 1915 he took command of the 1st Division and in 1917 succeeded General BYNG as general officer commanding the CANADIAN CORPS. Seen as a commanding officer who cared about his men, a rare breed in World War I, he was promoted general in Nov. 1919 and appointed inspector-general, Canadian militia. He was principal and vice-chancellor of McGill Univ. from 1920 until his death.

CUSTOMS UNION, arrangement in which all tariffs and duties between countries in the union are removed and a common schedule of tariffs is established to protect against trade from other countries. Customs union with the United States was advocated by the Liberal party of Canada in the late 1880s and early 1890s. During the 1891 federal election the Conservatives and others used the Liberal support for the policy to charge that the Liberals favoured annexation to the United States. Following the Conservative victory in the election, Liberal leader WILFRID LAURIER abandoned the policy.

CUT KNIFE HILL, BATTLE OF, battle between the forces of Cree Chief POUNDMAKER and the Canadian militia under Colonel W.D. OTTER on 2 May 1885 during the NORTH-WEST REBELLION about 48 km west of North Battleford. *See also* LOUIS RIEL; GABRIEL DUMONT; F. MIDDLETON.

CYPRESS HILLS MASSACRE, massacre of 36 Assiniboine Indians by American and Canadian wolf hunters in the Cypress Hills (now in southern Saskatchewan) in late May 1873. The event helped convince the federal government to form the NORTH-WEST MOUNTED POLICE.

DAFOE, ALLAN ROY (1883-1943), physician. Born at Madoc, Ont., and trained at the Univ. of Toronto, Dafoe delivered the DIONNE QUINTUPLETS in 1934 and kept the tiny infants alive. His success brought him fame and fortune as he became the quints' appointed protector, a broadcaster, and an author.

DAFOE, JOHN WESLEY (1866-1944), journalist. Legendary editor of the *Manitoba (Winnipeg) Free Press* from 1901 to 1944, Dafoe was born at Combermere, Canada West. He began as parliamentary correspondent for the Montreal *Star* in 1884, moved to the Ottawa *Evening Journal* in 1886, and to the *Free Press* later the same year. Dafoe developed a unique relationship with the owners of the paper, one that allowed him substantial editorial freedom. He was pro-

courtesy Manitoba Archives

John W. Dafoe

CONSCRIPTION in 1917, viciously anti-labour and anti-foreigner during the WINNIPEG GENERAL STRIKE, but generally liberal in sentiment, as shown in his support for Canadian autonomy and the LEAGUE OF NATIONS. Influential and widely respected in Canadian affairs, Dafoe served on the ROYAL COMMISSION ON DOMINION-PROVINCIAL RELATIONS. He wrote a number of books, including *Laurier: A Study in Canadian Politics* (1922), *Clifford Sifton in Relation to His Times* (1931), and *Canada: An American Nation* (1935).

DANDURAND, RAOUL (1861-1942), senator. A lawyer and a Liberal, he was named to the Senate by WILFRID LAURIER in 1898, became its speaker in 1905, and a member of the Privy Council in 1901. Prime Minister MACKENZIE KING brought him into the cabinet (without portfolio) in 1921 and he remained there as long as King governed until he died. Dandurand frequently represented Canada at the LEAGUE OF NATIONS in the 1920s, and he is best remembered today for telling the assembled nations that Canadians lived in a FIRE-PROOF HOUSE far from inflammable materials, the quintessential isolationist statement of the interwar period.

DASH 7 (DHC-7), four-engine inter-city aircraft. Built by DE HAVILLAND AIRCRAFT OF CANADA, the Dash 7 first flew in 1975. The federal govern-ment paid 80 per cent of the $120 million development cost but, despite its advanced design, the Dash 7 was not a financial success. Lessons learned in the design and development were applied to the more successful DASH 8.

DASH 8, twin-engined passenger aircraft manufactured by DE HAVILLAND AIRCRAFT OF CANADA in Toronto. Work on the Dash 8 began in the fall of 1980 and the aircraft has been sold to a large number of feeder airlines around the world. The design was based on that of the DASH 7, a four-engine plane that was also developed by de Havilland.

DAVEY, KEITH (1926–), politician. Born and educated in Toronto, Davey worked in radio while making his way up through the Toronto LIBERAL PARTY hierarchy in the 1950s. In 1961 he became national campaign director of the party, oversaw the election struggles of 1962, 1963, and 1965, and was appointed a senator in 1966. He shaped the majority Liberal victories of 1974 and 1980 but was unable to rescue Prime Minister JOHN TURNER's campaign in 1984.

DAVIDSON, JOE (1915-85), labour leader. Born in Shotts, Scot., Davidson was head of the Canadian Union of Postal Workers from 1974 to 1977. He was prominent in two national strikes of inside postal workers after the union won the right to strike in the mid-1960s.

DAVIES, ROBERTSON WILLIAM (1913–), writer. An outstanding Canadian literary figure, Davies was born at Thamesville, Ont., and attended Queen's and Oxford univs. He tried his hand at acting before returning to Canada in 1940 as literary editor of SATURDAY NIGHT. As editor and later publisher of the Peterborough *Examiner* from 1942 to 1965, Davies wrote 18 books. He joined the Univ. of Toronto in 1960 and taught literature for the next 21 years, most of them as master of Massey College. Davies won international recognition for his utilization of Jungian psychology in the novel *Fifth Business* (1970) and its sequels, *The Manticore* (1972) and *World of Wonders* (1975), collectively known as the Deptford Trilogy.

DAVIES CO., *see* WILLIAM DAVIES CO.

DAVIS, WILLIAM GRENVILLE (1929–), premier of Ontario. Davis was born at Brampton, Ont., and educated at the Univ. of Toronto. He was called to the bar in 1955 but entered Ontario politics and won a seat as a Conservative in 1959. Davis demonstrated his ability to preside over a big-spending department after premier JOHN ROBARTS handed him the difficult education portfolio in 1962. Chosen to succeed Robarts as leader of the BIG BLUE MACHINE in 1971, the deliberately bland Davis governed with relative success and stayed unchallenged in his party until he resigned in 1985.

DAWSON, GEORGE MERCER (1849-1901), geologist. Born in Pictou, N.S., and educated at McGill Univ. and in London, Dawson was appointed geologist and botanist to the North American Boundary Commission in 1873; two years later he joined the GEOLOGICAL SURVEY OF CANADA, becoming assistant director in 1883 and director 12 years later. His own work was largely in British Columbia and the Northwest Territories, and he published widely. His work in mapping accelerated settlement and resource development.

DAWSON, SIR JOHN WILLIAM (1820-99), geologist, educator. Dawson was born at Pictou, N.S., and educated in Edinburgh, Scot. A geologist, he became a world expert on fossil plants, but, despite that, remained vigorously opposed to Charles Darwin's evolutionary theories. He served as superintendent of education in Nova Scotia from 1850 to 1855 and as McGill Univ. principal from 1855 to 1893.

DAWSON, ROBERT MCGREGOR (1895-1958), political scientist. Born at Bridgewater, N.S., and educated at Dalhousie, Harvard, and the London School of Economics, McGregor Dawson taught at a number of universities before joining the staff at the Univ. of Toronto in 1937. He published widely, wrote the standard textbook on Canadian government, and was, until his death, the official biographer of MACKENZIE KING.

DEACON, THOMAS RUSS (1865-1955), engineer, manufacturer. Born in Perth, Ont., Deacon became a prominent manufacturer and politician in pre–World War I Winnipeg. He founded the

Manitoba Bridge and Ironworks, a company steadfastly opposed to the presence of unions and a hotbed of labour unrest. A strike of his workers in May 1919 helped touch off the WINNIPEG GENERAL STRIKE.

Amor de Cosmos

courtesy PABC #HP2625

DE COSMOS, AMOR (1825-97), premier of British Columbia. Born William Alexander Smith at Windsor, N.S., he ventured to the California gold fields in 1851 and changed his name while working as a photographer. De Cosmos followed the gold rush to British Columbia in 1858 and founded the *British Colonist* in Victoria. Critical of the colony's governor, JAMES DOUGLAS, and a strong advocate of the entry of the mainland united with Vancouver Island into CONFEDERATION, De Cosmos entered politics in 1863 as a member of the Island's Legislative Assembly and, four years later, he was a member of the British Columbia Legislative Council. In 1871 he won a seat in the legislature and became premier the next year, a post he retained until 1874. He had also been elected to the House of Commons in 1871 where he sat as a Liberal until 1882.

DE HAVILLAND AIRCRAFT OF CANADA LTD, aircraft manufacturer incorporated in 1929 as the Canadian branch of de Havilland Aircraft of Great Britain. It became a world leader in the design and production of small- and medium-sized transport aircraft, particularly with STOL (short takeoff and landing) capability. De Havilland produced the BEAVER, CARIBOU, DASH-7, DASH-8, and OTTER (now Twin Otter) aircraft. In 1974 the federal government purchased the company from its British owners, Hawker Siddeley Aviation, and in 1986 sold it to the Boeing Corp. of Seattle, Wash.

DE LA ROCHE, MAZO (1879-1961), writer. Born at Newmarket, Ont., and educated at the Univ. of Toronto, she published her first short story in *Atlantic Monthly* in 1915. She had written three novels before she won fame for *Jalna* in 1927. The book was so successful that she wrote sequel after sequel, popular all over the world. She wrote more than 23 novels, 50 short stories, and 13 plays with sales in the millions. In 1971 the *Whiteoaks of Jalna*, a series dramatizing the Jalna novels, was shown on Canadian television.

DEFENCE OF CANADA REGULATIONS, regulations giving the government sweeping authority to protect the country against subversion and to control dissent, proclaimed in force on the outbreak of war on 3 Sept. 1939 under authority of the WAR MEASURES ACT. They were drafted between March and July 1939 by an interdepartmental committee of bureaucrats and military officers.

DEFENCE PRODUCTION SHARING AGREEMENT, Canada-United States agreement to maintain a long-term balance in defence trade between the two. Negotiated by the DIEFENBAKER government in 1958, the DPSA gave Canada duty-free entry to the United States for defence products and exemption from the U.S. "Buy American" legislation.

DEMOBILIZATION, term for the return to civil life of men and women in the armed forces. Used more frequently in 1945 than in 1918, the term encompassed the physical separation of service personnel from the armed forces, as well as the process of their reintegration into civil life and the veterans' benefits that awaited them.

DENISON, FLORA MACDONALD (1867-1920), feminist. Born Flora Merrill in Hastings County, Canada West, Denison was a major figure in the WOMEN'S SUFFRAGE movement. While running a successful dress business, she was president of the Canadian Suffrage Assn from 1911 to 1914, a columnist in the *Toronto Sunday World*, and a leading free spirit of the day.

DENISON, GEORGE TAYLOR (1839-1925), soldier, magistrate. Born at Toronto, Denison was one of the great characters of his era. He saw service in the raids by the FENIANS and the NORTH-WEST REBELLION, he helped found CANADA FIRST, and was a supporter of imperial unity. He wrote an internationally renowned history of cavalry. In 1877 he became a police magistrate, renowned for his eccentric style in court.

DESJARDINS, ALPHONSE (1854-1920), journalist, founder of the caisses populaires. Born at Lévis, Canada East, Desjardins was French-language reporter for HANSARD in the House of Commons when in 1900 he founded the first CAISSE POPULAIRE in Lévis. It was to be a people's bank, a cooperative effort that would give ordinary people lower interest rates. The idea spread throughout Quebec, other parts of Canada, and around the world before his death.

DEUTSCH, JOHN JAMES (1911-76), civil servant, educator. Born at Quinton, Sask., Deutsch was educated at Queen's Univ. and took a job with the research staff of the BANK OF CANADA in 1936. He moved to External Affairs during World War II, then to Finance and the Treasury Board. He was the spark behind an abortive FREE TRADE effort in 1947-8. In 1956 he joined the economics department at the Univ. of British Columbia, moved to Queen's in 1959, and became principal in 1968. Deutsch was the pre-emininent practical economist of his day, a down-to-earth man of great force.

DEUX NATIONS, theory advocated by those who believed that Canada is, fundamentally, a union of two "nations," one English, the other French, and that Canada's constitutional, political, social, and cultural institutions should reflect that duality. Advocates of "two nations" thought, for example, that Quebec, as the homeland of the French-Canadian people, should be given special powers and privileges within CONFEDERATION not only over cultural and educational matters, but over economic development as well. The idea was adamantly opposed by Prime

Minister PIERRE TRUDEAU who believed that all of Canada should reflect the BILINGUALISM AND BICULTURALISM that resulted from the marriage of English and French in the union of 1867. The theory has become incorporated in the MEECH LAKE ACCORD arrived at by Conservative Prime Minister BRIAN MULRONEY and the premiers of the ten provinces in the spring of 1987.

DEVINE, DONALD GRANT (1944–), premier of Saskatchewan. Born at Regina, Sask., Devine graduated from the Univ. of Saskatchewan and Ohio State before returning to his native province in 1976 to farm near Moose Jaw and teach at the Univ. of Saskatchewan. He made a successful bid for the leadership of the Progressive Conservative party in 1979. Devine led his party to a resounding victory over ALLAN BLAKENEY's New Democratic Party in 1982, the first Conservative win since 1929, and won re-election four years later.

DEVONSHIRE, VICTOR CHRISTIAN WIL-LIAM CAVENDISH, 9TH DUKE OF (1868-1938), governor general of Canada. He entered the House of Commons in Great Britain in 1891 and sat as a Liberal Unionist until he succeeded his uncle as duke in 1908. As governor general from 1916 to 1921 he presided over the formation of ROBERT BORDEN's UNION GOVERNMENT. He later served as secretary of state for the colonies.

DEW LINE (Distant Early Warning Line), a line of radar stations completed in 1957 by Canada and the United States which stretches along the Arctic coast from Alaska to Greenland. The DEW line was part of North America's defences against the Soviet Union but the appearance of the intercontinental ballistic missile made it quickly obsolescent. In 1985, Prime Minister BRIAN MULRONEY and President Ronald Reagan agreed to update the DEW Line to counter the threat of Soviet Cruise missiles.

DEXTER, ALEXANDER GRANT (1896-1961), journalist. Born at St Andrews, Man., Dexter attended Brandon College and joined the *Manitoba Free Press* in 1912. He served in World War I, then resumed his career, becoming a protégé of J.W. DAFOE. His Ottawa reporting, always informed by his many confidential sources, made the *Free Press* indispensable reading, and Dexter

sent regular confidential memoranda to Winnipeg that remain a prime source for the history of the 1930s to 1950s. He was less successful as editor of the *Free Press* (1948-54).

DICKINS, GLENNELL HAGGERSTON, "PUNCH" (1899–), aviator. Dickins served with distinction in the Royal Flying Corps in World War I. After the war he became a legendary bush pilot, flying airmail and prospectors around the north. In World War II, he ran schools in the BRITISH COMMONWEALTH AIR TRAINING PLAN. After the war he joined the board of DE HAVILLAND AIRCRAFT OF CANADA.

courtesy Toronto Star Syndicate

John G. Diefenbaker

DIEFENBAKER, JOHN GEORGE (1895-1979), prime minister of Canada. He was born at Neustadt, Ont., and accompanied his family to the North-West Territories in 1903. His father failed at farming and moved to Saskatoon in 1910 where Diefenbaker completed schooling and attended the Univ. of Saskatchewan. Along with most of his classmates, he joined the army during World War I, but a training injury kept him out of the trenches. After his return to Canada, he completed law school in Saskatoon and began practice in Wakaw, Sask.

An aspiring CONSERVATIVE PARTY politician, he had no success in his first attempts at election. He lost federally in 1925 and 1926, provincially in 1929 and 1938, and municipally in Prince Albert in 1933. Not until the federal election of 1940, a disastrous one for the Conservatives nationally, did he win a seat in Lake Centre, Sask., and then he was greatly assisted by the charm of his wife Edna (who died in 1951). In Parliament, Diefenbaker developed a reputation for oratory and as a defender of civil liberties, but this was not enough to win him the party leadership at conventions in 1942 and 1948. In 1956, however, shortly after he married Olive Freeman, Diefenbaker swept the leadership convention.

Soon he swept the country too. In 1957 the Conservatives stunned the nation by defeating the government of Prime Minister LOUIS ST LAURENT and forming a minority administration. The next year, the crusading "Chief," proclaiming his "vision" of a new northern Canada, led his party to a smashing triumph–208 seats and the largest majority to that time. But the triumph turned quickly hollow. The economy slumped, unemployment rose, and there were difficulties with the cancellation of the CF-105 AVRO ARROW, with Britain over trade and Prime Minister Harold Macmillan's desire to join the Common Market, and with the United States over nuclear weapons. U.S. President John Kennedy wanted Canada to accept nuclear warheads, but although Diefenbaker had ordered BOMARC and Honest John missiles that were effective only with them, he began to balk. After a dilatory government response during the CUBAN MISSILE CRISIS in Oct. 1962, Diefenbaker came under stronger pressure from the United States, and in Feb. 1963 he was defeated in Parliament on a non-confidence motion.

Diefenbaker narrowly lost the election of 1963 to LESTER PEARSON and the LIBERAL PARTY, but he led a successful scandal-mongering opposition that largely frustrated the government, again denying the Pearson government majority status in 1965. By this time, however, dissidents within the Conservative party were calling for Diefenbaker to resign, and at the 1967 convention that chose ROBERT STANFIELD to replace him as leader, Diefenbaker did poorly, ultimately dropping from the ballot. Until his death in 1979, he remained

in Parliament as the MP for Prince Albert, and he gradually became a much-loved figure across the country, something he had been unable to achieve in power.

courtesy National Archives of Canada/C-14160

The beach at Dieppe, 1942

DIEPPE, 1942, a raid on the French port town on 19 Aug. 1942 by 4963 Canadian soldiers of the 2nd Canadian Division under the command of Major-General J.H. Roberts. The operation was a total disaster as the Germans controlled the heights above the beach and tanks could not get traction on the shale. Casualties totalled 3367 and included 907 killed and 1946 prisoners of war. The post facto justification for the raid was that the lessons learned made the NORMANDY INVASION, 1944, a success.

courtesy NEA Service
National Archives of Canada/C-36305

The Dionne Quintuplets

DIONNE QUINTUPLETS, the first quintuplets to survive more than a few days. Annette, Cécile, Émilie, Marie, and Yvonne were born to Olivia and Elzire Dionne at Corbeil, Ont., on 24 May, 1934. An overnight sensation, the quints were snatched from their impoverished parents by the Ontario government and placed in the protective custody of the doctor who delivered them, A.R. DAFOE. A special hospital was built to handle the tourists who flooded the area and brought the province millions of dollars each year. After a nine-year battle, the quintuplets were reunited with their parents in 1943 but unhappily. Annette, an epileptic, died in 1954 and the remaining four wrote a bitter autobiography, *We Were Five* (1963). Marie died in 1970, and the survivors split what remained of a trust fund in 1979.

DISALLOWANCE, federal power under the BRITISH NORTH AMERICA ACT, 1867, to disallow provincial legislation. Employed frequently and against all provinces (except Prince Edward Island) in the early years of the dominion as Ottawa struggled to maintain federal primacy, disallowance fell into disuse as relations between the federal and provincial governments settled down. Its last use was in 1943.

DISPLACED PERSONS, term used for post–World War II refugees displaced from their homes by the fighting. At the close of the war millions of refugees languished in refugee camps across Europe. Many eventually returned to their homes but many also sought to move elsewhere. In 1948, following a reappraisal of Canada's future manpower needs, Canadian immigration regulations were liberalized to allow a large number of these persons to enter the country.

DOFASCO, *see* DOMINION FOUNDRIES AND STEEL LTD

DOHERTY, CHARLES JOSEPH (1855-1931), politician. Born at Montreal and educated at McGill Univ., Doherty taught law there until he was named to the bench in 1891. He ran for Parliament in 1908 as a Conservative and was minister of justice in the administrations of Prime Ministers ROBERT BORDEN and ARTHUR MEIGHEN.

DOLLAR-A-YEAR MEN, term used to refer to the managers and executives from private corporations who were persuaded to go to Ottawa during WORLD WAR II by the minister of munitions and supply, C.D. HOWE, to help run the war effort. These people were paid $1 per year by the gov-

ernment while their own companies continued to pay their usual salary as a contribution to the war.

DOLLAR CRISIS, 1947, Canadian financial crisis. In 1947 Canada suddenly found itself suffering an acute shortage of U.S. dollars as a result of a major trade imbalance with the United States. The Canadian government was forced to impose currency controls and began discussing with the United States ways of lowering trade barriers between the two countries. Those discussions eventually led to a tentative FREE TRADE agreement that was eventually vetoed by Prime Minister MACKENZIE KING.

DOME PETROLEUM LTD, oil company founded in 1950 as Dome Exploration (Western) Ltd. In 1958 its name was changed to Dome Petroleum Ltd. Under Jack Gallagher, a Manitoba-born geologist, the company became a leader in BEAUFORT SEA exploration. Dome's acquisition of Hudson's Bay Oil and Gas Co. in 1981 placed great debt burdens on Dome when world oil prices began to fall late that year. By 1982 Dome was near bankruptcy, but was kept alive by creditors, in Canada and elsewhere. In the spring of 1987 the United States-based Amoco Petroleum Co. made an offer to buy Dome.

DOMINION COAL CO., Cape Breton company founded by H.M. Whitney in 1893 to secure a coal supply for his American utilities. A native of Boston, Whitney convinced a group of Montreal financiers to invest in the company which was to merge, reorganize, and manage a number of Cape Breton collieries. At the turn of the century the Dominion Coal Co. went public, and in 1920 was one of a number of companies acquired by the BRITISH EMPIRE STEEL CO. *See also* DOMINION IRON AND STEEL CO.

DOMINION DAY, original name for Canada Day, a national holiday celebrated 1 July to commemorate CONFEDERATION. In 1982 the name Canada Day was adopted. *See also* BRITISH NORTH AMERICA ACT.

DOMINION IRON AND STEEL CO., company founded in Nova Scotia by Boston's H.M. Whitney in 1899. It went on to become at one time the largest iron and steel producer in Canada. During the pre–World War I era the company's prosperity began to decline and by 1920 Dominion Iron and Steel, along with Whitney's DOMINION COAL, was forced to accept a take-over bid from Roy Wolvin's newly organized BRITISH EMPIRE STEEL CO. The Nova Scotia government later gained control of the Sydney operation, renaming it SYDNEY STEEL CORP.

DOMINION OF CANADA, official name of Canada, established by the BRITISH NORTH AMERICA ACT of 1867. The term "dominion" was suggested by SAMUEL LEONARD TILLEY, a FATHER OF CONFEDERATION, from Psalm 72: "He shall have dominion also from sea to sea . . ." The title is not much used although it remains Canada's official title and was reconfirmed as such by the CONSTITUTION ACT of 1982.

DOMINION EXPERIMENTAL FARM, agricultural research agency, established in Ottawa by the federal government on 2 June, 1886. The farm carried out experiments designed to improve crops and agricultural production in Canada. The first director was WILLIAM SAUNDERS who investigated cross breeding wheat in the search for a hardier and higher yielding strain. The research, continued by his son C.E. SAUNDERS, eventually led to the development of MARQUIS WHEAT. Although the first farm was located in Ottawa, many branch farms were established across Canada so that experiments could be carried out under local soil and climatic conditions. *See also* JOSEPH GRISDALE.

DOMINION GRANGE, farm organization founded in London, Ont., in June 1874 to promote the general welfare of Canadian farmers. A non-partisan organization, it was established following the spread into Canada of the U.S.-based National Grange of the Patrons of Husbandry. The Dominion Grange was opposed to monopolies and the "credit system." It reached its zenith soon after its founding but continued to exist until the early 20th century.

DOMINION LANDS ACT, federal legislation passed in 1872 to expedite settlement of the Canadian Prairies. The act provided for the surveying of western lands using the township pattern pioneered in the United States, which divided the Prairies into square townships of 36 sections

each, with each section containing 640 acres. Potential settlers, called "HOMESTEADERS," were invited to register for available 160-acre quarter sections of land by paying a $10 registration fee. If they lived permanently on that land for three years, erected a permanent dwelling, and raised crops on it, they were given clear title. *See also* "PROVE UP"; QUARTER SECTION; SOD SHACK.

DOMINION POLICE, federal government police force created in 1868 and charged with the protection of federal property and the enforcement of federal statutes. The jurisdiction of the police was limited to the central and Maritime provinces of Canada; enforcement of federal law in the west was the responsibility of the NORTH-WEST MOUNTED POLICE (later Royal North-West Mounted Police). In 1919 the Dominion Police united with the RNWMP to form the ROYAL CANADIAN MOUNTED POLICE.

DOMINION TEXTILE CO., company formed in 1905 when a number of small textile companies merged under the guidance of SIR CHARLES B. GORDON. Gordon became president and managing director of Dominion Textile in 1909. It soon grew into Canada's largest textile manufacturer producing about 20 per cent of the country's textiles in over 40 facilities located in Canada and abroad.

"DO NOT SHIP" LIST, black list used by the Seafarers' International Union under HAL BANKS to deny jobs to anti-SIU workers. The list was circulated to SIU hiring halls and passed to shipping companies.

DORION, SIR ANTOINE-AIMÉ (1818-91), politician. Born at Ste-Anne-de-la-Perade, Lower Canada, Dorion was first elected to the UNITED PROVINCE OF CANADA assembly in 1854 as a supporter of the PARTI ROUGE. He was a well-known opponent of CONFEDERATION and remained outside the GREAT COALITION of 1864. Although he led Canada East's opposition to the QUEBEC CONFERENCE proposals, he won election to the House of Commons in 1867. He was justice minister in Liberal Prime Minister ALEXANDER MACKENZIE's government until in 1874 he became chief justice of the Court of Queen's Bench in Quebec.

DOUGHTY, SIR ARTHUR GEORGE (1860-1936), archivist. Born in England, Doughty came to Canada in 1886. In 1897, he joined the Quebec public service and became dominion archivist in 1904. He greatly expanded the size and role of the Public Archives of Canada and, at the same time, was co-editor of CANADA AND ITS PROVINCES and launched the publication of archival records.

DOUGLAS, CLIFFORD HUGHES (1879-1952), English political theorist. Born in Manchester, Eng., Douglas worked as an aircraft engineer during World War I. In the early 1920s he originated the SOCIAL CREDIT movement in England. The movement was based on his belief that capitalism was being undermined by international bankers who were manipulating the money supply by charging interest on loans and not channelling that interest back into the economy. Douglas's solution was the establishment of a national dividend to be paid directly to the people by government. The theory of Social Credit was picked up and modified in Alberta by WILLIAM ABERHART who led the ALBERTA SOCIAL CREDIT LEAGUE to power in 1935. *See also* ERNEST MANNING; W.A.C. BENNETT.

courtesy National Archives of Canada

Thomas "Tommy" Douglas

DOUGLAS, THOMAS CLEMENT (1904-86), premier of Saskatchewan, national leader of the New Democratic Party. Born at Falkirk, Scot., Douglas came to Canada with his family in 1910.

He worked as a printer's apprentice until 1924, when he studied at Brandon College for the Baptist ministry. Ordained in 1930, he became a minister in Weyburn, Sask., where depression conditions were grim, and he found himself drawn into political activism. He helped found the CO-OPERATIVE COMMONWEALTH FEDERATION in 1932, ran unsuccessfully in a provincial election in 1934, but won a seat in the 1935 federal election. He made a solid impression in Ottawa as an orator, and he was a ready choice to head the CCF in Saskatchewan in 1944 when he led the party to victory. Forming the first social-democratic government in North America, Douglas recruited a small but able civil service and pioneered an array of social services, including hospital insurance. Before he resigned as premier in 1961 to lead the NEW DEMOCRATIC PARTY, he had laid the foundations for MEDICARE. As NDP leader, Douglas had a difficult task. He lost an attempt for his own seat in Regina in the 1962 election, but won a subsequent by-election in British Columbia. Until his retirement as party leader in 1971 and his leaving Parliament in 1979, Douglas worked to build the NDP's foundations. He was greatly admired for his wit and eloquence, and his record in Saskatchewan and Ottawa – hospital insurance, medicare, pension plans – bore the stamp of his commitment.

DOUKHOBORS, sect of Russian Anabaptists who arrived in Canada at the turn of the century. The Doukhobors insisted on having land granted to them on a bloc settlement basis and refused, because of their religious beliefs, to swear an oath of allegiance to the crown after their lands had been allocated to them. As a result, they were forced by the federal government to abandon their farms in 1908. The majority moved to the British Columbia interior under leader PETER VERIGIN. A radical anarchist sect of the Doukhobors, the Sons of Freedom, have been responsible for a number of acts of arson and bombing in the Kootenay region. They are well known for the nude protest parades and the hunger strikes mounted by their women.

D.P.'s, *see* DISPLACED PERSONS

DRAPEAU, JEAN (1916–), mayor of Montreal. He was born and educated in the city he governed for almost three decades. A participant in the LIGUE POUR LA DÉFENSE DU CANADA and unsuccessful in bids for federal and provincial seats, he succeeded to the mayoralty when CAMILLIEN HOUDE retired in 1954. Defeated in 1957, Drapeau formed the Montreal Civic party and won the 1960 election. Nicknamed "Mr Montreal," his accomplishments include the construction of the Place des Arts, EXPO 67 and the subway, the creation of the Montreal Expos baseball club, and the hosting of the 1976 Olympics. On his retirement in 1986, he was given a patronage posting in the Department of External Affairs.

DRAPER, PATRICK M. (1856-1943), labour leader. Born in Aylmer, Que., he devoted his life to the service of the TRADES AND LABOUR CONGRESS of Canada. He was active in the typographical union before being elected secretary of the TLC in 1900. A nationalist, he was also a realist in assessing the power of the American Federation of Labor in the North American labour movement. He retired in 1937, but not before serving one year as TLC president.

courtesy Arthur Roy/National Archives of Canada/C-11578

George A. Drew

DREW, GEORGE ALEXANDER (1894-1973), premier of Ontario. Born at Guelph, Ont., Drew was wounded in World War I. He was called to the bar in 1920 and practised law at Guelph until appointed assistant master of the Ontario Supreme Court in 1926 and master in 1929. In 1931 he became the first chairman of the Ontario Se-

curities Commission. Drew had entered politics as an alderman in Guelph in 1922 and was mayor in 1925. A contentious figure, he sparked the BREN GUN inquiry. Chosen leader of the Ontario Conservative party in 1938, he led it to victory in 1943 under a program of progressive change. In 1948 he resigned to become leader of the federal PROGRESSIVE CONSERVATIVE PARTY. Unable to defeat the Liberals in two successive elections, in part because of his pompous image and a reputation as an anti-francophone, he passed the leadership to JOHN DIEFENBAKER in 1956 and went to London as Canada's high commissioner. He retired in 1964. Drew also wrote a number of books about World War I and the munitions trade, notably *The Truth About The War* (1928), *Salesman of Death* (1933), and *Canada's Fighting Airmen* (1930).

DRUMMOND, WILLIAM HENRY (1854-1907), poet. Born in Ireland, Drummond came to Canada in 1864. A physician, he took up writing broken English verse that had a substantial vogue for a time. His best-known book was *The Habitant* (1897).

DRURY, ERNEST CHARLES (1878-1968), premier of Ontario. Born at Crown Hill, Ont., the son of Ontario's first minister of agriculture, he graduated from Ontario Agricultural College in 1900. Active in the farmers movement, he served as secretary of the CANADIAN COUNCIL OF AGRICULTURE before becoming the first president of the UNITED FARMERS OF ONTARIO in 1914. In 1919 the UFO, with the support of the INDEPENDENT LABOUR PARTY, astounded Ontario by winning the provincial election and Drury, who had not contested the election, was called upon to lead the government. His administration was well meaning and progressive but fell victim to opposition assaults and petty scandals. Drury retired from politics after his defeat in 1923 and became registrar and sheriff of Simcoe County from 1934 to 1957. His autobiography, *Farmer Premier*, appeared shortly before his death.

DRYBONES CASE, legal case concerning a native Indian, J. Drybones, who was found drunk off the reserve in the lobby of a Yellowknife hotel. In 1970 the SUPREME COURT of Canada held that Drybones was punished because of his racial origin under the Indian Act which did not apply to other Canadians. The Court ruled that no person could be tried under a federal law which infringed on rights granted by the BILL OF RIGHTS unless Parliament intervened.

DUCK LAKE, BATTLE OF, first battle of the NORTH-WEST REBELLION between a small party of Métis, led by LOUIS RIEL and GABRIEL DUMONT, and a larger group consisting of NORTH-WEST MOUNTED POLICE and white settlers from Prince Albert under the command of Supt. L.N.F. Crozier. The fighting took place at Duck Lake, approximately 50 km southwest of Prince Albert, on 26 March 1885. Crozier's force suffered 23 casualties, the Métis five. The victory emboldened Riel's forces.

DUFF, SIR LYMAN POORE (1865-1955), jurist. Born at Meaford, Ont., and educated at the Univ. of Toronto, Duff moved to Victoria, B.C., in 1894 to practise law. Appointed to the Supreme Court of British Columbia in 1904 and to the SUPREME COURT of Canada in 1906, he was chief justice from 1933 until his retirement in 1944. Duff also chaired the one-man 1942 royal commission investigating the Canadian expeditionary force to HONG KONG.

DUFFERIN AND AVA, FREDERICK TEMPLE BLACKWOOD, 1ST MARQUESS OF (1826-1902), governor general of Canada. Lord Dufferin was lord-in-waiting to Queen Victoria (1849-52 and 1854-8), a member of the House of Lords, and Gladstone's chancellor of the duchy of Lancaster before being appointed governor general in 1872. His term coincided with the PACIFIC SCANDAL and British Columbia's discontent with CONFEDERATION. He also granted amnesty to those involved in the RED RIVER REBELLION. Dufferin went on to a distinguished career as a diplomat and viceroy of India.

DUGGAN, ALPHONSUS GREGORY (1884-1970), labour leader. Born in Hollyrood, Nfld, Duggan was first president of the Newfoundland Trades and Labour Council in 1937. He had been a paper-mill worker and became active in union affairs before World War I.

DUMBELLS, Canadian soldiers of the 3rd Division who entertained front-line troops during WORLD WAR I. After the war the Dumbells went on vaudeville tours in Canada and the U.S.

DUMONT, GABRIEL (1837-1906), Métis military leader. Dumont was born at Red River and raised during the era of the buffalo hunt. He took no part in the RED RIVER REBELLION of 1869-70 but was one of the MÉTIS delegation sent to invite LOUIS RIEL back to Canada in 1884. Appointed Riel's adjutant-general during the NORTH-WEST REBELLION of 1885, Dumont conducted a clever campaign with victories at DUCK LAKE and FISH CREEK, where he stopped General MIDDLETON's army. Dumont fled to the United States following the Métis surrender at Batoche, toured with Buffalo Bill's famed Wild West Show as a marksman, and returned to Canada in 1888 after being granted amnesty.

DUNCAN, JAMES STUART (1893-1986), businessman. Born in Paris, France, Duncan began working for MASSEY-HARRIS in Berlin, Germany, in 1909. Two years later he was transferred to Canada where he continued to work for the company. In 1936 he was appointed general manager and was president 1941-56. During World War II Duncan served Canada as deputy minister of national defence for air and helped organize and operate the BRITISH COMMONWEALTH AIR TRAINING PLAN. He returned to Massey-Harris after the war.

DUNCAN, SARA JEANNETTE (1861-1922), writer. Born in Brantford, Canada West, she was the first full-time female employee of the Toronto *Globe*. On a world tour in 1888, Duncan married in India and lived there for a quarter-century. She is best remembered for her novel *The Imperialist* (1904), which looks shrewdly at small-town Ontario.

DUNKIN, CHRISTOPHER (1812-81), politician. Born in England and a lawyer, he was first elected to the assembly of the Province of Canada in 1858. A temperance advocate, Dunkin spoke for the Protestant Eastern Townships. He was one of the leaders of the opposition to CONFEDERATION, but he sought and won election to the Quebec legislature and Parliament in 1867, and he held ministerial posts in both Quebec City and Ottawa.

DUNN, SIR JAMES HAMET (1874-1956), capitalist. Dunn was born at Bathurst, N.B., and attended Dalhousie Univ. to study law. He turned to investment banking, moving to London, Eng., in 1905 where he made his fortune. In 1935 he took control of ALGOMA STEEL CORP., put it on its feet, and enhanced his fortune. The death duties on his estate helped create the CANADA COUNCIL.

Charles A. Dunning

DUNNING, CHARLES AVERY (1885-1958), premier of Saskatchewan, federal politician. Born at Croft, Eng., he came to Canada in 1903 to homestead in Saskatchewan. He joined the GRAIN GROWERS' movement in 1910, serving as vice-president (1911-14), and organized and managed the Saskatchewan Co-operative Elevator Co. from 1911 to 1916. He entered provincial politics as a Liberal in 1916 and held a number of portfolios before becoming premier in 1922. In 1926 Dunning resigned to enter federal politics, becoming Prime Minister MACKENZIE KING's minister of railways and canals (1926-9) and very conservative minister of finance (1929-30, 1935-9). He was named chancellor of Queen's Univ. in 1940 after ill health forced his retirement from politics.

DUNSMUIR, JAMES (1851-1920), mining entrepreneur, premier of British Columbia. Dunsmuir was born at Fort Vancouver, Wash., and educated in Ontario and Virginia. Inheriting his father's business in 1899, he directed operations, principally the Vancouver Island coal-mining interests, until 1910, when he sold the mines to WILLIAM MACKENZIE and DONALD MANN. He entered provincial politics in 1898 as a Conservative and was premier of British Columbia from 1900 to 1902. Appointed lieutenant-governor in 1906, he resigned in 1909 and retired to private life.

Robert Dunsmuir

DUNSMUIR, ROBERT (1825-89), industrialist, politician. Born in Hurlford, Scot., Dunsmuir moved to Vancouver Island in 1851 to work as a coal miner for the HUDSON'S BAY CO. In 1869 he discovered the rich Wellington coal seam and with backing from investor partners at the Esquimault Royal Navy base, he opened his own coal mine and built a town nearby. Dunsmuir was a shrewd entrepreneur and a tyrannical manager. He refused to recognize unions and successfully turned back several attempts to organize his men. In 1882 he was elected MLA for Nanaimo and, in 1888, he became president of the Executive Council of British Columbia. Through his various enterprises, Dunsmuir eventually owned about one quarter of the land on Vancouver Island.

DUNTON, ARNOLD DAVIDSON (1912-87), public servant. Dunton worked as a journalist in the 1930s and joined the WARTIME INFORMATION BOARD in 1942, becoming its general manager in 1944. In 1945 the MACKENZIE KING government made him chair of the CANADIAN BROADCASTING

CORP., and there he directed the development of its national television network. He became president of Carleton Univ. in 1958, co-chair of the ROYAL COMMISSION ON BILINGUALISM AND BICULTURALISM in 1963, and director of Carleton's Institute of Canadian Studies in 1973.

Maurice Duplessis

courtesy National Archives of Canada/C-9338

DUPLESSIS, MAURICE LE NOBLET (1890-1959), premier of Quebec. Known as "Le Chef," Duplessis was born at Trois-Rivières, Que., graduated from Univ. Laval and was called to the bar in 1913. He built a successful law practice in Trois-Rivières before entering provincial politics. Defeated in the 1923 election, he won a seat as a Conservative in 1927, becoming leader of the party in 1933. A master of political manoeuvring, Duplessis merged his party with PAUL GOUIN'S ACTION LIBÉRALE NATIONALE to form the UNION NATIONALE that brought down the government of L.A. TASCHEREAU in 1936. The UN failed in its first bid, but Duplessis, now firmly in control of the party, succeeded in toppling Taschereau in 1936 and soon drove out Gouin's reformers. Defeated in 1939 when the federal Liberals intervened in the provincial election, Duplessis returned to power in 1944 and governed the province through a close alliance with "anglo" business and the Roman Catholic church

until his death. Duplessis presided over a period of enormous growth in Quebec, but his regime did not long survive him.

DURNAN, WILLIAM ARNOLD (1915-72), hockey player. Durnan joined the Montreal Canadiens as a goalie in 1943 and won the VEZINA Trophy in six of the next seven years. He retired in 1950.

DUST BOWL, term originating in the United States but also used in Canada in the early 1930s to describe the area of the southern prairies known as PALLISER'S TRIANGLE. This region, which takes in southwestern Manitoba, much of southern Saskatchewan, and southeastern Alberta, has a low annual average rainfall. Poor soil conservation techniques and constant easterly winds allowed the soil to dry and erode in the early 1930s. Huge dust clouds were formed as the valuable top soil drifted away, and many farms were destroyed and abandoned. In 1935 the federal government established the PRAIRIE FARM REHABILITATION ADMINISTRATION to combat the dust bowl.

DYSART, A. ALLISON (1880-1962), premier of New Brunswick. Born at Cocagne, N.B., and educated at the Ontario Agricultural College, St Joseph's and Dalhousie univs., Dysart entered the New Brunswick legislature as a Liberal in 1917. He served as speaker (1921-5) and minister of lands and mines (1925) before becoming leader of the party and of the opposition in 1926. A decisive win in 1935 brought his party to power. His administration was reformist, and, after another election victory in 1939, Dysart resigned in 1940 to become a county court judge.

EATON, CYRUS S. (1883-1979), financier. Born in Pugwash, N.S., Eaton moved to the United States at an early age and entered the world of business and high finance. He was instrumental in the formation of the Republic Steel Corp. in the United States although he continued to invest heavily in Canadian mining. Eaton was probably best known for his efforts to stimulate international understanding and to help bring about an end to the Cold War. The annual conferences he sponsored at Pugwash from the 1950s brought together academics and public figures from the countries of the east and west in the pursuit of that goal.

EATON, SIR JOHN CRAIG (1876-1922), merchant. He became president of the T. Eaton Co. in 1907, and introduced a number of paternalistic measures designed to draw his employees closer to the company. He was probably better known for his philanthropic activities than as an innovator in merchandizing.

EATON, TIMOTHY (1834-1907), founder of the T. Eaton Co. department stores. He was born near Ballymena, Ireland, and immigrated to Canada in 1854. In 1868 he moved to Toronto and the following year opened the first Eaton's on Yonge St. Eaton revolutionized the dry-goods business by replacing the credit and barter system with a "fixed price" cash sales system and introduced catalogue sales in 1884. Before his death at Toronto, Eaton employed 9000 people in his stores and factories.

ECONOMIC ADVISORY COMMITTEE, set up in Sept. 1939 to advise the federal cabinet. Consisting of key bureaucrats (including O.D. SKELTON, CLIFFORD CLARK, GRAHAM TOWERS, and NORMAN ROBERTSON), the committee exercised great influence on economic policy during the early years of WORLD WAR II.

ECONOMIC COUNCIL OF CANADA, CROWN CORPORATION established in 1963 to provide economic forecasts for the federal government and to make recommendations concerning future economic policies.

EDDY, EZRA BUTLER (1827-1906), manufacturer. Born in Bristol, Vt, he came to Canada in 1851 to establish a friction-match factory near Hull, Canada East. He then entered local and provincial politics, serving as mayor of Hull and winning a seat in the Quebec assembly in 1871. His company became a major Canadian producer of wood and paper products.

courtesy Glenbow Archives, Calgary/NA-2607-1

Henrietta L. Edwards

EDWARDS, HENRIETTA LOUISE (1849-1931), feminist. Born in Montreal, Edwards founded the Working Girls' Assn to provide vocational training. She was a founder of the NATIONAL COUNCIL OF WOMEN in 1893 and the Victorian Order of Nurses. As one of the Alberta plaintiffs in the PERSONS CASE, the victory capped her career of trying to expand women's legal and political rights.

EDWARDS, ROBERT C. (1864-1922), newspaperman. Born in Edinburgh, Scot., Edwards settled in western Canada in 1894. Edwards was a hard drinking, reform-minded iconoclast who poked fun at many social institutions. He became known as "Eye Opener" Bob because of his ownership of the *Calgary Eye Opener* newspaper which he published in High River, Alta, before moving it to Calgary in 1897. He was the target of a number of lawsuits from local and provincial politicians and he was a strong supporter of HENRY WISE WOOD and the UNITED FARMERS OF ALBERTA.

ELDORADO GOLD MINE, *see* GILBERT LABINE

ELECTION EXPENSES ACT, 1974, federal legislation regulating election campaign spending. The act limits the amounts that can be spent by parties and individual candidates, encourages contributions by making donations tax-deductible, and provides for the filing of returns.

EMMERSON, HENRY ROBERT (1853-1914), premier of New Brunswick, federal politician. Born at Maugerville, N.B., Emmerson was a lawyer and businessman when he was elected to the legislature as a Liberal in 1888. In 1897 he became premier and attorney general, leaving for Ottawa in 1900. He served in SIR WILFRID LAURIER's cabinet in the railways portfolio from 1904 to 1907 and remained an MP until his death.

EMPIRE DAY, school holiday celebrated on the school day immediately before VICTORIA DAY. First observed at the height of the British Empire in 1899, Empire Day fell into decline following World War II.

EMPLOYEE REPRESENTATION PLANS, a form of company union designed to give workers the illusion that they have some say in determining wages and working conditions at their place of work. MACKENZIE KING designed one such plan for the Rockefeller-owned coal mines in Colorado in 1913, and it was copied by companies all over Canada and the United States in the following 20 years.

EMPRESS LINE, see CANADIAN PACIFIC STEAMSHIP CO.

ENEMY ALIENS, term used for people living in Canada who held citizenship in a country with which Canada was at war. The term was used most frequently during WORLD WAR I, when some enemy aliens were interned. Most were placed on a sort of parole. See also INTERNMENT.

ENGEL, MARIAN (1933-85), writer. Born in Toronto, Marian Passmore was educated at McMaster and McGill univs. She wrote six novels of which *Bear* (1976, Governor General's Award) and *Lunatic Villas* (1981) are probably the best known. She was a founder and first chair of the Writers' Union of Canada.

EQUAL RIGHTS ASSN, an Ontario-based Protestant movement founded in 1889 to fight passage of the JESUITS' ESTATES ACT. Its chief spokesperson, D'ALTON MCCARTHY, a Conservative MP, launched a crusade against Catholic "interference" in politics and SEPARATE SCHOOLS. The ERA ran candidates in the 1890 Ontario election but won only one seat. By 1891 it had lost its appeal although McCarthy continued to rail at the French-Canadian "threat."

EQUALIZATION PAYMENTS, federal payments to the provinces to ensure basic equality of services across Canada. Section 50 of the original BRITISH NORTH AMERICA ACT contained provision for the annual payment by the federal government to each of the original provinces of a specified sum of money plus a grant based on population. This was the birth of the equalization concept – that all Canadians are entitled to the same basic level of governmental services regardless of the wealth or poverty of their province, and that the federal government had the responsibility to ensure that basic equality. The ROYAL COMMISSION ON DOMINION-PROVINCIAL RELATIONS first recommended a formal apparatus for equalization payments in the late 1930s, and the first equalization program was introduced in 1957. Since then the equalization scheme has grown more complex, and it is now a major charge on the federal government's purse.

ERICKSON, ARTHUR CHARLES (1924-), architect. Born at Vancouver and trained at Univ. of British Columbia and McGill, Erickson began his practice in Vancouver in 1953. His first major assignment was the campus of Simon Fraser Univ., a project which won international attention. Other commissions followed at EXPO 67, the Univ. of Lethbridge, the Museum of Anthropology at the Univ. of British Columbia, and the Canadian Embassy in Washington (incomplete in 1988). Erickson is one of the few Canadian architects of world renown.

ESPOSITO, PHILIP ANTHONY (1942-), hockey player. Phil Esposito was born in Sault Ste Marie, Ont., and played in the National Hockey League with Chicago from 1963 to 1967. He was traded to Boston and led the Bruins to success, setting goal-scoring records. He was the team leader in the CANADA-SOVIET HOCKEY SERIES in 1972. In 1975 he was traded to New York, retired in 1982, and shortly thereafter became Rangers' general manager.

ESTEVAN MASSACRE, the killing of three miners in Estevan, Sask., 29 Sept. 1931 during a strike of coal miners organized by the MINE WORKERS UNION OF CANADA. That day the miners staged a parade through Estevan in defiance of a municipal ban and were fired upon by the ROYAL CANADIAN MOUNTED POLICE.

ESTEVAN STRIKE, *see* BIENFAIT STRIKE

EWART, JOHN SKIRVING (1849-1933), writer, constitutional theorist. Born and educated in Toronto, Ewart moved to Winnipeg in 1882 and practised law there. He was counsel to the French-speaking minority in the MANITOBA SCHOOLS QUESTION legal case. He moved to Ottawa in 1904 and began to write an extraordinary series of pamphlets and essays arguing for Canadian independence. Little read now, Ewart's work had influence in the 1920s.

EXAMINATION UNIT, a secret wireless intercept and code-breaking unit established by the Department of External Affairs in 1941 and concealed under the aegis of the NATIONAL RESEARCH COUNCIL. The unit worked on Vichy French codes, intercepted German messages, and cooperated with Canada's allies in decoding intercepted messages from the Japanese military. In 1945, after the GOUZENKO AFFAIR, the unit began to work on intercepts from the Soviet Union's embassy and those of its allies.

courtesy National Archives of Canada/C-18536

Expo 67

EXPO 67, the 1967 Montreal World Fair. Expo 67 was the only first-category world exhibition ever held in Canada. It opened on 28 April 1967 and by the time it closed on 27 Oct. 1967, it had attracted over 50 million visitors. The Expo site was located on a chain of man-made islands in the St Lawrence River off Montreal harbour. The exhibition was the brainchild of Montreal mayor JEAN DRAPEAU and became the focal point of the CENTENNIAL celebrations, marking the 100th anniversary of CONFEDERATION.

FAIRCLOUGH, ELLEN LOUKS (1905–), politician. Born in Hamilton, Ont., Fairclough was involved in Hamilton city politics and won election to Parliament in a 1950 by-election as a Conservative. In 1957, Prime Minister JOHN DIEFENBAKER named her secretary of state, the first woman cabinet minister in Canadian history. In 1958 she took over the citizenship and immigration portfolio and in 1962 the Post Office. She lost her seat in the 1963 election.

FAIRLEY, BARKER (1887-1986), scholar, artist. He joined the Univ. of Alberta in 1910 as a Goethe scholar and earned great distinction. He moved to the Univ. of Toronto in 1915 and became involved in the founding of the CANADIAN FORUM and wrote for it as an art critic. He took up painting late in life and became a noted portraitist and landscape artist.

FALAISE, BATTLE OF, the name given to the great battle in Normandy between 7 and 21 Aug. 1944 in which British, Canadian, and American forces tried, but failed, to destroy German strength in France. Breaking out from Caen where it had been pinned since shortly after the NORMANDY INVASION, II Canadian Corps under Lieutenant-General GUY SIMONDS began to press towards the town of Falaise on 7 Aug. in the face of increasingly desperate German opposition. Of some 100,000 Germans trapped on 16 Aug., fewer than half had escaped when the trap was finally closed on 21 Aug. Canadian losses from 8 to 21 Aug. were almost 5500.

FALCONBRIDGE NICKEL MINES LTD, mineral company located near Sudbury, Ont., established in 1928. It began operations in 1930, to challenge the nickel monopoly of the

INTERNATIONAL NICKEL CO. (Inco). Falconbridge expanded rapidly during World War II to become one of the largest nickel producers in the world.

FALCONER, SIR ROBERT (1867-1943), educator. He taught Greek at Pine Hill College, Halifax. In 1907, he was named president of the Univ. of Toronto, a post he filled for 25 years. Falconer essentially created an integrated university out of the collection of colleges that existed when he took over.

FALLON, MICHAEL FRANCIS (1867-1931), Roman Catholic bishop. Born at Kingston, Canada West, Fallon studied at the Univ. of Ottawa and was ordained in 1894. He taught at the Univ. of Ottawa, had a parish in Buffalo, N.Y., and was named bishop of London, Ont., in 1909. Fallon led Ontario Irish Catholics in their fights with French-speaking Catholics against bilingual schools.

FAMILY ALLOWANCES, universal social measure, passed by Prime Minister MACKENZIE KING's government in 1944 and operational in 1945. Family allowances (also known as the baby bonus) paid all Canadian mothers with children under 16 a monthly sum of between $5 and $7. In 1973 a new Family Allowance Act increased payments to an average $20 for dependent children under 18.

"FARM FORUM," national radio broadcasts initiated by the CANADIAN BROADCASTING CORP. during World War II to provide farmers with up-to-date information on markets and prices. The broadcasts were scheduled for the noon hour and included other features of interest to farm families across the country.

FARMERS' BANK OF CANADA, bank incorporated in 1904 to provide special loan services for farmers. Much of its paid-up capital was subscribed by farmers, and it began operations in Toronto in 1906. The bank ceased operations in 1910, and a subsequent inquiry revealed that the bank had made fraudulent claims to the federal government.

FARMERS' PLATFORM OF 1916, *see* CANADIAN COUNCIL OF AGRICULTURE

FATHERS OF CONFEDERATION, term for the political leaders who forged the CONFEDERATION of 1867. The most famous of these were GEORGE BROWN, JOHN A. MACDONALD, GEORGE ÉTIENNE CARTIER, ALEXANDER GALT, and OLIVER MOWAT, representing the UNITED PROVINCE OF CANADA, SAMUEL TILLEY, representing New Brunswick, and CHARLES TUPPER, representing Nova Scotia. *See also* BRITISH NORTH AMERICA ACT.

FAVREAU, GUY (1917-67), politician. Born at Montreal, Favreau was elected to Parliament as a Liberal in 1963. He served in a number of portfolios in the government of Prime Minister LESTER PEARSON, was House leader, and leader of the Quebec Liberal caucus. Favreau became a victim of a scandal involving Lucien Rivard, was savaged in a resulting Royal Commission, and left dangling by his leader. He resigned as justice minister in 1965 but was soon reappointed to cabinet despite his tarnished reputation.

FELLOWSHIP FOR A CHRISTIAN SOCIAL ORDER, Christian socialist group formed in 1934. Set up by many of those who had created the LEAGUE FOR SOCIAL RECONSTRUCTION, the FCSO drew most of its members from the United Church. The group published *Towards the Christian Revolution* (1936). It disbanded in the mid-1940s.

FEMALE SUFFRAGE, *see* WOMEN'S SUFFRAGE

courtesy National Archives of Canada/C-17196

Volunteers arriving to fight the Fenians

FENIANS, Irish-Americans who attempted to secure Ireland's independence from Britain by attacking Canada between 1866 and 1870. Organized in 1857, the Fenians conducted several raids into Canada and helped to give impetus to

CONFEDERATION. They met little success; one of their number was blamed for the assassination of D'ARCY MCGEE in 1868.

FERGUSON, GEORGE HOWARD (1870-1946), premier of Ontario, diplomat. Born at Kemptville, Ont., he was elected to the Ontario legislature in 1905 as a Conservative. He served as a controversial minister of lands and mines (1914-19) before assuming leadership of the party in 1920. He became premier after his party won the 1923 election; he resigned in 1930 to accept Prime Minister R.B. BENNETT's invitation to become Canadian high commissioner in London, a position he held until the Liberals came to power in 1935.

FERGUSON, GEORGE VICTOR (1897-1977), journalist. Born in Scotland, he was educated at the univs. of Alberta and Oxford. He served in World War I and joined the *Manitoba Free Press* in 1925. One of JOHN DAFOE's nationalist and internationalist protégés, Ferguson became managing editor in 1933 and executive editor in 1944 on Dafoe's death. He soon joined the *Montreal Star* where his attempts to explain what was happening in Quebec were important during the QUIET REVOLUTION.

FERNIE, WILLIAM (1837-1921), entrepreneur. He was born in Kimbolton, Eng., and came to Canada in 1860 to settle in British Columbia. In 1887 he discovered a rich coal seam in the Crow's Nest Pass that connects British Columbia with Alberta. He established the Crow's Nest Pass Coal Co. to mine the coal and founded the B.C. town that is named after him.

FESSENDEN, REGINALD AUBREY (1866-1932), inventor. Born in Milton-East, Canada East, Fessenden moved to the United States after graduating from Bishop's Univ. He worked on radio and invented wireless voice transmission in 1906.

FIELDING, WILLIAM STEVENS (1848-1929), premier of Nova Scotia, federal politician. Born and educated at Halifax, Fielding was editor of the Halifax *Morning Chronicle*. He entered politics in 1882 as a Liberal in the Nova Scotia legislature and served as minister without portfolio before becoming premier in 1884. Initially com-

William S. Fielding

mitted to pulling Nova Scotia out of CONFEDERATION, he reversed his stand, then resigned as premier in 1896 to become WILFRID LAURIER's finance minister. Defeated in the 1911 election, he broke with Laurier during the CONSCRIPTION CRISIS of 1917. Fielding's support for conscription probably cost him the Liberal leadership in 1919 but he was again finance minister under Prime Minister MACKENZIE KING from 1921 until he retired in 1925.

FILMON, GARY (1943-), premier of Manitoba. Born in Winnipeg and educated as an engineer at the Univ. of Toronto, Filmon was a businessman until in 1975 he entered Winnipeg city politics. Four years later he won election to the Manitoba Legislature as a Conservative, and became a minister in 1981. After the party's defeat in 1983 he succeeded STIRLING LYON as party leader, and in March 1986 Howard Pawley and the NEW DEMOCRATIC PARTY narrowly defeated him in his first election as leader. In the election of April 1988, however, Filmon squeaked into power with a minority government. Moderately progressive, Filmon leads a party and government more conservative than he is.

FINANCE ACT, 1914, federal legislation, taking Canada off the gold standard, passed as a wartime measure. It allowed the federal government to issue paper currency not backed by gold.

Canada returned to the gold standard in 1926 but went off it permanently during the GREAT DEPRESSION.

FINANCIAL POST, business newspaper established in Toronto in 1907 by J.B. MACLEAN. Initially intended for Toronto businessmen, by the 1930s it had established itself as aggressive and informed, privy to the secrets of Ottawa. That reputation continued during and after World War II. Maclean Hunter Ltd sold the *Post* to a group led by the *Toronto Sun* in 1987, and the venerable weekly was turned into a daily newspaper, beginning in Feb. 1988.

FINDLEY, TIMOTHY (1930-), writer. Born and educated at Toronto, Findley was an actor before he began writing. He published his first novel in 1967, becoming best known for *The Wars* (1977), which won a Governor General's Award. *Famous Last Words*, like *The Wars*, was a historical novel and an international success in 1981.

"FIRE-PROOF HOUSE," phrase in a speech made at the League of Nations in 1924 by Canada's delegate, Senator RAOUL DANDURAND. He was maintaining that Canada had nothing to worry about in international affairs because Canadians lived in "a fire-proof house, far from inflammable materials" and therefore remained unaffected by world crises.

FIRST CANADIAN ARMY, the largest-ever Canadian fighting unit, formed in England in 1942 under the command of General A.G.L. MCNAUGHTON. General H.D.G. CRERAR replaced him in March 1944. McNaughton had tried to keep the army together for the invasion of France, but it was split so that Canada could participate in the Sicilian and Italian campaigns. The First Canadian Army became operational in Normandy in late June 1944 and participated with distinction in the campaign in northwest Europe. The divisions in Italy were reunited with those in northwest Europe in March 1945.

FISH CREEK, BATTLE OF, battle of 25 April 1885 during the NORTH-WEST REBELLION. General FRED MIDDLETON's force, en route to Batoche, was attacked by MÉTIS and Indians led by GABRIEL DUMONT. Firing from trenches along Fish Creek, the Métis scored a victory against the superior arms of the Canadians, inflicting 55 casualties on Middleton's force of 350 against only 4 of their own.

FISHERMAN'S PROTECTIVE UNION, cooperative marketing organization founded in 1909. Based in Newfoundland, the union aimed to increase fishermens' earnings through cooperative marketing. It ceased to have any real influence in the 1920s but continued to exist until the 1940s.

FITZGERALD, LIONEL LEMOINE (1890-1956), painter. He was born in Winnipeg and trained there and in the United States. Though close to the GROUP OF SEVEN, with whom he exhibited briefly, he was not of them. His work had pointillist characteristics, he used a variety of media, and his later work was abstract.

FITZPATRICK, SIR CHARLES (1853-1942), politician, jurist. Born at Quebec City and a top criminal lawyer, he acted as chief counsel for LOUIS RIEL in 1885 and HONORÉ MERCIER in 1892. Elected to the Quebec legislature as a Liberal in 1890, he moved in 1896 to the House of Commons, serving as solicitor general (1896-1902) and minister of justice (1902-6) in the LAURIER government. In 1906 he became chief justice of Canada. Retired from the bench in 1918, he served as lieutenant governor of Quebec until 1923.

"FIVE-CENT" SPEECH, remark made by Liberal Prime Minister MACKENZIE KING in March 1930 in the House of Commons. When the Conservatives accused King of doing nothing about rising unemployment and suggested that his government give more money to the provinces for welfare, King said that he "would not give . . . a five cent piece" to Conservative provincial governments. The remark cost King heavily in the ensuing federal election.

FLAG DEBATE, debate in the House of Commons in late 1964 over the adoption of a distinctive Canadian flag. In 1963 the Liberal government of Prime Minister LESTER PEARSON decided to adopt a permanent national flag; until then Canada had used either the Union Jack or the RED ENSIGN. A design was chosen by a parliamentary committee and debate began in fall 1964. The Conservative party, led by JOHN DIEFENBAKER, bitterly opposed the new flag, and the government was forced to resort to closure. The new flag was officially proclaimed in 1965.

FLAVELLE, JOSEPH WESLEY (1858-1939), businessman. Born in Peterborough, Canada West, Flavelle began his commercial career as a small provisions merchant before becoming manager of the WILLIAM DAVIES CO., a leading packer and exporter of pork products, particularly bacon. Flavelle modernized the company, improved its products, and presided over a tremendous expansion of its export trade. Flavelle became president in 1900. He was also chairman of several companies and a noted philanthropist. During WORLD WAR I Flavelle headed the IMPERIAL MUNITIONS BOARD in Canada. His success in organizing war production brought him a baronetcy, although charges were raised that his own companies had benefited.

FLEMING, DONALD METHUEN (1905-87), politician. Born at Exeter, Ont., he practised law in Toronto, serving also on the board of education and city council. Elected to the House of Commons as a Progressive Conservative in 1945, he became finance minister in the government of Prime Minister JOHN DIEFENBAKER in 1957 and swung sharply between tight-fistedness and budget deficits. In 1962 he was made justice minister. Fleming contested the Conservative leadership in 1948, 1957, and 1967, always without success. Before his death he published a long memoir that vigorously attacked Diefenbaker (and others).

FLEMING, SIR SANDFORD (1827-1915), engineer. Born at Kirkcaldy, Scot., he immigrated to Canada in 1845 and became one of North America's greatest railway surveyors and engineers. He joined the Ontario, Simcoe and Huron Railway (later the Northern Railway), becoming chief engineer in 1857. Engineer-in-chief of the INTERCOLONIAL RAILWAY, he was appointed chief engineer of surveys for the CANADIAN PACIFIC RAILWAY in 1871. Fleming retired from the CPR in 1880 but continued to work on projects, helping to develop the twenty-four-hour system of telling time in use since 1884. He advocated inter-Empire telecommunications and designed the first Canadian postage stamp (issued in 1851). Before his death at Halifax he served as president of the Royal Society of Canada and chancellor of Queen's Univ.

FLEMMING, HUGH JOHN (1899-1982), premier of New Brunswick. Born at Peel, N.B., Flemming was a lumberman before entering politics in 1921 as municipal councillor for Carleton County, N.B. Elected to the provincial legislature as a Conservative in 1944, he became party leader in 1951 and ended 17 years of Liberal rule with his 1952 provincial election victory. Defeated in 1960, Flemming entered the House of Commons and served as minister of forestry and minister of national revenue in the government of Prime Minister JOHN DIEFENBAKER.

FLIN FLON STRIKE, metal miners' strike against Hudson's Bay Mining and Smelting in Flin Flon, Man., 11 June to 14 July 1934. The miners were members of the Communist-led WORKERS' UNITY LEAGUE. When, after three weeks, a number of workers tried to prevent a back-to-work vote, Premier JOHN BRACKEN of Manitoba sent in the ROYAL CANADIAN MOUNTED POLICE to maintain order.

FOOTE, JOHN WEIR (1904-88), army padre. Born in Madoc, Ont., he was ordained a Presbyterian minister in 1934. During WORLD WAR II he served as a padre with the Royal Hamilton Light Infantry. In Aug. 1942, he landed with his regiment during the DIEPPE raid, helped evacuate wounded to vessels offshore, and voluntarily remained with those who could not escape. Awarded the Victoria Cross for his heroism on the beaches. After his return to Canada, he sat in the Ontario Legislature and was Minister of Reform Institutions from 1950-57.

FORD, ROBERT ARTHUR DOUGLAS (1915–), diplomat, poet. Born at Ottawa, he joined the Department of External Affairs in 1940. A Soviet expert, Ford served in Moscow in 1946, 1951-4, and 1964-80, becoming the dean of the diplomatic corps. Other postings include Brazil, London, Yugoslavia, and Egypt. He is also a poet of note, the author of a number of volumes, including *A Window on the North* which won the Governor General's Award in 1956.

FOREIGN EXCHANGE CONTROL BOARD, board organized in Sept. 1939 by the federal government. Planning for the FECB began in Jan. 1939 under the direction of GRAHAM TOWERS, the governor of the BANK OF CANADA, and most of the board's directing personnel initially came from the bank and from the chartered banks. For the duration of WORLD WAR II, the board imposed strict controls on foreign exchange.

FOREIGN INVESTMENT REVIEW AGENCY, federal agency established by the Liberal government of Prime Minister PIERRE TRUDEAU in 1973 to monitor foreign investment in Canada. FIRA had a mandate to examine all foreign acquisitions of Canadian companies and to recommend to the government whether or not those acquisitions should be allowed to proceed. Although it approved almost all applications made to it, FIRA was strongly opposed by those who objected to impeding foreign investors. In 1984 the Conservative government of Prime Minister BRIAN MULRONEY changed its mandate so that it would encourage foreign investment and the agency's name was accordingly changed to Investment Canada.

FORGET, SIR JOSEPH-DAVID-RODOLPHE (1861-1919), stockbroker, politician. Born in Terrebonne, Canada East, he helped establish companies such as the Montreal Street Railway Co. and MONTREAL LIGHT, HEAT AND POWER CO., among others. After 1907 he became more involved in Quebec City-based establishments such as the Quebec Railway, Light and Power Co. From 1908 to 1911 he served as chairman of the MONTREAL STOCK EXCHANGE, and he sat in the House of Commons as a Conservative MP from 1904 to 1917.

FORGET, LOUIS-JOSEPH (1853-1911), businessman. Born in Terrebonne, Canada East, Forget sold securities in transportation and utility companies. With his nephew, Joseph-David-Rodolphe, he was involved in the organization of the MONTREAL LIGHT, HEAT AND POWER CO., served as president of the MONTREAL STOCK EXCHANGE in 1895 and 1896, and was appointed to the Senate in 1896.

FORKE, ROBERT (1860-1934), farm leader. He arrived in Canada in 1882 to begin farming grain near Brandon, Man. He eventually entered local politics and in 1921 was elected to the House of Commons as the PROGRESSIVE PARTY member for Brandon. When Progressive party leader T.A. CRERAR resigned from the party in Nov. 1922, Forke was elected house leader. He was re-elected as a Progressive in 1925 but then moved closer to the Liberals under Prime Minister MACKENZIE KING and ran as a Liberal-Progressive in the 1926 election. He was appointed minister of immigration and colonization in Sept. 1926 and entered the Senate in Dec. 1929.

FORRESTER, MAUREEN (1930–), singer. Forrester made her professional debut in Montreal at age 21. Her developing talent as a contralto was greatly assisted by the financial aid of sugar and newspaper magnate J.W. MCCONNELL, and after her New York City debut in 1956 her concert career took off, and she performed all over the world. In 1983 Forrester became chair of the CANADA COUNCIL and an effective and stubborn advocate for Canadian culture.

FORT FRANCES PULP AND POWER V. MANITOBA FREE PRESS, court case heard by the JUDICIAL COMMITTEE OF THE PRIVY COUNCIL in 1923. The JCPC ruled that Ottawa had the authority under the "PEACE, ORDER AND GOOD GOVERNMENT" provision of the BRITISH NORTH AMERICA ACT to intrude on provincial areas of jurisdiction during times of national emergency, such as war. The JCPC also held that Parliament alone has the power to decide when the emergency has started and when it has passed.

FORSEY, EUGENE ALFRED (1904–), constitutional expert. Born at Grand Bank, Nfld, he taught at McGill Univ., was involved in the LEAGUE FOR SOCIAL RECONSTRUCTION, and was an active member of the CO-OPERATIVE COMMONWEALTH FEDERATION. At the same time, he was a close friend of ARTHUR MEIGHEN, his hero in the KING-BYNG AFFAIR about which he wrote a book. Forsey became an inveterate article and letter writer, sometimes crabbily correcting others' errors but often pointing out the follies of federal-provincial diplomacy and of Quebec separatists. PIERRE TRUDEAU made him a senator in 1970.

FORT WALSH, NORTH-WEST MOUNTED POLICE post, located 170 km southwest of Swift Current, Sask. It was built in 1875 and was headquarters of the NWMP until it was abandoned in 1883. It was named for inspector James Walsh who received American Sioux Chief Sitting Bull there following the Sioux massacre of U.S. General George Custer in 1876.

FORT WHOOP-UP, post located in southern Alberta, not far from Fort Macleod, which was used as headquarters for whiskey traders operating out of Montana. The fort was abandoned at the approach of the NORTH-WEST MOUNTED POLICE in Oct. 1874.

FOSTER, SIR GEORGE EULAS (1847-1913), politician. Born in Carleton County, N.B., he was elected Conservative MP in 1882. He was a strong supporter of the NATIONAL POLICY and served as minister of marine and fisheries from 1885 to 1888 and minister of finance from 1888 to 1896. When the Conservative party was returned to power under ROBERT BORDEN in 1911, Foster was named minister of trade and commerce, a post he held until 1921 when he was appointed to the Senate. Foster was a Canadian delegate to the 1919 Paris Peace Conference.

FOSTER, WILLIAM ALEXANDER (1840-88), lawyer. Born in Toronto, he was a founding member of CANADA FIRST and wrote the movement's bible, a tract entitled *Canada First* which stressed the impact of the northern climate on the making of character and personality in Canada. Like other members of the movement, he emphasized the need for non-partisan action to enhance Canada's sense of purpose – a direction Canada First believed was lacking in the pragmatic and prosaic BRITISH NORTH AMERICA ACT and the bargaining which had led to CONFEDERATION.

FOULKES, CHARLES (1903-69), soldier. Born at Stockton-on-Tees, Eng., and educated in London, Ont., Foulkes joined the army in 1926. He went overseas with the 1st Canadian Division in 1939, returned to Canada as senior general staff officer of the 3rd Canadian Division in 1941 and went back to Europe in 1944 to command the 2nd Canadian Infantry Division. In Nov. 1944 he took over command of the I Canadian Corps and directed it in Italy and northwest Europe, accept-ing the German surrender in Holland in 1945. After WORLD WAR II he became chief of the General Staff and in 1951 the powerful chairman of the Chiefs of Staff. He is usually credited with pressing the new government of Prime Minister JOHN DIEFENBAKER into NORAD in July 1957.

FOWKE, VERNON CLIFFORD (1907-66), economic historian. Born at Parry Sound, Ont., Fowke was educated at the univs. of Saskatchewan, Chicago, and Washington, and taught at the Univ. of Saskatchewan. His major work was *The National Policy and the Wheat Economy* (1957), and he wrote a number of other books that firmly established him as the leading historian of Canadian agriculture.

FOWLER, ROBERT M. (1906-80), lawyer. He headed the 1956 Royal Commission on Broadcasting which recommended that the role of regulating broadcasting in Canada be taken from the CANADIAN BROADCASTING CORP. and placed in the hands of some new authority. Partly in response to these recommendations, the BOARD OF BROADCAST GOVERNORS was established in 1958. Fowler headed a second commission on broadcasting in 1965 which recommended further changes in the government's regulatory authority and which eventually led to the creation of the CANADIAN RADIO AND TELEVISION COMMISSION in 1967.

FOX, TERRANCE STANLEY (1958-81), runner. Terry Fox was born at Winnipeg, Man., and grew up on the west coast. While a student, he developed bone cancer and one leg was amputated. He then conceived the idea of a "Marathon of Hope"–a run across Canada to raise money for cancer research. The run began at St John's, Nfld, on 12 April 1980 and ended at Thunder Bay, Ont., on 1 Sept. after cancer had spread to his lungs. The gallant run drew national attention and raised millions, leading to annual fundraising runs.

FRAMEWORK AGREEMENT, term used to describe the Canada-European Economic Community agreement of 1976. Negotiated as a result of Canada's THIRD OPTION in 1972, the agreement sought to increase trade between Canada and the European Community. A similar agreement was signed with Japan. Neither has managed to divert trade or stop the increase in Canadian dependency on the U.S. market.

FRANCA, CELIA (1921–), ballet dancer. Born at London, Eng. (as Celia Franks), Franca trained in London. In 1951 she came to Canada as the founding artistic director of the National Ballet of Canada and built it from nothing and through periods of trial into a successful company. Franca left the company in 1974.

FRANCIS, ANNE, *see* BIRD, FLORENCE BAYARD

FRANCK, ALBERT JACQUES (1899-1973), painter. The painter of Toronto's backyards was born in Holland and emigrated to Canada in the 1920s. He came to Toronto after 1945 to set up shop as an art restorer and to display his own work, studies of the city's lanes and backyards.

FRANK SLIDE, rock slide that covered much of the mining town of Frank, Alta, in late April 1903, killing more than 80 people. Frank is located near the Crow's Nest Pass.

FRASER, BLAIR (1909-68), journalist. Born at Sydney, N.S., Fraser was educated at Acadia Univ. and worked as a journalist for Montreal newspapers from 1929 to 1943. During World War II, he began to cover the nation's capital for MACLEAN'S magazine. His close friendships with bureaucrats and politicians gave him unusual access. He left Ottawa in 1960, edited *MacLean's* for two years, and then became its London correspondent.

FRASER, GRAHAM (1846-1915), industrialist. Born in New Glasgow, N.S., he began his career working in a New Glasgow shipyard in 1867, but by 1872 he had become a partner in a small iron company. He later organized the NOVA SCOTIA STEEL CO. at Trenton, which used some of the most advanced methods of its day in its steelmaking operations.

FRÉCHETTE, LOUIS-HONORÉ (1839-1908), poet, playwright. Born at Lévis, Lower Canada, he studied law at Univ. Laval but failed at practise and moved to Chicago, Ill. Living there from 1866 to 1871, he wrote in many genres and on many subjects, including a denunciation of CONFEDERATION. He returned to Canada and won election to Parliament as a Liberal in 1874. He

continued to publish verse, won recognition in France, and was soon hailed as Quebec's poet laureate. His large body of work entitles him to rank as Quebec's major literary figure of the 19th century.

FREE VOTE, a vote in Parliament when MP's are allowed to vote their conscience. Held only rarely (as in the vote on capital punishment in June 1987), free votes see the constraints of party discipline lifted.

FREE TRADE, the tariff-free exchange of goods. The term came into use as the successor to RECIPROCITY, likely in the 1930s, and in Canada it is almost always employed to refer to trade between Canada and the United States. Trade agreements between Ottawa and Washington in 1935 and 1938 began reducing tariffs, and World War II also helped lower barriers. In 1947-8, secret negotiations begun to ease Canada's dollar crisis turned into free trade discussions but the resulting agreement was vetoed by Prime Minister Mackenzie King. The idea resurfaced in the 1950s, and then lay dormant until the 1980s when the government of Pierre Trudeau flirted with free trade in defined sectors of the economy. This notion did not fly, and it was succeeded in 1985 by an attempt, launched by the Progressive Conservative government of Brian Mulroney, to negotiate a full free trade pact. The effort met with success in Oct. 1987, and Mulroney and President Reagan signed the deal in Jan. 1988.

FREIGHT RATES, rates charged by the railways for shipping grain and other natural products from the Prairies to the east and for shipping finished goods from the east to the Prairies. These rates have long been a matter of contention in western Canada, with many westerners charging that they have been discriminated against by the railways which charged rates much higher than those in central and eastern Canada. Demands for government action to lower freight rates were raised as early as 1883 when the MANITOBA AND NORTHWEST FARMERS' PROTECTIVE UNION was formed. Every farm and progressive movement that followed sought similar government action. The issue remained alive into the 20th century and was even raised at the WESTERN ECONOMIC OPPORTUNITIES CONFERENCE of 1973. *See also* CROW'S NEST PASS AGREEMENT.

FRÈRE UNTEL (BROTHER JEAN-PAUL DESBIENS) (1927–), social critic. In Oct. 1959 *Le Devoir* published a letter attacking the teaching of the French language in Quebec schools, education generally, and the religious bureaucracy. Signed Frère Untel, or Brother Anonymous, the letter started an extraordinary furor, and Frère Untel soon wrote a book, *Les Insolences du Frère Untel*, which became a runaway bestseller. Untel, a Marist teaching brother named Jean-Paul Desbiens, was exiled to Europe, but his attack on repressive thinking in Quebec played a role in speeding the QUIET REVOLUTION. Desbiens published subsequent books and from 1972-4 was editor in chief of *La Presse*.

FROG LAKE "MASSACRE," killing of nine white settlers by a Cree band on 2 April 1885 during the NORTH-WEST REBELLION. Frog Lake is located 75 km west of Lloydminster, Sask. *See also* BIG BEAR; GABRIEL DUMONT; POUNDMAKER; LOUIS RIEL.

An FLQ bomb blows up a demolition expert in Montreal, 1963

FRONT DE LIBÉRATION DU QUÉBEC, terrorist organization that aimed to separate Quebec from Canada by violent revolution. It began its attacks on federal and anglophone institutions in Quebec in March 1963 by planting bombs in mailboxes in Westmount, a wealthy English-speaking suburb of Montreal. FLQ members eventually graduated to armed robbery and murder. Although police successfully broke up the organization a number of times, new members kept taking up the cause. In the fall of 1970 FLQ members kidnapped British trade commissioner James Cross and Quebec cabinet minister PIERRE LAPORTE, demanding large ransoms, safe passage from the country, and publication of the FLQ program. This sparked off the OCTOBER CRISIS which led to the disappearance of the FLQ.

FRONTIER COLLEGE, educational organization founded in 1899 by Alfred Fitzpatrick, a Nova Scotia minister concerned about the life of male immigrant workers who laboured in northern logging and railway construction camps. The college recruited university student volunteers who worked alongside these men during summer months and taught them subjects such as English or civics in the evenings.

FROST, LESLIE MISCAMPBELL (1895-1973), premier of Ontario. A product of small-town Ontario, he was born at Orillia. Severely wounded in World War I (about which he wrote a very good memoir), he returned home, graduated from Osgoode Hall in 1921, and with his brother bought a law practice in Lindsay. He entered the legislature in 1937 as a Conservative and served as treasurer of Ontario and mines minister in GEORGE DREW's 1943 cabinet. In 1949 Frost succeeded Thomas Kennedy as Conservative leader and premier of the province and until his resignation in 1961 he provided extraordinarily shrewd and careful government.

FRYE, HERMAN NORTHROP (1912–), educator, literary critic. Born at Sherbrooke, Que., and raised in Moncton, N.B., he studied at the univs. of Toronto and Oxford, and joined the staff at the Univ. of Toronto in 1939. His works on William Blake, the Bible, criticism, Shakespeare, and T.S. Eliot have made him influential around the world.

FULFORD, ROBERT MARSHALL BLOUNT (1932–), editor. He wrote for MACLEAN'S and the *Toronto Star*, and then became editor of SATURDAY NIGHT in 1968, a post he held until 1987. Fulford made that magazine the best liberal monthly in Canada, and his own movie reviews (written under the pseudonym of Marshall Delaney), political criticism, and general commentary gave *Saturday Night* much of its reputation.

FULTON, EDMUND DAVIE (1916–), politician, judge. Born at Kamloops, B.C., educated at the univs. of British Columbia and Oxford, Fulton served overseas in World War II, and won election to Parliament in 1945 as a Conservative. In 1957 he became a cerebral minister of justice, tried to succeed Prime Minister JOHN DIEFENBAKER in the cabinet crisis over nuclear weapons of 1963 but failed, and became leader of the B.C.

Conservative Party. Two years later he returned to Ottawa but failed to be elected Conservative leader at the 1967 convention. He was a justice of the B.C. Supreme Court, 1973-81.

FUNCTIONALISM, policy devised by Canada in WORLD WAR II to claim greater representation on Allied councils. Developed by HUME WRONG of the Department of External Affairs in 1942, the "functional principle" held that in certain areas smaller powers had as much to offer as the large powers (United States, Great Britain, and the Soviet Union), and had a right to full representation on the international policy-making bodies or agencies. Canada made its case successfully and secured access to the Combined Food Board, one of the British-U.S. COMBINED BOARDS. It had less success in other areas, but functionalism formed the basis of the MIDDLE POWER argument Canada posited after World War II.

FUNNY MONEY, *see* ALBERTA PROSPERITY CERTIFICATES

courtesy National Archives of Canada/C-22470

Sir Alexander Galt

G

GALBRAITH, JOHN KENNETH (1908–), economist. One of the world's best-known economists, Galbraith was born at Iona Station, Ont., and was educated at Ontario Agricultural College, Univ. of California, Berkeley, and Cambridge Univ. Since World War II, he has spent most of his time teaching at Harvard Univ., but has served as an adviser to Democratic presidents of the United States since Franklin Roosevelt. He was U.S. controller of prices during World War II and U.S. ambassador to India from 1961 to 1963. A writer of many books, including *The Affluent Society* (1958) and *The New Industrial State* (1967), he contributed to the ROYAL COMMISSION ON CANADA'S ECONOMIC PROSPECTS in 1956.

GALT, SIR ALEXANDER TILLOCH (1817-93), politician. Born in London, Eng., Galt came to Canada in 1835 and settled in Quebec where he was involved in a variety of land promotion and railway construction schemes. He was first elected to the legislature of the UNITED PROVINCE OF CANADA in 1849 as a follower of the Liberal Party. Galt was one of the earliest supporters of higher tariffs to protect developing industries and of a union of the British North American colonies. He became a member of the GREAT COALITION of 1864 and a FATHER OF CONFEDERATION. He was Canada's first minister of finance, serving in the Conservative government of Prime Minister JOHN A. MACDONALD, but he held the office for less than a year, resigning after a bank failure. Galt remained prominent in public life after he retired from Parliament in 1872. He was Canada's first HIGH COMMISSIONER to Britain, 1880-3.

GASCON, JEAN (1920-88), actor, director. A distinguished figure in Canadian theatre, Jean Gascon was born in Montreal. He established the Theatre du Nouveau Monde in 1951 and was co-founder of the National Theatre School in 1960. He acted in Quebec and at Stratford, Ont., was artistic director of the Stratford Shakespearian Festival from 1969 to 1974, and in 1977 became director of the theatre at the National Arts Centre, Ottawa. Much loved, Gascon was equally successful on stage and as a director in both of Canada's official languages.

GARDINER, FREDERICK GOLDWIN (1895-1983), civic politician. Born at Toronto and a graduate of Osgoode Hall Law School, Gardiner became first chair of Metropolitan Toronto in 1953 and bullied the new metropolis into adapting to growth. Known as "Big Daddy," Gardiner stepped down in 1961 and was appointed a Toronto Hydro commissioner four years later. Appropriately, he is memorialized by the Gardiner Expressway.

James G. Gardiner

GARDINER, JAMES GARFIELD (1883-1962), premier of Saskatchewan, federal politician. Born at Farquhar, Ont., "Jimmy" Gardiner left for the Prairies in 1903. He was elected to the Saskatchewan legislature in 1914, and served as minister of highways in CHARLES DUNNING's Liberal government from 1922 until succeeding Dunning as premier in 1926. Defeated in 1929 despite (or because of) having created a legendary political machine, Gardiner led his party back to power in 1934. He resigned in 1935 to enter the House of Commons. A powerful federal minister of agriculture from 1935 to 1957 and minister of national war services in 1940-1, Gardiner was responsible for getting the PRAIRIE FARM REHABILITATION ADMINISTRATION into operation. He left politics after losing the 1958 election.

GARNEAU, MARC (1949-), scientist, astronaut. Born in Quebec City, Garneau attended Collège militaire royal de St-Jean, the Royal Military College in Kingston and the Imperial War College in London, Eng. He pursued a dual career in both the military and aeronautical engineering before entering Canada's astronaut program. He was the first Canadian to fly in space when he participated in the U.S. *Challenger* Space Shuttle mission on 5 to 13 Oct. 1984.

GARNER, HUGH (1913-79), author. Born at Batley, Eng., he came to Canada in 1919 and grew up in the poorer sections of Toronto about which he later wrote. A colourful figure who rode the rails during the GREAT DEPRESSION and fought in the Spanish Civil War and World War II, Garner published more than 17 books, 100 short stories, and scores of articles and scripts. His best-known novel, *Cabbagetown* (1968), is a realistic portrayal of Toronto's urban lower class. He won the Governor General's Award for a short story collection in 1963.

GARSON, STUART SINCLAIR (1898-1977), premier of Manitoba, federal politician. Stuart Garson was born at St Catharines, Ont., and graduated from the Univ. of Manitoba and Manitoba Law School. He practised law until 1936, but entered the Manitoba legislature as a Liberal-Progressive in 1927. He became premier in 1943, and in 1948 resigned to sit in the House of Commons, serving as Prime Minister LOUIS ST LAURENT's minister of justice and attorney general. Defeated in the 1957 federal election, Garson returned to practise law.

GATT, *see* GENERAL AGREEMENT ON TARIFFS AND TRADE

GAUDAUR, JACOB GILL, JR (1920-), football player. He played football with the Royal Canadian Air Force in World War II, and with the Hamilton Tigers after the war. From 1954 to 1968, he was general manager of the Hamilton Tiger-Cats and from 1968 to 1984 commissioner of the Canadian Football League.

GAUDREAULT, LAURE (1889-1975), labour leader, teacher. Born at La Malbaie, Que., she became active in the Catholic union movement in Quebec in the late 1930s when she tried to organize rural schoolteachers. She later founded a journal for teachers and pushed for the amalgamation of teachers' unions in Quebec. She served as vice-president of the Corporation générale des instituteurs et des institutrices catholique du Québec from 1946 to 1965.

GAULT, ANDREW HAMILTON (1892-1958), soldier. Born in England of Canadian parents, he attended McGill Univ. before joining the Canadian Mounted Rifles during the BOER WAR. On the outbreak of WORLD WAR I, he raised the Princess Patricia's Canadian Light Infantry at a cost of $100,000, accompanying the battalion overseas as second in command. During WORLD WAR II he served on staff of the Canadian Army in England.

GÉLINAS, GRATIEN (1909–), actor, playwright. Born at St-Tite, Que., he created in 1937 Fridolin, a radio character of extraordinary life. Out of Fridolin sprang *Tit-Coq* (1948), the illegitimate conscript, a smashing stage success. Later work by Gélinas included *Bousille et les Justes* (1959) and *Hier, les enfants dansaient* (1966), an examination of the impact of the QUIET REVOLUTION on a family.

GENERAL AGREEMENT ON TARIFFS AND TRADE (GATT), international treaty signed by Canada and other nations in 1947 after extensive negotiations in Geneva, Switz. It established a mechanism for the multilateral negotiation of lower tariffs for purposes of stimulating international trade. In signing the agreement, Canada committed itself to a broad policy of lower tariffs. Major tariff reductions, especially between Canada and the United States, followed the Geneva Round negotiations in 1956, the Kennedy Round 1964-7, and the Tokyo Round 1974-9.

GEOFFRION, JOSEPH-ANDRÉ-BERNARD, "BOOM BOOM" (1931–), hockey player. He joined the Canadiens in 1950. Nicknamed Boom Boom because of his crashing shot, he was a high scorer for 14 years with the team. After a brief retirement, he played for two years with the New York Rangers.

GEOLOGICAL SURVEY OF CANADA, agency responsible for geological surveys and maps and for estimating the general mineral resources of Canada, was founded by the UNITED PROVINCE OF CANADA in 1842. It was intended to help the fledgling mining industry plan future exploration and development. As Canada expanded, so too did the scope and work of the agency. It became a separate department of government – the Department of Mines – headed by its own cabinet minister in 1907. The current title is Department of Energy, Mines and Resources.

GEORGE, DAN (1899-1981), actor. Born near Vancouver, B.C., he worked in a variety of trades until, in 1959, he began to play roles on Canadian televison and stage. His most notable role was in the Hollywood film *Little Big Man*. He was chief of the Squamish band from 1951 to 1963.

GINGER GROUP, farm and labour MPs who broke with the PROGRESSIVE PARTY in 1924. The group acquired its name for its feistiness. Led by J.S. WOODSWORTH, AGNES MACPHAIL, and WILLIAM IRVINE, the group had little influence in Parliament although it did squeeze Canada's first OLD AGE PENSIONS out of Prime Minister MACKENZIE KING in 1926. Its members, and especially Woodsworth, played a major role in forming the CO-OPERATIVE COMMONWEALTH FEDERATION.

GIRARD, MARC-AMABLE (1822-92), premier of Manitoba. Born at Varennes, Lower Canada, Girard went to Manitoba in 1870, becoming a member of the assembly and the Executive Council in that year. In 1871 he was named a senator. He became provincial premier in 1874, the first French Canadian to hold the post, but resigned before the year was out. He served in JOHN NORQUAY's cabinet from 1879 to 1883.

GIROUARD, SIR ÉDOUARD PERCY CRANWILL (1867-1932), colonial administrator. Born at Montreal and educated at the ROYAL MILITARY COLLEGE, Percy Girouard took a commission in the Royal Engineers. He served in the Sudan, and built railways in South Africa and Nigeria. He was governor of Northern Nigeria from 1907 to 1909 and then governor of the British East Africa Protectorate until 1912. After leaving the colonial service he was employed by Armstrong Whitworth, a British munitions firm.

GLADSTONE, JAMES (1887-1971), native leader, senator. Born at Mountain Hill, North-West Territories, into the Blood tribe, Gladstone was three times leader of the Indian Association of Alberta. In 1958 JOHN DIEFENBAKER named him a senator, the first Indian so honoured.

GLASSCO, JOHN (1909-81), writer. He fled Montreal for Paris at age 20 in search of a bohemian life, a period recalled in his *Memoirs of Montparnasse* (written 1932, published 1970). His *Selected Poems* won a Governor General's Award in 1971; he published erotic stories to earn money.

GODBOUT, JOSEPH-ADÉLARD (1892-1956), premier of Quebec. Born at St-Éloi, Que., and educated at Ste-Anne-de-la-Pocatière and Massachusetts Agricultural College, Godbout taught at Ste-Anne-de-la-Pocatière from 1918 to 1930 and was agronomist for L'Islet County between 1922 and 1925. Elected to the Quebec legislature as a Liberal in 1929, he served as minister of agriculture before succeeding L.-A. TASCHEREAU as premier in 1936. Defeated by the UNION NATIONALE in the 1936 provincial elections, Godbout's party, with the help of the federal Liberals, won the 1939 election but was again defeated by MAURICE DUPLESSIS and the UN in 1944. Godbout continued as opposition leader until called to the Senate in 1949.

GOOD, WILLIAM CHARLES (1876-1967), farm leader. Born near Brantford, Ont., he became active in the farm movement in Ontario early in the 20th century and helped draft the constitution of the CANADIAN COUNCIL OF AGRICULTURE in 1909. He helped organize, and was first president of, the United farmers' Co-operative Co. in Ontario, established in 1914. Good was elected to the House of Commons in 1921 as a PROGRESSIVE PARTY member and associated himself with the GINGER GROUP. From 1921 until 1945 he was president of the Co-operative Union of Canada.

GORDON, SIR CHARLES BLAIR (1867-1939), businessman. Born in Montreal, he was a skilled and daring entrepreneur involved in the organization of such major corporations as DOMINION TEXTILES and Dominion Glass. He worked with J.W. FLAVELLE on the IMPERIAL MUNITIONS BOARD during World War I, and he was appointed president of the BANK OF MONTREAL in 1927.

courtesy Glenbow Archives, Calgary/NA-4887-6

Charles W. Gordon (Ralph Connor)

GORDON, CHARLES WILLIAM (1860-1937), novelist. Better known by his pen name Ralph Connor, Charles Gordon was born at Glengarry County, Canada West, and educated at the Univ. of Toronto and Edinburgh Univ. Ordained a Presbyterian minister in 1890, he pursued missionary work in Alberta before becoming pastor of St Stephen's Church at Winnipeg in 1894. Gordon went overseas as a chaplain with the CANADIAN EXPEDITIONARY FORCE in World War I and returned to Canada to become moderator of the Presbyterian church in 1921. As Ralph Connor, Gordon published more than 30 novels, including such bestsellers as *Black Rock* (1898), *The Sky Pilot* (1899), *The Man From Glengarry* (1901), and *Glengarry School Days* (1902). His autobiography, *Postscript to Adventure*, was published in 1938.

GORDON, CRAWFORD (1914-67), civil servant, businessman. Born in Winnipeg, Man., he worked in the federal Department of Munitions and Supply during World War II and in the Department of Defence Production in the early 1950s. As president and general manager of AVRO CANADA, he coordinated production of the CF-100 fighter and the early experimental work on the AVRO ARROW.

GORDON, DONALD (1901-69), public servant. Born at Old Meldrum, Scot., Gordon came to Canada as a boy and worked for the Bank of Nova Scotia where his intelligence attracted attention. In 1935 the new BANK OF CANADA recruited him as secretary and in 1938 he became deputy governor. In 1941 he became head of the WARTIME PRICES AND TRADE BOARD, a critical job that he handled with great force and skill. After postwar service at the bank, he was named president of CANADIAN NATIONAL RAILWAYS in 1950, soon plunging into controversy when he slighted French Canadians. He retired in 1967 to head Brinco.

GORDON, WALTER LOCKHART (1906-87), politician. Born at Toronto and educated at ROYAL MILITARY COLLEGE, he was a partner in the accounting firm founded by his father before joining the finance department during World War II. He chaired the Royal Commission on Administrative Classification in the Public Service in 1946 and the ROYAL COMMISSION ON CANADA'S ECONOMIC PROSPECTS from 1955 to 1957. Elected to the House of Commons as a Liberal in 1962, Gordon became Prime Minister LESTER PEARSON's minister of finance in 1963 and instantly plunged into hot water when controversial proposals in his budget that June had to be withdrawn. After he advised Pearson to call the 1965 election and it produced yet another minority government, he resigned. In 1967 he returned to the cabinet as minister without portfolio and president of the privy council but resigned again in 1968. A founder of the nationalist COMMITTEE FOR AN INDEPENDENT CANADA in the 1970s, Gordon became a spokesperson for nuclear disarmament in the 1980s.

GOUIN, SIR JEAN-LOMER (1861-1929), premier of Quebec, federal politician. He was born at Grondines, Canada East, and educated at Univ. Laval. He practised law at Montreal and

courtesy *La Presse*

Sir Jean-Lomer Gouin

dabbled in local politics. In 1897 Gouin was elected to the Quebec legislature and served as minister of public works in SIMON PARENT's Liberal government before becoming premier in 1905. After 15 years as Premier he left provincial politics in 1920 to become Prime Minister MACKENZIE KING's very conservative minister of justice from 1921 to 1924, and his influence was believed responsible for King's failure to absorb the PROGRESSIVE PARTY and turn the Liberals into a low-tariff party. Gouin was lieutenant-governor of Quebec for a short time before his death.

GOUIN, PAUL (1898-1976), politician. The son of LOMER GOUIN and grandson of HONORÉ MERCIER, he was destined for politics. Trained as a lawyer, he founded the ACTION LIBÉRALE NATIONALE in 1934 to protest the corruption of the TASCHEREAU government, but his 1935 alliance with MAURICE DUPLESSIS and the Conservatives, while successful in the 1936 elections, saw Gouin's supporters swallowed whole or driven out of the UNION NATIONALE. Gouin helped found the BLOC POPULAIRE CANADIEN in 1942 but played little further part in public life.

GOULD, GLENN HERBERT (1932-82), pianist. Born in Toronto and trained at the Royal Conservatory of Music, he first played as a soloist with the Toronto Symphony in 1946. By 1955 he had made his debut in the United States, recorded Bach's *Goldberg Variations* for the first time, and attracted international acclaim. Idiosyncratic, Gould retired from the concert circuit in 1964 to concentrate on recordings, television documentaries on disparate subjects, and writing.

courtesy *Toronto Star*

Igor Gouzenko

GOUZENKO, IGOR SERGEIEVICH (1919-82), Soviet defector. Igor Gouzenko was born at Rogachov, U.S.S.R., and became a cypher clerk in the Soviet Embassy at Ottawa in 1943. In Sept. 1945 he defected with 109 documents demonstrating Soviet espionage activities in Canada. Gouzenko's revelations led to a number of arrests, a royal commission, and the subsequent conviction of 12 persons. In later years he occasionally appeared on television wearing a hood to conceal his appearance from the KGB. Gouzenko published *This Was My Choice* (1948) and *Fall of a Titan* (1953).

GOUZENKO AFFAIR, a Soviet spy scandal. Sparked by the revelations of IGOR GOUZENKO, a cypher clerk who defected from the Soviet embassy in Ottawa with 109 sensitive documents in Sept. 1945, the Gouzenko Affair established the existence of at least one and likely more Soviet spy rings in Canada. A royal commission was set up in 1946 to investigate the case and those named in the documents were toughly interrogated. Among those convicted as a result of the affair was FRED ROSE, a LABOUR PROGRESSIVE PARTY MP.

GRAHAM, HUGH, BARON ATHOLSTAN (1848-1938), newspaper publisher. Born at Atholstan, Canada East, he began working for the Montreal *Daily Telegraph* in 1863. In 1869 he helped found the Montreal *Evening Star*, which was the basis for his empire: the Montreal *Daily Star*, the *Family Herald*, and the *Weekly Star*. As head of Canada's largest and most profitable newspaper, Graham ran the operation for nearly 70 years. He was created Baron Atholstan in 1917.

GRAIN GROWERS' ASSOCIATIONS, farm organizations first formed in western Canada at the end of 1901 as the Territorial Grain Growers' Assn to pressure the federal government into improving the grain transportation and marketing system. It was followed, two years later, by the Manitoba Grain Growers' Assn. These organizations laid the foundations for the United Farmers organizations that emerged in the three prairie provinces between 1909 and 1926. The grain growers associations supported independent farm political action in the 1920s and organized cooperative elevator companies in the prairie provinces. *See also* UNITED FARMERS OF ALBERTA; UNITED FARMERS OF CANADA (SASKATCHEWAN SECTION); and UNITED FARMERS OF MANITOBA.

GRAIN GROWERS' GRAIN CO., a farmer-owned grain marketing cooperative founded by E.A. PARTRIDGE in 1906. The company was set up to give farmers a seat on the WINNIPEG GRAIN EXCHANGE but the exchange strongly resisted its entry and only conceded after strong pressure from the government of Manitoba. *See also* GRAIN GROWERS' GUIDE; T.A. CRERAR.

GRAIN GROWERS' GUIDE, farm newspaper, published between 1908 and 1928 by the GRAIN GROWERS' GRAIN CO. An important voice for political reform in western Canada, the *Guide* strongly supported both the establishment of farm cooperatives and, after World War I, independent farm political action, especially via the PROGRESSIVE PARTY. The political activism of the *Guide* began to decline along with the Progressive party in the mid-1920s, and it was replaced by the COUNTRY GUIDE in 1928.

GRAND TRUNK PACIFIC RAILWAY, the western subsidiary of the GRAND TRUNK RAILWAY. It was built because Liberal Prime Minister WILFRID LAURIER wanted to construct a second transcontinental railway in addition to the CANADIAN PACIFIC RAILWAY. Laurier's plan, announced in 1901, envisaged a privately owned railway – the Grand Trunk Pacific – to be built from Winnipeg to the west coast and linked with a government-owned line – the NATIONAL TRANS-CONTINENTAL RAILWAY – to be built from the Maritimes to Winnipeg. High costs, serious competition from the CPR and the CANADIAN NORTHERN RAILWAY, and the lack of adequate branch lines, doomed the Grand Trunk Pacific. It was nationalized by the federal government in 1919 and in 1923 became part of the CANADIAN NATIONAL RAILWAYS system.

GRAND TRUNK RAILWAY OF CANADA, Canada's most important commercial link for most of the 19th century. In 1852 a charter was granted to the company by the UNITED PROVINCE OF CANADA to build a line between Toronto and Montreal. The following year a railway from Montreal to Portland, Maine, was purchased by the Grand Trunk so that when the main line was completed to Toronto in 1856, the Grand Trunk stretched from Lake Ontario to the Atlantic Ocean. By the turn of the century it had expanded westward to Chicago. The Grand Trunk, largely owned by British investors, suffered chronic financial difficulties. Eventually high costs, absentee management, bad publicity resulting from poor service, and the costs of building a subsidiary – the GRAND TRUNK PACIFIC RAILWAY – led to the need for heavy subsidizing by the federal government. The railway was taken over by the government in 1919 and became a main part of the CANADIAN NATIONAL RAILWAYS system in 1923. *See also* CHARLES MEL-VILLE HAYS.

GRANT, GEORGE MONRO (1835-1902), educator. Born at Albion Mines, N.S., and educated at Glasgow Univ., he was ordained into the Church of Scotland in 1860. After serving as a Presbyterian minister in the Maritime provinces, he became principal of Queen's Univ. in 1877, a post he held for 25 years. Grant made Queen's into a first-class school, inculcating his students (and staff) with British ideals, imperialist beliefs, and a commitment to learning.

GRANT, GEORGE PARKIN (1918–), philosopher. Born at Toronto, the grandson of G.M. GRANT, George Grant was educated at Queen's and Oxford univs. He taught at Dalhousie and McMaster univs., returning to Halifax in 1980. His most notable Canadian book was *Lament for a Nation* (1965) which attracted considerable attention because of its conservative and anti-American character and its bitter conclusion that Canada was fated to disappear. *Technology and Empire* (1969) was equally gloomy, as was *English-Speaking Justice* (1978). Nationalist and a RED TORY, Grant remains a potent intellectual force in Canada.

GRAY REPORT, *see* TASK FORCE ON FOREIGN OWNERSHIP

GREAT COALITION, political alignment in the UNITED PROVINCE OF CANADA, created in 1864 when GEORGE BROWN, leader of the CLEAR GRIT party in the assembly, approached his political enemy, JOHN A. MACDONALD, leader of the Liberal-Conservative party, to propose a coalition government to break the political deadlock that had existed in the province since the late 1850s. Brown wanted the coalition to work either for a federal union of CANADA EAST and CANADA WEST or a federal union of Canada with the Maritime provinces. Macdonald agreed to join, and the stage was set for the CHARLOTTETOWN CONFERENCE and QUEBEC CONFERENCE, which led to the BRITISH NORTH AMERICA ACT of 1867 and the DOMINION OF CANADA. *See also* CONFEDERATION.

GREAT DEPRESSION, the world-wide economic depression that began with the Wall Street Crash of Oct. 1929. The exact cause of the Great Depression is still not known, but the collapse of the stock market in the United States was only one of many conditions that plunged the world into the greatest economic depression of modern times. That crash was sparked off by a number of European bank failures but was made worse by the large number of stockholders who were playing the market on margin and who had in fact borrowed to buy stock. Governments, especially the government of the United States, were unsure how to respond to the depression and quickly raised tariffs in the hope that the depression could be throttled by isolating it at its source. There was no one source, however, and this action only impeded international trade, and made the economic situation far worse. Canada was particularly hard hit because its economy was still largely based on the production and export of raw materials, and in any economic slowdown, manufacturers reduce their orders for raw materials. In Canada, popular disaffection with

courtesy National Archives of Canada/C-29397

A cry against unemployment during the Great Depression

the government of the day led to the defeat of Prime Minister MACKENZIE KING's Liberals in 1930 and the election of a Conservative government under R.B. BENNETT. Bennett did little to alleviate the high unemployment that accompanied the depression, and King was returned to power in 1935. Across the country provincial governments were defeated and protest movements such as SOCIAL CREDIT and the CO-OPERATIVE COMMONWEALTH FEDERATION rose up. The depression lasted until the outbreak of World War II and was not ended

by any act of any government anywhere. It was the war and the war-induced shortages of manpower, goods, and raw materials that brought economic recovery. *See also* BANK OF CANADA; BENNETT NEW DEAL; CANADIAN WHEAT BOARD; ESTEVAN MASSACRE; ON-TO-OTTAWA TREK; ROYAL COMMISSION ON DOMINION-PROVINCIAL RELATIONS.

GREAT WAR VETERANS' ASSN, the most important of the WORLD WAR I veterans' associations, formed in April 1917. The GWVA numbered perhaps 180,000 after the armistice. Its efforts, more moderate than those of some its rival organizations, were aimed at securing benefits for its members. By 1926, the GWVA and most of its rivals had united in the [ROYAL] CANADIAN LEGION.

GREAT WESTERN RAILWAY, railway centred on Hamilton, Upper Canada, that dated back to the early 1830s. By 1854 the company's main line stretched from Niagara Falls to Windsor, providing a base for further expansion throughout southwestern Ontario and into Michigan by the early 1880s. When American rivals began to cut rates in the late 1870s, the Great Western could not compete. It was forced to amalgamate with the GRAND TRUNK RAILWAY in 1882.

GREEN, HOWARD CHARLES (1895–), politician. Born at Kaslo, B.C., and educated at the Univ. of Toronto and Osgoode Hall, Howard Green practised law in Vancouver and fought in World War I before entering politics. Elected to the House of Commons as a Conservative in 1935, he served as Prime Minister JOHN DIEFENBAKER's minister of public works from 1957 to 1959 and as secretary of state for external affairs until the Conservative government fell in 1963. Green was an advocate of disarmament and strenuously opposed to nuclear weapons for Canada, and his stubborn convictions in the BOMARC MISSILE CRISIS helped destroy the Diefenbaker government. Green left politics after failing to win a seat in the 1963 and 1965 federal elections.

GREENE, LORNE HYMAN, (1915-87), actor. Born at Ottawa, he graduated from Queen's Univ. From 1939 to 1942 he was chief news announcer for CBC radio and after World War II helped found the Jupiter Theatre in Toronto. In 1953 he left Canada for the United States and spent five years on Broadway before landing the role as Ben Cartwright on "Bonanza," television's most successful weekly program, a role he would play for the next 14 years. "Bonanza" last aired on 23 Jan. 1972, and Greene continued his television appearances, hosting the series "Lorne Greene's New Wilderness."

GREENE, NANCY (1943–), skier. Born at Ottawa and raised in Rossland, B.C., she was selected for the 1960 Olympic ski team. Her talent developed fully in the mid-1960s, and in 1967 she won the World Cup. In 1968 she captured the Olympic gold medal in the giant slalom and a silver in the slalom and, with nine straight victories, won her second World Cup.

GREENFIELD, HERBERT (1867-1949), premier of Alberta. Born at Winchester, Eng., Greenfield established a homestead north of Edmonton in 1906. Soon involved in farmer politics, he was a vice-president of the UNITED FARMERS OF ALBERTA and, although he had not sought election in the 1921 contest, was asked to become premier. Greenfield led the UFA government for four years and passed the torch to J.E. BROWNLEE.

GREENWAY, THOMAS (1838-1908), premier of Manitoba. Born at Cornwall, Eng., he was a general merchant at Centralia, Canada West. From 1875 to 1878 he sat in the House of Commons and supported Prime Minister JOHN A. MACDONALD's government until breaking with the Conservatives over the NATIONAL POLICY. In 1879 Greenway moved to Manitoba, started farming, and entered the provincial legislature, becoming the first leader of the Manitoba Liberal party. He was premier from 1888 to 1900, and his government had to deal with the MANITOBA SCHOOLS QUESTION. He returned to the House of Commons in 1904 but did not seek re-election in 1908. Greenway served briefly on the BOARD OF RAILWAY COMMISSIONERS.

GRENFELL, SIR WILFRED THOMASON (1865-1940), missionary doctor. He was born at Parkgate, Eng., and attended London Medical School and Oxford Univ. He joined the National Mission for Deep-Sea Fisherman in 1888, becoming superintendent in 1889, and set out to tour Newfoundland and Labrador in 1892. Impressed with the plight of the outport people, Grenfell devoted the rest of his life to medical missionary work. He established the Labrador Mission, which included five hospitals, seven nursing stations, and three orphanages. Grenfell retired from active mission work in 1935. He wrote many books, including *Adrift on an Ice-pan* (1909), and his autobiography *A Labrador Doctor* (1919) and *Forty Years for Labrador* (1932).

GREY, ALBERT HENRY GEORGE GREY, 4th EARL (1851-1917), governor general of Canada. He sat in the British House of Commons before becoming administrator of Rhodesia (1894-7). Appointed governor general in 1904, he served until 1911, having his term twice extended. In 1909 he donated the Grey Cup for the Canadian football championship.

GREY OWL, *see* ARCHIBALD BELANEY

GRIERSON, JOHN (1898-1972), filmmaker. The "father of the documentary" in Canada, he was born at Deanston, Scot. and educated at Glasgow and Chicago univs. He came to Canada at the invitation of the government of Prime Minister MACKENZIE KING in 1938 and in 1939 was appointed first commissioner of the NATIONAL FILM BOARD of Canada, which he galvanized into an outstanding organization. From 1943 to 1945 Grierson headed the WARTIME INFORMATION BOARD. In 1945 he left Canada for New York and in 1947 returned to Europe as director of mass communications with UNESCO. He returned briefly to Canada to teach filmmaking at McGill Univ. before his death.

GRISDALE, JOSEPH HIRAM (1870-1939), agronomist. Born at Ste-Marthe, Que., Grisdale joined the DOMINION EXPERIMENTAL FARM in 1899 to work under WILLIAM SAUNDERS and succeeded Saunders as director in 1911. Grisdale later sat on the NATIONAL RESEARCH COUNCIL and attended the 1926 and 1931 imperial conferences as part of the Canadian delegation.

GRIT, colloquial name for a Liberal party member. The name is derived from the Clear Grit party, founded in CANADA WEST in the late 1840s. The Clear Grits were a republican-leaning farm-based party which advocated greater democracy and freer trade. Their name came from their anti-patronage, anti-corruption stance. One version of the origin of the name had it that they were "all sand and no dirt, clear grit all the way through." In the late 1860s they were led by GEORGE BROWN.

GROULX, LIONEL-ADOLPHE (1878-1967), historian, priest. One of Quebec's most famous historians and nationalists, he was born at Vaudreuil, Que., and ordained a Roman Catholic priest in 1903. He taught at Valleyfield seminary before pursuing further studies at Rome, Freiburg, and Paris. Appointed professor of history at the Univ. de Montréal in 1915, Groulx founded the *Action française* in 1920, the Institut d'histoire de l'Amérique française in 1946, and its journal which he edited for 20 years, *Revue d'histoire de l'Amérique française* in 1947. Groulx wrote some 30 books, including *Histoire du Canada français* (4 parts, 1950-2) and the novel, *L'Appel de la race* (1922). Prominent in Groulx's writings was the theme of survival.

GROUP GOVERNMENT, theory developed by Alberta farm leader HENRY WISE WOOD. Wood concluded that the problems created by the rise of industrialism in a competitive society could be resolved only by cooperation between organized economic groups. The commercial and financial classes had already organized; therefore, other groups, such as farmers, had to organize in turn. Wood also believed that each group should elect representatives to the legislatures, replacing representation by geographic constituencies. This theory, which ultimately would see farmers bargaining for their rights in a parliament of groups, clashed with the "BROADENING OUT" ideas of others in the PROGRESSIVE PARTY.

GROUP OF SEVEN, Canadian art movement organized in 1920 by A.Y. JACKSON, LAWREN HARRIS, FRANK CARMICHAEL, FRANZ JOHNSTON, ARTHUR LISMER, J.E.H. MACDONALD, and F.H. VARLEY. It later included A.J. CASSON (1926), and EDWIN HOLGATE (1930). TOM THOMSON was influential in the early stages of the formation but died before the group was organized. Many of the original members worked as designers at Grip Ltd in Toronto. Inspired by a show MacDonald gave in 1911 and by tendencies in Scandinavian art, the friends decided to exhibit together, holding their first show

at the Art Gallery of Toronto in 1920. The Seven were primarily landscape painters, and together they presented a new approach to painting in Canada, one that scorned the fat Dutch cows that had hitherto been considered high taste. The group disbanded in 1933, leaving an enduring mark on Canadian art.

GROVE, FREDERICK PHILIP (1879-1948), author. Born at Randomno, East Prussia, under the name of Felix Paul Berthold Friedrich Greve, he attended university in Germany and settled in Manitoba in 1913 under his anglicized name. He taught school for 10 years, then turned to full-time writing. His most notable novels are *Over Prairie Trails* (1922), *Settlers of the Marsh* (1925), *A Search for America* (1927), and an extraordinarily fictionalized autobiography *In Search of Myself* (1946) that won the Governor General's Award.

GUARANTEED INCOME SUPPLEMENT, *see* OLD AGE PENSIONS

GUIBORD AFFAIR, term used to refer to the events surrounding the death and burial of Joseph Guibord, which took place in Montreal between 1869 and 1875 and which were part of the epic struggle between liberalism and the Roman Catholic Church in Quebec in the 19th century. Guibord, a printer, was a member of the INSTITUT CANADIEN, a liberal reading and discussion club which had been proscribed by Roman Catholic BISHOP IGNACE BOURGET. When Guibord died the Catholic church refused to grant him extreme unction, thus preventing his family from burying him in a Catholic cemetery. Guibord's widow went to court over the issue and eventually the JUDICIAL COMMITTEE OF THE PRIVY COUNCIL ordered Bourget's ruling overturned. Outraged by this decision, many Montreal Catholics physically prevented a first attempt by the government to bury Guibord in Oct. 1875. The following month, however, Guibord's body was escorted to the grave by armed troops. The incident was a great political embarrassment to the Liberal government of Prime Minister ALEXANDER MACKENZIE, which was forced by the JCPC's decision to violate the sensitivities of the Montreal Catholic community.

GUTTERIDGE, HELENA ROSE (1880-1960), labour leader, feminist. Born in London, Eng., Gutteridge founded the British Columbia Women's Suffrage League and was an active union member and socialist. In 1937 she was elected to the Vancouver City Council under the CO-OPERATIVE COMMONWEALTH FEDERATION banner.

GZOWSKI, SIR CASIMIR STANISLAUS (1813-98), engineer. Born in St Petersburg, Russia, he came to Canada in 1841 and worked as an engineer before taking up a post as a superintendent of public works for the UNITED PROVINCE OF CANADA. He worked on a large number of railway and canal projects including the GRAND TRUNK RAILWAY. Gzowski was the first chairman of the Niagara Parks Commission which was responsible for the extensive parks that line the Canadian bank of the Niagara River. He was a founder and president of the Canadian Society of Civil Engineers and was an active member of the Canadian militia.

HAIG-BROWN, RODERICK (1908-76), conservationist, writer. Born in England, he came to British Columbia in 1931 and earned his living by logging, guiding, and writing. His early fiction included animal stories, children's books and later essays and books on fishing. He was a noted supporter of conservation of wilderness areas.

HAINSWORTH, GEORGE (1895-1950), hockey player. Born at Toronto, Hainsworth played goal for the Montreal Canadiens (1926-33), Toronto Maple Leafs (1933-6), and again briefly for Montreal. He won the VEZINA Trophy three times and had a remarkable 94 shutouts in 464 games.

HALF-BREED, *see* MÉTIS

HALIBUT TREATY, treaty signed 2 March 1923 between Canada and the United States covering fishing rights in the north Pacific Ocean. It was the first treaty negotiated and signed by Canada. Although the British government,

which had hitherto controlled the foreign policy and treaty-making powers of the empire, was unhappy that it could not also sign the treaty, Prime Minister MACKENZIE KING's government insisted on Canada's right to sole signature.

HALIFAX EXPLOSION, disaster that occurred on 6 Dec. 1917 when a French munitions ship, the SS *Mont Blanc*, exploded in Halifax harbour, levelling much of the northern part of the city. The French ship had collided with a Belgian ship carrying relief supplies. Over 1600 people were killed, 9000 were injured, and more than 25,000 were left without adequate shelter.

HALIFAX RIOT, civil disturbance on 7 May 1945, following celebrations over the end of the war in Europe. More than 10,000 servicemen, mostly sailors, ran amok, looting and vandalizing much of the city's downtown.

HALL, EMMETT MATTHEW (1898-), jurist, royal commissioner. Born at St Colomban, Que., he moved to Saskatoon in 1910 where he was a classmate of JOHN DIEFENBAKER at the Univ. of Saskatchewan. He practised law, became chief justice of the Court of Queen's Bench in Saskatchewan in 1957, chief justice of Saskatchewan in 1961, and a justice of the SUPREME COURT of Canada the next year. Diefenbaker named him to head the ROYAL COMMISSION ON HEALTH SERVICES, and he headed numerous other commissions as well, both before and after his retirement from the Supreme Court in 1973.

HALL, FRANK (1895-1972), labour leader. Born in Norfolk, Eng., he was leader of the Canadian Brotherhood of Railway and Steamship Clerks. After World War II he organized a powerful coalition of NON-OPERATING UNIONS that brought about one of the largest strikes in Canadian history in Aug. 1950, involving 125,000 workers. The walkout was ended after one week when Parliament forced the strikers back to work.

HAMILTON, FRANCIS ALVIN GEORGE (1912-), politician. Born at Kenora and educated at the Univ. of Saskatchewan, he was elected to Parliament in 1957. As minister of northern affairs, he galvanized his department, provided most of the ideas for JOHN DIEFENBAKER's Northern Vision in 1958, and after 1960 had the same impact on the agriculture department. Hamilton pressed for grain sales to China, legislated the AGRICULTURAL REHABILITATION AND DEVELOPMENT ACT, and made an impact wherever he was. In 1967 he failed to be elected Conservative leader.

HANLAN, EDWARD, "NED" (1855-1908), sculler. Born at Toronto, he learned to row on Toronto harbour. By 1873 he was Ontario's best sculler, and four years later he captured the dominion championship. The next year he won the American title, and he held the world title for five years until defeated in 1884. A great popular hero and the first Canadian world champion, Hanlan is memorialized by Hanlan's Point on the Toronto Islands.

HANSARD, the colloquial name for the record of Parliamentary debates. Derived from T.C. Hansard, the printer of the British debates from 1812 to 1892, the term now covers the printed record of the Canadian House of Commons and Senate. Prior to 1875 only a newspaper *Hansard* exists; after that date, a printed version is available, though the 1875-80 Hansard was not entirely reliable.

HARDY, ARTHUR STURGIS, (1837-1901), premier of Ontario. Born at Mount Pleasant near Brantford, Upper Canada, he became a successful lawyer in Brantford. He entered the Ontario legislature as a Liberal in 1873 and served as provincial secretary (1877-89) and commissioner of crown lands (1889-96) before succeeding SIR OLIVER MOWAT as premier in 1896. He was forced to retire because of ill health in 1899.

HARKNESS, DOUGLAS SCOTT (1903-), politician. Born in Toronto, Harkness taught school and farmed in Alberta until World War II when he served overseas with the artillery and won the George Medal. Elected to Parliament in 1945 as a Conservative, he became agriculture minister in 1957 and defence minister in 1960. A strong advocate of nuclear weapons, he clashed with Prime Minister JOHN DIEFENBAKER during the BOMARC MISSILE CRISIS, and his resignation provoked the fall of the government in 1963. He bitterly opposed Diefenbaker's leadership until 1967 and remained in the House until 1972.

HARRINGTON, GORDON SIDNEY (1883-1943), premier of Nova Scotia. Born at Halifax and educated at Dalhousie Univ., Harrington practised law in Glace Bay, N.S. After war service, he was elected to the provincial legislature as a Conservative in 1925 and became labour minister. He succeeded E.N. RHODES as premier in 1930 but his government has defeated in 1933 and later charged with rigging the voters' lists.

HARRIS, ALANSON (1816-94), manufacturer. Born in Brantford, Upper Canada, Harris worked in a local sawmill before opening his own foundry in Beamsville in 1857. He successfully produced farm implements from American patents as well as designing his own. In the 1870s and 1880s his company relocated to Brantford and expanded production to serve the growing western Canadian and United States markets. In 1890 he amalgamated with his rival MASSEY MANUFACTURING CO., and the new company became MASSEY-HARRIS CO. LTD.

HARRIS, LAWREN STEWART (1885-1970), artist. A founder and leading member of the GROUP OF SEVEN, he was born at Brantford, Ont., into a well-off manufacturing family and attended the Univ. of Toronto before going to Berlin to study art for four years. In 1908 Harris returned to Canada and befriended J.E.H. MACDONALD and TOM THOMSON. Inspired by an exhibition of Scandinavian art at the Albright Art Gallery in Buffalo, Harris and others began to tour and paint together. World War I intervened but the group reassembled to exhibit together as the Group of Seven in 1920. Harris had a tremendous impact on Canadian painting as he moved from landscape to abstract mediums.

HARRIS, ROBERT (1849-1919), painter. Born in Wales, Harris came to Prince Edward Island in 1856. He trained in Boston, Paris and Rome, worked for publishers in Canada and the United States, and became one of the country's leading portrait artists. His best-known painting, though destroyed when the Parliament Buildings burned in 1916, was "The Fathers of Confederation."

HARRIS, WALTER EDWARD (1904-), politician. Born at Kimberley, Ont., and trained as a lawyer, he was elected to Parliament in 1940 as a Liberal. He served in World War II, was named to the cabinet in 1950, and became finance minister in 1954. He was notably successful in that post, but won bitter criticism in 1957 for limiting pensioners to a $5 increase, a decision that played its part in the 1957 Liberal defeat.

HART, JOHN (1879-1957), premier of British Columbia. Born at Mohill, Ireland, he came to Canada in 1898 and established a successful brokerage and financial business in Victoria. He entered the B.C. legislature in 1916 and, except for a nine-year retirement from politics (1924-33), served as Liberal minister of finance from 1917 to 1941, when he became premier. Hart's government established the B.C. Power Commission and began a program of highway building.

HARVEST EXCURSIONS, special trips arranged by the railways between 1890 and 1930 to carry men to western Canada from as far away as Britain to work on the harvest. Large numbers of workers were needed and the railways sold special low harvest fares to attract them. The work was hard but easy to find, and the pay was good. Harvest excursions became known for their drunkenness and rowdiness. They peaked before World War I. After the war, as more farms mechanized, there was less demand for outside labour.

HARVEY, DOUGLAS (1924–), hockey player. He played for the Montreal Canadiens from 1947 to 1961, and was thought the best defenceman of his time. He won the Norris Trophy as top defenceman in the National Hockey League seven times, led the club to the STANLEY CUP repeatedly, but was traded to the New York Rangers in 1961 after he became active in the players' association.

HARVEY, JEAN-CHARLES (1891-1967), journalist. Born at La Malbaie, Que., he worked for a number of newspapers, as well as writing novels. His *Les Demi-civilisés* was put on the index by CARDINAL VILLENEUVE in 1934. As founder of *Le Jour* in 1937, he supported Canada's role in World War II in direct contrast to most of his fellow Quebec journalists. After the war, he continued to write and broadcast.

HATFIELD, RICHARD BENNETT (1931–) premier of New Brunswick. The longest reigning premier of his province, Hatfield was born at Woodstock, N.B., and educated at Acadia Univ. and Dalhousie Law School. Elected to the N.B. legislature as a Conservative in 1961, he assumed leadership of the party in 1969 and took it to victory in 1970, ending 10 years of Liberal government. His government, reformist in tone and sensitive to bilingualism and national issues, was decisively defeated in 1987, winning no seats.

courtesy Glenbow Archives, Calgary/NA-510-2

Sir Frederick W. Haultain

HAULTAIN, SIR FREDERICK WILLIAM (1857-1942), politician, jurist. Born at Woolwich, Eng., Haultain was educated at the Univ. of Toronto. He was called to the bar in 1882, moved west soon after, and sat in the legislature of the North-West Territories from 1888 to 1905. For the last eight years of this period he was president of the Executive Council or de facto premier. When Saskatchewan was created in 1905, he led the Provincial Rights party in opposition. In 1912 he was appointed chief justice of the Superior Court of Saskatchewan and in 1917 of the Court of Appeal.

HAYS, CHARLES MELVILLE (1856-1912), railway executive. Born in Rock Island, Ill., he came to Canada in 1896 to become general manager and later president of the GRAND TRUNK RAILWAY. Hays was closely involved with the creation of the GRAND TRUNK PACIFIC RAILWAY and became its president in 1905. He opposed organized labour and guided his company through a major strike in 1910, incurring the wrath of the federal government because of his refusal to compromise with his employees. Hays drowned in the sinking of the *Titanic*.

HAZEN, SIR JOHN DOUGLAS (1860-1937), premier of New Brunswick, federal politician. Born at Oromocto, N.B., and educated at the Univ. of New Brunswick, he practised law at Fredericton and Saint John. He served as mayor of Saint John before being elected to the House of Commons in 1891 as a Conservative. Defeated in 1896, he entered the N.B. legislature in 1899 and became leader of the opposition. Hazen put together an effective party that took power in 1908. In 1911 he resigned as premier and returned to the House of Commons, serving as SIR ROBERT BORDEN's minister of marine and fisheries and minister of naval affairs from 1911 to 1917. Appointed chief justice of New Brunswick in 1917, he retired in 1935.

HEAD, IVAN LEIGH (1930-), public servant. Born at Calgary and educated in law at the Univ. of Alberta, Head served in the Department of External Affairs and taught at the Univ. of Alberta. In 1967 he was constitutional adviser to justice minister PIERRE TRUDEAU, and he became a special assistant in 1968 after Trudeau became prime minister. Head's special interest was foreign policy, and he played a major role in the foreign policy review of 1968-72, undertook special missions abroad for the prime minister, and spearheaded Trudeau's call for North-South dialogue. In 1978 he became president of the International Development Research Centre.

HEAPS, ABRAHAM ALBERT (1885-1954), labour leader, politician. Born in Leeds, Eng., Heaps was an upholsterer and became active in union affairs in Winnipeg before World War I. He was one of the leaders of the WINNIPEG GENERAL STRIKE and was arrested and charged with seditious conspiracy. He was cleared of the charge and was elected to represent Winnipeg North for the INDEPENDENT LABOUR PARTY OF MANITOBA and the CO-OPERATIVE COMMONWEALTH FEDERATION from 1925 to 1940.

HEARST, SIR WILLIAM HOWARD (1864-1941), premier of Ontario. He was born at Arran Township, Canada West, and practised law at Sault Ste Marie before entering provincial politics in 1908. Minister of lands, forests and mines in SIR JAMES WHITNEY's Conservative government, he became premier in 1914 when Whitney died. Hearst's government enfranchised women, introduced PROHIBITION, established a Department of Labour, and promoted hydroelectric projects. Defeated in 1919, he returned to his law practice. Before his death he served on the INTERNATIONAL JOINT COMMISSION.

HÉBERT, JACQUES (1923-), publisher, writer, and social activitist. He was born in Montreal and educated in Prince Edward Island and Montreal. He ran the newspaper *Vrai*, established the publishing houses of Éditions de l'Homme and Éditions du Jour, and wrote a number of books, including one on the notorious Coffin affair and a journal (with his old friend PIERRE TRUDEAU) of a trip to China in 1960. He founded Canada World Youth, an organization for cultural interchange, was co-chair of the Federal Cultural Policy Review Committee, and was named to the Senate by Trudeau.

HEENEY, ARNOLD DANFORD PATRICK (1902-70), public servant. Born in Montreal, Heeney grew up in Winnipeg where he attended the Univ. of Manitoba. He won a Rhodes Scholarship to Oxford, became a lawyer in Montreal, and in 1938 became principal secretary to Prime Minister MACKENZIE KING. Two years later he became clerk of the Privy Council, implementing the administrative reforms that let Canada's leaders efficiently run the war. Under-secretary of state for external affairs in 1949, he then served as ambassador to the United States twice, as chair of the CIVIL SERVICE COMMISSION, and as head of the INTERNATIONAL JOINT COMMISSION and the PERMANENT JOINT BOARD ON DEFENCE.

HEENEY-MERCHANT REPORT, 1965, a study of the "Principles for Partnership" between Canada and the United States. ARNOLD HEENEY, a senior Canadian public servant, and Livingston Merchant, twice U.S. ambassador to Canada, were commissioned by Prime Minister LESTER PEARSON and President Lyndon Johnson to study the problems in the relations between the two countries that had become evident during the

Conservative government of JOHN DIEFENBAKER. Their report recommended that Canada pursue "quiet diplomacy" when it disagreed with U.S. actions and policies, a recommendation that the Johnson administration thought would limit Ottawa's grumbling about Vietnam policy and that many Canadians wrongly interpreted as calling for virtual surrender to American directives.

HELLYER, PAUL THEODORE (1923–), politician. Born at Waterford, Ont., Hellyer served in the air force and army in World War II. Elected to the House of Commons in 1949 as a Liberal, he was briefly associate defence minister in 1957. He became defence minister in 1963 and launched the armed forces on a process of INTEGRATION and UNIFICATION that involved him in great controversy. He lost the Liberal leadership in 1968 to PIERRE TRUDEAU, then served as minister of transport until he resigned from the Trudeau government in 1969. He founded a new party, Action Canada, and then unsuccessfully sought the Conservative leadership in 1976.

HÉMON, LOUIS (1880-1913), writer. Born at Brest, France, Hémon came to Canada in 1911. He worked briefly in Montreal, then moved to the Lac St-Jean district where he wrote *Maria Chapdelaine*, a work that appeared in 1914 after his accidental death. By the 1920s the novel had achieved great renown for its depiction of habitant life.

HENRY, GEORGE STEWART (1871-1953), premier of Ontario. Born in King Township, Ont., and educated at the Univ. of Toronto and Ontario Agricultural College, "Honest George" became a farmer. He entered the provincial legislature as a Conservative in 1913 and over the next 30 years served as minister of agriculture (1918-19), minister of public works and highways (1923-30), and as premier from 1930 to 1934. After his party was defeated in 1934 by MITCH HEPBURN's Liberals, Henry sat as opposition leader until retiring in 1937.

HENRY, ROBERT ALEXANDER CECIL (1884-1962), civil servant, businessman. Born in Montreal, Henry entered the public service in 1908 and from then until the 1930s held a number of posts in the government and in the CANADIAN NATIONAL RAILWAYS. In 1930 he left government service to become general manager of

the Beauharnois Light, Heat and Power Co. but he rejoined the government to work with C.D. HOWE in World War II.

Mitchell Hepburn

courtesy CBC/National Archives of Canada/C-19518

HEPBURN, MITCHELL FREDERICK (1896-1953), premier of Ontario. One of the most flamboyant Ontario premiers, "Mitch" was born at St Thomas, Ont., and was a bank clerk before brief military service in World War I. He then established himself as an onion farmer and entered the House of Commons as a Liberal in 1926. Chosen leader of the Ontario Liberal party in 1930, he resigned his seat in Parliament in 1934 and took the party to a decisive victory in the provincial election. Hepburn introduced a number of popular measures, selling off government limousines, for example, but his differences with Prime Minister MACKENZIE KING and a tempestuous personal life eventually led to his resignation in 1942. In 1944 Hepburn returned as opposition house leader but was defeated in 1945 and retired to his St Thomas farm.

HEPBURN'S HUSSARS, derogatory name given by General Motors' strikers to a detachment of Ontario Provincial Police dispatched to Ottawa on the orders of Ontario Premier MITCHELL HEPBURN during the OSHAWA STRIKE of 1937. They were also called "sons of mitches."

HERRIDGE, WILLIAM DUNCAN (1888-1961), political adviser. Born at Ottawa, a lawyer, and a decorated veteran of World War I, Herridge was brother-in-law of Prime Minister R.B. BENNETT. He wrote speeches for Bennett in the 1930 election, was named minister to Washington, and counselled Bennett to emulate President Roosevelt's New Deal. The result was the BENNETT NEW DEAL speeches of 1935. In 1939 the mercurial Herridge tried to launch the NEW DEMOCRACY party, a quasi–SOCIAL CREDIT movement that went nowhere.

HERZBERG, GERHARD (1904–), scientist. Born at Hamburg, Germany, he immigrated to Canada in 1935 as a refugee from Hitler and taught physics at the Univ. of Saskatchewan. In 1945 he went to Chicago but returned to Canada in 1948 and joined the NATIONAL RESEARCH COUNCIL, becoming director of physics from 1949 to 1969. Herzberg's work in molecular spectroscopy won him the Nobel Prize for chemistry in 1971 and in 1975 the astronomy and spectroscopy divisions of NRC were renamed in his honour as the Herzberg Institute of Astrophysics.

HICKMAN, ALBERT EDGAR (1875-1943), politician. Born at Grand Bank, Nfld, Hicks entered politics in 1913 and held a number of cabinet posts before being elected prime minister of Newfoundland in June 1924. He was defeated in a general election less than six weeks later.

HICKS, HENRY DAVIES (1915–), premier of Nova Scotia. Born at Bridgetown, N.S., and educated at Mount Allison, Dalhousie and Oxford univs., he served in the artillery in World War II before entering the N.S. legislature in 1945. He was minister of education from 1949 until succeeding ANGUS MACDONALD as Liberal premier in 1954. Defeated in 1956, Hicks led the opposition until resigning in 1960 to become dean at Dalhousie and president in 1963, a position he held until 1980. From 1963 to 1967 he sat on the CANADA COUNCIL and was also president of the Canadian Commission to UNESCO. In 1972 he was made a senator.

HIGH COMMISSIONER, diplomatic representatives from one Commonwealth country to another are known as high commissioners. The office was created by the Conservative govern-ment of Prime Minister JOHN A. MACDONALD in the spring of 1880 to allow Canada to maintain a permanent official representative in Britain. Canada's first high commissioner to the United Kingdom was SIR ALEXANDER GALT.

HILL, JAMES JEROME (1838-1916), railway magnate. "J.J." Hill was born at Rockwood, Upper Canada, but settled in St Paul, Minn. In 1870 he formed the Red River Transportation Co., a steamboat line on the Red River. With others he took control of the St Paul and Pacific Railway in 1878 and reorganized it as the ST PAUL, MINNEAPOLIS AND MANITOBA RAILWAY in 1879 with himself as general manager and later president. A director of the CANADIAN PACIFIC RAILWAY, he resigned in 1883 and expanded the St Paul into the Great Northern Railway in 1893.

HILLCREST EXPLOSION, explosion in a coal mine in Hillcrest, Alta, on 19 June 1914 that killed 189 miners. It was the worst mine disaster in Canadian history. The cause of the explosion was never determined but methane gas was strongly suspected.

HILLIARD, ANNA MARION (1902-58), physician. Born at Morrisburg, Ont., Hillard studied medicine at the Univ. of Toronto and in Britain. She worked at Women's College Hospital in Toronto, devised a simple Pap test, and published books on gynecological problems that made her extremely well respected.

HINCKS, CLARENCE MEREDITH (1885-1964), psychiatrist. Hincks, born at St Mary's, Ont., and educated in medicine at the Univ. of Toronto, introduced intelligence testing into the Toronto school system in 1913. Five years later, with CHARLES CLARKE, he started the Canadian National Commission for Mental Hygiene. He then helped begin the first institute for child study at the Univ. of Toronto, became a world authority on mental health, and a campaigner for funds necessary to treat the mentally ill.

HINCKS, SIR FRANCIS (1807-85), politician, colonial administrator. Born at Cork, Ireland, Hincks came to Canada in 1832 and worked for the People's Bank before establishing the Toronto *Examiner* in 1838 and the Montreal *Pilot* in 1844. He was elected to the assembly of the

UNITED PROVINCE OF CANADA in 1841 and with Robert Baldwin and L.-H. LaFontaine founded the Reform party. Resigning in 1843, Hincks returned as inspector general in the second Baldwin-LaFontaine ministry in 1848, becoming leader when Baldwin and LaFontaine retired in 1851. Defeated in 1854, Hincks later become governor of Barbados and Windward Islands, and British Guyana. He returned to Canada in 1869 and entered SIR JOHN A. MACDONALD's government as minister of finance but resigned in 1873 and served as a bank president from 1873 to 1879. His autobiography, *Reminiscences*, was published shortly before his death.

courtesy Glenbow Archives, Calgary/NA-1451-10

E. Cora Hind

HIND, ELLA CORA (1861-1942), journalist. She was born at Toronto and moved to Winnipeg. Initially denied a position with the Manitoba *Free Press*, she became agricultural editor in 1901, renowned for her ability to predict wheat crop yields. President of the Canadian Women's Press Club, Hind worked for WOMEN'S SUFFRAGE. Before her death at Winnipeg she published a number of books, notably *Red River Jottings* (1905) and *Seeing For Myself* (1937).

HIND, HENRY YOULE (1823-1908), geologist. Born at Nottingham, Eng., Hind was educated at Cambridge and came to Canada in 1846 to teach at the Toronto Normal School, later moving to Trinity College. After 1863 Hind worked as a consulting geologist and became an author of popular works on science and exploration. He joined two expeditions to the Prairies in 1857

and 1858 as scientist, producing works that gave British North Americans a sense of the area's potential.

HIRSHHORN, JOSEPH HERMAN (1900-81), businessman. Born in Latvia, he came to the United States as a young man. In the early 1930s he began to invest in mineral exploration in Canada and after World War II participated in the largest uranium strike in Canadian history at Blind River, Ont. His art collection was notable.

HODGE V. THE QUEEN, a federal-provincial legal dispute over licensing power. In 1883 the JUDICIAL COMMITTEE OF THE PRIVY COUNCIL ruled that provincial governments were sovereign, not subordinate, to the federal government in their areas of jurisdiction. The case replaced the concept of federal supremacy with the principle of coordinate and separate provincial sovereignty.

HOGTOWN, derogatory name for Toronto given because of the pork-packing plants established in the city in the late 19th century. The current meaning suggests Toronto's efforts to hog everything in Canada for itself.

HOLT, SIR HERBERT SAMUEL (1856-1941), banker, capitalist. Born at Geashill, Ireland, and educated as a civil engineer, Holt immigrated to Canada in 1873 and worked on a number of construction projects, including the prairie and mountain sections of the CANADIAN PACIFIC RAILWAY. He turned to banking, becoming president of the Sovereign Bank (1902-4) and the ROYAL BANK of Canada (1908-34). Under his direction the Royal Bank became the largest in Canada. His main financial interest was in utility companies, notably the immensely profitable MONTREAL LIGHT, HEAT AND POWER CO. which he formed in 1902 and built into a much hated monopoly.

HOME BANK OF CANADA, a Toronto-based bank which failed in Aug. 1923, sending shock waves through the Canadian banking community. It was the first outright failure of a Canadian bank since 1911 and was to be the last until the failures of the Canadian Commercial Bank and the Northland Bank in 1985. The collapse of the Home Bank led to a revision of the BANK ACT and the establishment of the Office of Inspector General of Banks, responsible to the minister of finance.

HOMESTEADER, term originating in the United States and used in Canada to describe a potential settler who paid a $10 registration fee to qualify for a free QUARTER SECTION of prairie land under the DOMINION LANDS ACT.

HONDERICH, BELAND HUGH (1918–), newspaper publisher. He began his newspaper career with the Kitchener-Waterloo *Record* in 1935. In 1943 he joined the Toronto *Star*, becoming editor in chief in 1955, president and publisher in 1966, and chairman and publisher in 1969. Honderich made the *Star* into Canada's largest circulation newspaper.

HONG KONG, BATTLE OF, WORLD WAR II military disaster when Japan attacked the colony on 7 Dec. 1941 and it surrendered Christmas Day. In 1941 the MACKENZIE KING government had agreed to a United Kingdom request to send two battalions of troops and a brigade headquarters to help defend the Crown Colony of Hong Kong. In the battle that December, 290 Canadians were killed, and of the 1683 officers and men taken prisoner, 557 perished in Japanese camps before the end of the war. The government set up a royal commission under SIR LYMAN DUFF in 1942 to investigate the disaster after GEORGE DREW charged that ill-prepared troops had been sent. Duff's report largely exonerated the government, but the defeat still stirs controversy.

HOODLESS, ADELAIDE (1857-1910), women's educational reformer. Born at St George, Canada West, Hoodless lost a child after he drank contaminated milk. This spurred her to crusade for better women's education as homemakers, and this led in 1897 to her founding the first Women's Institute at Stoney Creek, Ont., in 1897, a movement that quickly spread across Canada. She helped found the NATIONAL COUNCIL OF WOMEN and the Victorian Order of Nurses, as well as the Young Women's Christian Assn.

HOSE, WALTER (1875-1965), naval officer. Born at sea, an ideal birth place for a future sailor, he served in the Royal Navy for 21 years, transferring to the ROYAL CANADIAN NAVY in 1912.

During WORLD WAR I, he commanded naval defences on the Atlantic coast and in 1921 he became director of the naval staff, an appointment he held until 1934. He struggled manfully to preserve the Navy against attempts to absorb it or sink it with spending cuts in the GREAT DEPRESSION.

HOUDE, CAMILLIEN (1889-1958), politician. Houde, born at Montreal, had a political career spanning three decades. He entered politics in 1923 when elected to the Quebec legislature and was leader of the provincial Conservatives from 1929 to 1932. Elected to the House of Commons in 1949, he sat in it until 1953. But it was as mayor of Montreal that Houde is best remembered. He held the position almost continuously from 1928 to 1954, except for four years spent in an INTERNMENT camp during WORLD WAR II, after he called for resistance to registration for military service.

HOWE, CLARENCE DECATUR (1886-1960), politician. One of the most successful and powerful businessman-politicians in Canadian history, he was born at Waltham, Mass., and graduated from the Massachusetts Institute of Technology as a civil engineer. He came to Canada in 1908 and taught at Dalhousie Univ. until leaving to join the Canadian BOARD OF GRAIN COMMISSIONERS in 1913. In 1916 Howe formed his own company and became wealthy building grain elevators across Canada. Hit hard by the Depression, he entered the House of Commons as a Liberal in 1935. Known as the "Minister of Everything," he served as minister of railways and canals and minister of marine (1935-6), minister of transport (1936-40), minister of munitions and supply (1940-5), minister of reconstruction (1944-5), minister of reconstruction and supply (1946-8), minister of trade and commerce (1948-57), and minister of defence production (1951-7). During WORLD WAR II Howe mobilized the economy in magnificent style, and he ran postwar reconstruction almost as well. His contempt for political niceties earned him (and the Liberal government) the reputation for arrogance that, after the PIPELINE DEBATE, brought down the ST LAURENT government in 1957. Defeated in that election, Howe did not return to Parliament.

HOWE, GORDON (1928–), hockey player. Arguably the greatest hockey player in history, he joined the Detroit Red Wings in 1946 and by 1950 was a league-leading scorer, a man of extraordinary strength and agility. Winner of every hockey award (and most several times), Howe retired from the Red Wings in 1971 but two years later joined the Houston Aeros of the World Hockey Assn to play with his two sons. Known for his sharp elbows in the corners, he finally retired at age 52 (after 32 seasons of professional hockey) from the Hartford Whalers.

courtesy National Archives of Canada

Joseph Howe

HOWE, JOSEPH (1804-73), journalist, politician. Born at Halifax, N.S., he worked in his father's printing shop before taking over the Halifax *Nova Scotian* in 1828. He entered provincial politics in 1836 after winning a celebrated libel case brought against him by the government and sat in the legislature for almost 30 years. A conservative Reformer, Howe led the fight for responsible government in Nova Scotia and became provincial secretary when it was granted in 1848. He was chairman of the Railway Commission from 1854 to 1857, and premier from 1860 to 1863, the year he was appointed imperial fisheries commissioner. The foremost agitator against CONFEDERATION between 1866 and 1868, Howe entered JOHN A. MACDONALD's government as secretary of state for the provinces when the movement to have it repealed failed. Ill-health

forced him to resign in 1873, and he served briefly as lieutenant-governor in his province.

HUDSON BAY RAILWAY, railway to provide access from the Prairies to Hudson Bay first chartered in 1880 and started several times between the early 1880s and the 1920s. It had long been demanded by prairie wheat farmers who bridled under the CPR monopoly. It was finally completed by CANADIAN NATIONAL RAILWAYS in 1929 and connected Churchill, Man., to Winnipeg.

HUDSON'S BAY CO., fur-trading company granted a royal charter on 2 May 1670. Two French explorers and traders, Pierre-Esprit Radisson and Médard Chouart Des Groseilliers, proposed the company to a group of British investors after exploring the fur-producing areas of southern Hudson Bay and James Bay in the late 1660s. The 1670 charter granted the "Governor and Company of Adventurers" of Hudson Bay title to an area to be known as RUPERT'S LAND (all of western and northern Canada draining into Hudson Bay). The company set up trading posts on Hudson and James bays. In 1774 the first inland post was established at Cumberland House (Sask.) to keep the HBC competitive with its Montreal-based rival, the North West Co. The two companies merged in 1821 giving the Hudson's Bay Co. a monopoly of the western Canadian fur trade. As title-holder to Rupert's Land, the HBC was involved in the government of the Red River Colony. In 1870 the company sold Rupert's Land to Canada for a number of concessions including the retention of the land around its posts, a cash payment of £300,000, and title to one-twentieth of the fertile land in the soon-to-be surveyed southern prairies. As a result of the transaction the company became a wealthy landowner and developer in western Canada. During the 1880s the HBC moved rapidly into the retail trade. It formed the subsidiary Hudson's Bay Oil and Gas Company (HBOG) in 1926, an asset it sold to DOME PETROLEUM in 1982. In 1970 the HBC head office was moved to Winnipeg from London, Eng. A few years later the company increased its retail holdings with the purchase of Simpson's Ltd and Zeller's. Today the company has diversified interests but remains one of the largest fur-trading companies in the world. *See also* RED RIVER REBELLION; LOUIS RIEL.

HUDSON'S BAY MINING AND SMELTING CO. LTD, mining company, originally formed as a subsidiary of the HUDSON'S BAY CO. to explore for minerals on lands acquired when the HBC sold RUPERT'S LAND to Canada. The company was involved in the initial discovery of mineral deposits near Flin Flon, Man., in 1915. In 1930 Hudson's Bay Mining and Smelting began large-scale mining operations in Flin Flon. The company was taken over by the South African company, Anglo-American Corp., in 1962.

courtesy National Archives of Canada/C-20240

Sir Samuel Hughes

HUGHES, SIR SAMUEL (1853-1921), journalist, soldier, politician. One of the most contentious figures in Canadian history, Hughes was born at Darlington, Canada West, and educated in Toronto. He ran a newspaper in Lindsay, Ont., and won election to Parliament as a Conservative in 1892. Interested in the MILITIA in which he served, and convinced that militia officers were far superior to hidebound regulars, he wangled a staff job in the BOER WAR and afterwards claimed that he was entitled to two Victoria Crosses for his service there which was, however, most useful. Involved in the ROSS RIFLE affair, Hughes became minister of militia in the government of Prime Minister ROBERT BORDEN in 1911 and played an important role in mobilizing the CANADIAN EXPEDITIONARY FORCE and in a major armaments scandal. Nearly driving his prime minister to distraction, he was finally sacked in late 1916, thus allowing order to be brought to the war effort.

HULL, ROBERT MARVIN (1939-), hockey player. The popularizer of the slapshot, Bobby Hull was born at Point Anne, Ont. He joined the Chicago Black Hawks in 1957 and became one of the highest scoring players in the game. He won many awards and joined the Winnipeg Jets of the fledgling World Hockey Assn in 1972. By 1981, he was out of hockey entirely.

HUNGERFORD, SAMUEL JAMES (1854-1933), railway executive. Born at Bedford, Canada East, he worked for several railways before joining the CANADIAN NORTHERN RAILWAY in 1910. He stayed with it after it was taken over by the federal government and in 1934 was named president of CANADIAN NATIONAL RAILWAYS, a post he held until 1941. Hungerford was the first president of TRANS-CANADA AIRLINES and president of National Munitions Ltd, a World War II crown corporation.

HUTCHISON, LEONARD (1896-1980), artist. Born in Manchester, Eng., Hutchison came to Canada in 1912. He studied at the Hamilton School of Art and chose woodblock prints as his principal medium, his best work recording the lives of workers during the GREAT DEPRESSION.

HUTCHISON, WILLIAM BRUCE (1901-), journalist. Born at Prescott, Ont., he grew up in the Kootenays and in Victoria, B.C., and became a reporter for the Victoria *Times* in 1918. He was an active Liberal, close to the politicians and key bureaucrats, and in the 1940s and 1950s his writing in the Sifton newspapers was influential. He wrote a number of books, including a biography of MACKENZIE KING and a memoir.

HUTTON, SIR EDWARD THOMAS HENRY (1848-1923), soldier. Born at Torquay, Eng., he came to Canada as general officer commanding the Canadian MILITIA in 1898. He was active in pressing his reluctant government into a commitment of troops for the BOER WAR, fought with his ministers about patronage, and was recalled at Ottawa's request after only two years.

HYDE PARK DECLARATION, 1941, WORLD WAR II agreement reached between U.S. President Franklin Roosevelt and Prime Minister MACKENZIE KING on 20 April 1941. The declaration committed the United States to buy more in Canada, thus easing Canada's shortage of U.S. dollars. Roosevelt also agreed that the goods Canada imported from the United States for inclusion in exports destined for Britain could be charged to Britain's LEND-LEASE account. The agreement freed the Canadian economy for its extraordinary contribution to the war.

HYDRO-QUÉBEC, a crown corporation created in April 1944 when the Quebec government took control of MONTREAL LIGHT, HEAT AND POWER and its subsidiary, Beauharnois Light, Heat and Power. Until 1963 the company provided power in the Montreal area, but the rest of Quebec was served by private power companies. In 1963, under the direction of the Liberal resource minister RENÉ LÉVESQUE, Hydro-Québec took over all privately owned electrical utilities in the province making the company the largest utility in Canada. Further expansion occurred in the 1970s and 1980s including the controversial JAMES BAY PROJECT. *See also* QUIET REVOLUTION.

IGNATIEFF, GEORGE (1913–), diplomat. Born at St Petersburg, Russia, into a noble family, Ignatieff came to Canada with his family in the mid-1920s. He was educated at the univs. of Toronto and Oxford and joined the Department of External Affairs in 1940. He served in London, Ottawa, Yugoslavia, Brussels, and New York and took a hard line on defence questions. After he left the service in 1972, he became a crusader for nuclear disarmament.

ILSLEY, JAMES LORIMER (1894-1967), politician. Born at Somerset, N.S., and educated at Acadia and Dalhousie Univs., he practised law in Halifax before entering the House of Commons as a Liberal in 1926. In 1935 he became minister of national revenue and served as a remarkably popular minister of finance in Prime Minister MACKENZIE KING's wartime cabinet. Ilsley accepted the justice portfolio in 1946 but retired from politics in 1948 to practise law. He was appointed chief justice of the Supreme Court of Nova Scotia in 1950.

I'M ALONE **INCIDENT,** a PROHIBITION-era diplomatic dispute between Canada and the United States. The *I'm Alone* was a Nova Scotia-based rumrunner, shipping liquor surreptitiously to the United States. In 1929, in contravention of international law, the U.S. Coast Guard chased the ship into international waters, sank it, and killed one crew member. The United States finally paid damages in 1935.

IMPERIAL CONFERENCES, *see* COLONIAL AND IMPERIAL CONFERENCES

IMPERIAL ECONOMIC CONFERENCE, 1932, *see* OTTAWA CONFERENCE

IMPERIAL FEDERATION LEAGUE, league formed in Britain in 1884, with branches in Canada. Its members, imbued with the spirit of IMPERIALISM, worked for a federation of the self-governing dominions of the British Empire, such as Canada, New Zealand, and the Australian and South African colonies.

IMPERIAL MUNITIONS BOARD, board created by the British Ministry of Munitions during WORLD WAR I to handle British contracts for the manufacture of war material in Canada. After the scandals that had initially characterized munitions contracts under Sam Hughes's administration became politically embarrassing, the IMB was established in Nov. 1915. It was headed by Toronto businessman J.W. FLAVELLE. *See also* SHELL COMMITTEE.

IMPERIAL OIL LTD, company founded by a group of Toronto investors in 1880. John D. Rockefeller's Standard Oil Co. gained control of Imperial in 1898. Imperial Oil was involved in the exploration and development of such frontier areas as the LEDUC oil field which proved to be a major Canadian oil-producing area in the years following World War II. It has become the largest refiner of petroleum in Canada and an important producer of crude oil. The company is also involved in the ATHABASCA TAR SANDS project with a 25 per cent share in Syncrude Canada Ltd.

IMPERIAL PREFERENCES, tariff concessions extended by one British Empire country to another, first extended by Canada to British products in 1897. Since Britain continued to follow the free trade policy first adopted in 1849, it did not reciprocate until 1919. The OTTAWA CONFERENCE of 1932 entrenched the custom, and Canada thereafter spent substantial time negotiating out of the preferences, largely to secure increased access to the U.S. market. Britain stopped giving preferences after entering the European Economic Community in 1973, but many Commonwealth countries, including Canada, continue the practice in minor ways.

IMPERIAL WAR CABINET, a meeting of British and dominion prime ministers convened by British Prime Minister David Lloyd George in London on 2 March 1917 to discuss matters relating to WORLD WAR I. The Imperial War Cabinet met concurrently with the IMPERIAL WAR CONFERENCE. SIR ROBERT BORDEN attended for Canada and described the meetings as a "Cabinet of Governments. Every Prime Minister . . . is responsible to his own Parliament and to his own people . . . in this may be found the genesis of a development in the constitutional relations of the Empire, which will form the basis of its unity in the years to come."

IMPERIAL WAR CONFERENCE, meetings convened in London by British Prime Minister David Lloyd George to discuss imperial matters unrelated to WORLD WAR I. Meeting concurrently (but on alternate days) with the IMPERIAL WAR CABINET, the conference was most notable for its passage of RESOLUTION IX which attempted to set the Empire's future course.

IMPERIALISM, term for the drive on the part of western countries such as Britain, France, Germany, and the United States to acquire colonies in the late 19th century. This drive was accompanied by the development of various rationalizations that made it easier to subject certain people to a second-class or colonial status. Among those was that known as "the white man's burden," after a poem written by British author Rudyard Kipling which asserted that it was the responsibility of white peoples to care for and "civilize" non-whites. In Canada, imperialism brought glorification of the British Empire, of which Canada was a part, and calls for greater empire unity. *See also* EMPIRE DAY, IMPERIAL FEDERATION LEAGUE.

INCO, *see* INTERNATIONAL NICKEL CO.

INCOME TAX, direct tax on personal and business income, introduced as a temporary wartime measure by the Conservative government of Prime Minister ROBERT BORDEN in 1917 to pay for the war effort. The federal government's authority to tax was not limited by the BRITISH NORTH AMERICA ACT, but until 1917 federal revenues had been raised through indirect taxes, such as customs duties. The provinces are also entitled to levy direct taxes according to the constitution. In all provinces but one, the federal government collects both the federal and provincial income tax and passes on the provincial share. Quebec levies its own income tax.

INDÉPENDANTISTE, Quebec political term to characterize those supporting an independent Quebec nation. Coming into widespread use in the 1970s, *indépendantiste* was roughly equivalent to separatist in English-Canadian usage, though without the derogatory overtones that term usually had.

INDEPENDENT LABOUR PARTY OF MANITOBA, political party founded in 1895, but largely moribund until near the end of World War I. In 1921 J.S. WOODSWORTH ran successfully for Parliament under the ILP banner. The ILP was one of the organizations that helped found the CO-OPERATIVE COMMONWEALTH FEDERATION in 1932.

INDEPENDENT LABOUR PARTY OF ONTARIO, political party founded in 1918. It was for a time affiliated to the CANADIAN LABOUR PARTY but withdrew from the CLP because of the latter's domination by the COMMUNIST PARTY of Canada. In the 1919 Ontario provincial election the ILP cooperated with the UNITED FARMERS OF ONTARIO. The coalition governed until 1923.

INDIAN TREATIES, legal agreements between native peoples and the crown. In the colonial era these were treaties of alliance or friendship between more or less equal partners. Following the American Revolution, they were increasingly based on the idea of aboriginal rights. This is the notion that native people possess certain rights by virtue of having owned or occupied Canada (i.e., they held aboriginal title) prior to the arrival of European colonizers and settlers. The treaties thus evolved into arrangements involving the surrender of aboriginal title in exchange for a variety of obligations assumed by the

courtesy National Archives of Canada/C-17185

Discussion prior to signing of the Manitoba Indian Treaty, 1871

crown, generally including the setting aside of a reserve for the Indians and the payment of annuities. During the 1870s the federal government began to negotiate the first of the so-called "numbered treaties" – Treaties 1–11 – which extinguished aboriginal title to most of western and northern Canada east of the Rocky Mountains. The first of these numbered treaties was concluded in 1871, the last in 1921. Two of these were especially noteworthy: Treaty 6, concluded between the crown and the Plains Indians of central Alberta and Saskatchewan in 1876, which committed Ottawa to providing health services and food in the event of famine; and Treaty 7, between the Indians of southern Alberta and the crown, signed at Blackfoot Crossing in the summer of 1876 by the powerful Chief CROWFOOT. Native LAND CLAIMS are based both on the concept of aboriginal title and on rights explicitly laid out in treaties. Aboriginal rights in general were guaranteed by the CONSTITUTION ACT of 1982, but specific rights such as native self-government have not been explicitly defined because of the failure of native people, the federal government, and the provinces to reach agreement on the terms of such rights.

INDUSTRIAL BANNER, labour newspaper published in Toronto during World War I. The paper was owned by James Simpson, a socialist and prohibitionist.

INDUSTRIAL DEFENCE BOARD, body created by the federal government in 1948 to advise on the war potential of industry and plan for war production.

INDUSTRIAL DISPUTES INVESTIGATION ACT, labour legislation passed by the federal Parliament in 1907. The IDIA was drawn up by MACKENZIE KING, the deputy minister of labour, and modelled on conciliation laws then in effect in Australia and Britain and in use on Canadian railways. The IDIA forced labour and/or management to undergo compulsory investigation of its case and compulsory conciliation before any work disruption could be allowed. In 1925 the JUDICIAL COMMITTEE OF THE PRIVY COUNCIL limited the IDIA to employees under direct federal jurisdiction. The act was replaced by the INDUSTRIAL RELATIONS AND DISPUTES INVESTIGATION ACT in 1948. The IDIA was also called the Lemieux Act because it was introduced while RODOLPHE LEMIEUX was minister of labour. *See also* LETHBRIDGE STRIKE.

INDUSTRIAL RELATIONS AND DISPUTES INVESTIGATION ACT, labour law, passed by the Federal Parliament in 1948 to replace the INDUSTRIAL DISPUTES INVESTIGATION ACT. The IRDIA combined the compulsory investigation and conciliation provisions of the IDIA with legalization of collective bargaining. The CANADA LABOUR RELATIONS BOARD was established to certify unions and enforce unfair labour practice laws; employers under federal jurisdiction were henceforth compelled to bargain with bona fide unions of their employees if the CLRB certified those unions.

INDUSTRY AND HUMANITY, book written by MACKENZIE KING and published in 1917, in which he outlined a plan for a welfare state and his ideas on maintaining peace in the workplace.

INNIS, HAROLD ADAMS (1894-1952), scholar. Canada's greatest economic historian, Innis was born at Otterville, Ont., attended McMaster Univ., and served overseas in World War I. Wounded, he returned to Canada and, after further study at the Univ. of Chicago, joined the political economy department at the Univ. of Toronto in 1920. *The Fur Trade in Canada*, published in 1930, introduced the staple thesis and established his reputation as an outstanding thinker. This book was followed, among others, by *Problems of Staple Production in Canada* (1933) and *The Cod Fisheries* (1940). During World War II Innis moved away from economic history and began to study the role communications and technology played in history, work that was carried forward by MARSHALL MCLUHAN. Innis published *Empire and Communications* in 1950 and *The Bias of Communication* in 1951. He was a dedicated scholar who, unlike many of his peers, was chary of seeing academics involved in government.

INSTITUT CANADIEN, ROUGE social and political club, organized in 1844 in Montreal. The Institut soon spread across Lower Canada. Radical in politics and religion, the Institut was bitterly opposed by the Roman Catholic hierarchy, so bitterly in fact that in 1858 BISHOP BOURGET's opposition led to mass resignations. The Institut found itself caught in the GUIBORD affair, and by 1885 it had been forced out of existence.

INTEGRATION, a policy of eliminating triplication from the Canadian armed forces. Introduced by defence minister PAUL HELLYER in a *White Paper on Defence* in spring 1964, the policy tried to free funds for new equipment by more effective coordination. Integration was soon followed by UNIFICATION, a far more contentious attempt to combine three services into one force.

INTERCOLONIAL RAILWAY, rail link between the Atlantic colonies and the UNITED PROVINCE OF CANADA completed June 1876. Schemes for such a railway had been mooted in the 1840s, but it was not until the late 1850s that a number of sections of track were constructed. The completion of a rail link was a condition of CONFEDERATION and work on the Intercolonial Railway began in earnest shortly after Confederation, under the direction of SANDFORD FLEMING. The line, completed after many delays caused by patronage and scandal, was never profitable. It was operated as part of CANADIAN GOVERNMENT RAILWAYS and was absorbed into the CANADIAN NATIONAL RAILWAYS system in 1923.

INTERNATIONAL CONTROL COMMISSIONS, observer bodies set up by the Geneva Conference, 1954, to supervise the three successor states – Laos, Cambodia, and Vietnam – to French Indochina. Canada was asked to participate along with Poland and India. The International Commissions for Supervision and Control (the formal but rarely used name) in Laos and Cambodia did their work with relative ease, but that in Vietnam turned into a draining commitment as the regimes in the north and south solidified into hostility. The ICC continued futilely in existence until 1974. Meanwhile in early 1973, to cover the American withdrawal from South Vietnam, a new International Commission of Control and Supervision was formed by Poland, Hungary, Indonesia, and Canada. Ottawa reluctantly provided just under 300 men. The new ICC was as helpless as its predecessor and the Canadian government withdrew from it in June. The unhappy dénouement reinforced the growing Canadian disillusionment with PEACEKEEPING.

INTERNATIONAL JOINT COMMISSION, a joint Canada-United States organization formed in 1911 under the terms of the BOUNDARY WATERS TREATY, 1909, to deal with disputes on the development of water resources along the Canada-U.S. border.

INTERNATIONAL MONETARY FUND, body formed by a number of the Allied Powers in 1944 to stabilize international exchange rates. Anticipating the end of the war, the participants were interested in avoiding the restrictive trade practices of the 1930s which had intensified the GREAT DEPRESSION and which had, in the opinion of some, led to war. The IMF was supposed to work with the WORLD BANK in helping less-developed countries improve their economic and financial positions.

INTERNATIONAL NICKEL CO., mining company established in 1902 by the merger of the Canadian Copper Co. and the Orford Copper Co., both American-owned. It was set up to mine and refine nickel ore in the Sudbury basin in central Ontario. Its operations expanded to the point where, by 1929, it approached a world monopoly of nickel production. Since then other companies, such as FALCONBRIDGE NICKEL, have made inroads into the production of nickel, but Inco remains one of the world's largest producers.

INTERNMENT, forcible confinement in time of war. In WORLD WAR I, persons of "ENEMY ALIEN" origin, that is, those citizens of countries with which Canada was at war, were subject to internment if reasonable grounds could be advanced that they might engage in espionage. In all, 8579 were interned. In WORLD WAR II, the minister of justice had the power under the DEFENCE OF CANADA REGULATIONS to intern anyone acting in a manner "prejudicial to the public safety or the safety of the state," a phrasing that permitted Canadian citizens as well as aliens to be locked up. The regulations were applied to Nazi supporters, fascists, communists, and mayor CAMILLIEN HOUDE of Montreal, who had urged his compatriots not to participate in the 1940 national registration for military service. In addition, Japanese Canadians in some numbers were interned. After the attack on Pearl Harbor 38 were arrested, and a further 720 were subsequently put under guard in northern Ontario for resisting evacuation from the west coast or other reasons. *See also* JAPANESE EVACUATIONS.

INUIT TAPIRISAT OF CANADA, founded in 1971 to represent Inuit in negotiations and lobby activities with Ottawa and the provinces, the organization is headquartered in Ottawa and works towards the strengthening of the Inuit people and rational development of the Canadian Arctic. It currently represents more than 25,000 Inuit.

IRVINE, WILLIAM (1885-1962), minister, politician. A Unitarian minister, he was elected to the House of Commons to represent Calgary East on the labour ticket in 1921. In Ottawa he joined the J.S. WOODSWORTH and farm representatives to form the GINGER GROUP. He was defeated in the 1935 federal election but continued to be active in the CO-OPERATIVE COMMONWEALTH FEDERATION.

IRVING, KENNETH COLIN (1899-), industrialist. Born in Buctouche, N.B., Irving returned from service overseas in World War I to open a small automobile sales agency and a gas station. In 1924 he established the Irving Oil Co. In the following decades he expanded its refining and retail operations and used it as a base to build a massive commercial and industrial empire including everything from newspapers to bus companies.

JACKSON, ALEXANDER YOUNG (1882-1974), artist. A member of the GROUP OF SEVEN, he was born at Montreal and worked at various designer firms from 1895 to 1907. He studied art in Paris, returned to Montreal in 1909, and moved to Toronto in 1913, where he met and painted with TOM THOMSON and others. In 1915 he went overseas, was wounded, and became a war artist with the Canadian War Records. After the war, Jackson joined with other members of the Group of Seven to hold their first exhibition in Toronto on 7 May 1920. His more famous paintings include *Terre Sauvage* (1913), *The Red Maple* (1914), and *Barns* (1926). His autobiography, *A Painter's Country*, was published in 1958.

JACKSON, CLARENCE SHIRLEY (1906-), labour leader. Born at Fort William, Ont., he was head of the United Electrical Workers union. A one-time organizer for the CANADIAN CONGRESS OF LABOUR, Jackson was a strong supporter of the COMMUNIST PARTY and his union was expelled from the CCL for its Communist leanings in 1949. The UE was reinstated into the CANADIAN LABOUR CONGRESS in 1972.

JACKSON, DONALD (1940-), figure skater. He held the Canadian senior men's title when he went on to win the bronze at the 1960 Olympics. He won the silver in the world championships that year and the gold at the 1962 world championships. Like most Canadian skaters, his strength was in free skating, something that facilitated his entry into professional skating in 1962.

JACKSON, RUSSELL STANLEY (1936-), football player. Born at Hamilton, Ont., he graduated from McMaster Univ. He joined the Ottawa Roughriders in 1958 and became starting quarterback in 1962. For seven years he led the

Riders, becoming the finest quarterback yet produced in Canada. He coached the Toronto Argonauts in 1975-76 with little success.

JACKSON, WILLIAM HENRY (1861-1952), a leader of the NORTH WEST REBELLION of 1885, secretary to LOUIS RIEL; also known as Honoré-Joseph Jaxon. Born in Toronto, Jackson was a local farm leader in Saskatchewan when he was attracted to Riel's cause in 1884. He escaped punishment for his role in the rebellion by reason of insanity. In later life, he was a union organizer in the United States.

JAMES BAY AGREEMENT, treaty signed in 1975 between the province of Quebec and Cree and Inuit living in northern Quebec adjacent to James Bay. The agreement transferred aboriginal rights from the native people to Quebec in return for $225 million, hunting and fishing rights, and substantial self-government. The treaty was necessary to pave the way for the massive JAMES BAY PROJECT announced by Liberal Premier ROBERT BOURASSA in 1971.

JAMES BAY PROJECT, a massive construction project to harness the hydroelectric potential of several river systems emptying into James Bay, announced in 1971 by Quebec Liberal Premier ROBERT BOURASSA. The work got underway after negotiation of the JAMES BAY AGREEMENT between Quebec and the native people of the region. The project has diverted rivers, created the world's largest underground powerhouse, and built dams and dikes. Most of the power generated by the project is intended to be sold to customers in the United States.

JAMIESON, DONALD (1921-86), politician. Born at St John's, Nfld, he was a prominent radio broadcaster in the 1940s and an opponent of Confederation with Canada. He was first elected to Parliament as a Liberal in 1966 and held a number of cabinet posts until 1979, including secretary of state for external affairs for the last three years. He led the Newfoundland Liberals to defeat in the 1979 provincial election and in 1983 he was named high commissioner to Britain, a post he held until the Conservative government took over in 1984.

courtesy Vancouver Public Library/1364

Japanese Canadians being checked before evacuation, 1942

JAPANESE EVACUATION, evacuation of all Japanese Canadians living on the west coast into the interior, ordered by the federal government in Feb. 1942. The order was partly the result of fears that an invasion of the west coast by Japanese forces was imminent – and that Japanese Canadians would aid the invaders – and partly the result of the deeply ingrained, anti-oriental racism that had existed on the coast for decades. The evacuation was carried out under the authority of the WAR MEASURES ACT and affected more than 20,000 people, most of whom were moved to small communities in the British Columbia interior. After the evacuation, the property of the Japanese Canadians was seized and sold by the government at bargain basement prices. Although many of the internees returned to the coast after the war, the government offered virtually no compensation for its seizure of their property. *See also* INTERNMENT.

JENKINS, FERGUSON ARTHUR (1943-), baseball player. Born at Chatham, Ont., he was the finest pitcher produced in Canada. In seasons with the Chicago Cubs and Texas Rangers, he won 284 games, won over 20 games in six different years, and captured the Cy Young Award in 1971. He retired as an active major league player in 1984.

JENNESS, DIAMOND (1886-1969), anthropologist. Born at Wellington, N.Z., Jenness came to Canada in 1913 to join VILHJALMUR STEFANSSON's expedition to the Arctic. He joined the National Museum of Canada after World War I service, and began his impressive series of publications on Canadian Inuit and Indians. In 1926 he became chief anthropologist at the museum, and he drafted the legislation protecting archaeological sites in the north.

JESUITS' ESTATES QUESTION, political controversy over the 1888 Quebec act to compensate the Jesuit order for the confiscation of property by the British crown after the Conquest. The monetary settlement, mediated by Pope Leo XIII at the request of Premier HONORÉ MERCIER, provided $160,000 for the Jesuits, gave Univ. Laval $140,000, other orders $100,000, and Protestant schools in Quebec $60,000. The papal "interference" produced cries of outrage from proponents of NATIVISM in Ontario, and some organized the EQUAL RIGHTS ASSN as a result.

JODOIN, CLAUDE (1913-75), labour leader. Born in Westmount, Que., he worked as an organizer for the International Ladies Garment Workers Union and later became involved in the TRADES AND LABOUR CONGRESS. He was elected president of the TLC in 1954 and was first president of the CANADIAN LABOUR CONGRESS from 1956 to 1966.

JOHN LABATT CORP., holding company. The company was established by John Kinder Labatt, an Ontario farmer, who purchased a small brewery near London, Canada West, in 1847. The company went public in 1945 but with the Labatt family maintaining a controlling interest in it.

JOHNSON, BYRON INGEMAR, "BOSS" (1890-1964), premier of British Columbia. Born at Victoria, he became a partner in a building supply business following service in World War I. He entered the B.C. legislature as a Liberal in 1933 but was defeated in 1937. During World War II he was in charge of airfield construction in the province. Re-elected in 1945, he succeeded JOHN HART as premier of a coalition government in 1947 until defeated by W.A.C. BENNETT'S SOCIAL CREDIT party in the 1952 provincial election.

JOHNSON, DANIEL (1915-68), premier of Quebec. Born at Ste-Anne-de-Danville, Que., he attended the Univ. de Montréal. Elected to the Quebec legislature in 1946 for the UNION NATIONALE, he became parliamentary secretary to

Premier MAURICE DUPLESSIS in 1955 and in 1956 entered the cabinet as minister for hydraulic resources. Johnson won leadership of the UN in 1961, rebuilt the party, and led it to victory over JEAN LESAGE's Liberals in 1966. Not a separatist, he vigorously fought for Quebec's rights, most notably in a televised confrontation with then minister of justice PIERRE TRUDEAU.

JOHNSON, EDWARD (1878-1959), opera singer. Born at Guelph, Ont., he trained in Italy and made his debut as a tenor in Padua. In 1919 he went to the Chicago Opera and three years later to the Metropolitan. In 1935 he became general manager of the Metropolitan Opera, a post he held for 15 years. His daughter Fiorenza married GEORGE DREW.

JOHNSON, EMILY PAULINE (1861-1913), poet. Daughter of a Six Nations chief and an Englishwoman, she was educated at the Brantford Normal School. Her poetry was extraordinarily popular in her day, and she toured widely, giving readings. Her first book was *White Wampum* (1895); her collected poems are in *Flint and Feather* (1912).

JOHNSTON, FRANCIS HANS (1888-1949), artist. Franz Johnston, born at Toronto, was a commercial artist at Grip Ltd from 1908 to 1910, when he left to study in Philadelphia. He worked in New York, returning to Canada in 1915. He was commissioned in 1917 as a war artist. Although a charter member of the GROUP OF SEVEN, Johnston participated only in the group's first exhibition and resigned in 1924. Between 1922 and 1924 he was principal of the Winnipeg School of Art and from 1927 to 1929 taught at the Ontario College of Art. His notable works include *Fire-Swept Algoma* (1920) and *The Fire Ranger* (1920).

JONES, JOHN WALTER (1878-1954), premier of Prince Edward Island. Jones was born at Pownal, P.E.I., and educated at the univs. of Acadia, Toronto, Chicago, Cornell, Columbia, and Clark. He worked for the U.S. Department of Agriculture in 1911-12 before returning to P.E.I. in 1914. He entered the legislature as a Liberal in 1935 after failing to win a federal seat as a Progressive in 1921. He was premier 1943-53, and was made a senator in 1953.

JUDICIAL COMMITTEE OF THE PRIVY COUNCIL, the court of last resort for Canada until 1949. Situated in London, the JCPC was composed of British high court judges, and cases could be brought to it either directly from lower courts in Canada or from the SUPREME COURT of Canada. The JCPC was important in determining the nature of Canada's governmental system because of the cases brought before it arising out of jurisdictional disputes between provincial and federal governments. In early cases such as RUSSELL V. THE QUEEN, the council interpreted the BRITISH NORTH AMERICA ACT in such a way as to sustain the broad powers given the federal government at Confederation. But later, with cases such as TORONTO ELECTRIC COMMISSIONERS V. SNIDER, the JCPC gave a much narrower interpretation of federal powers and provincial powers were expanded as a result. With passage of the STATUTE OF WESTMINSTER, Canada acquired the power to abolish appeals to the JCPC, an action taken only in 1949.

JULIEN, OCTAVE-HENRI (1852-1908), illustrator. Born at Quebec City, he worked as an engraver-lithographer. He accompanied the NORTH-WEST MOUNTED POLICE expedition west in 1874 to produce drawings for the *Canadian Illustrated News*, and became the art director of the Montreal *Star* in 1888. His cartoons of government figures became extraordinarily popular and are still frequently reproduced.

JUTRA, CLAUDE (1930-87), filmmaker. Born in Montreal, he joined the NATIONAL FILM BOARD in 1956 and later turned to feature films. His *Mon Oncle Antoine* (1971) is arguably the best Canadian film yet, and *Kamouraska* (1973) was thought by many to be equally good, although *Surfacing* (1981) was not hailed. He also produced television films for the CANADIAN BROADCASTING CORP. Suffering from Alzheimer's disease, he disappeared in 1987 and was found drowned.

KAPYONG, BATTLE OF, 1951, a major battle fought by the Princess Patricia's Canadian Light Infantry during the KOREAN WAR. As part of the 27th British Commonwealth Infantry Brigade, the Princess Pats had the task of protecting the withdrawal of a Korean division under heavy Chinese pressure. Situated on hills on the west side of the Kapyong River valley, the Princess Pats fought superbly through the night of 24-25 April and halted the Chinese advance. Casualties were 10 killed and 23 wounded.

KARSH, YOUSUF (1908–), photographer. Born in Armenia, Karsh came to Canada in 1924. He opened a studio in Ottawa in 1932 and cultivated the powerful. His glowering photo of Winston Churchill in 1941 established his reputation. He has published several books of his work and his reputation for portrait photography remains high.

KEEFER, THOMAS COLTRIN (1821-1915), civil engineer. Born at Thorold, Upper Canada, Keefer was one of Canada's first experts on railroading. He published *The Philosophy of Railroads* (1849), extolling the construction of railways for progress and prosperity. He worked on a variety of railway and hydraulic engineering projects in subsequent years, and designed the water system of Hamilton, Ont. He helped found and was first president of the Canadian Society of Civil Engineers in 1887.

KEENLEYSIDE, HUGH LLEWELLYN (1898–), public servant. Born at Toronto and raised in British Columbia, Keenleyside attended the Univ. of British Columbia and Clark Univ. from which he received a doctorate in history. He joined the Department of External Affairs in 1928, and served in Japan, Ottawa, and Mexico. After the war he became deputy minister of mines and resources and had great influence on northern development. He then worked for the United Nations and for British Columbia Hydro as chair of its Power Authority. He helped negotiate the COLUMBIA RIVER TREATY. A committed and liberal man, Keenleyside did not rise as high as his talents justified.

KELSO, JOHN JOSEPH (1864-1935), social reformer. Born at Dundalk, Ireland, he was a reporter for Toronto newspapers. Alarmed at the state of the poor, he founded the Humane Society, the Fresh Air Fund, and the Santa Claus Fund in 1887-8 in an attempt to alleviate conditions. He then created the Children's Aid Society in 1891 and two years later was named the superintendent of neglected children in Ontario. He spread the Children's Aid Society across the province and advocated reform of children's punishment and adoption.

KEMP, SIR ALBERT EDWARD (1858-1929), politician. Born at Clarenceville, Canada East, he built a flourishing sheet metal operation in Toronto. He was elected to Parliament as a Conservative in 1900, became minister of militia in 1916 and went to London in 1917 as minister for the overseas military forces of Canada. In England, his main task was to restore order where SAM HUGHES and his cronies had created chaos, a task he accomplished. He became a senator in 1921.

KENT, THOMAS WORRAL (1922–), journalist, public servant. Born at Stafford, Eng., Kent attended Oxford Univ. and came to Canada as editor of the Winnipeg *Free Press* in 1954. He became a close adviser to Prime Minister LESTER PEARSON and was deputy minister in two departments from 1966 to 1971. He then headed the Cape Breton Development Corp. to 1977 and SYDNEY STEEL CORP. to 1979. In 1980, he joined the faculty at Dalhousie Univ. and published a first-rate memoir in 1988.

KIERANS, ERIC WILLIAM (1914–), businessman, politician, born in Montreal. He was president of the MONTREAL STOCK EXCHANGE when Quebec Liberal Premier JEAN LESAGE appointed him minister of revenue in Aug. 1963. In 1965 Lesage named him minister of health, a post he held until the defeat of the Liberal government the following year. Kierans was a strong supporter of the QUIET REVOLUTION, but he opposed his friend RENÉ LÉVESQUE when he opted for SOVEREIGNTY-ASSOCIATION in 1968. That same year Kierans was elected to the House of Commons,

serving as postmaster general and minister of communications in the Liberal government of Prime Minister PIERRE TRUDEAU until 1971.

KICKING HORSE PASS, pass through the Rocky Mountains from Lake Louise, Alta, to Field, B.C. The pass was used by the CANADIAN PACIFIC RAILWAY and the TRANS-CANADA HIGHWAY.

KILLAM, IZAAK WALTON (1885-1955), capitalist. Born at Yarmouth, N.S., he worked at the Union Bank of Halifax before moving to Montreal. He managed the London office of MAX AITKEN's Royal Securities from 1909 to 1913, becoming president in 1915 and owner in 1919. An entrepreneurial genius, Killam built an enormous financial empire in Canada and Latin America. With holdings in publishing, utilities, construction firms, pulp and paper, and the film industry, he was probably the richest Canadian of his day. After his death, inheritance taxes on his estate helped establish the CANADA COUNCIL, and since 1973, at the bequest of his widow, Dorothy Killam (d. 1965), the council's Killam Program has awarded fellowships to support the work of eminent scholars in the humanities, social sciences, and natural sciences.

Mackenzie King chatting with Franklin Roosevelt, 1936

KING, WILLIAM LYON MACKENZIE (1874-1950), prime minister of Canada. Canada's longest reigning prime minister was born at Berlin (Kitchener), Ont., the grandson of William Lyon Mackenzie, leader of the 1837 Rebellion. He attended the univs. of Toronto, Chicago, and Harvard. In 1900 King entered government service as the first deputy minister in the new Department of Labour and edited the *Labour Gazette*. Elected to the House of Commons in 1908 as a Liberal, he became SIR WILFRID LAURIER's minister of labour in 1909 but was defeated in the 1911 RECIPROCITY election and went to work for the Rockefeller Foundation as a labour consultant. In 1919, after Laurier's death, King won a party convention and became Liberal leader. He subsequently won the 1921 federal election, defeating ARTHUR MEIGHEN and the Conservative remnants of the UNION GOVERNMENT. He was then victorious in the elections of 1925, 1926, 1935, 1940, and 1945, thanks in substantial part to the unwavering support of French Canada, losing only in 1930 to R.B. BENNETT.

His early governments were cautious and undistinguished, although he showed great guile and nerve in his handling of the KING-BYNG AFFAIR in 1926. After the 1935 victory, King's government began to show interest in Keynesian economics and tinkered with deficit financing, as well as implementing such measures as the NATIONAL HOUSING ACT. King came into his own during WORLD WAR II when his administration, certainly the strongest in Canadian history, ran a superb economic war effort and mounted a massive military force without running aground on the shoals of CONSCRIPTION, despite the political crises of 1942 and 1944. As secretary of state for external affairs (a post he held until 1946), King presided over the emergence of Canada as an independent nation within the Commonwealth, a process he had directed and controlled through the CHANAK CRISIS, the BALFOUR DECLARATION, and constant reiteration that "PARLIAMENT WILL DECIDE." King also brought Canada closer to the United States through his friendship with President Franklin Roosevelt and such measures as trade agreements in the 1930s and the PERMANENT JOINT BOARD ON DEFENCE and the HYDE PARK DECLARATION. King's election victory in 1945 was testimony to his political skills. Canadians did not admire King, but they recognized his abilities and his concern for Canadian unity.

Leader of the Liberal party for 29 years, King retired in 1948, passing the torch to his chosen successor, LOUIS ST LAURENT, at a Liberal convention. He wrote a number books, including *The Secret of Heroism* (1906), INDUSTRY AND HUMANITY (1918), and *Canada at Britain's Side* (1941), and for most of his life kept a remarkable diary, portions of which have been published.

KING-BYNG AFFAIR, political crisis which erupted in the summer of 1926 and which pitted Liberal Prime Minister MACKENZIE KING against governor general LORD BYNG. The crisis had its roots in the 1925 federal election in which King's Liberals placed second to ARTHUR MEIGHEN's Conservatives in the number of seats won. King clung to power with the expectation of support from the PROGRESSIVE PARTY. When, in June 1926, his government appeared in danger of losing a motion of censure, King sought a dissolution. Byng refused and called on Meighen to form a government. In a minority situation, Meighen was defeated in the House and soon sought a dissolution himself. In the ensuing general election King claimed that the governor general had interferred in the political process by refusing to grant him a dissolution, and the Liberals won the election. Henceforth the governor general ceased being a representative of the British government in Canada, a role then assumed by a British HIGH COMMISSIONER. The first high commissioner to Canada was appointed in 1927.

"KING OR CHAOS," campaign slogan used by MACKENZIE KING's Liberals in the 1935 election. The Liberals had few policies to deal with the GREAT DEPRESSION, yet managed to take 173 seats, completely destroying R.B. BENNETT and the Conservatives.

KIRK, LAWRENCE ELDRED (1886-1969), agronomist. Born in Bracebridge, Ont., he was primarily responsible for the development of Fairway, a crested wheat grass used by Prairie grain farmers to control soil erosion. He had worked for the DOMINION EXPERIMENTAL FARM for years before developing Fairway in 1932 and he is credited with much of the research on grasses that was applied by the PRAIRIE FARM REHABILITATION ADMINISTRATION to fight the DUST BOWL of the 1930s.

KIRKLAND LAKE STRIKE, strike between Nov. 1941 and Jan. 1942 of gold miners belonging to the International Union of Mine, Mill and Smelter workers against eight gold mines in the Kirkland Lake region. The total failure of the strike angered organized labour across Canada, which accused Prime Minister MACKENZIE KING of a lack of regard for labour during wartime. One result was King's replacement of Norman

McLarty with labour leader HUMPHREY MITCHELL as labour minister.

KLEIN, ABRAHAM MOSES (1909-72), poet. Born in Russia, he grew up in the Montreal Jewish ghetto and studied at McGill Univ. and the Univ. de Montréal. He supported himself by practising law, but his real interest was in writing, the CO-OPERATIVE COMMONWEALTH FEDERATION, and Zionist causes. He edited the *Canadian Jewish Chronicle* and ghosted speeches for SAMUEL BRONFMAN. His poetry worked over Jewish themes. *Hath Not a Jew* . . . (1940), *The Hitleriad* (1944), and *The Rocking Chair* (1948) established his reputation.

courtesy RCMP Photo Archives

Quiet scene at the Sulphur Creek NWMP post, NWT, during the Klondike Gold Rush

KLONDIKE GOLD RUSH, gold stampede begun in 1896 when gold was discovered on a tributary of the Klondike River. Word of the find reached the west coast in mid-1897 and some 100,000 joined the rush to the north. Men and women travelled overland from Edmonton or by sea via Skagway, Alaska, over the CHILKOOT TRAIL. The city of Dawson sprang up instantly, its population reaching 30,000 and providing every manner of pleasure and vice known to man (and woman). The YUKON FIELD FORCE, sent by Ottawa to maintain federal authority and to discourage American adventurism, presided. By the turn of the century, the rush was over, some $5 million in gold having been extracted.

KNIGHTS OF LABOR, labour union organized in the United States in the late 1860s and in Canada in the 1870s. The Knights wanted to bring all wage earners into one union and worked for various reform measures such as temperance and votes for women. Officially the Knights rejected strikes as a means of settling wage disputes. In Canada the order eventually included over 400 local assemblies; it grew particularly strong in Quebec because its anti-strike, anti-international union attitude appealed greatly to Catholic workers. The Knights were part of the TRADES AND LABOUR CONGRESS of Canada when it was organized in 1886 but were expelled from the TLC after the BERLIN CONVENTION of 1902. They then joined the National Trades and Labour Congress until they disappeared before World War I.

KNIGHTS OF ST CRISPIN, labour union, formed by shoemakers in the United States in 1867, which by 1870 had 16 locals in Canada. The union was similar to many early craft unions in its use of elaborate rituals and the establishment of a burial society.

KNOWLES, STANLEY HOWARD (1908-), politician. Before retiring in 1984, Knowles sat in the House of Commons for almost 40 years. Born at Los Angeles, he came to Canada in 1924 and was a United Church minister at Winnipeg before joining the CO-OPERATIVE COMMONWEALTH FEDERATION in 1935. Elected to the House of Commons in J.S. WOODSWORTH's Winnipeg North seat in a 1942 by-election, Knowles was defeated in 1958, but not before his mastery of procedure had played an important part in the PIPELINE DEBATE of 1956. From 1958 to 1962 he served as executive vice-president of the CANADIAN LABOUR CONGRESS and chaired the founding convention of the NEW DEMOCRATIC PARTY in 1961. Re-elected to Parliament in 1962, he retired from politics in 1984 having suffered a stroke in 1981. Parliament made him an honorary officer of the House. In 1961 he published *The New Party*.

KOERNER, LEON JOSEPH (1892-1972), lumberman. Born in what is now Czechoslovakia, Koerner came to Canada in 1938. The next year, he bought a mill in New Westminster, B.C., applied European techniques, and built a prosperous lumber empire. He became a major philanthropist in the areas of education and the arts.

KOREAN WAR, fought between United Nations forces and the North Korean-Chinese Communist armies, 1950-3. On 25 June 1950, North Korea invaded South Korea. The United States secured the UN Security Council's authority, when the Soviet Union boycotted the council's meetings, for member states to assist South Korea. Initially Canada contributed three destroyers and an air transport squadron, but the United States, its forces under heavy pressure from the North Koreans, made demands of Canada for a large army contribution. On 7 Aug. Prime Minister LOUIS ST LAURENT announced plans to recruit a Canadian Army Special Force for Korea. By Sept., after U.S. General Douglas MacArthur's brilliantly successful Inchon invasion and after the North Koreans were forced back over the 38th parallel, it seemed possible that Canadian forces might not be ready in time to see action. But in late Oct., large Chinese Communist forces crossed the Yalu River and the UN forces were driven south.

The first Canadian unit to arrive was the Princess Patricia's Canadian Light Infantry which landed in Feb. 1951. In May, the remainder of the 25th Canadian Infantry Brigade reached Korea. The Princess Pats fought well at KAPYONG in April 1951, but the brigade as a whole engaged mainly in small but vicious struggles as the battle line stabilized close to the 38th parallel. In all, 21,940 Canadian troops served in Korea along with 3621 naval personnel and a few ROYAL CANADIAN AIR FORCE pilots on exchange with the U.S. Air Force before the war drew to a close with an armistice on 8 June 1953.

On the political front, secretary of state for external affairs LESTER PEARSON attempted to moderate American leadership, which Ottawa believed was sometimes too aggressive. At the UN, Pearson earned the enmity of U.S. secretary of state Dean Acheson with his efforts to achieve a truce.

KRIEGHOFF, CORNELIUS DAVID (1815-72), painter. Born in Holland and trained in Germany, he came to America in the 1830s and moved to the Montreal area about 1840. His paintings of habitant life became immensely popular in his day and have continued to be so popular that forgeries are widespread.

KURELEK, WILLIAM (1927-77), painter. Born near Whitford, Alta, of Ukrainian immigrant parents, he suffered from psychiatric problems but established himself as an important painter in Toronto by the early 1960s. His paintings, done in a naive style, portrayed complex messages and became popular, although some were extraordinarily didactic. He wrote an autobiography and a number of illustrated books.

LABATT BREWING CO., *see* JOHN LABATT CORP.

LABELLE, FRANÇOIS-XAVIER-ANTOINE (1833-91), colonizer-priest. Born at Ste-Rose, Lower Canada, educated at the Collège de Ste-Thérèse, and ordained in 1856, Labelle worked with great energy to discourage *Canadien* emigration to the cotton mills of the "Boston States" and to encourage the settlement of areas of Quebec north of Montreal. In 1888 the government of HONORÉ MERCIER named him deputy minister of agriculture and colonization.

LABERGE, LOUIS (1924-), labour leader. Born at Ste-Martine, Que., and an aviation mechanic, he was elected president of the Fédération des travailleurs du Québec / Quebec Federation of Labour in 1964, a position he held in 1988. He fought inroads from the CONFÉDÉRATION DES SYNDICATS NATIONAUX / CONFEDERATION OF NATIONAL TRADE UNIONS by bringing more nationalist rhetoric and objectives into the QFL.

LABINE, GILBERT (1890-1977), prospector. Born in Westmeath, Ont., he became well known for the Eldorado Gold Mine which he formed in 1926 with his brother. The Manitoba mine was profitable at first and became the base of the Eldorado Mining Co. LaBine continued prospecting and made a major discovery in 1930 at Great Bear Lake where he found large silver and pitchblende deposits. He set up a refinery at Port Hope, Ont., to produce radium from pitchblende but had a difficult time selling the product until nuclear weapons research during WORLD WAR II created a demand for uranium. The federal government bought control of his company in 1942 and nationalized it two years later as Eldorado Mining and Refining Ltd. LaBine stayed as president until 1947.

LABOUR GAZETTE, a monthly journal published by the federal Department of Labour from 1900 to 1978. It was established at the suggestion of MACKENZIE KING, who was its first editor until 1908. It collected and published a variety of statistics including wholesale and retail costs of commodities and reports on strikes and lockouts.

LABOUR DAY, holiday honouring working people. In 1894 Parliament proclaimed the first Monday in Sept. to be Labour Day, in contrast to the European practice of celebrating 1 May as a labour holiday.

LABOUR PROGRESSIVE PARTY, name adopted by the COMMUNIST PARTY of Canada when it was outlawed in 1940. The LPP elected FRED ROSE to Parliament in a 1943 Montreal by-election, but the party's growth was stalled by the GOUZENKO AFFAIR, Rose's conviction for spying, and the cold war.

LAFLÈCHE, LEO RICHER (1888-1956), soldier. Born in Kansas, he came to Canada as a child. He joined the civil service, then served overseas in World War I and was severely wounded. He was president of the [ROYAL] CANADIAN LEGION from 1928 to 1931, and was deputy minister of national defence from 1932 to 1940. From 1942 to 1945, General LaFlèche served in the cabinet as minister of national war services, and after the war he was an ambassador abroad until 1955.

LAFLÈCHE, LOUIS-FRANÇOIS (1818-98), Roman Catholic bishop. Born at Ste-Anne-de-la-Pérade, Lower Canada, he was ordained in 1844. He served as a missionary in the west, as a professor at the Collège de Nicolet, and as bishop of Trois-Rivières from 1867. A stern supporter of ULTRAMONTANISM, he battled liberalism and led the forces of reaction. He fought WILFRID LAURIER's policy on the MANITOBA SCHOOLS QUESTION but could not secure Rome's support for his unyielding stand.

LAMARSH, JUDY VERLYN (1924-80), politician. Born at Niagara Falls, Ont., and educated at the Univ. of Toronto, she served in the CANADIAN WOMEN'S ARMY CORPS in World War II. She was called to the bar in 1950, was elected to the House of Commons as a Liberal in 1960, and entered the cabinet in 1963 as health and welfare minister. She was secretary of state during the preparations for the CENTENNIAL and left politics after PIERRE TRUDEAU's selection as Liberal leader. She then wrote a revealing memoir and a novel.

LAMONTAGNE, MAURICE (1917-83), politician. Educated at the Univ. Laval and Harvard as an economist, he taught at Laval until 1954 when he joined the public service as an adviser to Prime Minister ST LAURENT. He was an adviser to Liberal leader LESTER PEARSON from 1958 to 1963, and won election to Parliament as a Liberal in 1963. He held two cabinet posts but was tarred in a minor scandal in 1965. He was appointed a senator in 1967. A committed federalist, he argued tellingly against separatism.

LAMPMAN, ARCHIBALD (1861-99), poet. Lampman was born in Morpeth, Canada West, and educated at Trinity College. He then joined the Post Office department in Ottawa. He wrote three volumes of poetry, *Among the Millet* (1888), *Lyrics of Earth* (1893), and *Alcyone* (1899), that led to his being called the "Canadian Keats." He was the best of the Canadian nature poets.

LAND CLAIMS, claims made by native peoples arising out of their aboriginal title. These claims are usually made during negotiations with governments over the existence or size of a reserve. *See also* INDIAN TREATIES.

LANDYMORE, WILLIAM MOSS (1916–), naval officer. He joined the ROYAL CANADIAN NAVY in 1936 and served through WORLD WAR II and the KOREAN WAR. After a variety of postings, in 1965 he became head of Maritime Command, based in Halifax, and led the opposition to defence minister PAUL HELLYER's plans for UNIFICATION. He retired prematurely in 1966.

LANE, GEORGE (1856-1925), rancher. Born in Des Moines, Iowa, Lane came to Canada in 1883 and established a ranch in southern Alberta in 1891. He was one of the BIG FOUR CATTLEMEN who helped finance the first CALGARY STAMPEDE.

LANGEVIN, SIR HECTOR-LOUIS (1826-1906), politician. Born at Quebec City and trained in the law, he worked as a journalist, editor, and newspaper owner. He was elected mayor of Quebec in 1857 and in the same year to the assembly of the Province of Canada. He held cabinet posts in pre-Confederation governments, attended the Charlottetown, Quebec, and London conferences that created CONFEDERATION, and was a member of Prime Minister JOHN A. MACDONALD's first cabinet. He succeeded GEORGE-ÉTIENNE

Sir Hector Langevin

courtesy National Archives of Canada/C-23373

CARTIER as Quebec leader in 1873, found himself implicated in the PACIFIC SCANDAL, and withdrew from politics. In 1878, however, he was re-elected, headed major patronage departments, and, again implicated in scandal, was forced out of the cabinet in 1891.

LANGTON, JOHN (1808-94), public servant. Born in England and educated at Cambridge Univ., he came to Canada in 1833 and settled near Peterborough. He was elected to the assembly of the Province of Canada in 1851, and in 1855 he was appointed first auditor of public accounts. In 1867, he became dominion auditor general, a post he held until 1878 while simultaneously being deputy minister of finance.

LANSDOWNE, HENRY CHARLES KEITH PETTY-FITZMAURICE, 5TH MARQUESS OF (1845-1927), governor general of Canada. He came to Canada as governor general in 1883 after service as under-secretary for war and under-secretary for India in Gladstone's Liberal government. He remained in Ottawa for five years, presiding over the fierce politics that surrounded the final stages of the construction of the CANADIAN PACIFIC RAILWAY and the NORTH-WEST REBELLION. After his departure from Canada he became viceroy of India.

LAPALME, GEORGES-ÉMILE (1907-), politician. Born in Montreal and educated at the Univ. de Montréal, he was elected to the House

of Commons as a Liberal in 1945. In 1950, he became Quebec Liberal leader, won election to the legislature in 1953, but stepped down in 1958 after two defeats. In the JEAN LESAGE government, he was deputy premier, attorney general, and minister of cultural affairs. The federal government made him chair of the Canadian Film Development Corp. in 1968.

Ernest Lapointe

courtesy NFB

LAPOINTE, ERNEST (1876-1941), politician. Born at St-Éloi, Que., and educated at Univ. Laval, Lapointe was a lawyer when first elected to Parliament in 1904 as a Liberal. He played an increasingly important role as an opposition member under WILFRID LAURIER, and MACKENZIE KING made him his key Quebec adviser once he formed a government. As minister of justice from 1924, Lapointe had the virtual deciding voice on questions involving Quebec, and he shared King's views on Canadian autonomy. In 1939, he was instrumental in bringing a united country into WORLD WAR II, thanks to his assurances to French Canada that there would be no overseas CONSCRIPTION in this war. He died before that pledge was broken.

LAPORTE, PIERRE (1921-70), politician. Born at Montreal, he worked as a journalist for *Le Devoir* from 1945 to 1961, becoming one of the fiercest opponents of Quebec premier MAURICE DUPLESSIS and his government. Elected to the provincial legislature as a Liberal in 1961, he held two portfolios under JEAN LESAGE. After he failed to win the Liberal leadership in 1970, he served as labour minister under ROBERT BOURASSA. During the OCTOBER CRISIS of 1970, he was kidnapped by the FRONT DE LIBÉRATION DU QUÉBEC and murdered one week later.

LASH, ZEBULON AITON (1846-1920), lawyer. Born and educated in Newfoundland, he joined the federal public service in 1872 and was deputy minister of justice, 1876-82. He then began practising law in Toronto and became the most important corporation counsel in the country, representing the CANADIAN NORTHERN RAILWAY, the Canadian Bank of Commerce and the like. Lash was also a strong supporter of the IMPERIAL FEDERATION LEAGUE and he broke with the Liberals in the RECIPROCITY election of 1911, becoming one of the TORONTO EIGHTEEN.

LASKIN, BORA (1912-84), lawyer, judge. Born in Fort William, Ont., he attended the Univ. of Toronto, Osgoode Hall, and Harvard Univ. He taught law at the Univ. of Toronto from 1940 to 1965 (except for four years at Osgoode Hall), establishing a reputation as the country's foremost constitutional lawyer and expert on civil rights. In 1965, he was appointed to the Ontario Court of Appeal and five years later to the SUPREME COURT of Canada. He became chief justice in 1973.

LAST SPIKE, iron railway spike driven by DONALD A. SMITH of the CANADIAN PACIFIC RAILWAY to mark the completion of the CPR main line from Ontario to the west coast, on 7 Nov. 1885. The event took place at CRAIGELLACHIE, B.C., in the EAGLE PASS. Contrary to popular belief, the last spike was iron, not gold.

LAURENCE, MARGARET (1926-87), author. Born at Neepawa, Man., and educated at United College, Margaret Wemyss married Jack Laurence in 1947. They moved to England and then Africa where he worked on water development and she began to write. In 1954, she published translations of Somali folk tales; this was followed by *This Side Jordan* (1960) and *The Tomorrow-Tamer* (1963), short stories set in Ghana. Her first book to attract national attention was *The Stone Angel* (1964), followed by *A*

courtesy *Quill & Quire*/photo by Lori Spring

Margaret Laurence

Jest of God (1966) which became a film. *The Diviners* (1974), which followed other writings, definitely established Laurence as one of Canada's great writers. She was active in the Writers' Union of Canada and a strong supporter of disarmament.

LAURENDEAU, JOSEPH-EDMOND-ANDRÉ (1912-68), journalist. André Laurendeau was born at Montreal and educated at the Univ. de Montréal and in France. He returned to Canada to become editor of *L'Action nationale*, a nationalist magazine that propounded social Catholicism. An anti-conscriptionist, Laurendeau helped create the LIGUE POUR LA DÉFENCE DU CANADA to mobilize the "non" vote in the CONSCRIPTION plebiscite of 1942. Its success led to the formation of the BLOC POPULAIRE CANADIEN of which Laurendeau became provincial leader in 1944. He won a seat in the legislature in the election that year, but the party made little headway. Laurendeau resigned from the legislature in 1947 to join *Le Devoir* of which he became editor in 1958. He fought against Quebec premier MAURICE DUPLESSIS, was disturbed by the DIEFENBAKER government's lack of understanding of Quebec, and accepted Prime Minister LESTER PEARSON's offer in 1963 to co-chair the ROYAL COM-

MISSION ON BILINGUALISM AND BICULTURALISM. His diaries and papers reflect his growing despair at English Canada's inability to comprehend Quebec.

LAURENTIAN THESIS, theory advanced by some Canadian historians and economists to explain the political evolution of Canada. The Laurentian thesis is based on the idea that Canada developed along lines of trade and communication that linked metropolitian centres in Europe, principally London, with the Canadian interior via the St Lawrence River. Economist HAROLD A. INNIS was one of the first to explore the idea, but historian DONALD G. CREIGHTON became its champion. The theory was used to claim that the east-to-west political structure of Canada was not "artificial" and did not fly in the face of "natural" north-south lines of communication that ought to have linked the British-American colonies to the United States – the CONTINENTALIST interpretation of Canadian development. *See also* METRO-POLITAN-HINTERLAND THESIS.

courtesy National Archives of Canada/C-1969

Wilfred Laurier as a young man

LAURIER, SIR WILFRID (1841-1919), prime minister of Canada. Born at St-Lin, Canada East, Laurier became Canada's first French-speaking prime minister and a much-loved figure. He perfected his English at Montreal's McGill Univ. where he studied law, graduating in 1864. He practised in that city and, when his health failed, in Arthabaska. There he edited a

It took Laurier nine years to win power. The government of JOHN A. MACDONALD had been fraying at the edges for years, particularly since the 1885 execution of LOUIS RIEL, but even after the Old Chieftain's death Conservatism remained a powerful force. By 1896, however, Laurier had managed to moderate the free trade zealotry of his Ontario supporters and had obfuscated his party's policy on the contentious MANITOBA SCHOOLS QUESTION sufficiently to allow Liberals in English and French Canada to feel comfortable. The result was victory at the polls.

For the next 15 years Laurier governed with a sure hand, convinced that the 20th century was Canada's. He resolved the schools question and encouraged the exploitation of the country's resources. He granted Alberta and Saskatchewan provincial status in 1905, but not before losing one of his most powerful ministers, CLIFFORD SIFTON, to a recurrence of difficulties over denominational schooling in those provinces. Under his administration, two new transcontinental railways joined the CANADIAN PACIFIC RAILWAY, more than the still lightly populated nation could support. He steered a course between nationalism and imperialism during the BOER WAR, sending volunteers but resisting the demands of English Canada. His government sought to develop a pan-Canadian nationalism, but his negotiation of a RECIPROCITY arrangement with the United States in 1911, at the same time as he was resisting British demands for contributions to the Royal Navy, allowed the opposition to combine. ROBERT BORDEN's Conservatives, joined by HENRI BOURASSA and his *nationalistes*, toppled Laurier. In English Canada, the cry had been "No Truck or Trade with the Yankees." In Quebec, opponents had charged that "M. Laurier's newspaper, upheld the policies of the PARTI ROUGE, and opposed CONFEDERATION. In 1871, he won election to the provincial legislature, and three years later to the House of Commons. Intelligent and capable of brilliant oratory, Laurier did not instantly make his mark. In 1877, however, his speech in Quebec City on political liberalism firmly linked the LIBERAL PARTY to the moderate traditions of British liberalism. Soon after he was brought into Prime Minister ALEXANDER MACKENZIE's cabinet, and ten years later, when EDWARD BLAKE stepped down as party leader, Laurier became the first French Canadian to head one of the national parties.

navy," the small Canadian navy that Laurier had begun in order to resist British demands for Canadian contributions to the Royal Navy, would lead to conscription. "Perhaps we have governed too long," a wistful Laurier said when the results were in.

For the remaining years of his life, he led his party in opposition. The dreadful WORLD WAR I years and the resurgence of difficulties over schooling, this time primarily in Ontario, as well as the CONSCRIPTION CRISIS of 1917 split his party into linguistic wings, and it was crushed by Borden's UNION GOVERNMENT in that year's general election. Two years later, at 77, Laurier died in Ottawa. Dispirited and saddened by the war years, he nonetheless left his party a great reputation for conciliation to build upon. *See also* AUTONOMY BILLS; CUSTOMS UNION; NATIONAL TRANSCONTINENTAL RAILWAY.

LAVALLÉE, CALIXA (1842-91), musician, composer. Born at Verchères, Canada East, Lavallée studied music in the United States and Europe. Although he lived much of his adult life in Boston, Lavallée is best remembered for composing the music to "O CANADA," initially a popular song and now the national anthem of the country.

LAVERGNE, ARMAND-RENAUD (1880-1935), politician. Born at Arthabaskaville, Que., he was believed by many to have been fathered by WILFRID LAURIER. He studied at Univ. Laval and was called to the bar in 1903. In 1904, he was elected to Parliament as a Liberal, but he moved away from Laurier and became a supporter of HENRI BOURASSA. He sat in the Quebec legislature from 1908 to 1912 as a *nationaliste*. From 1930 to 1935, he was a Conservative MP and deputy speaker of the Commons.

LAYTON, IRVING PETER (1912–), poet. Born in Romania, he was raised in Montreal. A vigorous writer, Layton captured attention with his frankly sexual poetry and his anti-bourgeois sensibility. His many volumes of poetry include *A Red Carpet for the Sun* (1959) which took the Governor General's Award, *Balls for a One-Armed Juggler* (1963), and *Droppings from Heaven* (1979).

Stephen Leacock

LEACOCK, STEPHEN BUTLER (1869-1944), educator, author. Born at Swanmore, Eng., he came to Canada as a boy and was educated at the univs. of Toronto and Chicago. An economist, he was hired by McGill Univ. in 1903 and remained there until he retired in 1936. Leacock wrote widely in his field and produced a best-selling political science text, but he became an international public figure because of his humorous writings and lecture tours. Beginning in 1910, Leacock produced almost a book a year, most based on magazine pieces. The most famous of his books are *Sunshine Sketches of a Little Town* (1912) and *Arcadian Adventures of the Idle Rich* (1914). Mariposa, the fictional town of *Sunshine Sketches*, has assumed a mythic stature in Canada, and Orillia, Ont., where Leacock had a summer home, is certain that it is the model. Leacock's non-humorous work was often offensive, his views verging on racism in his condemnation of non-British migrants to Canada.

LEAGUE FOR SOCIAL RECONSTRUCTION, study group created by Montreal and Toronto intellectuals, mostly connected with McGill Univ. and the Univ. of Toronto, in Jan. 1932. Prominent members included FRANK UNDERHILL and F.R. SCOTT. The league advanced the idea that Canada needed democratic socialism to survive the GREAT DEPRESSION and it named J.S. WOODSWORTH, labour member of the House of Commons, as its honorary leader. The LSR worked closely with the CO-OPERATIVE COMMONWEALTH FEDERATION, after its creation in Aug. 1932, although it never formally joined the CCF; the league prepared the REGINA MANIFESTO which was adopted as the CCF platform in the summer of 1933.

LEAGUE OF NATIONS, an international organization created at the Paris Peace Conference in

1919. The brainchild of U.S. President Woodrow Wilson (though the United States was never a member), the league was an attempt to put into practice the concept of collective security, which held that aggression against one nation would be considered aggression against all nations and the response would be collective economic or military action against the aggressor. Canada never lent its support to collective security and feared its implications, but nonetheless was a member of the league until it was replaced by the UNITED NATIONS in 1945.

LEAGUE OF NATIONS SOCIETY, organized in Canada in 1921 to promote world peace. The society, based in Ottawa, attracted notable Canadians such as SIR ROBERT BORDEN, ERNEST LAPOINTE, and J.W. DAFOE to its presidency. Its aims were educational and it sponsored speakers and broadcasts until it disbanded in 1942.

LEASED BASES AGREEMENT, 1940, agreement between Britain and the United States in which Britain gave the Americans rights to use a number of bases in its colonial territories in exchange for 50 over-age U.S. destroyers. The arrangement was made in summer 1940 but not finalized until 27 March 1941; it included six areas leased for 99 years in Newfoundland, most notably the naval base at ARGENTIA, the air base at Stephenville, and the army base, Fort Pepperrell, on Quidi Vidi Lake.

LEDUC, town located 30 km south of Edmonton, Alta, and site of a large oil deposit discovered in Feb. 1947. This discovery sparked the Alberta oil boom. *See also* IMPERIAL OIL.

LEE, DENNIS (1939–), writer, editor. As a writer of fiction, poetry, and children's books and as an editor, Dennis Lee has been influential. Born in Toronto and educated at the Univ. of Toronto, Lee founded the House of Anansi Press where his editing won acclaim. He won the Governor General's Award for *Civil Elegies* in 1968. His children's books, *Alligator Pie* and *Nicholas Knock and Other People* won him new audiences, as did his scripts for television's "Fraggle Rock."

LÉGER, JULES (1913-80), diplomat, governor general of Canada. Born at St-Anicet, Que., brother of PAUL-ÉMILE LÉGER, he was educated at

the Univ. de Montréal and the Sorbonne. He worked as a journalist with Ottawa's *Le Droit*, and then joined the Department of External Affairs in 1940. After service in Chile, London, Paris, and Mexico City, he became the first French-speaking under-secretary of state for external affairs in 1954, and as such he had to handle the transition between the ST LAURENT and DIEFENBAKER regimes. From 1964 to 1968, he was ambassador in Paris where he had the difficult task of dealing with President de Gaulle's trouble-making in Quebec. On his return to Ottawa, he became under-secretary of state, and helped implement Prime Minister PIERRE TRUDEAU's bilingualism policies. After service in Brussels, in 1974 he was named governor general and early in his term suffered a stroke. Aided by his wife, Gabrielle, however, he completed his term in 1979.

Paul-Émile, Cardinal Léger

courtesy La Presse

LÉGER, PAUL-ÉMILE (1904–), Roman Catholic cardinal. Born at Valleyfield, Que., brother of JULES LÉGER, he was educated in Montreal and Paris and ordained in 1929. He taught philosophy in Japan in the 1930s, then was vicar-general of the Sulpicians in Valleyfield, Que., and rector of the Canadian College in Rome. In 1950 he was named archbishop of Montreal and in 1953 a cardinal. When Léger took over in Montreal, the church was all powerful, but the QUIET REVOLUTION shook the province and by the time Leger stepped down in 1967 to become a missionary to African lepers, the Roman Catholic Church in Quebec had been altered by the secularism of the times. Léger had tried to control the press and to retard change, but he was not the most conservative of Quebec's cardinals.

LEMIEUX, JEAN-PAUL (1904–), painter. He was born at Quebec City and studied in Montreal and Paris. He taught briefly in Montreal and then moved in 1937 to the École des beaux-arts in Quebec where he remained until 1965. His art cries out aloneness, spare figures presented against flat backgrounds. The effect is powerful and moving.

LEMIEUX ACT, see INDUSTRIAL DISPUTES INVESTIGATION ACT

LEMIEUX, RODOLPHE (1866-1937), federal politician. A lawyer and a Liberal, Lemieux was educated at the Collège de Nicolet and Univ. Laval. He was a law partner of HONORÉ MERCIER and LOMER GOUIN, a professor of law at Laval, and an MP from 1896 to 1930 when he was elevated to the Senate. Lemieux held a number of posts in the government of SIR WILFRID LAURIER between 1906 and 1911, put through the INDUSTRIAL DISPUTES INVESTIGATION ACT while labour minister, and led a notable mission to Japan to discuss immigration questions. He then served as speaker of the House of Commons from 1922 to 1930.

LEND-LEASE, act pushed through the U.S. Congress in March 1941 which allowed Britain to "take now and pay later" for American war material. The act posed an economic threat to Canada because Britain would no longer have to buy Canadian-made munitions if it could secure American supplies free. The problem was resolved by the HYDE PARK DECLARATION, April 1941, which charged the British lend-lease account for the American components Canada needed to incorporate into munitions for Britain.

LESAGE, JEAN (1912-80), federal politician, premier of Quebec. Born at Montreal, he was one of the most attractive MPs from Quebec from 1945 until he left federal politics and became leader of the provincial Liberals in 1958. Lesage rebuilt the party, preparing it so that it was able to take advantage of the opportunity that arose upon the deaths of MAURICE DUPLESSIS and PAUL

Jean Lesage

SAUVÉ of the UNION NATIONALE. When his party won the 1960 election, Lesage gave the QUIET REVOLUTION its legislative shape with his policies of nationalization of electricity, electoral redistribution, secularization of education, and a massive assault on political corruption. Lesage was re-elected in 1962 but was surprisingly defeated in 1966. He retired from politics in 1970, returning just before his death to campaign against SOVEREIGNTY-ASSOCIATION in the 1980 referendum.

LESUEUR, WILLIAM DAWSON (1840-1917), historian, public servant. LeSueur was educated at the Univ. of Toronto, becoming a civil servant in the Post Office in 1856. As a critic and historian, he published widely in the English-speaking world on literature, science, philosophy, and religion. His critical portrayal of William Lyon Mackenzie, in a book written for the *Makers of Canada* series, created enormous controversy among Liberals, and its publication was blocked by an injunction.

LETHBRIDGE STRIKE, strike of coal-miners in and around Lethbridge, Alta, for union recognition and higher wages, from March to Dec. 1906. When the strike produced a coal shortage on the Prairies as winter approached, deputy minister of labour MACKENZIE KING intervened to try to bring about a settlement. He eventually succeeded in ending the strike, but without winning union recognition. The strike convinced King that Canada needed a new law to protect citizens from work stoppages. That law, passed in 1907, was the INDUSTRIAL DISPUTES INVESTIGATION ACT.

LÉVESQUE, GEORGES-HENRI (1903–), educator. He was born at Roberval, Que., and studied at the Dominican College in Ottawa and in France. He taught at the Dominican College and at Laval, organizing the school of social sciences, and serving as dean of the faculty from 1943 to 1956. A liberal and a scholar, he was extremely unpopular with the government and its hangers-on during the MAURICE DUPLESSIS regime for his role in training social science critics and for his federalism. In 1949 he was co-chair of the ROYAL COMMISSION ON NATIONAL DEVELOPMENT IN THE ARTS, LETTERS AND SCIENCES, and he was named to the CANADA COUNCIL which had been recommended by the commission. From 1963 to 1972, he worked in Africa, founding a university in Rwanda.

LÉVESQUE, RENÉ (1922-87), premier of Quebec. Born at New Carlisle, Que., he served as a war correspondent with the U.S. armed forces during World War II and then joined Radio-Canada in 1946 where he established a reputation as a radio reporter and television journalist. In 1960, running for the Liberals led by JEAN LESAGE, he won a seat in the Quebec legislature, later becoming public works minister, minister of natural resources, and minister of family and social welfare. Lévesque pressed his premier to nationalize the province's hydroelectric power companies, the central issue in the 1962 election. Shortly thereafter he became increasingly disillusioned with the difficulties of dealing with the federal government, and he left the Liberals in 1967 to found the Mouvement souveraineté-association. He united disparate separatist groups into the PARTI QUÉBÉCOIS in 1968 and led it to a stunning victory in 1976 over ROBERT BOURASSA and the Liberals. His government was progressive and active, strong in defence of French language rights, relatively free of corruption, and shrewd in its tactics of fighting the federal government under Prime Minister PIERRE TRUDEAU. But the referendum on SOVEREIGNTY-ASSOCIATION in May 1980 was lost, thanks to a strong federal campaign (and Trudeau's stunning return to power in the 1980 election). Although Lévesque won re-election the next year, by this time the economy was in difficulty and when he cut back on salaries of public sector workers, his government's unpopularity greatly increased. At the same time, Lévesque was outsmarted by Trudeau in the negotiations on patriation of the CONSTITUTION in 1981-2. By 1985, Lévesque and his team were worn out, the premier sometimes erratic in public situations, and he gave up the leadership to Pierre-Marc Johnson who lost power to the Liberals under ROBERT BOURASSA in Dec. 1985. His years in politics had been astonishing ones, even if he failed to achieve his ultimate goal of independence for Quebec. *See also* QUIET REVOLUTION.

LEWIS, DAVID (1909-81), politician. Born in Russia, he came to Canada in 1921. He became a brilliant student at McGill Univ., a Rhodes Scholar, and a lawyer. When he returned to Canada in 1935, Lewis was appointed national secretary of the CO-OPERATIVE COMMONWEALTH FEDERATION, a party that he galvanized through his organizational ability and great will. He was unable to win election himself, however, in four tries between 1940 and 1949. Lewis stayed active in the CCF, helped turn it into the NEW DEMOCRATIC PARTY, and tried again for Parliament in Toronto in 1962 with more success this time. In 1971 he ran for party leader, defeating a WAFFLE challenge from Jim Laxer. Utilizing a brilliant campaign that attacked "corporate welfare bums," he led the party to a position of substantial power in the 1972 election, holding the balance in a minority Parliament. The Liberal government danced to the Lewis tune for two years, moving on social questions and creating PETRO-CANADA, a government-owned oil company. Personally defeated in 1974, Lewis resigned as party leader in 1975.

LEWIS, STEPHEN HENRY (1937–), politician, diplomat. Born at Ottawa, he was the son of CO-OPERATIVE COMMONWEALTH FEDERATION activist DAVID LEWIS. In 1970, after teaching in Africa, he became leader of the Ontario NEW DEMOCRATIC PARTY where his oratory helped push the party to opposition status in 1975. In 1978 he resigned the leadership. To the surprise of all, BRIAN MULRONEY in 1984 named Lewis Canadian ambassador to the UNITED NATIONS, a post he filled with great eloquence and notable success, and one in which his knowledge of and concern for Africa had full scope.

courtesy National Archives of Canada/C-22831

Jimmy Gardiner addressing Liberal Convention delegates, 1948

LIBERAL PARTY, successful centrist political party. The Liberal party grew out of reformist parties in the British North American colonies that agitated for responsible government against the entrenched compacts and oligarchies who held power. The heart of the movement was in Canada West where the CLEAR GRIT tradition was strong, and the reformers in Canada West (if not those in Canada East) cooperated with JOHN A. MACDONALD in the GREAT COALITION that produced CONFEDERATION. The Liberals as a party took shape in the 1870s as the opposition to Macdonald's Conservative-coalition government, much of their support coming from those who had been against Confederation. In 1873, under Prime Minister ALEXANDER MACKENZIE, the Liberals formed their first administration, a dour and cheerless one. Not until the arrival of WILFRID LAURIER as party leader in 1887 did the party truly become established. Laurier muted the free trade enthusiasms of his caucus, made Liberalism acceptable in Quebec by accenting its moderation, and with his charm became a much-loved leader. In office from 1896 to 1911, Laurier established the party's principles: national unity between French and English, increased autonomy for Canada, efforts at accommodation with the United States, and the triumphant exploitation of the economy. The CONSCRIPTION CRISIS of 1917, like other crises before, demonstrated both the fragility of national unity and the urgent necessity for it, and Laurier's successor, MACKENZIE KING, raised the techniques of his predecessor to a pinnacle. Relying on Quebec's support, King created a political system that kept him in power from 1921 to 1948 with only five years in opposition by absorbing free trade westerners into his centrist party, by offering something for every region, by building a superb civil service, by making his party the creator of the social welfare state, and by finding strong ministers and letting them run their departments and manage their regions. So powerful was King that he could steer the country through World War II without the great divisions that had split the country in World War I and bring it into the peace ready to ride the new economic boom. In 1948 King turned office over to LOUIS ST LAURENT, a Quebec lawyer. Under these two leaders, the Liberals became, in Professor Reg Whitaker's phrase, the government party, an efficient mix of politician and bureaucrat that scarcely brooked criticism from the opposition or recognized the dividing line between them. The Liberals lost in 1957 but returned a mere half dozen years later, ready to begin yet another 21 years in office under LESTER PEARSON and PIERRE TRUDEAU. The latter's government, with its arrogant style, was more in keeping with the government party thesis than was Pearson's, which was notably inefficient despite the large number of former senior bureaucrats in key posts. Trudeau's government devoted itself to constitutional reform, and it picked up the thrust begun under Pearson of turning the public service into a bilingual operation. The Liberals' crushing defeat in the 1984 election created fears that the party might be doomed to a generation in the wilderness, but the many failures of the BRIAN MULRONEY government stirred optimism. All the more remarkable, this renewed hope took place despite the lacklustre leadership of JOHN TURNER, at the helm since 1984.

LIGUE POUR LA DÉFENSE DU CANADA, a French Canadian nationalist movement that fought for a "non" vote during the April 1942 CONSCRIPTION plebiscite called by Mackenzie King. Canadians were asked to decide whether the government should be released from its pledge against conscription for overseas service. Quebec voted 72.9 per cent against releasing the government.

LINCH-PIN THEORY, the thesis that Canada has played a critical part in bringing Britain and the United States together. A staple of after-dinner speakers for at least 75 years, the role of Canada in bringing these two English-speaking nations together has been of some import. But except on the rarest of occasions (as during the SUEZ CRISIS), London and Washington have never had difficulty talking with each other; when they disagreed, Canada ordinarily could play little part in resolving differences.

courtesy National Archives of Canada/C-3619

Sir John Young, Baron Lisgar

LISGAR, SIR JOHN YOUNG, BARON (1807-76), governor general of Canada. As a British Tory MP, he was chief secretary for Ireland from 1852 to 1855, and he held colonial appointments before his appointment to Canada in 1869. Opinionated and independent, Lisgar played a minor role in bringing Manitoba into CONFEDERATION in 1870 and he helped encourage British Columbia to join the following year. His term in Ottawa ended in 1872.

LISMER, ARTHUR (1885-1969), painter. Born at Sheffield, Eng., he studied there and in Antwerp before coming to Canada in 1911 to work as an illustrator. In Toronto, he met other artists who would influence his work and with him form the GROUP OF SEVEN in 1920. He taught in Halifax from 1916 to 1919 and then returned to Toronto to the Ontario College of Art. For the rest of his career he worked in art education in Toronto, New York, and Montreal. Like his colleagues in the Group, his paintings of the Canadian landscape had power and strength.

LIVESAY, DOROTHY (1909–), writer. Born at Winnipeg and educated at the univs. of Toronto, British Columbia, and the Sorbonne, she became one of Canada's major left-wing writers. Her poetry won two Governor General's Awards and she published an interesting memoir. She has worked for UNESCO and taught in Africa.

LLOYD, WOODROW STANLEY (1913-72), premier of Saskatchewan. Born near Webb, Sask., he was a schoolteacher and teacher's federation president. In 1944 he became education minister in TOMMY DOUGLAS's CO-OPERATIVE COMMONWEALTH FEDERATION government and, when Douglas moved to Ottawa to lead the NEW DEMOCRATIC PARTY, Lloyd became premier in Nov. 1961. Almost at once he plunged into the difficult struggle with the province's doctors over MEDICARE. It culminated in the Saskatchewan doctors' strike of 1-23 July 1962 that was settled with a compromise favouring the government position. Nonetheless the medicare battle helped defeat Lloyd's government in 1964. He retired from the leadership in 1970 and from politics in 1971.

LORD'S DAY ACT, federal legislation passed in 1907 that forbade stores and other businesses from staying open on Sundays. It followed an intense lobbying campaign by the Lord's Day Alliance, which succeeded in winning the support of labour unions and Catholic leaders despite its Protestant origins.

LORNE, JOHN DOUGLAS SUTHERLAND CAMPBELL, MARQUESS OF (1845-1914), governor general of Canada. In 1871 he married Princess Louise, Queen Victoria's fourth daughter, and his reward came in 1878 when he was made the vice-regal representative in Ottawa. Interested in the arts, he founded the Royal Canadian Academy of the Arts in 1880 and the Royal Society of Canada in 1882, and, after his term ended in 1883, he wrote several books that discussed his time here.

LOMBARDO, GUY (1902-77), bandleader. Born at London, Ont., Lombardo, with his brothers and others, formed a dance band and went to Cleveland in 1923. As the Royal Canadians, Lombardo and his crew with their syrupy style became extraordinarily popular and, thanks to radio and television, a fixture of New Year's Eve broadcasts.

LONGBOAT, THOMAS CHARLES (1887-1949), runner. Born at the Six Nations Reserve in Ontario, he was a popular champion long-distance runner. After winning local races in Ontario, he won the Boston Marathon in 1907 and the world marathon championship in 1909. He collapsed during the 1908 Olympics, however. A professional runner from 1908, Longboat served as a despatch runner in World War I in France.

LOUGHEED, EDGAR PETER (1928–), premier of Alberta. Grandson of SIR JAMES LOUGHEED, he was born at Calgary and educated at the univs. of Alberta and Harvard. A lawyer and corporation executive, he became leader of the ineffectual Alberta Progressive Conservative party in 1965 and led it to power in 1971. He won re-election with huge majorities until he retired in 1986. As premier, Lougheed benefited enormously from the oil revenues generated in his province, using them to keep taxes down and to establish a multi-billion dollar ALBERTA HERITAGE SAVINGS TRUST FUND to cushion the shock when the oil inevitably runs out. With the strong support of his province behind him, Lougheed fought bitterly with the federal government of Prime Minister PIERRE TRUDEAU over oil policies, especially over the NATIONAL ENERGY PROGRAM and the constitution.

LOUGHEED, SIR JAMES ALEXANDER (1854-1925), lawyer, senator. Born at Brampton, Canada West, he practised law in Toronto and then in Calgary, latterly in partnership with R.B. BENNETT. He was named to the Senate by SIR JOHN A. MACDONALD in 1889, sat in SIR ROBERT BORDEN's cabinet as minister without portfolio from 1911 to 1918, held four portfolios at various times until 1920, and was acting minister of soldiers' civil

re-establishment in the MEIGHEN government. He was in addition Tory leader in the Senate from 1906 to 1921. His grandson EDGAR PETER LOUGHEED became premier of Alberta in 1971.

LOWER, ARTHUR REGINALD MARSDEN (1889-1988), historian. He was educated at the univs. of Toronto and Harvard, served overseas in World War I with the Royal Navy, and taught at United College and Queen's Univ. His writings on the lumber trade and on Canadian social history established his reputation, as did a successful textbook, *Colony to Nation*. Other writings, including some under the pseudonym L.E.G. Upper, were often humorous.

LOWER CANADA, name from 1791 to 1841 of the British colony centred on present-day Quebec. In 1841 the name was changed to Canada East and in 1867 to Quebec. *See also* UNITED PROVINCE OF CANADA.

LUMBER WORKERS INDUSTRIAL UNION, labour union organized by west coast loggers during World War I. The LWIU was strongest in British Columbia but also enjoyed support in northern Ontario. It affiliated to the ONE BIG UNION in 1919 but withdrew shortly after. It joined the ALL-CANADIAN CONGRESS OF LABOUR in the 1920s and the WORKERS' UNITY LEAGUE in the 1930s.

LYON, STERLING RUFUS (1927–), premier of Manitoba. Born at Windsor, Ont., he practised law in Winnipeg and was elected to the Manitoba legislature as a Conservative in 1958, holding ministerial posts until 1969. He became leader of the provincial Progressive Conservative party in 1975 and premier in 1977. His government tried to restrain spending, and Lyon fought vigorously against Prime Minister PIERRE TRUDEAU's CANADIAN CHARTER OF RIGHTS AND FREEDOMS. He was defeated in the 1981 election and resigned from the leadership in 1983.

MAASS, OTTO (1890-1961), scientist. Born in New York City, he joined McGill Univ.'s Department of Chemistry in 1920. An energetic educator and scientist, he worked both in pure and applied science areas. In the latter field he was particularly active as an adviser to the government during World War II, heading the Directorate of Chemical Warfare and Smoke. Maass also helped establish the Defence Research Board and was assistant to the president of the NATIONAL RESEARCH COUNCIL from 1940 to 1946.

MCADOO AWARD, wage schedule for Canadian rail workers introduced by government order in 1918. Named after William McAdoo, director of the U.S. Railroad Administration, the McAdoo Award gave Canadian railworkers wage parity with U.S. rail workers.

MCBRIDE, SIR RICHARD (1870-1917), premier of British Columbia. Born at New Westminster, B.C., McBride received his law degree from Dalhousie Univ. He was elected MLA in 1898, served briefly in the ministry of JAMES DUNSMUIR, and in 1903 he formed the first party government in British Columbia, a Conservative one. His administration was initially tightfisted, but there were gestures towards trade unions that won him support. He created the Univ. of British Columbia, built roads and railways, and campaigned for ROBERT BORDEN in 1911. The downturn in the provincial economy by 1913 posed difficulties, and McBride, suffering from Bright's disease, resigned in 1915, going to London as B.C. agent general.

MCCARTHY, D'ALTON (1836-98), politician. Born at Oakley Park, near Dublin, Ireland, he came to Canada as a boy. First elected to Parliament as a Conservative in 1876, he represented North Simcoe until his death. In 1889 he broke with his party over the JESUITS' ESTATES QUESTION and launched the EQUAL RIGHTS ASSN. An opponent of the French language and Catholicism, a proponent of imperial federation, McCarthy was a near-perfect embodiment of Anglo-Canadian politics in his time. *See also* MANITOBA SCHOOLS QUESTION.

MCCLUNG, NELLIE LETITIA (1873-1951), advocate of WOMEN'S SUFFRAGE and prohibition. Born Nellie Mooney at Chatsworth, Ont., she was raised on a Manitoba homestead. She taught school, became involved in the WOMAN'S CHRISTIAN TEMPERANCE UNION, and began to write. Her first novel, published in 1908, was a great success, and three years later she moved to Winnipeg and became more directly involved in women's causes. By 1915, she had moved to Alberta, continuing her campaigning and writing and winning a legislature seat which she held 1921-6. Her published works amounted to 16 books.

MCCLURE, ROBERT BAIRD (1900-), medical missionary. He was born in Oregon, the child of Canadian missionaries to the Chinese. He studied medicine at the Univ. of Toronto and in Edinburgh and went to China in 1923. At the outbreak of the Sino-Japanese war in 1937 he worked for the Red Cross and later attacked the Canadian government (wrongly) for its policies of shipping strategic metals to Japan. From 1941 to 1946, he directed the Friends Ambulance Unit in China. After the Communist victory, he worked in Palestine and India and became moderator of the United Church from 1968 to 1971.

MCCONACHIE, GEORGE WILLIAM GRANT (1909-65), airline executive. Born in Hamilton, Ont., he organized a small airline, Yukon Southern Air Transport, in the 1930s. In 1941 his company was purchased by Canadian Pacific which acquired a number of small airlines. In 1947, McConachie was named president of CANADIAN PACIFIC AIRLINES, presiding over its post-war expansion into Asia and the South Pacific. McConachie fought hard against TRANS-CANADA AIRLINES' government-sponsored monopoly of transcontinental air services and spearheaded the modernization of CP Air's equipment at the dawn of the jet age.

MCCONNELL, JOHN WILSON (1877-1963), publisher. He made his fortune in Montreal where he entered the business world in 1900. He purchased the Montreal *Star* in 1938 and used it to support the Liberal government of Prime Minister MACKENZIE KING during World War II.

MCCRAE, JOHN (1872-1918), physician, soldier, poet. Born at Guelph, Ont., he was educated at the Univ. of Toronto. He served in the BOER WAR in the artillery, and joined McGill Univ. as a pathologist in 1900. He enlisted in the CANADIAN EXPEDITIONARY FORCE in 1914 and went overseas as a medical officer. "In Flanders Fields," his most famous poem, was published in 1915 and became the most quoted poem of the war. McCrae died of pneumonia in 1918 at his military hospital in France.

MCCURDY, JOHN ALEXANDER DOUGLAS (1886-1961), aviator. Born at Baddeck, N.S., and educated at the Univ. of Toronto and at the N.S. Technical College, McCurdy worked with ALEXANDER GRAHAM BELL and F.W. Baldwin in the AERIAL EXPERIMENT ASSN that sought to test the practicality of powered flight. The SILVER DART which he designed and flew made the first successful flight in the British Empire in 1909. He worked in aircraft production in World War II and was lieutenant governor of Nova Scotia, 1947-52.

MACDONALD, ANGUS L. (1890-1954), premier of Nova Scotia, federal politician. Born at Dunvegan, N.S., educated at St Francis Xavier, Dalhousie, and Harvard univs., he went overseas in World War I. He served in the provincial public service, 1921-4, as a professor at Dalhousie Law School, 1924-30, and he was elected provincial Liberal leader in 1930. He won the election of 1933 and ran a progressive administration during the Great Depression. In 1940 MACKENZIE KING made him minister of national defence (naval services), and he had a stormy relationship with the prime minister, notably over CONSCRIPTION. In 1945 he returned to Halifax and the premiership, this time opposing King's centralizing policies. He died in office in 1954.

MACDONALD, SIR HUGH JOHN (1850-1929), premier of Manitoba. The only son of JOHN A. MACDONALD, he was born at Kingston, Canada West and educated at the Univ. of Toronto; he practised law from 1872. In 1882 he moved to Winnipeg, and there was elected to Parliament in 1891, briefly serving in SIR CHARLES TUPPER's government. He led the Manitoba Conservatives to power in 1899, but retired to run unsuccessfully against CLIFFORD SIFTON in the 1900 general election. After his defeat, he returned to the practice of law.

MACDONALD, JAMES EDWARD HERVEY (1873-1932), painter. A founder of the GROUP OF SEVEN, Ned MacDonald was born in England, coming to Canada at age 13. He studied painting in Hamilton and Toronto, and worked at Grip Ltd from 1895. The Scandinavian landscape painters, to whose work he was introduced before World War I, influenced his style greatly, as it did all of the members of the Group, and MacDonald spent time sketching in the rough but beautiful Algoma country and later in the Rocky Mountains. He was principal of the Ontario College of Art, 1929-32.

courtesy National Archives of Canada/C-9078

Sir John A. Macdonald

MACDONALD, SIR JOHN ALEXANDER (1815-91), prime minister of Canada. Born in Scotland, he accompanied his parents to Kingston, Upper Canada, when he was five. Within 10 years he was articling with a local lawyer and was called to the bar at 21 where he gradually built a substantial reputation. His political career began municipally in 1843, and the next year he won election to the Legislative Assembly of the Province of Canada. Four years later, he received his first cabinet position. Macdonald's talents for political manoeuvre were shown by his role in the creation of the Liberal-Conservative party after 1854 and by the way he encouraged Sir Allan MacNab to retire in his favour as premier. Governing jointly with a Lower Canadian leader, most notably GEORGE-ÉTIENNE CARTIER, the shrewd and practical Macdonald came to believe that French and English could work together but only if the proper governmental structure could be found. A federal structure had to accommodate racial, religious, and sectional differences; simultaneously, the central government had to be strong enough to lead and direct. The CONFEDERATION bargain, worked out under Macdonald's lead, brought Nova Scotia and New Brunswick into union with Quebec and Ontario in 1867, and, before his death in 1891, extended Canada from sea unto sea.

Knighted and chosen first prime minister of the Dominion of Canada, Sir John had to create the political infrastructure for a new country, a goal he achieved through a brilliant use of patronage. He had to build the nation and patronage was grease for the wheels. One early challenge to unity came on the Red River where LOUIS RIEL led a MÉTIS rebellion in 1869-70 that was suppressed by British troops. That produced the new province of Manitoba, to which were soon added British Columbia, Prince Edward Island, and the North-West Territories. Another challenge was to tie the ramshackle dominion together, a necessity that could only be met by a great railway. His efforts to achieve this plunged Macdonald into the PACIFIC SCANDAL and he lost office in 1873 to ALEXANDER MACKENZIE's Liberals.

In opposition, Sir John campaigned for a NATIONAL POLICY of tariff protection and, returned to office in 1878, he implemented his pledge the next year. Canadian manufacturers received all the protection they sought, business was firmly tied to the CONSERVATIVE PARTY, and Macdonald ruled unchallenged for a dozen years. The tariff notwithstanding, however, economic growth remained slow. The CANADIAN PACIFIC RAILWAY was completed with heavy government assistance in 1885, just in time to carry troops from the east to put down another Riel-led rebellion in the North-

West. Pressed by insistent demands from Ontario for the rebel's death, Macdonald agreed to Louis Riel's execution, creating a firestorm of protest in French Canada. The Conservatives won the election of 1887, however, and Macdonald, now old, often ill, and occasionally drinking too much, continued his rule. Rebuffed in his efforts to strike a RECIPROCITY arrangement with the United States, Macdonald went to the hustings for the last time in 1891 and campaigned for his policy of protection once more. Exhausted but victorious, the Grand Old Man, the father of his country, died in Ottawa on 6 June 1891. *See also* FATHERS OF CONFEDERATION; GREAT COALITION.

MACDONALD, JOHN SANDFIELD (1812-72), premier of Ontario. Born at St Raphael, Upper Canada, he was called to the bar in 1840 and practised in Cornwall. Elected as a Conservative to the assembly of the Province of Canada in 1841, he switched to the Reform side in 1843, serving as Robert Baldwin's solicitor general, 1849-51. He feuded with GEORGE BROWN, the other great Reform leader, preferring the "double majority" to Brown's "REP-BY-POP." In 1862 he formed the government with L.-V. Sicotte, and then with A.-A. Dorion. The government fell in 1864. He was slow to join in the GREAT COALITION that brought about CONFEDERATION but did in 1867. He became first premier of Ontario and resigned in ill-health in 1871.

MACDOUGALD, JOHN ANGUS, "BUD" (1908-78), businessman. Born into a wealthy family in Toronto, he entered the securities business in the mid-1920s. He later formed a number of business partnerships with E.P. TAYLOR and became chairman of Argus Corp. in 1969.

MCDOUGALL, WILLIAM (1822-1905), politician. Born near York, Upper Canada, he was educated at Victoria College and admitted to the bar in 1847. Elected a CLEAR GRIT member of the assembly of the Province of Canada in 1858, he held cabinet portfolios and participated in the Charlottetown, Quebec, and London conferences that led to CONFEDERATION. Named public works minister in the first JOHN A. MACDONALD cabinet, McDougall was nominated as lieutenant governor of the North-West Territories in 1869, but his effort to reach Fort Garry was blocked by

LOUIS RIEL, and the failure blighted his political career. *See also* RED RIVER REBELLION.

MACEACHEN, ALLAN JOSEPH (1921–), politician. He was born at Inverness, N.S., and educated at St Francis Xavier Univ. and the univs. of Toronto and Chicago. He taught at his alma mater from 1946, was elected to Parliament as a Liberal in 1953, and from 1963 on was the leading Liberal from his province. He held a number of portfolios, including external affairs (where he had great interest in north-south questions) and finance (where his 1981 budget involved him in great controversy). He is credited with masterminding Prime Minister PIERRE TRUDEAU's resurrection as Liberal leader in Dec. 1980. Trudeau named him a senator in 1984.

courtesy Gordon/National Archives of Canada/C-6109

T. D'Arcy McGee

MCGEE, THOMAS D'ARCY (1825-68), politician. Born at Carlingford, Ireland, he came to Montreal from the United States in 1857 to edit the *New Era*, a newspaper. A proponent of British North American federation and a great orator, McGee was elected to the assembly of the Province of Canada in 1858 as a Reformer. In 1863 he became a minister in the MACDONALD-CARTIER government and attended both the CHARLOTTETOWN CONFERENCE and QUEBEC CONFERENCE. An opponent of the FENIANS, McGee was assassinated in April 1868 and was widely believed to have fallen victim to a Fenian plot.

MCGILL FENCE, radar defence system developed by scientists at McGill Univ. and installed on the MID-CANADA LINE, authorized by Ottawa in June 1954.

MCGUIGAN, JAMES CHARLES (1894-1974), Roman Catholic cardinal. Born at Hunter River, P.E.I., he was educated at St Dunstan's College, Univ. Laval, and the Grand Séminaire de Québec. He was ordained in 1918, became secretary to Bishop O'Leary of Charlottetown and accompanied the bishop to Edmonton in 1920. McGuigan became archibishop of Regina in 1930 and transferred to Toronto in 1934. He was created a cardinal in 1945, the first English-speaking Catholic so designated in Canada.

MACKAY, ANGUS (1841-1931), agronomist. Born in Pickering, Upper Canada, he took up grain farming in the North-West Territories in the early 1880s and is credited with discovering (or rediscovering) the summer-fallowing technique. This involves plowing a field but not planting it for a full season to allow it to recoup the moisture lost in normal crop cultivation. MacKay was appointed to head the DOMINION EXPERIMENTAL FARM branch established at Indian Head (Sask.) in 1888.

MACKAY, ROBERT ALEXANDER (1894-1979), educator, diplomat. Educated at the univs. of Toronto and Princeton, he taught political science at Dalhousie Univ. from 1927 to 1947, publishing books on foreign policy and the Senate. He was a commissioner on the ROYAL COMMISSION ON DOMINION-PROVINCIAL RELATIONS. In 1941 he joined the Department of External Affairs, left briefly at the end of the war, then returned in 1947. He was a key figure in bringing Newfoundland into Confederation and was permanent representative at the United Nations and ambassador to Norway.

MACKENZIE, ALEXANDER (1822-92), prime minister of Canada. He emigrated to Canada from Scotland at age 20. Eventually settling near Sarnia, Canada West, Mackenzie initially worked as a stone mason until in the early 1850s he became editor of the GRIT newspaper, the *Lambton Shield*. Elected to the Province of Canada's Legislative Assembly in 1861 as a supporter of GEORGE BROWN, he became a proponent of CONFEDERATION and won election to the first House of Commons in 1867. After SIR JOHN A. MACDONALD became enmeshed in the PACIFIC SCANDAL in 1873, Mackenzie and his LIBERAL PARTY formed the government. Hardworking and

Alexander Mackenzie

honorable, Mackenzie was not blessed with luck. The economy was stagnant, a condition that obliged him to go slow on building the transcontinental railway that all agreed was necessary. That slow-down led inevitably to charges that he lacked vision, and his lacklustre administration was toppled when a forgiving electorate reinstated Macdonald in 1878. In 1880, the Liberals selected EDWARD BLAKE as their leader, and Mackenzie drifted into obscurity.

MACKENZIE, SIR ALEXANDER (1860-1943), businessman. Born in Kincardine, Canada West, he was called to the bar in 1883. At the turn of the century he went to work for Toronto businessman ZEBULON LASH, overseeing Lash's Brazilian interests. In 1915 he became president of Brazilian Traction which controlled power and traction monopolies in several major Brazilian cities.

MACKENZIE, CHALMERS JACK (1888-1984), engineer, public servant. He was born at St Stephen, N.B., and educated at Dalhousie and Harvard univs. After World War I service, he moved to the Univ. of Saskatchewan as a part-time lecturer in engineering, eventually becoming dean of the faculty. Named to the NATIONAL RESEARCH COUNCIL in 1935, he became acting president in 1939 and as such the government's chief scientific adviser in World War II. He was involved in atomic research planning and in the manifold activities of government, a role he continued as president of ATOMIC ENERGY OF CANADA LTD and the Atomic Energy Control Board until his retirement in 1961. An organizer rather than a leading researcher, Mackenzie was the most powerful scientific figure in Ottawa for almost a quarter century.

MACKENZIE, IAN ALISTAIR (1890-1949), politician. Born at Assynt, Scot., he served in the CANADIAN EXPEDITIONARY FORCE in World War I. Elected to the British Columbia legislature in 1920 as a Liberal, he won a seat in Parliament in 1930, and became defence minister in 1935. Not a success as an administrator, involved in the BREN GUN SCANDAL, Mackenzie was moved to pensions and national health on the outbreak of war in 1939. As B.C.'s cabinet minister, he called for evacuation of the Japanese Canadians in early 1942. He pressed social reform on the government, and as veterans' affairs minister, 1944-8, oversaw the extraordinary package of benefits given veterans. He became a senator in 1948.

MACKENZIE, NORMAN ARCHIBALD MACRAE (1894-1986), educator. Born at Pugwash, N.S., he served with great distinction in World War I. He was educated at Dalhousie, Harvard, and Cambridge univs., taught law at the Univ. of Toronto from 1927 to 1940, and became president of the Univ. of New Brunswick. Much involved in international affairs associations and well connected in Liberal Ottawa, MacKenzie served on a variety of commissions and boards, including the WARTIME INFORMATION BOARD, the ROYAL COMMISSION ON NATIONAL DEVELOPMENT IN THE ARTS, LETTERS AND SCIENCES, and the CANADA COUNCIL. He moved to the Univ. of British Columbia in 1944 where he was president until 1962. He became a senator in 1966.

MACKENZIE, SIR WILLIAM (1849-1923), railway capitalist. Born at Eldon Township, Canada West, he began in business owning a gristmill in rural Ontario. By 1874, he had become a railway contractor in Canada and the United States, and he then invested heavily in street railways in Toronto and Brazil, becoming one of the founders of Brazilian Traction. With his partner DONALD MANN, he put prairie rail lines together to form the CANADIAN NORTHERN RAILWAY, the third transcontinental. The Northern quickly fell into financial difficulty during the war and was nationalized.

MACKENZIE-PAPINEAU BATTALION, Canadian unit, familiarly known as the Mac-Paps, that fought with the International Brigades against Franco's Fascists during the Spanish Civil War. The volunteers of the Mackenzie-Papineau Battalion, which derived its name from the leaders of the 1837 Rebellion, were involved in five campaigns between 1937 and 1938. The government's response to the formation of the battalion was to pass the Foreign Enlistment Act of 1937 prohibiting Canadians from fighting in foreign wars.

MACKENZIE VALLEY PIPELINE, a controversial proposal, first advanced by the federal government in 1970, to pipe natural gas from the BEAUFORT SEA to southern Canada. It was met with objections from native people and others who worried about the pipeline's impact on the fragile ecological system of the north. A royal commission, chaired by Judge THOMAS BERGER, was launched in 1974 and, after its detailed investigation, the proposal was shelved.

MACKINTOSH, WILLIAM ARCHIBALD (1895-1970), economic historian, bureaucrat. He was born in Madoc, Ont., and attended Queen's and Harvard univs. He returned to Queen's in 1920 and began to establish himself as one of Canada's great economic historians, writing on such subjects as agricultural cooperation in western Canada, prairie settlement and, for the ROYAL COMMISSION ON DOMINION-PROVINCIAL RELATIONS, *The Economic Background of Dominion-Provincial Relations*. In 1926 he helped the Advisory Board on Tariff and Taxation, and in 1936 he was a member of the National Employment Commission. With the outbreak of war in 1939, he went to Ottawa full-time, serving as special assistant to the deputy minister of finance, CLIFFORD CLARK, and then in the Department of Reconstruction where he drafted the WHITE PAPER ON EMPLOYMENT AND INCOME. He returned to Queen's after the war, becoming principal in 1951.

MCLACHLAN, JAMES BRYSON (1869-1937), labour leader, founder and editor of the *Maritime Labour Herald*. He emigrated to Nova Scotia in 1902 to work in the Cape Breton coal fields. In 1909 he became secretary-treasurer of the United Mine Workers District 26, which was just organizing in the region. In 1923 he was fired by union president John L. Lewis for leading coalminers on a sympathy strike to back Cape Breton steelworkers. He later joined the COMMUNIST PARTY of Canada and served as president of the WORKERS' UNITY LEAGUE from 1930 to 1936.

MCLAREN, NORMAN (1914-87), film animator. Born in Scotland, he came to the NATIONAL FILM BOARD in 1941. He made his own technically innovative animated films and set up the NFB's animation unit. His most famous film, *Neighbours* won an Oscar in 1953; his later work concentrated on pure design.

MCLARNIN, JAMES (1907-), boxer. He came to Canada as a child and began boxing in Vancouver at age 12. He turned professional at 16, moved to Los Angeles and New York, and won the welterweight championship in 1933. He lost the crown to Barney Ross in 1934, recaptured it, and then lost again to Ross in 1935.

courtesy General Motors/neg. no. 234

R. Samuel McLaughlin

MCLAUGHLIN, ROBERT SAMUEL (1871-1972), industrialist. McLaughlin was born in Enniskillen, Ont. He entered the family carriage and motor business and concluded an agreement to build General Motors car bodies in 1908. McLaughlin sold the business to General Motors in 1918 but remained as president of the Canadian operation. During the 1920s McLaughlin became the largest automobile producer in the Commonwealth. He retired in 1942 but remained on the General Motors board until 1967. He was a noted philanthropist.

MCLEAN, JAMES STANLEY (1876-1954), meat packer. Educated at the Univ. of Toronto, he took a job with the Harris Abattoir Co., a packing house, and under the guidance of JOSEPH FLAVELLE, he eventually became its president. In 1927 McLean organized the merger that created CANADA PACKERS, a company he headed from its founding until his death.

MACLEAN, JOHN ANGUS (1914–), federal politician, premier of Prince Edward Island. Born at Lewes, P.E.I., he served overseas in World War II. In 1951 he won a by-election to Parliament, and in 1957 he became fisheries minister in the DIEFENBAKER government. MacLean was a Diefenbaker loyalist through 1967, and in 1979 he returned to P.E.I., became Conservative leader, and won the election. In 1981 he resigned as premier.

MACLEAN, JOHN BAYNE (1862-1950), publisher. Born at Crieff, Canada West, he gained experience as a newspaperman before launching *Canadian Grocer* in 1887, the first of a number of trade publications which formed the basis of the Maclean Hunter publishing empire. In partnership with Horace Hunter, Maclean also began the *FINANCIAL POST, MACLEAN'S,* and *Chatelaine.* Maclean himself was more than slightly eccentric, writing fanciful tales of a German plot to invade Canada.

MACLEAN'S, popular magazine, started in 1905 by J.B. MACLEAN. *Maclean's* assumed its present title in 1911 and by 1914 it had become a nationalist vehicle, profiling important Canadian personalities and focusing on politics. Before television cut into the magazine market, *Maclean's* had substantial influence, thanks in part to the reputation of its Ottawa reporter, BLAIR FRASER, and the skilful editing of RALPH ALLEN. The magazine was saved from TV's inroads by its conversion into a weekly news magazine in the 1970s and, although the format is modelled on that of *Time, Maclean's* still provides unique coverage of Canadian news.

MCLENNAN, SIR JOHN CUNNINGHAM (1867-1935), physicist. He graduated with a PhD in physics from the Univ. of Toronto in 1900. Specializing in radioactivity, he pioneered in the use of radium therapy to fight cancer and was a founding member of the NATIONAL RESEARCH COUNCIL.

MACLENNAN, JOHN HUGH (1907–), author. He was born at Glace Bay, N.S., and educated at Dalhousie, Oxford, and Princeton univs. He taught at Lower Canada College from the middle 1930s and in 1941 published his first novel, *Barometer Rising,* about the HALIFAX EXPLOSION. The novel was a success, as was his next one, *Two Solitudes* (1945), about the clash between French and English Canadians in World War I. *Two Solitudes* won Maclennan his first (of three) Governor General's Awards. Maclennan's later novels were publishing events, especially the apocalyptic *Voices in Time* (1980).

MACLEOD, JAMES FARQUHARSON (1836-1894), policeman. Born in Scotland, he practised law in Ontario and served in the Canadian MILITIA before joining the newly created NORTH-WEST MOUNTED POLICE in 1874. He accompanied the police on their first march west, founded Fort Macleod in southern Alberta, and gave the city of Calgary its name. He resigned from the NWMP in 1880 and then served as a magistrate and judge.

MACLEOD, JOHN JAMES RICKARD (1876-1935), physiologist, codiscoverer of insulin. Born in Cluny, Scot., Macleod was appointed professor of physiology at the Univ. of Toronto in 1918. Macleod allowed FREDERICK B. BANTING the use of laboratory space and equipment in the spring of 1921 for experiments seeking a cure for diabetes. Macleod later joined the research team which included J.B. COLLIP and C.H. BEST and played an important role in discovering a usable form of insulin. In 1923 he and Banting were awarded the Nobel Prize for their discovery; he chose to share his award with Collip.

MCLUHAN, HERBERT MARSHALL (1911-80), educator. Born at Edmonton, McLuhan was educated at the univs. of Manitoba and Cambridge. He taught at Wisconsin and St Louis univs. and at Assumption College in Windsor, Ont., until in 1946 he came to the Univ. of Toronto. Although he was originally a conventional linguistic scholar in English, his work took a new turn with *The Mechanical Bride* (1951), *The Gutenberg Galaxy* (1961), and *Understanding Media* (1964). Influenced by HAROLD INNIS, McLuhan propounded theories to explain the impact of the "hot" or "cool" media, and he became the leading communciations theorist of his day, attaining such celebrity that he even found his way into a Woody Allen film.

MCMAHON, FRANCIS MURRAY PATRICK (1902–), industrialist. Born in Moyie, B.C., McMahon began working as a driller and then a drilling contractor in that province. During the 1930s he discovered oil in Turner Valley, Alta, for his company Pacific Petroleum Ltd. After building the company into a western success story he sold out in 1979 to PETRO CANADA. McMahon was also involved in the construction of Westcoast Transmission, Canada's first long-distance gas pipeline.

MCMASTER, ROSS HUNTINGTON (1880-1962), industrialist. He worked for a paint company in Montreal before joining the Montreal Rolling Mills. His outstanding abilities led him to a management position when the mill became part of the giant Steel Co. of Canada (STELCO) in 1910. He was an intense, innovative leader both as president of the company, a position he held from 1926, and as chairman in the post-World War II period.

MCMASTER, WILLIAM (1811-87), businessman. McMaster emigrated to Canada from Ireland in 1833 and became a successful dry-goods wholesaler. He was one of the founders of the CANADIAN BANK OF COMMERCE in 1867. Funds from his estate were used to establish McMaster Univ. (now in Hamilton, Ont.) in 1890.

MACMILLAN, ALEXANDER STIRLING (1871-1955), premier of Nova Scotia. Born at Upper South River, N.S., Macmillan made his mark as a lumberman and in construction. A member of the Legislative Council from 1925 to 1928, minister of highways in 1925, and MLA from 1928 to 1945, Macmillan became premier when ANGUS L. MACDONALD went to Ottawa in 1940. Holding several other portfolios at the same time wore him down, and when Macdonald returned in 1945, Macmillan readily retired.

MACMILLAN, SIR ERNEST ALEXANDER CAMPBELL (1893-1973), conductor. Born at Mimico, Ont., he was a child prodigy, composing for and playing the organ. He graduated from Edinburgh and Oxford univs. and was interned in Germany through World War I. Returning to Canada, he performed widely, composed, and conducted. He became principal of the Toronto Conservatory in 1926 and dean of the music faculty at the Univ. of Toronto in 1927. From 1931 to 1956 he was conductor of the Toronto Symphony and from 1942 conductor of the Mendelssohn Choir.

MACMILLAN, HARVEY REGINALD (1885-1976), businessman. Born in Newmarket, Ont., he trained in forestry before entering the forest industry in 1907. He was chief forester for British Columbia and was timber-trade commissioner for Canada during World War I. He founded H.R. MacMilllan Export Co. in 1919 and became an important lumber exporter. During World War II he was appointed chairman of Wartime Shipping Ltd, a CROWN CORPORATION. He merged his company with Bloedel, Stewart and Welch in 1951 and remained a director of the new MACMILLAN BLOEDEL until 1970.

MACMILLAN BLOEDEL LTD, lumber company formed in 1951 when H.R. MACMILLAN's export company merged with Bloedel, Stewart and Welch. During the 1960s MacMillan Bloedel expanded rapidly, acquiring lumber and paper companies as well as its own timberland. In 1981 NORANDA MINES gained control of the company, Canada's largest timber corporation.

MCNAIR, JOHN BABBITT (1889-1968), premier of New Brunswick. He was born at Andover, N.B., and first elected to the legislature in 1935. He served as attorney general in A.A. DYSART's Liberal government and succeeded him as premier in 1940. His government stayed in power until 1952 when it was defeated by the Conservatives. McNair was named chief justice of the province three years later; in 1965 he became lieutenant governor.

MCNAUGHTON, ANDREW GEORGE LATTA (1887-1966), soldier. Born at Moosomin, Sask., he studied engineering at McGill Univ. A militiaman since 1909, he went overseas with the artillery in the CANADIAN EXPEDITIONARY FORCE in 1914. A brilliant gunner, McNaughton applied science to the task of locating enemy guns. He ended the war a brigadier in charge of the CANADIAN CORPS' guns. McNaughton remained in the forces, becoming deputy chief of the General Staff of the CANADIAN ARMY in 1922 and chief in 1929, creating camps for unemployed men in the GREAT DEPRESSION. In 1935 he became president of the NATIONAL RESEARCH COUNCIL, an ideal post for one with his restless mind. On the outbreak of war in 1939, McNaughton was named commander of the 1st Canadian Division which he took overseas. He was successively corps commander and army commander, resisting all efforts to divide his Canadians between theatres. Enormously popular with the troops and at home, his performance on exercises was criticized by British officers, and in 1943 he was relieved, returning to Canada. In Nov. 1944, during the early stages of the CONSCRIPTION CRISIS, Prime Minister MACKENZIE KING made McNaughton defence minister, but the general could not find sufficient volunteers for overseas service among the ZOMBIES, and he was sorely embarrassed when the prime minister decided to send conscripts overseas. He subsequently lost a by-election. He became Canadian representative on the United Nations Atomic Energy Commission, Canadian permanent representative to the UN, and chair of the INTERNATIONAL JOINT COMMISSION and the PERMANENT JOINT BOARD ON DEFENCE. In his last battle, he campaigned vigorously against the COLUMBIA RIVER TREATY which he viewed as a sell-out.

MACOUN, JOHN (1831-1920), naturalist. Born in Ireland, he came to Canada in 1850 to farm. In 1868, he was named professor of botany and geology at Albert College, Belleville, Ont., and four years later he accompanied SANDFORD FLEMING on his expedition to the Pacific. In 1879, Macoun was named the Canadian government's explorer in the North-West Territories and in 1882 botanist to the GEOLOGICAL SURVEY OF CANADA. He concluded that the Canadian Prairies would be excellent for farming and urged that they be opened to settlement as quickly as possible. This contrasted with earlier reports from Captain John Palliser that the southern Prairies were arid and unsuitable for agriculture. Macoun published catalogues of flora and fauna and a book on Manitoba and the Prairies.

MACPHAIL, AGNES CAMPBELL (1890-1954), politician. Born in Grey County, Ont., she became a country schoolteacher and was active in the COOPERATIVE MOVEMENT when she became the first woman elected to Parliament in Canada in 1921. She sat in the House from 1921 to 1940, first as a PROGRESSIVE, then as an independent, and finally as a CO-OPERATIVE COMMONWEALTH FEDERATION MP. A feminist and an anti-militarist, she had some impact in Ottawa where she was respected. In 1943 and 1948 she won election to the Ontario legislature under the CCF banner.

MACPHAIL, SIR ANDREW (1864-1938), physician, soldier. Born at Orwell, P.E.I., he trained as a doctor at McGill Univ. He taught at Bishop's Univ. from 1893 to 1905 and then went to McGill as professor of the history of medicine. He wrote a number of books, published innumerable articles on subjects as disparate as imperialism (pro) and feminism (anti) in the *University Magazine* which he edited, and he served overseas in World War I with the medical corps.

MAINGUY, EDMOND ROLLO (1901-79), sailor. Born at Chemainus, B.C., he graduated from the Royal Naval College of Canada. He served in the ROYAL CANADIAN NAVY, commanding destroyers, a cruiser, and filling staff posts in World War II. In 1947, he headed a committee examining mutinies in the fleet, and his report recommended, among other things, an end to pseudo-British traditions in the RCN. In 1951, he became chief of the naval staff, a post he held for five years.

MAIR, CHARLES (1838-1927), poet, public servant. Born at Lanark, Upper Canada, Mair was educated at Queen's Univ. He became a journalist, helped found CANADA FIRST, and reported for the Montreal *Gazette* from Red River where he was notorious for his contempt of the MÉTIS. He subsequently lived in the west, served in the militia during the NORTH-WEST REBELLION of 1885, and took a public service post. He wrote volumes of poetry and drama, an account of the buffalo, and travel literature.

MALONE, RICHARD SANKEY (1909-85), publisher. Malone worked as a journalist for Toronto and Prairie newspapers. In 1939, he enlisted with the infantry, served as an aide to the minister of national defence, and participated in the invasion of SICILY. He was an aide to Field Marshal Montgomery, in charge of Canadian public relations, and the head of a mission to U.S. General MacArthur's headquarters in the Pacific. As such he rescued Canadian prisoners of war taken at HONG KONG. After the war he returned to the Winnipeg *Free Press*, becoming its publisher in 1961 and chair of F.P. Publications in 1975. Malone wrote a war account and two volumes of memoirs.

MANDARINS, term for the bureaucratic elite, used since the 1940s and 1950s to refer to a group of key public servants – e.g., CLIFFORD CLARK, R.B. BRYCE, NORMAN ROBERTSON, ARNOLD HEENEY – who had enormous influence, especially in the KING and ST LAURENT governments.

courtesy National Archives of Canada/C-7774

Robert Manion

MANION, ROBERT JAMES (1881-1943), politician. Educated at the Univ. of Toronto, he practised medicine at Fort William, Ont., served as a medical officer in World War I, and was decorated for gallantry. Elected to Parliament as a Unionist in 1917, Manion held cabinet posts under MEIGHEN and BENNETT, and in 1938 was elected leader of the CONSERVATIVE PARTY. In the 1940 election, however, he changed his party's name to NATIONAL GOVERNMENT and, despite denouncing CONSCRIPTION, lost badly. He was driven

from the leadership soon after, and MACKENZIE KING made him director of air raid precautions.

MANITOBA ACT, legislation passed in 1870 to amend the BRITISH NORTH AMERICA ACT and create the province of Manitoba. The measure was forced on the federal government by LOUIS RIEL who led his MÉTIS followers in the RED RIVER REBELLION of 1869. The act provided Manitoba with a bicameral government, two seats in the Senate and two in the House of Commons, bilingualism in the provincial legislature, two tax-supported school systems, one public and the other separate, and no control over the lands and resources in the province which remained under the federal government The new province was deliberately made small so that the federal government could continue to exercise a large degree of control over the remainder of western Canada through the NORTH-WEST TERRITORIES ACT.

MANITOBA AND NORTHWEST FARMERS' PROTECTIVE UNION, farm organization formed in Winnipeg in Dec. 1883, the first Canadian-based western protest movement. The union demanded provincial control over lands and natural resources, provincial chartering of local grain-carrying railways, improvements in the grading, storage, and transportation of grain, and freer trade with the United States. The union was short-lived and disappeared by 1887.

MANITOBA GRAIN ACT, federal legislation passed by Parliament in July 1900 to establish general supervision of the grain trade on the Canadian Prairies by a federal commissioner. It provided for government inspection of the weighing and grading of grain and the construction of flat warehouses to allow farmers to use facilities other than grain elevators to store and load grain onto trains.

MANITOBA NUMBER 1 HARD, the highest quality classification for western Canadian wheat. If wheat was found by graders to contain the proper mix of moisture and hardness, it was given this classification.

MANITOBA SCHOOLS QUESTION, political controversy which arose following the abolition of tax-supported SEPARATE SCHOOLS in Manitoba by the Liberal government of Premier THOMAS

GREENWAY in 1890. The MANITOBA ACT had provided for such schools, but anti-Catholic agitation by the EQUAL RIGHTS ASSN, and the paucity of Catholic settlers in Manitoba, prompted Greenway to act. The move precipitated an immediate outcry in Quebec and court challenges from Manitoba Catholics. In ruling on the constitutionality of the abolition, the JUDICIAL COMMITTEE OF THE PRIVY COUNCIL upheld Manitoba's right to end tax support for separate schools but also affirmed the federal government's right to intervene in the dispute to protect Manitoba Catholics. In March 1896, the federal government, under Prime Minister SIR CHARLES TUPPER, introduced remedial legislation to repeal the Manitoba law. Protestant nativists such as D'ALTON MCCARTHY fought the bill as did Liberal leader WILFRID LAURIER, and because the term of the current Parliament ran out before the bill could be passed, the schools question became a federal election issue. In English Canada Tupper claimed that he was only following the dictates of the JCPC; in Quebec he posed as a champion of Catholic rights. Laurier told Quebecers that Tupper's harsh measures would not be effective and that he could better protect Manitoba Catholics with "sunny ways," while in English Canada he attacked Tupper for interfering in the provincially controlled area of education. Laurier won the election and entered into negotiations with the Greenway government. A compromise of sorts was reached that allowed optional religious teaching in the public schools, after school hours, where requested.

MANN, SIR DONALD (1853-1934), businessman. Born in Acton, Canada West, he worked on the Pacific railway even before the CANADIAN PACIFIC RAILWAY was formed in 1880. Later, in partnership with WILLIAM MACKENZIE, Mann subcontracted to build a number of sections of the CPR main line on the Prairies and in British Columbia. Mann and Mackenzie founded the CANADIAN NORTHERN RAILWAY in 1899.

MANNING, ERNEST CHARLES (1908-), premier of Alberta. Born at Carnduff, Sask., he was a student at the Prophetic Bible Institute run by WILLIAM ABERHART in Calgary. When Aberhart took SOCIAL CREDIT to the province, Manning went along, becoming provincial secretary in Aberhart's cabinet. After Aberhart's death in 1943, Manning became premier, a post he held until

1968. His government moved away from Social Credit dogma towards cautious fiscal conservatism, aided immeasurably by the post-war oil boom that permitted low taxes and relatively good social services. Manning, however, resisted national MEDICARE as a left-wing policy. In 1970, he was appointed to the Senate.

MARCHAND, JEAN (1918-), labour leader, politician. He studied labour relations at Univ. Laval before joining the Catholic Pulp and Paper Workers as a union organizer. In 1947 he was elected secretary general of the CONFÉDÉRATION DES TRAVAILLEURS CATHOLIQUES DU CANADA / CANADIAN CATHOLIC CONFEDERATION OF LABOUR and, in 1961, president of the CONFÉDÉRATION DES SYNDICATS NATIONAUX / CONFEDERATION OF NATIONAL TRADE UNIONS. In 1965 Marchand, PIERRE TRUDEAU, and GÉRARD PELLETIER joined the federal Liberal party and were elected to Parliament. He was convinced that Quebecers had to be persuaded to look to Ottawa for political leadership or CONFEDERATION was in danger. He subsequently served in a number of cabinet posts. In 1976 Marchand resigned his seat in the House of Commons to run unsuccessfully against the PARTI QUÉBÉCOIS in the Quebec provincial election. He was then appointed to the Senate where he served until 1983 when he was named to head the CANADIAN TRANSPORT COMMISSION.

MARINE INDUSTRIES LTD, shipyards located at Sorel, Que., approximately 50 km northeast of Montreal on the St Lawrence River. The company was developed by Joseph Simard who garnered major shipbuilding contracts from the federal government during World War II and who ran the operation with the help of brother Édouard.

MARITIME RIGHTS, Atlantic protest movement that reached its peak in the 1920s. The Maritime provinces' decline in population and economic power after 1867 created agitation to get federal support for improved transportation, changes in tariffs, and larger subsidies. The campaign may have encouraged voters in the region to penalize the unsympathetic federal parties (although it is difficult to determine why electors voted as they did). In 1926 the government of Prime Minister MACKENZIE KING appointed a royal commission to investigate the discontent, and although railway freight rates were lowered and subsidies increased as a result, the commission's main recommendations for linking subsidies to fiscal need were overlooked.

MARQUIS WHEAT, strain of wheat developed by CHARLES E. SAUNDERS at the DOMINION EXPERIMENTAL FARM in Ottawa and tested at the branch at Indian Head, Sask., in the early 1900s. It was a high-quality wheat that matured early, allowing prairie farmers to escape early frost damage. It was placed in general distribution in 1909 and became the standard spring wheat in North America until the 1940s.

MARSH, LEONARD CHARLES (1906-82), social scientist. Born at London, Eng., and educated at the London School of Economics, he came to McGill Univ. in 1930 as director of a social science research program. He wrote *Canadians in and out of Work* (1940), contributed to the LEAGUE FOR SOCIAL RECONSTRUCTION's work, and during World War II was author of the *Report on Social Security for Canada*, an effort to prepare a blueprint for social welfare. Marsh worked for the United Nations Relief and Rehabilitation Administration and taught at the Univ. of British Columbia from 1948 to 1972.

MARTIN, PAUL JOSEPH JAMES (1903–), federal politician. Martin was born at Ottawa and educated at the Univ. of Toronto, Osgoode Hall, Harvard, and Cambridge. He won election to Parliament as a Liberal in 1935 and became secretary of state and then health and welfare minister in Prime Minister MACKENZIE KING's and LOUIS ST LAURENT's governments. Among his achievements were the CANADIAN CITIZENSHIP ACT and hospital insurance. Martin also played an important role in diplomacy, notably his 1955 success in pressing expanded membership on the United Nations. He tried for the Liberal leadership in 1958 but lost to LESTER PEARSON; nonetheless he was a key Liberal in the destruction of the DIEFENBAKER government. In 1963 he became secretary of state for external affairs, but his tenure was made difficult by the Vietnam War and by increasing difficulties with France. He lost the 1968 leadership race to PIERRE TRUDEAU, was made senate leader and from 1975 to 1979 HIGH COMMISSIONER in London. He published two successful volumes of memoirs in the 1980s.

MARTIN, WILLIAM MELVILLE (1876-1970), premier of Saskatchewan. Martin, born at Norwich, Ont., was educated at the Univ. of Toronto and Osgoode Hall. He moved to Regina after the turn of the century, and was elected to Parliament in 1908 and 1911 as a Liberal. In 1916, he became leader of the Saskatchewan Liberal party and premier, guiding the province through the war and post-war PROGRESSIVE uprising. In 1922, afer he had left the premiership, he became a judge and in 1941 chief justice of Saskatchewan, a post he held for 20 years.

courtesy National Archives of Canada/C-8354

Vincent Massey

MASSEY, CHARLES VINCENT (1887-1967), politician, diplomat, governor general of Canada. He was the grandson of HART MASSEY, the founder of the powerful farm implement dynasty. Educated at the Univ. of Toronto and Oxford, he taught history at the Univ. of Toronto from 1913 to 1915. During World War I, he served in the army in Canada and worked for a time in the Privy Council Office in Ottawa. From 1921 he was president of MASSEY-HARRIS CO., a position he resigned to join MACKENZIE KING's cabinet in 1925. But the voters rejected his attempts at election, and King in 1926 named him Canada's first minister to the United States. He was more successful there in the social and public relations role than in doing the hard work of diplomacy, and his term ended with the election of R.B. BENNETT and the Conservatives in 1930. He headed the National Liberal Federation through the election of 1935, at times thinking of displacing King and turning the Liberal party in reform directions. After the election, King sent him to London as HIGH COMMISSIONER where he remained until 1946, representing Canada and seeking honours. His judgment on political questions between Canada and Britain was not highly thought of by King. After his return to Canada in 1946, Prime Minister ST LAURENT named him the head of the ROYAL COMMISSION ON NATIONAL DEVELOPMENT IN THE ARTS, LETTERS AND SCIENCES and the Massey Commission report, produced in 1951, recommended creation of the CANADA COUNCIL. When that cultural body was formed in 1957, Massey had already been governor general for five years, the first Canadian to hold the post. He filled the post in a fashion that minimized the break with tradition that having a Canadian governor general represented. In 1959, his term over, he went into active retirement, establishing, among other things, Massey College, an ersatz Oxford college, at the Univ. of Toronto.

MASSEY, DANIEL (1798-1856), manufacturer. Born in Windsor, Vt, Massey immigrated to Upper Canada to farm. In 1849 he set up Newcastle Foundry and Machine Manufactory and three years later his son, HART ALMEURIN MASSEY, joined the business. This was the basis of the MASSEY MANUFACTURING CO., which specialized in agricultural implements. In 1890 the firm merged with A. Harris Co. to form MASSEY-HARRIS.

MASSEY, HART ALMEURIN (1823-1896), manufacturer. Son of DANIEL MASSEY, Hart Massey was born in Haldimand Township, Upper Canada. After joining his father's foundry business, Hart launched the family company into the manufacture of agricultural implements. After his father's death he changed the company name to Newcastle Agricultural Works and then, in 1870, to MASSEY MANUFACTURING CO. In 1890 he merged his company with A. Harris to form MASSEY-HARRIS CO. He assumed the presidency until his death. Massey is also known for the Massey Music Hall in Toronto and the Massey Foundation, formed in 1918 out of his estate.

MASSEY, RAYMOND HART (1896-1983), actor. Grandson of HART MASSEY and brother of VINCENT MASSEY, Raymond was born in Toronto. After acting at Oxford Univ., he turned professional in 1922 in England, beginning a distinguished stage career. He began in films in 1931 and is best remembered for his portrayals of Lincoln and Dr. Gillespie on the "Doctor Kildare" U.S. television series.

MASSEY-FERGUSON LTD, company formed in 1953 when Argus Corp. amalgamated the Harry Ferguson tractor company and MASSEY-HARRIS. The company rivaled the giant International Harvester tractor and implements manufacturer in world markets. A change in management occurred in 1956, and the company continued to prosper through the 1960s but fell into insolvency in the late 1970s. Conrad Black, an Argus partner, took charge of the failing company but in 1980 he sold the company to the Massey pension fund. Massey received bail-outs from two levels of government in 1981, and by 1986 the salvagable portion of the company was restructured as Verity Corp. The farm machinery production lines closed down in 1988.

MASSEY-HARRIS CO. LTD, company formed in 1890 when manufacturer HART A. MASSEY merged MASSEY MANUFACTURING CO. with A. Harris, Son and Co. The company produced a variety of top-quality farm implements. After a number of acquisitions, the business became the largest of its kind in the British empire. A bicycle division was also set up which was purchased by CANADA CYCLE AND MOTOR CO LTD. (CCM) in 1899. VINCENT MASSEY became president from 1921 to 1925 and JAMES DUNCAN from 1941 to 1956. In 1953 the company merged with Harry Ferguson's tractor company forming MASSEY-FERGUSON.

MASSEY MANUFACTURING CO., name in 1870 for company founded by DANIEL MASSEY as the Newcastle Foundry and Machine Manufactory in 1849. It was under HART MASSEY that the company name was changed. By 1880 the company headquarters was in Toronto. The company expanded its production of agricultural implements, especially reapers and mowers, in the 1880s as settlers began to spread across the Canadian west; it also successfully penetrated the large American market. In 1890 Hart Massey merged the company with A. HARRIS's farming implement company to form MASSEY-HARRIS CO. Ltd, for many years Canada's largest implement dealer.

MATHERS COMMISSION, the 1919 federal Royal Commission on Industrial Relations headed by T.G. Mathers, chief justice of Manitoba. It investigated the state of labour-management relations in Canada and recommended that unions be recognized and that labour peace be established by means of factory councils representing unions and management.

MAVOR, JAMES (1854-1925), educator. Born at Stanraer, Scot., he came to Canada in 1892 to become professor of political economy at the Univ. of Toronto. He began the teaching of commerce, wrote on Russian economic history, Ontario hydro, Manitoba telephones, and the wheat economy, but he was probably best known for his interest in the plight of Russian DOUKHOBORS, an interest that led to substantial immigration to Canada. His memoirs are entitled *My Windows on the Street of the World* (1923).

MEDICAL RESEARCH COUNCIL, federal crown corporation founded in 1969 to help stimulate medical research in Canada through grants and awards.

MEDICARE, comprehensive, universal, prepaid medical care. It was first implemented in Saskatchewan by the governments of T.C. DOUGLAS and WOODROW LLOYD in 1961-62, despite a doctors' strike. Nationally, the government of Prime Minister LESTER PEARSON moved towards medicare at a federal-provincial conference in July 1965, introduced legislation in Parliament in July 1966, and Pearson's successor brought the plan into effect on 1 July 1968. Under the terms of the act British Columbia and Saskatchewan were eligible for federal reimbursement of 50 per cent of the cost of their provincial plans; Manitoba, Nova Scotia, and Newfoundland joined in 1969; and the others came in soon after. *See also* SASKATCHEWAN DOCTORS' STRIKE.

MEECH LAKE ACCORD, 1987, constitutional agreement between the federal and provincial governments. Prime Minister BRIAN MULRONEY had as one of his aims the reconciliation of Que-

bec to the 1982 CONSTITUTION, which he achieved through an agreement negotiated in a meeting at Meech Lake on 30 April 1987, and revised on 3 June 1987. The accord declared Quebec a "distinct society," without defining the phrase. It also gave provincial governments the right to nominate SUPREME COURT of Canada justices and to present a slate of names from which senators would be chosen. Each province was also given a veto over future constitutional change in defined areas. Although all ten premiers and the leaders of the federal Liberal and New Democratic parties accepted the accord which was hailed in Quebec and the west, there was soon sharp criticism from some federal Liberals unhappy at the destruction of PIERRE TRUDEAU's 1982 constitution and the loss of a strong federal power, from women's groups concerned that the CANADIAN CHARTER OF RIGHTS AND FREEDOMS was now subordinate to the "distinct society" clause, and from the Northwest Territories and Yukon governments that feared unanimous consent from the ten provinces would never be secured for their eventual transformation into provinces. The accord must be ratified by Ottawa and all ten provinces within three years before it comes into effect.

courtesy NFB / National Archives of Canada

Arthur Meighen

MEIGHEN, ARTHUR (1874-1960), prime minister. Clear-headed and logical, Meighen won neither the affection nor the trust of the Canadian people. Born in Anderson, Ont., Meighen attended the Univ. of Toronto and then moved to Portage la Prairie, Man., to practise law. Elected to Parliament in 1908 as a Conservative, he began to build a reputation for powerful oratory. Made solicitor general in SIR ROBERT BORDEN's government, he soon added the portfolio of secretary of state. Meighen was one of the creators of the device of CLOSURE, the principal draftsman of the MILITARY SERVICE ACT, 1917, the chief defender of the WARTIME ELECTIONS ACT, 1917, and the bill nationalizing near-bankrupt railways and creating the CANADIAN NATIONAL RAILWAYS, all measures that were hotly opposed and that firmly fixed his reputation for extreme partisanship. When Borden stepped down he became prime minister in 1920. His one notable achievement in office was to urge Britain not to renew the Anglo-Japanese Alliance, an entanglement that Meighen believed was certain to involve Canada in difficulties with the United States.

His first term in office was brief. In the election of 1921, Meighen, bereft of support in Quebec, where his conscriptionist role was clearly remembered, and assailed for his defence of high tariffs by the PROGRESSIVE PARTY in Ontario and the West, suffered a crushing defeat. The Conservative party fell to third place in party standing, and MACKENZIE KING and the Liberal party formed the government. But Meighen did well in opposition, revitalizing and reorganizing his party, creating an image of decisiveness in sharp contrast to King's platitudes and drift. In the 1925 election, Meighen won more seats than King, but the Progressives held the balance and King refused to abandon the prime ministership. When Parliament met, King soon faced defeat in the House, and when Governor General VISCOUNT BYNG refused to agree to a new election, King abandoned office. Meighen became prime minister as a result of this KING-BYNG affair, but he soon lost a vote of confidence and faced an election. In 1926, the voters, evidently preferring a pliant King to the rigid Meighen, handed power back to the Liberals, and in 1927 Meighen stepped down as leader.

Prime Minister R.B. BENNETT made him a senator in 1932, and in 1941, with his party in virtual ruin after the disastrous elections of 1935 and 1940, an element of the party drafted Meighen to lead the Conservatives once more in a campaign for CONSCRIPTION and national government. His tenure ended abruptly when he was defeated by a CO-OPERATIVE COMMONWEALTH FEDERATION candidate in a Feb. 1942 by-election, and Meighen left politics for good.

MEN IN SHEEPSKIN COATS, phrase used by minister of the interior CLIFFORD SIFTON to describe the type of immigrant he wanted to settle western Canada at the turn of the century. Sifton spoke of "stalwart peasants in sheepskin coats" to refer to eastern Europeans who would come to western Canada to farm.

MERCANTILE BANK AFFAIR, 1963 row between First National City Bank (Citibank) of New York and the federal government. In that year, the bank told Ottawa that it proposed to buy the Mercantile Bank of Canada, a small Dutch-owned bank. WALTER GORDON, the finance minister, opposed the sale, but the bank completed the purchase. The government then proposed to amend the BANK ACT to freeze the growth of any bank, including Mercantile, owned more than 25 per cent by non-residents. Lengthy negotiations followed, and Citibank was given five years to reduce its ownership to 25 per cent.

MERCHANTS' BANK OF CANADA, bank established in 1861 by SIR HUGH ALLAN and a number of Montreal investors. Seven years later it acquired the failing Commercial Bank and became a major banking institution. It struggled through hard times in the late 1870s, regained its prosperity by the turn of the century, but had sunk into insolvency by 1921. It was then taken over by the BANK OF MONTREAL which assumed its $8 million debt.

courtesy Livernois/National Archives of Canada/C-3304

Honoré Mercier

MERCIER, HONORÉ (1840-94), premier of Quebec. Born at St-Athanase, Lower Canada, Mercier was a founder of the PARTI NATIONAL in 1871 and under its banner won election to Parliament. In 1878, he lost his riding, turned to provincial politics and won a seat in the legislature in 1879. In 1883, he became Liberal leader, first receiving national attention for his part in mobilizing Quebecers against the execution of LOUIS RIEL in 1885. Recreating the Parti national to bring in anti-Ottawa dissidents of all parties, Mercier won the 1886 provincial election. He resolved the JESUITS' ESTATES QUESTION, encouraged development and settlement of the province, and in 1887 called a premiers' meeting at which the COMPACT THEORY OF CONFEDERATION was proclaimed. Mercier was implicated in the BAIE DES CHALEURS SCANDAL in 1891 and his government lost office.

MESSER, DONALD CHARLES FREDERICK (1909-73), country musician. Born at Tweedside, N.B., he played the fiddle as a child and by the end of the 1920s was performing on radio. In 1939, he formed "The Islanders" for Charlottetown radio and 20 years later moved to television. From 1959 to 1969, Don Messer's "Jubilee" was a popular staple of the CANADIAN BROADCASTING CORP., and its cancellation stirred protest.

MÉTIS, mixed-race people who emerged out of the intermarriage of white fur traders and native women. These people were the children of French fur traders and native women and British — usually Scottish — fur traders and native women, and were known as Métis and country-born, respectively. The terms half-breeds and bois-brûlés were also used. The Métis lived in small communities in what became Manitoba and Saskatchewan but were concentrated near the Hudson's Bay Co. posts on the Red River in the Red River Settlement. In 1869, under LOUIS RIEL, they resisted annexation of their settlements to Canada without adequate guarantees of their rights and land titles. The RED RIVER REBELLION forced Prime Minister JOHN A. MACDONALD to introduce the MANITOBA ACT in March 1870.

MICHENER, DANIEL ROLAND (1900-), politician, governor general of Canada. Born at Lacombe, Alta., he was educated at the Univ. of Alberta and at Oxford as a Rhodes Scholar. He practised law in Toronto from 1924, was elected to the Ontario legislature as a Conservative in 1945 for one term, and to the House of Commons

courtesy *Globe & Mail*/Patriquen

Roland Michener

in 1953. When JOHN DIEFENBAKER formed his government in 1957, Michener was not given a cabinet post because he was thought to be too close to LESTER PEARSON; instead he became speaker of the House of Commons, a post he filled with impartiality, thus reinforcing the enmity Diefenbaker felt towards him. After Michener's defeat in the election of 1963, the Liberal government sent him to India as high commissioner in 1964 and then appointed him governor general in 1967. For seven years, he and his wife Norah tried to democratize Rideau Hall, a task he carried out with distinction.

MID-CANADA LINE, radar line built by Canada across the 55th parallel, using the MCGILL FENCE. Construction was authorized in June 1954.

MIDDLE POWER, term used during and after WORLD WAR II, first by Canadians and then by others, to describe countries such as Canada which were influential beyond their borders for various reasons but were clearly not world-scale powers. The phrase neatly fit a world with five "great" powers — the United States, Britain, the Soviet Union, France, and China. Now that there are two superpowers — United States and the Soviet Union — the term no longer describes any reality.

courtesy Manitoba Archives

General Middleton accepts Poundmaker's surrender, 1885

MIDDLETON, SIR FREDERICK DOBSON
(1825-98), soldier. He was commissioned in the British Army in 1842 and came to Canada in 1868 to instruct the MILITIA. In 1884 he became commander of the Canadian militia and organized and led the expedition to the NORTH-WEST REBELLION in 1885. Not a brilliant commander, the ponderous (and portly) Middleton eventually crushed the MÉTIS and Indians by sheer weight. His accomplishment was diminished by his involvement in the misappropriation of spoils during the rebellion.

MILITARY SERVICE ACT, 1917, act passed
in the House of Commons in July 1917 and signed on 29 Aug that declared all men between the ages of 20 and 45 eligible for overseas military service. As a device for reinforcing the CANADIAN EXPEDITIONARY FORCE, the act was a failure (only 24,132 men reached units in France); as a device to help Prime Minister SIR ROBERT BORDEN to form a UNION GOVERNMENT, it was a short-term success. *See also* CONSCRIPTION CRISIS.

MILITARY VOTERS' ACT, 1917, legislation
passed in Sept. 1917 giving soldiers the right to vote. The act allowed soldiers to vote only for the government or the opposition; the votes of soldiers who did not know their constituency could be allocated where they were needed. The Liberals made serious charges of UNION GOVERNMENT misuse of this act during the 1917 election.

MILITIA, volunteers for part-time army service. Under a variety of MILITIA ACTS before and after Confederation and under a number of names, men were enlisted in local units across the country, training in the evenings or on weekends. In both WORLD WAR I and WORLD WAR II, the militia provided most of the first contingents for overseas service, large numbers of the officers of the army, and much of the training expertise. Often scorned by regulars and by the public as "Saturday night soldiers," the reserve forces have struggled on despite scanty budgets and obsolete equipment. The MULRONEY government has pledged to upgrade the reserves.

MILITIA ACTS, legislation governing the raising of manpower for the defence of Canada. Pre-Confederation Militia Acts in British North America provided for a levy en masse of all males between ages 16 and 50, usually calling for a one-day muster that was more honoured in the breach than the observance. Acts provided as well for active militia composed of volunteers or those drawn by lot. During the Crimean War, the Province of Canada enacted laws to provide for an active militia of 5000 to be trained and paid, unusual additions in that day. The threat posed by the American Civil War led JOHN A. MACDONALD's government to ask for a 50,000-man active militia to be trained and paid for 28 days, but this proposal was defeated, the government falling. The first Militia Act of the Dominion of Canada, 1868, provided for a militia of 40,000 volunteers, and a subsequent act in 1883 laid the basis for a permanent force by providing for staffing of militia training schools. The 1904 act established a militia council, a chief of the general staff, and authorized a permanent force of 4000. After World War I, the 1922 National Defence Act brought the three services together under the Department of National Defence.

MILLARD, CHARLES HIBBERT (1896-1978), labour leader. Born in St Thomas, Ont., he helped organize the General Motors auto workers in Oshawa, Ont., and led them in a strike for union recognition in 1937. In 1938 and 1939 he was Canadian director of the United Auto Workers and he filled a number of important labour posts in subsequent years. He was elected vice-president of the CANADIAN LABOUR CONGRESS at its founding in 1956.

MILNE, DAVID BROWN (1882-1953), painter. Born at Paisley, Ont., he studied at the Art Students League in New York. After service in the CANADIAN EXPEDITIONARY FORCE, he returned to New York State, beginning to develop his linear style. Milne returned to Canada in 1929, and VINCENT MASSEY became his patron. His work is evenly divided between his oils and luminescent watercolours, and he also produced superb dry point prints.

MINE WORKERS UNION OF CANADA, labour union founded by coal-miners in Alberta in 1925. The miners had left the United Mine Workers of America when it opposed pay cuts in the Alberta coal fields during a time of severe depression in the industry. The MWUC affiliated with the ALL-CANADIAN CONGRESS OF LABOUR after it was formed in 1926 but then joined the Communist-led WORKERS' UNITY LEAGUE in 1930. It merged with the UMW after the WUL disbanded in 1936. *See also* ESTEVAN MASSACRE.

courtesy Topley/National Archives of Canada/C-8466

Lord Minto

MINTO, GILBERT JOHN MURRAY KYNYNMOND ELLIOT, 4TH EARL OF (1845-1914), governor general of Canada. He served as military secretary to LORD LANSDOWNE in Ottawa and as the chief of staff to General FRED MIDDLETON, the commander of the Canadian forces during the NORTH-WEST REBELLION, 1885. Governor general from 1898 to 1904, Minto was not a success. He was unhappy with SIR WILFRED

LAURIER's cautious policy towards committing Canadian troops to the BOER WAR, and he was an avid supporter of British schemes for IMPERIAL FEDERATION. Minto did not understand that the role of a modern vice-regal representative was properly limited only to such things as the donation of a Minto Cup for lacrosse supremacy.

MITCHELL, HUMPHREY (1894-1950), labour leader, politician. Born in Old Shoreham, Eng., Mitchell came to Canada after World War I and became an active trade unionist. He was elected to the House of Commons as an independent in 1931 and in late 1941 was named minister of labour after the KIRKLAND LAKE STRIKE intensified union criticism of the federal government.

MITCHELL, PETER (1824-99), premier of New Brunswick, federal politician. Born at Newcastle, N.B., he was a strong proponent of CONFEDERATION in politics. He was briefly premier in 1866 and, appointed a senator, he joined the government of SIR JOHN A. MACDONALD in 1867 as fisheries minister. In 1872 he left the Senate and won election to the House, but his career was destroyed by the PACIFIC SCANDAL.

MITCHELL, WILLIAM ORMOND (1914–), writer. Born at Weyburn, Sask., he attended the univs. of Manitoba and Alberta. He taught school for a time, and published his first novel, *Who Has Seen the Wind*, in 1947, a book that has achieved continuing readership. His other novels have not had similar success, although his radio plays on "Jake and the Kid," based on stories written for *MACLEAN'S*, had a substantial vogue. Eccentric, Mitchell is well known in the Canadian media.

MOCK PARLIAMENT, *see* WOMEN'S PARLIAMENT

MOLSON COMPANIES LTD, conglomerate based on the brewery established by John Molson in 1786. The Molson family became one of the leading clans of the Montreal business community when, in the early 19th century, Molson's sons, William, Thomas, and John, extended the family's activities into investment banking through Molson's Bank and the BANK OF MONTREAL. In the 1960s the Molsons expanded into hardware, lumber, and chemical sales. The present name was adopted in 1973, and the Molson family still retains a large minority interest in the company.

MONCK, CHARLES STANLEY MONCK, 4TH VISCOUNT (1819-94), governor general of Canada. A Liberal MP at Westminster from 1849, Monck was governor general of British North America from 1861 to 1867 and of the Dominion of Canada from 1867 to 1868. Appointed to British North America, he showed talent in managing the difficult Canadian-American relationship during the Civil War years and, most notably, in helping to bring together the GREAT COALITION in the Canadas that pressed CONFEDERATION to fruition. Monck also tried, with less success, to moderate opposition to Confederation in the Maritimes.

MONK, FREDERICK DEBARTZCH (1856-1914), politician. Born at Montreal and educated in law at McGill Univ., Monk was first elected to Parliament as a Conservative in 1896. He led the provincial party in Quebec from 1900 to 1904, simultaneously sitting in the Commons. In 1911, he became public works minister in the BORDEN government, but he resigned the next year in protest at the government's naval policy.

MONTGOMERY, LUCY MAUD (1874-1942), writer. Best remembered for her phenomenally successful story of a young girl on Prince Edward Island, *Anne of Green Gables*, Montgomery was a successful Canadian author at a time when that was a rare species. Extraordinarily productive — her corpus consisted of over 20 novels and hundreds of poems and short stories — she mastered the knack of writing for the audience of her day. Her plots were maudlin, her characters' virtues always triumphed, but she clearly gave readers what they wanted. The cult of Anne, the plucky P.E.I. redhead, continues to this day, greatly enhanced by the successful CBC television shows. Montgomery's own life, as her diaries, published in 1987, make clear, had fewer triumphs and more personal tragedy.

MONTREAL CITY AND DISTRICT SAVINGS BANK, founded as a savings bank for small depositors in 1846 at a time when most Canadian banks dealt only with wealthy investors. BISHOP IGNACE BOURGET was instrumental in its founding, and the bank was intended to marshall the savings of francophones into projects compatible with Catholic philosophy.

MONTREAL LIGHT, HEAT AND POWER CO., formed in 1901-2 when the FORGET brokerage firm consolidated a number of Quebec utilities. Under the direction of SIR HERBERT S. HOLT, the company acquired a monopoly of the hydroelectric power generation and distribution in the Montreal area. In 1944 the company and its subsidiary Beauharnois Light Heat and Power were taken over by the Quebec government to form the basis of HYDRO-QUÉBEC.

MONTREAL STOCK EXCHANGE, incorporated under a Quebec charter in 1874. The exchange opened in May 1832, selling stocks in the Champlain and St Lawrence Railway. In 1863 an 11-man board of brokers was formed. The exchange listed stocks in the CANADIAN PACIFIC RAILWAY in 1883 and listed its first mining stocks in 1896. In 1965 the exchange amalgamated with its rival, the Canadian Stock Exchange.

MOORE, DORA MAVOR (1888-1979), actress, teacher. Born at Glasgow, Scot., Dora Mavor studied acting in Toronto and at the Royal Academy of Dramatic Arts in London, Eng. She acted in Canada, the United States, and Britain and then began teaching and directing in Toronto. She founded the Village Players and the New Play Society which produced "Spring Thaw," an annual satirical review.

MOORE, TOM (1878-1943), labour leader. Born in Leeds, Eng., Moore came to Canada in 1909 and was soon active in the labour movement. He was elected TRADES AND LABOUR CONGRESS president in 1918, a position he held until 1935, and then again from 1938 to 1943. He was a strong supporter of the American Federation of Labor and led the battle against the ONE BIG UNION in 1919.

MOORES, FRANK DUFF (1933-), premier of Newfoundland. Born at Carbonear, Nfld, he entered politics in 1968 when he won election to the House of Commons. Two years later he became leader of the provincial Progressive Conservative party. There was a virtual tie in seats with the Liberals in the 1971 election, and early in 1972 Premier JOSEPH SMALLWOOD resigned, Moores then being asked to form the government. He won clear victories in 1972 and 1975 and left electoral politics in 1979. Moores supported BRIAN MULRONEY's bid to capture the Conservative national leadership, and he has worked as a lobbyist in Ottawa during Mulroney's government.

MORENZ, HOWARTH WILLIAM (1902-37), hockey player. Howie Morenz joined the Montreal Canadiens in 1923, quickly becoming the fans' favorite because of his speed and scoring. Traded away in 1934, he came back to Montreal in 1936, but died as a result of injuries suffered in a game in Jan. 1937.

MORGAN, HENRY (1819-93), businessman. Born in Saline, Scot., Morgan opened a dry-goods store in Montreal in the mid-1840s. The establishment, which became known as Henry Morgan & Co., grew to become one of the largest retail stores in the city. Morgan was also the founder of the Morgan Trust Co. which he established to offer trust and financial services to Montreal's upper crust.

MORGENTALER, HENRY (1923–), physician. Born in Poland and a survivor of Nazi death camps, Morgentaler came to Canada in 1950, beginning the practice of medicine in Montreal. By 1969, he had become an open advocate of abortion, carrying out thousands himself and ceaselessly preaching it across the land. Tried repeatedly since 1973 for violating the Criminal Code's prohibition against abortion without consent of a hospital committee, he was found not guilty by juries but suffered at the hands of judges, his legal difficulties stirring up concern among lawyers. In 1988 the Supreme Court of Canada overturned his last conviction and the law against abortion, vindicating his long struggle. Morgentaler has tried to set up abortion clinics across Canada, drawing protests and praise.

MORRICE, JAMES WILSON (1865-1924), painter. Born at Montreal, Morrice studied art in Paris and decided to live abroad, although he regularly returned to Canada and painted some of his best work here. Morrice's painting was initially influenced by the Impressionists and then

by Matisse. He worked as a Canadian war artist in World War I.

MORRIS, LESLIE (1904-64), Communist leader. Born in Somerset, Eng., Morris worked on the railway out of Winnipeg, helped found the Young Workers' League in 1922, and participated in the underground convention of the COMMUNIST PARTY in 1923. Morris held innumerable positions on the party executive and, in 1962, he became leader.

MORRIS, JOE (1913–), labour leader. Born in Lancashire, Eng., Morris became active in the labour movement through the International Woodworkers of America. He served as president of the CANADIAN LABOUR CONGRESS from 1974 until 1978. Under his leadership, the CLC organized a one-day national strike against wage and price controls in 1976.

MORRISON, JAMES "J.J." (1861-1936), farm leader. Born in Arthur, Canada West, he helped found the UNITED FARMERS OF ONTARIO in 1914 and held the post of UFO secretary from 1914 to 1933. Morrison was instrumental in the entry of the UFO into politics in 1919 but he opposed the UFO government's policy of cooperating with labour and urban progressives (BROADENING OUT). This opposition split the ranks of the UFO in the Ontario legislature and led to the downfall of the farm government in 1923. *See also* E.C. DRURY.

MORTON, WILLIAM LEWIS (1908-80), historian. Born at Gladstone, Man., and educated at the univs. of Manitoba and Oxford, Morton began his career with a classic study of the PROGRESSIVE PARTY (1950) which won a Governor General's Award. His history of Manitoba (1957), his study of 1857-73, *The Critical Years* (1974), and his text, *The Kingdom of Canada* (1963), established him as one of the leading Conservative interpreters of Canada's past, one who had a concern for regional differences.

MOSHER, AARON ROLAND (1881-1959), labour leader. Born in Halifax County, N.S., he was president of the CANADIAN BROTHERHOOD OF RAILWAY EMPLOYEES from its founding in 1908 until 1952. In 1926 he started the ALL-CANADIAN CONGRESS OF LABOUR, which was composed of a number of Canadian unions denied membership in the TRADES AND LABOUR CONGRESS. He steered the ACCL into a merger with Canadian branches of the Congress of Industrial Organizations in 1940 to found the CANADIAN CONGRESS OF LABOUR, and was its president from 1940 to 1956. Mosher was a strong labour nationalist, favoured industrial unions, and fought the Communists all his life.

MOTHERWELL, WILLIAM RICHARD (1860-1943), farm leader. Born in Perth, Canada West, he helped found the TERRITORIAL GRAIN GROWERS' ASSN in 1901 and was named minister of agriculture in the first Saskatchewan government. Motherwell was a champion of farmers' rights and an opponent of the monopolistic hold of railways and elevator companies on the western grain trade. He served two terms as minister of agriculture in the government of Prime Minister MACKENZIE KING from 1921 to 1926 and from 1926 to 1930.

MOUSSEAU, JOSEPH-ALFRED (1838-86), premier of Quebec. A *bleu*, Mousseau supported CONFEDERATION. He ran for the Conservative party in 1874, won election, and entered the cabinet in 1880. In 1882, he and J.-A. CHAPLEAU changed posts, and Mousseau thus became premier of Quebec. His contentious and unhappy term lasted only two years before he was forced out of office and onto the bench.

MOWAT, FARLEY (1921-), author. A very popular writer, Mowat was born at Belleville, Ont., and served overseas in World War II with the Hastings and Prince Edward Regiment, the subject of two of his best books. Mowat first won acclaim, however, for *People of the Deer* (1952), a sharp attack on Ottawa's treatment of the Inuit, and he followed that popular success with a flood of works, including several written for children. A showman, Mowat has engaged in widely publicized jousts with officialdom in Canada and the United States, his very presence sometimes crystallizing popular support for his causes which include whales, wolves, endangered species, and native peoples.

MOWAT, SIR OLIVER (1820-1903), premier of Ontario, federal politician. Born at Kingston, Upper Canada, he articled as a lawyer under JOHN A. MACDONALD. Beginning a practice in Toronto, Mo-

wat became a Reformer and sat in the assembly of the Province of Canada, 1858-64, holding ministerial posts. He participated in the conferences that produced CONFEDERATION, and in 1872 he began his long tenure as premier of Ontario. He practised moderation in politics, turning the Liberal party into the embodiment of his virtues. His government was development-oriented, moderately reformist for its day, interested in increasing the province's power vis-à-vis Ottawa, and inordinately successful. In 1896, Mowat left Ontario for the House of Commons, running in the election as WILFRID LAURIER's right-hand man. He was minister of justice until becoming lieutenant governor of Ontario in 1897.

MULOCK, SIR WILLIAM (1844-1944), lawyer, politician. Born at Bond Head, Canada West. Mulock, a Liberal, was first elected to the House of Commons in 1882. He was named postmaster general in the government of WILFRID LAURIER in 1896 and became Canada's first minister of labour in 1900, holding the two posts simultaneously. Mulock was responsible for bringing MACKENZIE KING into government service in 1900 as deputy minister of labour. He retired from politics in 1905 to sit on the Supreme Court of Ontario.

MULRONEY, MARTIN BRIAN (1939-), prime minister of Canada. Mulroney was born in Baie-Comeau, Que., the son of Irish immigrants. He attended local schools, St Francis Xavier Univ., and Univ. Laval law school. Long involved in student politics, he worked as an aide to ALVIN HAMILTON, a minister in the DIEFENBAKER government, and he built a role for himself as an adviser on Quebec politics to the Chief and later as an adviser to E. DAVIE FULTON. While Mulroney established himself as a respected labour lawyer and arbitrator in Montreal, however, he was content to stay in the backrooms. In 1976, by then married to Mila Pivnicki for three years, he ran a glitzy campaign for the Conservative leadership, losing to JOE CLARK. The next year he was named president of the Iron Ore Co. of Canada, a U.S. subsidiary, and in this role he amicably negotiated the shutdown of operations in Schefferville, Que. When Clark's government lost power in 1980 after its brief tenure, Mulroney manoeuvred quietly in the background. A new leadership convention was called in 1983, and he ran and narrowly won on the last ballot. Elected in a by-election in Central Nova, N.S., the novice parliamentarian performed creditably in the House against Prime Minister PIERRE TRUDEAU where he also imposed discipline on a fractious Tory caucus and mobilized a formidable electoral machine. In the election of Sept. 1984, assisted by his superb performances in television debates, he crushed Prime Minister JOHN TURNER, Trudeau's successor, and the Liberals, winning an overwhelming majority.

His government quickly ran into difficulties when it tried to eliminate the indexing of OLD AGE PENSIONS, however, and a succession of patronage scandals and ministerial resignations gave the prime minister a sleazy image that reduced his and his government's standings in the opinion polls to record lows by 1986. In the policy area, Mulroney negotiated a free trade agreement with the United States, and his government secured Quebec's adherence to the Constitution of 1982 in the MEECH LAKE ACCORD, produced a clear blueprint for defence, and essayed tax reform.

MULTICULTURALISM, a term expressing the varied ethnic heritages of Canadians. First heard widely in the 1960s as a counter to the emphasis on BILINGUALISM AND BICULTURALISM that characterized the Liberal government, multiculturalism became government policy in 1971, with a minister put in charge the next year and the Canadian Consultative Council of Multiculturalism created in 1973. The ethos of multiculturalism is that every Canadian, whatever his or her origin, has the right to honour his or her heritage in Canada. But French Canada has been suspicious of the idea, seeing it as an attempt to dilute the place of the French language and as encouraging immigration that lowers the percentage of French-speakers. Others have seen multiculturalism as a political tool, an attempt to divide and rule by using federal funds.

MUNRO, ALICE (1931–), writer. Born at Wingham, Ont., and educated at the Univ. of Western Ontario, she reflects small-town southwestern Ontario in her work. Her short stories have won widespread acclaim, notably *Lives of Girls and Women* (1971), and she publishes regularly in the *New Yorker*.

courtesy Duncan Cameron/
National Archives of Canada/PA-112770

Gerda Munsinger on television

MUNSINGER AFFAIR, political controversy which developed in 1966 after Liberal minister of justice LUCIEN CARDIN revealed that PIERRE SÉVIGNY, associate minister of national defence in the Conservative government of Prime Minister JOHN DIEFENBAKER, had had an affair in the late 1950s and early 1960s with a prostitute named Gerda Munsinger with vague connections in East European intelligence circles. A royal commission found that no breaches of security had occurred. The affair was, however, important for demonstrating how low Canadian politics had sunk in the mid-sixties.

MURDOCHVILLE STRIKE, strike of miners belonging to the United Steelworkers of America against Gaspé Copper Mines from March to Oct. 1957. The company employed strike-breakers protected by the Quebec Provincial Police and much violence ensued. Although both the CONFÉDÉRATION DES TRAVAILLEURS CATHOLIQUES DU CANADA / CANADIAN CATHOLIC CONFEDERATION OF LABOUR and the Fédération des travailleurs de Québec / Quebec Federation of Labour supported the strike, the workers were defeated.

MURPHY, EMILY GOWAN (1868-1933), writer, feminist. Born at Cookstown, Ont., Emily Ferguson married in 1887 and moved in 1904 with her family to Manitoba and then Alberta. Her writing, often under the pen name of "Janey Canuck," had already become popular in the press and *The Impressions of Janey Canuck Abroad* had been published in 1901. Four further books followed. She campaigned for the protection of dower rights, played a role in the WOMEN'S SUFFRAGE campaign, and was active in women's associations. In 1916 she became a police magistrate in Edmonton, the first woman magistrate in the Empire, and she led the fight in the PERSONS CASE that was finally successful in 1929.

MURRAY, ANNE (1945–), singer. Personable and wholesome, she won extraordinary acclaim as a pop singer in the 1970s and 1980s. "Snowbird," her first major hit, catapulted her to public attention, and her subsequent career blossomed in both pop and country fields. Her squeaky clean image greatly aided her rise.

MURRAY, GEORGE HENRY (1861-1929), premier of Nova Scotia. Born at Grand Narrows, N.S., he became Liberal leader and premier in 1896 when W.S. FIELDING joined the cabinet at Ottawa. Murray remained in power without a break until 1923; careful and cautious, he inspired few but continued to get votes. His government stressed development, education, and moderate reformism, including WOMEN'S SUFFRAGE in 1917.

MUTCHMOR, JAMES RALPH (1892-1980), United Church clergyman. Born on Manitoulin Island, Ont., Mutchmor was educated at the Univ. of Toronto, Columbia Univ., and, after war service, at the Union Theological Seminary. He was a minister in Winnipeg until 1936 then became associate secretary and later secretary of the United Church's Board of Evangelism and Social Service. A crusader against vice of all kinds, real or imaginary, he was a popular figure and in 1962 became moderator of his church.

MUTUAL AID, the Canadian aid program for the Allies in WORLD WAR II. Begun in May 1943, it followed on the BILLION DOLLAR GIFT of 1942 and provided, free of cost, Canadian munitions and supplies to the Allies. While there were critics of the scheme in Quebec, their force was lessened because, although Britain received most of the more than $2 billion, other countries including the Soviet Union and China also received aid. Mutual Aid allowed Canadian production and employment to remain at peak levels during the last years of war.

MYNARSKI, ANDREW CHARLES (1916-44), airman. Born in Winnipeg, he was an air gunner in the ROYAL CANADIAN AIR FORCE. When his Lan-

caster was hit by enemy fire, Mynarski, although he could have parachuted to safety, tried to free one of his fellows. His equipment caught fire and he died of burns, but the trapped airman survived the crash. Mynarski was awarded a posthumous Victoria Cross.

NAISMITH, JAMES A. (1861-1939), inventor of basketball. Born in Ontario, Naismith attended McGill Univ. and studied for the Presbyterian ministry before taking a post as athletic instructor at the International YMCA Training School at Springfield, Mass. In 1891 Naismith invented basketball to keep physical education students active and entertained between football and baseball seasons.

NANAIMO COAL STRIKE, strike of miners belonging to the United Mine Workers of America against Vancouver Island coal mines from Sept. 1912 to Aug. 1914. The main issue was union recognition. The mine owners expelled miners from company-owned towns and used strike-breakers. In Aug. 1914, riots broke out at several locations on Vancouver Island and the provincial government ordered the militia to occupy the towns and restore order. Many union leaders were arrested and the strike collapsed.

NATIONAL COUNCIL OF WOMEN OF CANADA, organization founded in 1893. The council's first president was LADY ABERDEEN and under her and her successors, it championed the rights of women and children. Conservative and middle-class, the NCWC did not call for WOMEN'S SUFFRAGE until 1910. Still in existence, the council is now a somewhat less conservative lobby group; it pressed for creation of the ROYAL COMMISSION ON THE STATUS OF WOMEN in the 1960s and for entrenchment of women's rights in the CONSTITUTION, 1982.

NATIONAL ENERGY BOARD, federal agency established in 1959 to regulate the energy industry and advise the federal government on energy matters. All interprovincial and international energy transactions fall within its jurisdiction.

NATIONAL ENERGY PROGRAM, federal program introduced by the Liberal government of Prime Minister PIERRE TRUDEAU in fall 1980 following the failure of federal and provincial governments to reach agreement on the sharing of energy revenues. The NEP was designed to increase Canadian ownership of the resource industry, achieve Canadian self-sufficiency in energy, shield Canadians from high world prices for oil and gas, and increase Ottawa's share of resource revenues. Among the measures it introduced was the Petroleum and Gas Revenue Tax which was a tax on the gross revenue of energy companies, rather than a tax on their net income. The NEP and especially the PGRT became an important point of contention between Ottawa and the energy-rich provinces, particularly Alberta. The program was dismantled by the Conservative government of BRIAN MULRONEY after it came to power in Sept. 1984. *See also* PETER LOUGHEED.

NATIONAL FARMERS UNION, organization founded in 1969 as an amalgam of farm organizations from British Columbia, Saskatchewan, Manitoba and Ontario. It is considered a militant advocate of farmers' rights.

NATIONAL FARM RADIO FORUM, *see* "FARM FORUM"

NATIONAL FILM BOARD, agency established 2 May 1939 with the passage of the National Film Act to advise on government film activities. The first commissioner was JOHN GRIERSON, one of the pioneers of documentary film and a social visionary, who brought all government filmmaking under his control. During WORLD WAR II the NFB produced hundreds of propaganda films. After the war, the NFB interpreted Canada to Canadians and the world, developed formidable expertise in animation, and continued its documentary tradition. During the QUIET REVOLUTION, Quebec filmmakers blossomed in the NFB, thus helping create a Quebec cinema that flourished in the next decade. Feature films began to be produced early in the 1960s. In the 1970s, women's films were produced by Studio D.

NATIONAL GOVERNMENT PARTY, name used by the CONSERVATIVE PARTY in the 1940 election. Led by R.J. MANION, the Conservatives campaigned in the 1940 election on the need for Canada to fight WORLD WAR II with a national government made up of the "best brains." MACKENZIE KING mocked Manion by asking him to name the best brains who had agreed to serve, and for Quebec national government was too evocative of the UNION GOVERNMENT of 1917.

NATIONAL HARBOURS BOARD, crown corporation created in 1936 to oversee those harbours and harbour properties under federal jurisdiction.

NATIONAL HOUSING ACT, 1938, government legislation to encourage low-cost housing. Passed by the MACKENZIE KING government, the NHA increased federal guarantees for first mortgages to 90 per cent on low cost housing and thus encouraged construction.

NATIONAL METEOROLOGICAL SERVICE, federal agency established in 1871 to provide weather forecasting services. It was the forerunner to Environment Canada.

courtesy National Archives of Canada/C-13211

The National Policy by J.W. Bengough

NATIONAL POLICY, policy initiated by Conservative Prime Minister JOHN A. MACDONALD in 1879 with the introduction of a protective tariff designed to foster industrialization in Canada. The National Policy tariff raised existing overall tariff rates from approximately 20 per cent to close to 40 per cent to shield Canadian manufacturers from foreign, mostly American, competition, thus giving them a protected Canadian market in which to sell their goods. The National Policy remained basic Canadian policy until the 1930s even though successive governments continued to seek RECIPROCITY in non-manufactured goods with the United States. In later years Macdonald linked the National Policy tariff with his policy of stimulating western settlement and underwriting the cost of the construction of a transcontinental railway in what was promoted as a three-phased approach to national development.

NATIONAL RESEARCH COUNCIL, formed in 1916 to advise on wartime research. The NRC set up its first laboratory in Ottawa in 1928 under its president, H.M. TORY. Under his successor, General A.G.L. MCNAUGHTON, staff was increased and the NRC began to prepare for its role during WORLD WAR II. The council directed research into weapons, radar, and nuclear fission, and even hid such organizations as the EXAMINATION UNIT under its wing. NRC's head from 1939 to 1952, C.J. MACKENZIE, became an Ottawa power-broker, and the council grew and created a strong pure-science orientation. In 1988 the council was a crown corporation reporting through the minister of state for science and technology.

NATIONAL RESOURCES MOBILIZATION ACT, 1940, CONSCRIPTION measure passed by the House of Commons on 21 June 1940, shortly after France surrendered to Germany. It introduced a policy of conscription for home defence and was amended in 1942 when BILL 80 gave the government power to conscript for overseas service. Soldiers raised under the act were known as ZOMBIES and in Nov. 1944, during the CONSCRIPTION CRISIS, the government ordered up to 16,000 overseas.

NATIONAL SELECTIVE SERVICE, WORLD WAR II manpower control system that began in March 1942. Under the Department of Labour, the NSS had power to control who worked where, changed jobs, and was called up for military service under the NATIONAL RESOURCES MOBILIZATION ACT. In Sept. 1942, women between 20 and 24 came under NSS rules.

NATIONAL TRADES AND LABOUR CONGRESS, *see* CANADIAN FEDERATION OF LABOUR

NATIONAL TRANSCONTINENTAL RAILWAY, railway constructed and owned by the Liberal government of Prime Minister WILFRID LAURIER. Laurier announced in 1901 that his government would develop a new transcontinental railway in two parts. The government would build and operate the NTR from Moncton, N.B., to Winnipeg and would subsidize the construction of a new line from Winnipeg to the west coast to be built and operated by the GRAND TRUNK RAILWAY of Canada. That line, to be known as the GRAND TRUNK PACIFIC, was supposed to lease the NTR from Ottawa. Owing primarily to patronage and poor management, the NTR was far more expensive to build than originally anticipated, and the Grand Trunk Pacific refused to lease it because of the high costs. The NTR was run as part of CANADIAN GOVERNMENT RAILWAYS until it was absorbed into the CANADIAN NATIONAL RAILWAYS system in 1923.

NATIONAL WAR LABOUR BOARD, federal government agency responsible for setting and enforcing government wage orders, established during WORLD WAR II. After the government legalized collective bargaining by issuing the NATIONAL WAR LABOUR ORDER (P.C. 1003), the board assumed responsibility for regulating industrial relations in war industries and among federal employees.

NATIONAL WAR LABOUR ORDER (P.C. 1003), order in council issued by the federal cabinet in Feb. 1944, which provided that workers could form unions and that employers would have to bargain with those unions if they were certified by the NATIONAL WAR LABOUR BOARD. The order was replaced in 1948 by the INDUSTRIAL RELATIONS AND DISPUTES INVESTIGATION ACT.

NATIONALIST LEAGUE — Ligue nationaliste, a Quebec-based political movement founded in 1903 primarily to resist the rise of IMPERIALISM in Canada. Its formative influence was HENRI BOURASSA, who never formally joined it; its leaders included ARMAND LAVERGNE and OLIVAR ASSELIN. In its early years the league developed a three-pronged program: resistance to imperialism and the promotion of a British commonwealth of self-governing dominions; the stimulation of bilingualism across Canada; the modernization of Quebec society through commercial and scientific education in Quebec schools, and the use of governmental powers to regulate and control the province's natural resources. In the 1911 federal election Bourassa rallied Quebec voters under the league's banner to oppose SIR WILFRID LAURIER. League members elected in the campaign became, in effect, a rump of the Conservative party under ROBERT BORDEN.

NATIVE COUNCIL OF CANADA, Métis organization formed in 1970 as an outgrowth of earlier organizations designed to promote MÉTIS interests in Canada.

NATIVISM, an amalgam of ethnic and racial prejudice and nationalism which in Canada most often took the form of Protestant, English-speaking prejudice towards Catholics, French-Canadians, eastern-European and oriental immigrants, and Jews. Nineteenth-century nativist groups in Canada included the ORANGE ORDER, the Protestant Protective Assn and the EQUAL RIGHTS ASSN. *See also* JESUITS' ESTATES QUESTION; D'ALTON MCCARTHY.

NATO, NORTH ATLANTIC TREATY ORGANIZATION, an international defence organization created when the North Atlantic Treaty was signed in Washington in March 1949 by the United States, Canada, Britain, France, The Netherlands, Belgium, Norway, Portugal, Italy, and Luxembourg. Greece and Turkey joined later. NATO is a military alliance in which the member countries pledge to come to each other's defence in case of attack. Canada participated in the tripartite discussions with Britain and the United States in 1948 which laid the groundwork for NATO. In 1951 Canada sent a brigade of troops and an air division to Europe as part of its military commitment to NATO; Canadian forces, though reduced in the early Trudeau years, have been stationed there ever since.

NAVAL AID BILL, 1913, federal legislation introduced by the Conservative government of ROBERT BORDEN in May 1913. It authorized a cash donation of $35 million to Great Britain for the construction of dreadnaught class warships. Because of opposition from SIR WILFRID LAURIER's Liberals, Borden used CLOSURE for the first time in Canadian history to have the bill passed by the House of Commons but it was rejected by the Liberal-dominated senate. *See also* NAVAL SERVICE ACT.

NAVAL SERVICE ACT, 1910, legislation establishing a Canadian navy. The act created a tiny navy under Canadian control. SIR WILFRID LAURIER had introduced the measure to defuse pressure to make a contribution of dreadnaughts to the Royal Navy, but his navy did not satisfy imperialists or HENRI BOURASSA's nationalists who charged in a 1911 by-election that the navy would result in CONSCRIPTION.

NEATBY, HILDA MARION, (1904-75), historian. Born at Sutton, Eng., and educated at the univs. of Saskatchewan, the Sorbonne, and Minnesota, Neatby taught at univs. in Regina, Saskatoon, and Kingston. Her historical work, notably *Quebec: The Revolutionary Age, 1760-91* (1966) established her credentials in the historical profession. She was, however, best known for her attack on modern, permissive education, *So Little for the Mind* (1953), and for her service on the ROYAL COMMISSION ON NATIONAL DEVELOPMENT IN THE ARTS, LETTERS, AND SCIENCES.

NELLIGAN, ÉMILE (1879-1941), poet. Born in Montreal, Nelligan began writing poetry in his teens. His first publication came in 1896, and he was elected a member of École littéraire de Montréal in 1897 and read there to great acclaim on several occasions. But his health and mind broke and he was institutionalized in 1899. He remained in asylums until his death.

NEW BRUNSWICK SCHOOL QUESTION, political controversy in May 1871, when a new school act ended government support for SEPARATE SCHOOLS. Despite significant opposition, the bill was held to be legal by the courts and New Brunswick has ever since been one of three provinces, along with British Columbia and Manitoba, with only one tax-supported school system. *See also* MANITOBA SCHOOLS QUESTION.

"NEW" CANADIANS, term used in the 1950s and 1960s to refer to Canadians of non-French or non-British background. With the rise of MULTICULTURALISM, the term has fallen into disuse.

NEW DEMOCRACY, political movement in 1939-40 founded by W.D. HERRIDGE. He had become disillusioned by the Conservative party's unwillingness to follow the ideas he had gleaned from the New Deal in Washington, and the New Democracy attracted support of SOCIAL CREDIT adherents who thought Herridge was a monetary reformer. In Sept. 1939, Social Credit MPs began to call themselves members of New Democracy, but the election of 1940 reduced the Social Credit contingent to 10, all Albertans. Herridge, who failed to win a seat, was quickly rejected by his erstwhile followers.

NEW DEMOCRATIC PARTY, political party founded in 1961 when the CO-OPERATIVE COMMONWEALTH FEDERATION and the CANADIAN LABOUR CONGRESS united to create a democratic socialist party committed to government planning, public ownership, universal MEDICARE, old age pensions, unemployment insurance, and workers' compensation. The party lukewarmly opposes Canadian participation in NATO and NORAD and advocates the establishment of Canada as a nuclear free zone. It is also critical of the level of foreign investment in Canada. The NDP has achieved its greatest electoral success provincially: forming administrations in Saskatchewan (1944-64; 1971-82), Manitoba (1969-77; 1981-8), and British Columbia (1972-5). Federally, the party performs best during minority governments when it holds the balance of power, although in mid-1987 the NDP led the Liberals and Conservatives in the opinion polls. Leaders of the NDP have been T.C. DOUGLAS (1961-71), DAVID LEWIS (1971-5) and ED BROADBENT (1975–).

NEWFIE BULLET, nickname for the cross-Newfoundland rail passenger service operated by the CANADIAN NATIONAL RAILWAYS until the late 1960s. The train was reputed to be the slowest in Canada.

NEW NATIONAL POLICY, the agricultural counter to the NATIONAL POLICY. The 'Farmers' Platform' was a program first formulated by western and Ontario agricultural leaders in 1916, and pressed with greatest vigour after World War I. It called for greater government intervention in the economy, public ownership of utilities and transportation, lower tariffs and regulation of the grain trade, and was the banner under which the PROGRESSIVE PARTY ran. *See also* CANADIAN COUNCIL OF AGRICULTURE.

NILE VOYAGEURS, Canadian lumbermen recruited for the British force to relieve General Charles Gordon in Khartoum. In March 1884, Britain organized a rescue expedition under General GARNET WOLSELEY who had commanded the 1870 force that put down the RED RIVER REBELLION and who believed that Canadian voyageurs could ensure safe passage down the Nile to Khartoum. The Canadian government permitted the recruitment of 386 volunteers. Wolseley's expedition arrived too late to save Gordon.

NINE-HOUR MOVEMENT, launched by Canadian workers in Hamilton, Ont., in 1872 to achieve a nine-hour limit on the working day at the same daily pay as workers were then receiving for much longer days. It was patterned after the Eight-Hour movement in the United States and the Nine-Hour movement in Britain. The TORONTO TRADES ASSEMBLY was especially active in the movement, particularly during the TORONTO PRINTERS' STRIKE, which grew out of an attempt on the part of Toronto printers to win the nine-hour day.

NOBLE, CHARLES S. (1873-1957), farm inventor. Noble was born in State Center, Iowa, and emigrated to Alberta in 1902. He was a highly successful farmer and farm land developer before World War I, but he went bankrupt in the 1920s due to over-expansion. By 1930 Noble was pushing the idea that soil erosion on the Prairies during the DUST BOWL had to be combatted by new cultivating techniques that preserved the surface of the soil. The NOBLE BLADE was designed to achieve that end.

NOBLE BLADE, agricultural implement invented by Alberta farmer CHARLES S. NOBLE in 1935. The Noble Blade allowed farmers to cultivate the soil without disturbing the surface. It consisted of a horizontal sub-surface blade designed to cut weed roots, killing them and pushing them to the surface. This was necessary both to preserve the moisture in the ground and to prevent the wind erosion that took place following more conventional plowing methods.

NON-OPERATING UNIONS, bargaining federation of railway unions organized by FRANK HALL in the late 1940s. The "non-ops," as they were called, encompassed workers who did not actually run trains but worked as clerks, shippers, car repairers, and so on. In 1950 a strike of the non-operating unions paralysed rail transport in Canada and the federal government ended the strike by ordering them back to work.

NON-PARTISAN LEAGUE, farm protest movement which originated in North Dakota and captured the North Dakota state legislature in 1916. Western Canadian farmers, especially in Alberta, started their own branches of the league in Canada. Towards the end of World War I Non-Partisan League members in Alberta began to push for independent farm political action and to publish the *Alberta Non-Partisan* newspaper. This agitation was instrumental in the entry of the UNITED FARMERS OF ALBERTA into politics during the 1921 provincial election. *See also* HENRY WISE WOOD.

NON-PERMANENT ACTIVE MILITIA, term used for the volunteer Canadian militia between the two world wars. Its authorized strength was approximately 140,000, but its actual strength was less; for example, in 1931 it was 51,000.

NOORDUYN NORSEMAN, single-engine bush airplane designed and built in Montreal by aircraft engineer R. Noorduyn in the late 1930s and the 1940s. The plane's excellent load-carrying abilities made it a favourite of the United States Army Air Force during and after World War II.

NORAD, NORTH AMERICAN AIR DEFENCE COMMAND, created by a Canada-United States agreement negotiated by the Liberal government of LOUIS ST LAURENT but accepted by the DIEFENBAKER government at the end of July 1957. It integrated the home defence squadrons of the Canadian and American air forces under an American commander and a Canadian deputy, with headquarters at Colorado Springs, Colo. In 1981 the name was changed to North American Aerospace Defence Command.

NORANDA MINES LTD, a publicly-owned company created in 1922 to acquire and consolidate mineral-bearing properties in the Rouyn-Noranda areas of Ontario and Quebec. By the 1930s Canadians had replaced Americans as the company's principal investors. In 1964 Noranda merged with Geco Mines Ltd to become a major corporation with interests in manufacturing, forestry, and sales as well as mining.

NORMAN, EGERTON HERBERT (1909-57), diplomat. Born in Japan to missionary parents, Norman studied at the univs. of Toronto, Cambridge, and Harvard, becoming a specialist on Japan, and one whose books rank with the finest in English. He joined the Department of External Affairs, served in the legation in Tokyo, was interned on the outbreak of war, and repatriated. He then worked on counter-intelligence duties in Ottawa and went to Japan again in 1946 to serve on General MacArthur's staff. While in Tokyo, charges that he had been a communist were raised against him. The charges were true, but although Norman dissembled, his career was checked. He was posted to New Zealand and Egypt where his services during the SUEZ CRISIS were distinguished. Disturbed by a renewal of charges against him in the U.S. Congress, he killed himself. Norman continues to be a subject of great controversy, two diametrically opposed biographies of him having appeared in 1986.

NORMANDY INVASION, 1944, D-Day, the Allied invasion of France on 6 June by American-British-Canadian forces. Under the command of General Dwight Eisenhower, Allied forces landed on the Normandy coast in a five-division assault (supplemented by airborne invasion) that constituted the largest seaborne invasion in history. In the attacking force was 3rd Canadian Division which made good gains on D-Day, but soon ran into fierce German opposition near Caen where it and the British were stalled. Not until late July and early Aug. did the Allies make real progress, culminating in the battle of the FALAISE GAP, when the opportunity to destroy the German Army in France was narrowly missed.

NORQUAY, JOHN (1841-89), premier of Manitoba. Born at St Andrews, Man., of Métis ancestry, Norquay farmed, taught school, and trapped before winning election to the legislature in 1870. After serving in the cabinet, he became premier in 1878. Norquay extended Manitoba's boundaries substantially, but he foundered when

courtesy Manitoba Archives

John Norquay

he opposed SIR JOHN A. MACDONALD's railway policy. By building a line south to the United States, he provoked the prime minister's intervention and in 1887 the fall of his own government.

NORRIS, TOBIAS CRAWFORD (1861-1936), premier of Manitoba. Born at Brampton, Canada West, Norris homesteaded in Manitoba and set up a successful auction business. He first won election to the Manitoba legislature in 1896, became Liberal leader in 1910 and premier in 1915. His government was progressive, passing temperance and minimum wage laws, so much so that he roused opposition among farmers who were the heart of the PROGRESSIVE movement. His government, in office during the war and the postwar labour unrest, ran afoul of the farmers in the election of 1922. He remained in the legislature until 1928 when he was named to the Board of Railway Commissioners.

NORRIS INQUIRY, the Industrial Inquiry Commission on the Disruption of Shipping headed by T.G. Norris that investigated labour activities on the Great Lakes. The inquiry, held in 1962 and 1963, was prompted by an upsurge of labour violence in the lake shipping industry resulting from the attempts of HAL BANK's Seafarers' International Union to eliminate its rivals, particularly the CANADIAN SEAMEN'S UNION. The inquiry uncovered widespread violence and corruption and led to charges against Banks.

NORTH AMERICAN AIR DEFENCE COMMAND, see NORAD

NORTH ATLANTIC TREATY ORGANIZATION, see NATO

NORTH ATLANTIC TRIANGLE, the interrelationship among Canada, the United States, and Britain. A term popularized by historian J.B. BREBNER, the North Atlantic Triangle aptly describes the symbiotic relationship between the three countries. Historically trade has been extensive, defence cooperation in the 20th century has been close, and, when one country ails, the others suffer. As the weak corner, Canada has probably benefited most in good times and suffered most in bad from the relationship.

NORTHERN DANCER, racehorse. Owned by EDWARD PLUNKETT TAYLOR, Northern Dancer was the first Canadian-bred thoroughbred to win the Kentucky Derby, a feat accomplished in 1964.

NORTH STAR, a four-engine transport aircraft developed by CANADAIR LTD in Montreal after World War II. It combined the airframe of the American-designed Douglas DC-4 and engines produced by Rolls Royce. The North Star was used extensively by TRANS-CANADA AIRLINES, CANADIAN PACIFIC AIRLINES, and the ROYAL CANADIAN AIR FORCE, and a number were acquired by the British Overseas Airways Corp.

NORTH-WEST MOUNTED POLICE, see ROYAL CANADIAN MOUNTED POLICE

NORTHWEST PASSAGE, water route across the northern edge of North America, through the ARCTIC ARCHIPELAGO. From the 16th century on, European explorers such as Martin Frobisher (1576) searched for a navigable passage to shorten the sea route from Europe to the east but were constantly frustrated by weather and ice. Despite their failure, much of the waters of the eastern archipelago were explored and mapped as was Hudson Bay. Sporadic efforts to find the passage continued into the 19th century, but success was not achieved until 1906 when Norwegian explorer Roald Amundsen finally sailed the passage from east to west. Canada has claimed sovereignty over the passage and other archipelago waters since the area was transferred to

Canada by Britain in 1880 but the United States considers the passage an international waterway. In 1986 the U.S. sent an icebreaker, the *Polar Sea*, through it without first seeking Canadian permission.

NORTHWEST REBELLION, political insurrection in 1885 led by LOUIS RIEL. On 19 March, 1885 Riel proclaimed the existence of a MÉTIS provisional government at BATOCHE, in the North-West Territories. The rebellion was the result of growing unrest among Métis who thought they had been cheated by the Canadian government following the RED RIVER REBELLION of 1869 and the proclamation of the MANITOBA ACT in March 1870. Their chief grievance arose from Ottawa's failure to settle Métis land claims in Manitoba or the Saskatchewan country. The first fighting in the North-West Rebellion took place on 26 March when a small mixed detachment of NORTH-WEST MOUNTED POLICE and MILITIA marched on DUCK LAKE and were intercepted by Métis riflemen led by GABRIEL DUMONT. The Métis prevailed while the force of police and militia lost one quarter of their men dead or wounded in a 15-minute engagement. The federal government, led by Prime Minister JOHN A. MACDONALD, quickly raised a field force of approximately 7000 men under the command of General FREDERICK MIDDLETON and dispatched it to the west on the almost completed CANADIAN PACIFIC RAILWAY. Although small bands of native peoples under Cree chiefs BIG BEAR and POUNDMAKER joined Riel's forces, the Métis were vastly outnumbered and lacked supplies. Middleton's caution and Dumont's military skills delayed the inevitable outcome until the Canadian troops finally closed in on Batoche and subdued it on 12 May. Riel surrendered on 15 May and was hanged for treason in Nov. 1885; Dumont fled to the United States. *See also* WILLIAM H. JACKSON.

NORTH WEST AIR STAGING ROUTE, air route stretching across northern Alberta, the Yukon, and Alaska to the Soviet Union. The North West Air Staging Route was established during WORLD WAR II to send aircraft to the Soviet Union from the United States and consisted of a chain of airstrips, radio stations, and navigational aids built by the U.S. government.

NORTH-WEST SCHOOLS QUESTION, political controversy arising out of the AUTONOMY BILLS, federal legislation introduced in 1905. The North-West Territories Act of 1875 had provided the North-West Territories with the same provision for tax-supported SEPARATE SCHOOLS as existed in the MANITOBA ACT, but in 1901 these schools were eliminated in the North-West and one public school system was introduced. Within that system, Catholic or Protestant religious instruction was permited at the end of each day according to the wishes of the majority in each school district. The minority was free to set up its own tax-supported school with its choice of religious instruction. In introducing the 1905 Autonomy Bills, Prime Minister WILFRID LAURIER bowed to Catholic demands to restore the pre-1901 status quo, overruling CLIFFORD SIFTON, his minister of the interior. Sifton resigned and led a caucus revolt against the Autonomy Bills. Laurier was forced to retreat and allowed Sifton to rewrite the educational clauses of the bills which emerged virtually unchanged from the 1901 provisions.

NORTH-WEST TERRITORIES ACT, federal statute passed in 1875. The act came into force in 1876 to organize the northwest region of Canada acquired from the HUDSON'S BAY CO. in 1870 for administrative and governmental purposes. The act provided for a governor, appointed by Ottawa, and an appointed council which would be replaced by elected members as the population grew. The North-West Territories Act was amended many times in subsequent years as portions of the region were allocated to the provinces of Manitoba, Saskatchewan, and Alberta.

NOTMAN, WILLIAM (1826-91), photographer. Born at Paisley, Scot., Notman came to Canada in 1856. He set up a daguerreotype studio in Montreal and won plaudits for his portraits. He soon moved outdoors, recording the events of his time, and building a substantial staff. His archive at the McCord Museum in Montreal, comprising almost a half million photographs, is a treasure of Canada's 19th century.

NOVA SCOTIA STEEL CO., company formed in 1882 by several families in Pictou County, N.S. The following year, it cast Canada's first steel ingots. The company expanded in the 1890s and, at the turn of the century, bought its own collieries on Cape Breton Island and constructed a new steel plant at Sydney Mines. In 1920 the company was taken over by BRITISH EMPIRE STEEL CO.

NOWLAN, GEORGE CLYDE (1898-1965), politician. Born at Havelock, N.S., and educated at Acadia and Dalhousie univs., Nowlan served overseas in World War I and then practised law. Elected to the Nova Scotia legislature in 1925 as a Conservative, he held a seat until 1933. In 1948 he won a seat in Parliament and served in several portfolios in JOHN DIEFENBAKER's cabinet, ultimately as minister of finance.

OAKES, SIR HARRY (1874-1943), mining entrepreneur. Born in Maine, he prospected in the KLONDIKE GOLD RUSH in 1898 but made his fortune in properties in northern Ontario, notably from the Lakeshore mine. In 1935 he moved to the Bahamas where he was murdered in 1943 in an unsolved case that still excites controversy.

O CANADA, national anthem. The original version, with lyrics in French only, was composed by CALIXA LAVALLÉE and first performed on 24 June, 1880. The English lyrics were written by Robert Stanley Weir in 1908. The song came into increasing use after World War II but it was not officially adopted as the national anthem until June 1980.

OCTOBER CRISIS, major crisis in Oct. 1970 when the FRONT DE LIBÉRATION DU QUÉBEC kidnapped British trade commissioner James Cross and Quebec cabinet minister PIERRE LAPORTE. Cross was seized on 5 Oct., Laporte on 10 Oct. The FLQ demanded large ransoms, safe passage from the country for its members, and publicization of the FLQ program, in return for the release of the two men. Prime Minister PIERRE TRUDEAU refused to negotiate and on 16 Oct., after consulting with Quebec Premier ROBERT BOURASSA, invoked the WAR MEASURES ACT and sent

the army to Montreal to help the Royal Canadian Mounted Police and the Quebec Provincial Police maintain order and search for the kidnappers. More than 400 people in Quebec and elsewhere were arrested under the War Measures Act. The FLQ responded by murdering Laporte, whose body was found 17 Oct. On 6 Nov. the first arrest was made in connection with the Laporte murder and on 3 Dec. Cross's whereabouts were discovered and a deal was struck in which his release was exchanged for safe passage to Cuba for his kidnappers. Laporte's killers were eventually prosecuted for murder. The October Crisis destroyed the FLQ but increased resentment of Trudeau among Quebec separatists and intellectuals.

O'DONOGHUE, DANIEL JOHN (1844-1907), labour leader, politician. O'Donoghue is known as "the father of the Canadian labour movement" because of his role in 19th century Ontario labour politics. He became active in the labour movement in the 1860s and was elected to the Ontario legislature in 1874. O'Donoghue joined the KNIGHTS OF LABOR in the early 1880s and became a strong supporter of the LIBERAL PARTY.

OFFICIAL LANGUAGES ACT, federal legislation passed in 1969 following recommendations of the ROYAL COMMISSION ON BILINGUALISM AND BICULTURALISM. The act stipulated that all federal institutions and crown corporations provide services in English and French across Canada and established a commissioner of official languages to monitor its implementation. *See also* PIERRE TRUDEAU.

OFFICIAL SECRETS ACT, legislation to protect state security passed in 1890, revised in the Official Secrets Act 1939, and amended on several occasions subsequently. The act protects information of official character from unauthorized disclosure, but it is vague and unclear in definition. The most notable example of the act's use occurred in the GOUZENKO AFFAIR.

OGDENSBURG AGREEMENT, 1940, term used to describe the result of the meeting between Prime Minister MACKENZIE KING and President Franklin Roosevelt at Ogdensburg, N.Y., on 18 Aug. The agreement, drafted in the aftermath of the Anglo-French defeat in Europe, produced the PERMANENT JOINT BOARD ON DEFENCE. In retrospect the agreement can be seen as marking Canada's switch from the British to the American sphere of interest.

OGILVIE, ALEXANDER WALKER (1829-1902), businessman. Born at St Michel, Lower Canada, he worked in his uncle's flour-milling business before setting up his own company, A.W. Ogilvie Ltd, in 1854. This later became Ogilvie Flour Mills. In 1867 he was elected to the Quebec legislature, eventually serving two terms. He retired from his company in 1871, turning it over to his brothers, and was appointed to the Senate in 1881.

O'KEEFE, EUGENE (1827-1913), brewer. Born in Ireland, O'Keefe was brought to Toronto as a boy. He worked in a bank and then borrowed money to start a brewery in 1861. Within 30 years, O'Keefe was one of Canada's leading brewers, heavily into technology. He sold the O'Keefe Brewing Co. in 1911, but the name survives.

OLD AGE PENSIONS, federal program agreed to by the Liberal government of Prime Minister MACKENZIE KING in 1926 to repay the GINGER GROUP for its support of the minority Liberal government over the preceding years. The pensions were paid to any Canadian 70 years of age or older who could pass a means test. Means tests were abolished in 1951, and the age limit was gradually reduced to 65 during the 1960s. In 1966 a Guaranteed Income Supplement was introduced which paid an extra amount to pensioners determined by need.

O'LEARY, MICHAEL GRATTON (1889-1976), journalist. Born at Gaspé, Que., he worked as a journalist in Saint John, N.B., before joining the Ottawa *Journal* in 1911. A devoted Conservative, O'Leary was a confidante of the party leaders whose interests he assiduously served in his newspaper. In 1961 he was named to head the ROYAL COMMISSION ON PUBLICATIONS, and JOHN DIEFENBAKER made him a senator in 1962. He returned the favour in Feb. 1963 when his speech in caucus, according to observers, was instrumental in keeping Diefenbaker as leader during the BOMARC MISSILE CRISIS and cabinet collapse.

OLIVER, FRANK (1853-1933), politician, publisher. Born in Peel County, Canada West, Oliver started the Edmonton *Bulletin* in 1880 and remained its publisher for more than 40 years. He was a member of the North-West Territories council and then the legislature in the 1880s and 1890s. He won election to the House of Commons as a Liberal in 1896 and succeeded SIR CLIFFORD SIFTON as interior minister in 1905.

John Oliver

OLIVER, JOHN (1856-1927), premier of British Columbia. "Honest John" Oliver was born at Harrington, Eng., and moved to Ontario with his parents in 1870. He went to British Columbia in 1877 and farmed, first winning a seat in the legislature in 1900. He became Liberal leader in 1905 but lost his seat in 1909. Seven years later, the Liberals returned to power and after serving in two portfolios Oliver became premier in 1918 and led the province with integrity through the post-war unrest and prosperity of the 1920s until his death in office.

OLYMPIC GAMES, 1976, first Olympics held in Canada. Montreal hosted the summer games in lavish new facilities built with substantial cost overruns. The games were held in an atmosphere marred by tight security (and memories of the murder of Israeli athletes at the 1972 Munich Games). Canadian athletes won five medals, the public highlight being a silver in the men's high jump earned by Greg Joy.

OLYMPIC GAMES, 1988, first winter Olympics staged in Canada. Superbly mounted in Calgary, the winter games overcame the vagaries of weather. Excellent facilities and a massive volunteer effort by local citizens, aided by national interest generated by a cross-country marathon of Canadians carrying the Olympic torch, provided the atmosphere. Canadian athletes won five medals in games dominated by the Soviets and East Germans.

ONE BIG UNION, labour organization founded in Calgary in June 1919. The OBU was formed principally by radical western workers who rejected the craft unionism of the TRADES AND LABOUR CONGRESS. In theory the OBU was intended to be a federation of industrial unions, but in practice no true industrial structure was ever established. At first, westerners and others disenchanted with the conservative TLC flocked to the OBU, and its membership quickly swelled to over 40,000. But the OBU withered under AFL and TLC counterattacks. By 1922 it held the allegiance of fewer than 5000. It joined the ALL-CANADIAN CONGRESS OF LABOUR briefly in the late 1920s and merged itself into the CANADIAN LABOUR CONGRESS when it was founded in 1956. The OBU formally dissolved in 1964. *See also* R.B. RUSSELL; WESTERN LABOR CONFERENCE.

ONTARIO FACTORY ACT, provincial labour law regulating conditions in the workplace, passed in 1884 and proclaimed in 1887. It was the first such legislation in Canada.

ONTARIO HYDRO, Ontario CROWN CORPORATION, created in 1906 as the Hydro-Electric Power Commission of Ontario. Established by the Conservative government of Premier JAMES P. WHITNEY, it was the world's first government-owned electricity company. Whitney was responding to rising demands from consumers, businessmen, and manufacturers who wanted their electric power at cost. At first the HEPC provided power at cost to only a portion of Ontario's consumers but ADAM BECK, the first president, transformed the company into a monopoly by the early 1920s. In 1988, the company was one of the largest in Canada.

ONTARIO NORTHLAND TRANSPORTATION COMMISSION, Ontario crown corporation established as the Timiskaming and Northern Ontario Railway in 1902. It connected southern Ontario with timber and mineral areas further north and eventually reached James Bay in 1932. The railway became an essential part of the development of the Timmins-Porcupine mining boom and of the pulp and paper industry in the region. In 1946 the name was changed to the Ontario Northland Transportation Commission.

ON-TO-OTTAWA TREK, demonstration intended to be a cross-country march organized by the Communist-led RELIEF CAMP WORKERS' UNION of the WORKERS' UNITY LEAGUE to bring unemployed demonstrators to Ottawa in the summer of 1935. The march began in British Columbia in June 1935, as unemployed men left relief camps to board east-bound freight trains. The marchers halted at Regina as march leader Arthur Evans and others went to Ottawa to present their demands to Prime Minister R.B. BENNETT. Bennett had little sympathy for the marchers, and the meeting ended in an angry confrontation. Bennett then gave orders to the ROYAL CANADIAN MOUNTED POLICE to ensure that the marchers returned from whence they had come. When the police tried to enforce Bennett's orders, the REGINA RIOT ensued on 1 July, 1935. This marked the effective end to the trek. *See also* RELIEF CAMP.

OPTING OUT, term describing the process under which a province declines to participate in a federal-provincial shared-cost program. The process began in 1965 when, at Quebec's insistence, Ottawa allowed provinces to opt out of such programs as hospital insurance and aid to the disabled; only Quebec chose to do so, accepting instead a direct payment of the money the federal government would have contributed to the program in Quebec. *See also* COOPERATIVE FEDERALISM.

ORANGE ORDER, Protestant nativist organization which began in Ireland in 1795 and spread to Canada in the early 19th century. Especially strong in Ontario, the order consistently attacked what it saw as an activist Catholic presence in Canadian political life and opposed the extension of special rights to Catholics inside Quebec or elsewhere in Canada. Although the order still exists, it has long ceased to play an important role in Canadian politics. *See also* EQUAL RIGHTS ASSN; MANITOBA SCHOOLS QUESTION; NATIVISM.

ORDER OF CANADA, means of honouring individual Canadians for achievement, established 1 July, 1967 as part of the CENTENNIAL celebrations.

ORR, ROBERT GORDON (1948–), hockey player. Born at Parry Sound, Ont., Bobby Orr joined the Boston Bruins in 1967 as a rushing defenceman. A superb skater and scorer, he remains the only defenceman to win the National Hockey League scoring title. He left Boston to play for Chicago in 1976 but knee injuries, the first of which occurred in 1967, forced his retirement that season.

ORTONA, BATTLE OF, 1943, major battle of the 1st Canadian Division in Italy in Dec. The capture of Ortona from German paratroops was the culmination of a month-long advance from the Moro River to the Riccio River, a campaign that cost 176 officers and 2163 men killed, wounded, or captured.

OSHAWA STRIKE, 1937, strike of United Automobile Workers local 222 against General Motors, 8-23 April. The strike, principally for union recognition, ended with a victory for the union. Although General Motors refused to recognize local 222 as a branch of the UAW, it did agree to bargain collectively with the local instead of with a company union. The strike received the moral support of the Congress of Industrial Organizations (although no material aid) and was strongly opposed by Ontario premier MITCHELL HEPBURN. *See also* DAVID CROLL; HEPBURN'S HUSSARS.

OSLER, SIR WILLIAM (1849-1919), physician. Born at Bond Head, Canada West, Osler was educated at the univs. of Toronto and McGill. He taught at McGill until 1884 when he went to the United States, eventually becoming professor of medicine at Johns Hopkins Univ. A superb clinician, teacher, and medical writer, Osler in 1905 became Regius professor of medicine at Oxford Univ.

OTTAWA AGREEMENTS, 1932, a complex of trade agreements negotiated at the Imperial Eco-

nomic Conference, held from 20 July to 20 Aug. The Ottawa Conference produced 12 bilateral trade agreements among Commonwealth countries that cumulatively amounted to the entrenchment of IMPERIAL PREFERENCES. Although sectors such as automobile production and wheat benefited from the accords, the United States was furious at what it saw as an imperial gang-up. Even the BENNETT government that had negotiated the agreements for Canada was seeking a trade agreement with the United States by 1933. Prime Minister MACKENZIE KING, however, was the first to begin watering down the agreements, in late 1935. Further dilution occurred in 1937, 1938, and subsequent years.

OTTAWA CONFERENCE, 1932, the Imperial Economic Conference of Britain and the dominions that produced the OTTAWA AGREEMENTS on tariff policy.

courtesy National Archives of Canada/C-14234

Sir William D. Otter

OTTER, SIR WILLIAM DILLON (1843-1929), soldier. Born at Clinton, Canada West, Otter was a militiaman who fought against the FENIANS in 1866. He joined the permanent force in 1883, commanded one of the columns of the NORTH-WEST REBELLION, and led the first Canadian contingent to the BOER WAR in 1899. By 1908 he was the first Canadian chief of the general staff. He directed INTERNMENT operations in WORLD WAR I and attained the rank of general.

OTTER (DHC-3), single-engine aircraft built by DE HAVILLAND AIRCRAFT OF CANADA in the 1950s. It was an especially versatile plane and was used extensively for search and rescue work as well as bush flying. A twin-engine version, the Twin Otter, was developed in the 1960s.

OUIMET, JOSEPH-ALPHONSE (1908–), public servant. Born in Montreal and trained as an electrical engineer at McGill Univ., he joined the CANADIAN RADIO BROADCASTING COMMISSION, the forerunner of the CANADIAN BROADCASTING CORP., in 1934 and became its chief engineer. In 1953 he became CBC general manager and in 1958 president. He resigned in 1967 after the CBC's "rotten" management was denounced by the responsible minister, JUDY LAMARSH. He went on to become chairman of TELESAT CANADA.

PAARDEBERG, BATTLE OF, 1900, the first major British victory in the BOER WAR and the initial action of the first Canadian contingent. Under renewed British assault directed at the Boer capitals, the Afrikaners under General Piet Cronje chose a strong defensive position on the Modder River. Led by Colonel W.D. OTTER, the Royal Canadian Regiment suffered heavily in an attack at Paardeburg Drift on 18 Feb. but fared better on 27 Feb. when the Canadians held their position under deadly Boer fire and forced the surrender of General Cronje's force. Canadian fatalities in the two engagements were 34.

PACIFIC SCANDAL, political scandal which developed as a result of the lobbying of SIR HUGH ALLAN for a federal government contract to build a railway from central Canada to the Pacific in 1872. Allan headed a syndicate of American entrepreneurs anxious to secure the contract who secretly donated approximately $360,000 to Prime Minister JOHN A. MACDONALD and the Conservative party in the 1872 federal election. When news of the secret donations was made public by the Liberal party in 1873, Macdonald was forced to resign and hand power over to

ALEXANDER MACKENZIE. *See also* CANADIAN PACIFIC RAILWAY.

PACIFIC WESTERN AIRLINES LTD, airline begun as Central British Columbia Airways in 1946. Its name was changed to PWA in 1953. From its base in Vancouver, the airline developed into an important regional carrier covering Alberta, B.C., the Yukon, and the western Northwest Territories. In 1974 the Alberta government purchased the airline and moved its head offices to Calgary. In 1983 PWA was privatized through the sale of shares to the public, and in 1987 the company shocked the financial world by taking over the larger CANADIAN PACIFIC AIRLINES, forming the new Canadian Airlines International.

PADLOCK LAW, Quebec legislation passed in 1937 that allowed the government arbitrarily to close (padlock) for up to one year any building it claimed was being used by Communists. It also allowed the government to imprison persons without appeal for one year if convicted of spreading Communism. The law was ruled unconstitutional by the SUPREME COURT of Canada in 1957.

PALLADIUM OF LABOR, official organ of KNIGHTS OF LABOR District Assembly 61 in Hamilton and an important voice of the labour movement in Canada in the 1880s. It gave voice to labour reformers such as T. PHILLIPS THOMPSON in its columns.

PALLISER, JOHN (1817-87), explorer. Born at Dublin, Ireland, Palliser explored the Canadian West from 1857 to 1859 as leader of the British North American Exploring expedition. He and his colleagues collected data on flora and fauna and assessed the capacity of the Prairies from the Red River to the Rockies for settlement. Reports were published in 1859-60 and 1863. *See also* PALLISER'S TRIANGLE.

PALLISER'S TRIANGLE, a semi-arid region of the southern Prairies that encompasses southwestern Manitoba, southern Saskatchewan, and southeastern Alberta, named for Captain JOHN PALLISER who headed a British exploring party in western Canada in 1857-9. Palliser reported that the southern Prairies were too dry for agriculture, a report later contradicted by JOHN MACOUN. During the 1930s low rainfall and soil erosion produced the DUST BOWL in the triangle region.

PANNETON, PHILIPPE, "RINGUET" (1895-1960), author. Trained as a physician at the Univ. de Montréal, Panneton used the pseudonym Ringuet to write *Trente Arpents* (1938) on the transition in Quebec from a rural to urban society. The book won numerous prizes, including a Governor General's Award. He wrote many other books and articles and was appointed ambassador to Portugal in 1957.

PAPINEAU, TALBOT-MERCER (1883-1917), lawyer, soldier. The great-grandson of Louis-Joseph Papineau, he attended Oxford Univ. and was called to the bar in 1908. In 1914, he joined the CANADIAN EXPEDITIONARY FORCE. He wrote articles from the front denouncing the anti-war activities of HENRI BOURASSA. An infantry major with the Military Cross, he was killed in action.

PARENT, MADELEINE (1918–), labour leader. Parent began organizing for the United Textile Workers of America in Quebec in the early 1940s. In 1947 she was convicted of seditious conspiracy for her role in the 1946 Dominion Textile strike but she was acquitted after a new trial in 1954. She helped found the Confederation of Canadian Unions in 1969.

PARENT, SIMON-NAPOLÉON (1855-1920), premier of Quebec. A lawyer, Parent was mayor of Quebec City while simultaneously sitting in the legislature and serving as minister of lands and forests. He became premier in 1900, still serving as mayor, but was forced out of office after five years, his critics denouncing him for selling out Quebec to foreign capital.

PARKIN, SIR GEORGE ROBERT (1846-1922), educator. Born at Salisbury, N.B., Parkin was educated at the univs. of New Brunswick and Oxford. In 1895 he became head of Upper Canada College, Toronto. A propagandist for IMPERIAL FEDERATION and the author of several books, Parkin toured the Empire making speeches. In 1902 he organized the Rhodes Scholarship Trust and remained at its head until his death.

"PARLIAMENT WILL DECIDE", a famous phrase of Prime Minister MACKENZIE KING that expressed his approach to foreign policy. First used in 1922 when Britain sought Canadian participation in the CHANAK crisis at a time when Parliament was out of session, King came to take shelter behind the necessity for the elected House of Commons to approve action of which he was leery. A good principle in and of itself (and one largely honoured when Canada went to war in Sept. 1939), the phrase became used by the Prime Minister's critics as a shorthand expression to describe King's inaction during the interwar years.

PARTI BLEU, political party formed about 1850 by a group of moderate French Canadian reformers seeking to establish a separate identity from the more radical PARTI ROUGE. The *bleus*, led by GEORGE-ÉTIENNE CARTIER, provided the backbone for the Quebec wing of the Conservative party. The name *bleu* has become the nickname of the Conservative party in Quebec to this day.

PARTI NATIONAL, political party originally formed in 1871 by Quebec Liberals led by HONORÉ MERCIER. It floundered until the hanging of LOUIS RIEL in 1885 alienated Quebec Conservatives, who then joined Mercier to win the 1886 provincial election. Mercier's administration governed until 1892, when it was dismissed over the BAIE DES CHALEURS SCANDAL.

PARTI QUÉBÉCOIS, political party founded in 1968 when the Mouvement souveraineté-association merged with the Ralliement national and the RASSEMBLEMENT POUR L'INDÉPENDANCE NATIONALE under the leadership of RENÉ LÉVESQUE, a former Liberal minister in the JEAN LESAGE government, committed to making Quebec a sovereign nation. It suffered two defeats before taking 71 of 110 seats in the Nov. 1976 provincial election. After governing efficiently for four years, in 1980 the government held a referendum in which it sought a mandate to negotiate SOVEREIGNTY-ASSOCIATION with the federal government. The vote was 60 per cent "non" but the PQ was returned with 82 seats in the 1981 election. The PQ suffered a number of crises in its second term, including the resignation of key cabinet ministers and then of Lévesque, and it was defeated by ROBERT BOURASSA's Liberals in 1985.

PARTI ROUGE, political party formed in Quebec in 1848 by a group of anticlerical French Canadian intellectuals led by ANTOINE-AIMÉ DORION. Their commitment to universal suffrage, abolition of the seigneurial system, repeal of the Act of Union of Canada East and Canada West, anti-ULTRAMONTANISM, and annexation of Canada to the United States did not win them popular success. In the 1870s the *rouges* joined with the CLEAR GRITS of Ontario to form the LIBERAL PARTY. *Rouge* is still the Quebec term for the Liberal party.

PARTRIDGE, EDWARD ALEXANDER (1862-1931), farm leader. Born near Barrie, Canada West, he homesteaded in Saskatchewan where he became active in the farmers' movement in the mid-1890s. In 1906 he helped found the GRAIN GROWERS GRAIN CO., a farmer-owned grain-selling cooperative, as a means of gaining farmer representation on the WINNIPEG GRAIN EXCHANGE. He was also a founder of the GRAIN GROWERS' GUIDE in 1908. Partridge believed that government should own and control the grain elevators, which were so essential to the grain-marketing system, and he advocated the construction of a railway linking the Prairies with Hudson Bay as an additional means of transporting grain to Europe. After World War I he encouraged farmers to enter politics.

PASSCHENDAELE, BATTLE OF, 1917, Canadian battle in Belgium. Fighting in appallingly muddy conditions, the CANADIAN CORPS, commanded by General SIR ARTHUR CURRIE struggled between 26 Oct. and 7 Nov. to capture the ruins of what was once Passchendaele. The Corps did the job at a cost of 7000 casualties, but the battle was yet another sample of strategic futility.

PATRONS OF INDUSTRY, a U.S.-based farm organization which entered Ontario in 1889. When the DOMINION GRANGE refused to engage in partisan politics in the 1890s, farmers turned to the more activist Patrons in large numbers and it grew phenomenally. The Patrons favoured low tariffs, more popular control of the judicial and legislative process, and simplification of government, and opposed monopolies and trusts. The organization disappeared just after the turn of the century.

PATTERSON, HARRY THOMAS (1920–), arts consultant. Born at Stratford, Ont., in 1952 he won authorization of Stratford City Council to attempt to create a Shakespearean festival. He persuaded Tyrone Guthrie to come from Britain to direct and Alec Guinness to star in the first season, which opened in a tent in 1953. Patterson subsequently helped other cities create theatrical festivals.

PATTERSON, WILLIAM JOHN (1886-1976), premier of Saskatchewan. Born at Grenfell, Sask., Patterson first was elected to the legislature as a Liberal in 1921 and became premier in 1935. The party machine, created by JAMES G. GARDINER, was reputedly formidable, but Patterson did little with it or with power. His government was lacklustre, proving easy meat for the CO-OPERATIVE COMMONWEALTH FEDERATION under T.C. DOUGLAS in 1944. Resigning as leader in 1946, Patterson was lieutenant governor from 1951-8.

PATTULLO, THOMAS DUFFERIN (1873-1956), premier of British Columbia. Born at Woodstock, Ont., Duff Pattullo moved to Prince Rupert, B.C., in 1908, became mayor, and in 1916 was elected to the legislature as a Liberal. In 1928, he became opposition leader, and he led his reorganized party to victory in 1933 during the depression. Attempting to implement a "little new deal" to cope with B.C.'s economic problems, Pattullo found himself in difficulty with the federal government, something that was exacerbated by his pressure for a road to Alaska through British Columbia. In 1941, his own party forced him out of the premiership after he rejected a coalition with the Tories, and in 1945 he lost his seat in the legislature.

P.C. 1003, *see* NATIONAL WAR LABOUR ORDER

"PEACE, ORDER, AND GOOD GOVERNMENT," the introductory phrase of section 91 of the BRITISH NORTH AMERICA ACT, 1867. The phrase set out the legislative jurisdiction of the federal parliament, giving Ottawa the power to act on matters not specifically given to the provinces. The phrase has also served as a convenient (and slightly ironic) way to compare Canada and the United States. In the American constitution, the state is to work for life, liberty, and the pursuit of happiness. In sombre Canada, it is peace, order, and good government that are to prevail. *See also* "PROPERTY AND CIVIL RIGHTS."

PEACEKEEPING, the term ordinarily applied to United Nations military operations. The UN Charter of 1945 included elaborate provisions for the maintenance of collective security, but the Cold War blocked efforts to implement them. Nonetheless, the UN was able to deploy a Military Observer Group to the India-Pakistan border during the Kashmir dispute that began in 1948 and to the Arab-Israeli borders the same year. An early if unenthusiastic supporter, Canada provided officers for both observer groups. Canada also sent large contingents to the KOREAN WAR, a different type of peacekeeping that was possible only because the Soviet Union was boycotting the Security Council.

In 1954, the Geneva Conference (and not the UN) created the INTERNATIONAL CONTROL COMMISSIONS to operate in the three successor states of French Indochina, and a "troika" of three countries — one Communist, one democratic, one neutral — took the field. Canada, India, and Poland participated in a largely futile effort to bring peace to the area, bedevilled by the escalation of the Vietnam War. Despite that experience, Canada again provided observers for another largely unsuccessful control commission from Feb. to June 1973 to cover the United States' withdrawal from Vietnam.

In 1956, more successfully, Prime Minister LESTER PEARSON proposed the establishment of the UNITED NATIONS EMERGENCY FORCE to separate the invading British-French-Israeli force from the defending Egyptians during the SUEZ CRISIS. General E.L.M. BURNS was the first UNEF commander, and Canadians made up a substantial portion of the multinational force. The initial Canadian offer of a battalion of infantry from the Queen's Own Rifles was refused by Egypt's President Nasser on the grounds that Egyptians would not be able to differentiate those soldiers and their RED ENSIGN from the similar-appearing British invaders under the Union Jack. Despite that, the UNEF's success and the Nobel Peace Prize Pearson won convinced Canadians that they were especially suited for peacekeeping, and there was public pressure on the DIEFENBAKER government to provide troops to the UN's Congo force in 1960. The government reluctantly acquiesced, sending signallers. Later, small numbers of Ca-

nadians served with UN forces in West Irian and Yemen, and in 1964 a battalion was supplied for duty in Cyprus, a commitment that continues. Observers and units (including 1145 men in UNEF II that operated in the Sinai desert from 1973 to 1979) also served in a large array of UN and non-UN operations along Arab-Israeli borders.

In 1967, President Nasser ordered Canada's UNEF contingent out of Egypt just prior to the outbreak of renewed war with Israel. That blow, seen by some Canadians as a national humiliation, began to dissipate enthusiasm for peacekeeping which suddenly took on the appearance of a difficult, thankless job. The armed forces, never enthusiastic at commitments that frittered away manpower, were similarly unimpressed. Peacekeeping continued, but Canada's special skills were no longer talked of.

PEARKES, GEORGE RANDOLPH (1883-1984), soldier, politician. Pearkes came to Canada from England in 1906, homesteaded in Alberta, then joined the ROYAL NORTH-WEST MOUNTED POLICE. He enlisted in 1915 in the CANADIAN EXPEDITIONARY FORCE, ending as a battalion commander with the Victoria Cross. He remained in the permanent force, commanded a division in Britain from 1940 to 1942, and was then put in command on the Pacific Coast. He opposed the policy of MACKENZIE KING's government on CONSCRIPTION and left the army in 1945 to run for Parliament as a Conservative. He won his seat, became defence minister under JOHN DIEFENBAKER from 1957 to 1960 and as such cancelled the AVRO ARROW. He served as lieutenant governor of British Columbia until 1968.

PEARSON, LESTER BOWLES (1897-1972), diplomat, prime minister of Canada. "Mike" Pearson was born at Newtonbrook, Ont., the son of a Methodist parson. His education at the Univ. of Toronto was interrupted by enlistment in the Canadian Army Medical Corps during World War I where he served on the Salonika front as a stretcher-bearer. When boredom and horror overcame him, he transferred to the Royal Flying Corps for pilot training. His chances of survival as a pilot would have been slim, but a collision with a bus in a blackout invalided him home. Pearson then completed his undergraduate work at Toronto, won a fellowship to Oxford, and was

courtesy National Archives of Canada/C-10435

Lester B. Pearson

hired by the Univ. of Toronto as a history instructor. In 1927, married and with a young family, he wrote the examinations for the fledgling Department of External Affairs and was hired as a first secretary.

For the next two decades, he worked his way up through the foreign service. He quickly attracted the attention of O.D. SKELTON, the under-secretary, for his intelligence, capacity for work, and great charm, and he also became favourably known to both MACKENZIE KING and R.B. BENNETT. In 1935, he went to London as first secretary at Canada's high commission; his views were nationalist and neutralist, and Pearson was as slow to recognize the threat posed by the Nazis as everyone in Canada (or England). But by the time of the Munich crisis he had made the turn and now favoured war, if necessary, to stop Hitler. In 1941, having been passed over for the under-secretaryship that came vacant on Skelton's death, he returned to Canada, and the next year he went to Washington as second in command at the legation. In 1945, he became Canada's first ambassador to the United States and a delegate to the founding conference of the United Nations where he was talked of as a possible secretary-general.

That was not to be. Instead Pearson became under-secretary in external affairs in 1946 where he struck a close working and personal relationship with LOUIS ST LAURENT, the secretary of state for external affairs. The two men carried Canada into the negotiations that produced the North Atlantic Treaty and, when St Laurent was chosen prime minister, Pearson entered LIBERAL PARTY politics and the cabinet in St Laurent's old post. As foreign minister, Pearson played an important role at the United Nations in securing an armistice in the KOREAN WAR, in NATO, and around the world. In 1956, his efforts during the SUEZ CRISIS to create the UNITED NATIONS EMERGENCY FORCE in Egypt as a device to halt the Israeli-British-French invasion won him plaudits, the Nobel Peace Prize, and in Jan. 1958 the leadership of the Liberal party.

JOHN DIEFENBAKER crushed Pearson's Liberals in the election of 1958, but Pearson harassed the ill-led government and galvanized the Liberal organization. In 1962, Diefenbaker was reduced to minority status and the next year, Pearson guided the Liberals to a narrow victory, thanks to the Tories' bungling of defence questions and relations with the United States. In power, however, Pearson quickly ran into serious difficulty. His "Sixty Days of Decision" turned to ashes when WALTER GORDON's budget had to be revised under attack, and a series of scandals rocked his cabinet. Nonetheless, Pearson did create the ROYAL COMMISSION ON BILINGUALISM AND BICULTURALISM as an effort to deal with Quebec's QUIET REVOLUTION, the ROYAL COMMISSION ON THE STATUS OF WOMEN, and he gave Canada its distinctive new flag in 1965. His government strengthened the nation's social welfare system with the CANADA PENSION PLAN, the cause of a crisis with JEAN LESAGE's government in Quebec, and MEDICARE. Pearson also presided over the UNIFICATION of the armed forces, and he negotiated the CANADA-U.S. AUTO PACT in 1965. The policy record was good, but so intense had been the confrontations between Pearson and Diefenbaker that there was a national sigh of relief when the two warriors gave up their posts. Pearson, unlike his opponent, went at a time of his own choosing, turning over power to PIERRE TRUDEAU after a party convention in early 1968.

PEDEN, WILLIAM J., "TORCHY" (1906-80), cyclist. Born at Victoria, B.C., Peden was a member of the Canadian cycling team at the 1928

Olympics. He then won races in Europe, turned professional in 1929, and won fame and competitions in North America on the Six-Day racing circuit.

courtesy NFB Phototheque/Marcel Cognac

Alfred Pellan

PELLAN, ALFRED (1906–), painter. Born at Quebec City and trained at the École des beaux-arts there, Pellan in 1926 won a Quebec government fellowship to study in Paris and remained there until 1940. His work was surrealist and abstract, almost cubist, and was not well received on his return to Montreal. In 1952 he went to Paris for three years and exhibited widely. By the time of his return to Canada, critical taste had caught up to him, and he was hailed as one of Canada's major artists.

PELLATT, SIR HENRY MILL (1859-1939), financier. Born at Kingston, Canada West, Pellatt joined his father's financial firm. He organized and financed hydro and street railway companies and Canadian General Electric, was active in the Queen's Own Rifles in the militia, and built Toronto's only castle, the astonishing Casa Loma. Pellatt went broke and ended his days living in a modest duplex in Toronto.

PELLETIER, GÉRARD (1919–), journalist, politician. Born at Victoriaville, Que., Pelletier

was educated at the Univ. de Montréal. He worked in Catholic youth organizations as a young man, then became a journalist at *Le Devoir*, involved in the growing ferment against MAURICE DUPLESSIS. His friendship with PIERRE TRUDEAU developed at the time of the ASBESTOS STRIKE, and he helped found *CITÉ LIBRE* to provide a forum for their opposition to Duplessis. In 1965 he ran for the Liberals federally with a view to helping Ottawa find the strength to check separatism. He held cabinet posts under Trudeau (1968-75), was ambassador to France and to the UN, and has published two able volumes of memoirs.

PELLETIER, WILFRID (1896-1982), musical administrator. Pelletier was born at Montreal and trained as a pianist. Beginning in 1935, he was the first director of the Société des concerts symphoniques de Montréal, director of the Quebec Symphonic Orchestra, and from 1961 to 1970 director of musical education for the Ministry of Cultural Affairs. An important figure in Jeunesses musicales du Canada, Pelletier also worked with the Metropolitan Opera in New York.

PENFIELD, WILDER GRAVES (1891-1976), neurosurgeon. The founder of the famed Montreal Neurosurgical Institute, Penfield was born at Spokane, Wash., and educated at Oxford and Johns Hopkins univs. He came to Montreal in 1928, established his reputation and credibility with funding agencies, and opened his institute in 1934. His major innovations were in the surgical treatment of epilepsy, and his studies of the brain were important. After retiring from the institute in 1960, Penfield wrote fiction, an autobiography, and medical books for laymen.

PERMANENT JOINT BOARD ON DEFENCE, a Canada-U.S. body created by the Ogdensburg Agreement of 18 Aug. 1940 by Prime Minister MACKENZIE KING and President Franklin Roosevelt. After Britain had been driven from the European continent by Germany in June 1940, Canada had to secure its own safety. This necessitated a defensive alliance with the United States and the board was the outward symbol of the changed relationship. Made up of civilian and military members, it began meeting on 26 Aug. 1940 and continues to this day as the agency that studies and reports on defence questions to the two governments.

PERSONS CASE, reference case brought to the SUPREME COURT of Canada by feminist leaders in 1927 to determine whether or not it was constitutional for the government of Canada to appoint women to the Senate. The question revolved around the interpretation of the word "persons" in section 24 of the BRITISH NORTH AMERICA ACT which specified how senators were to be appointed. In 1928 the court ruled that women were not "persons" as specified in the act, but the ruling was overturned by the JUDICIAL COMMITTEE OF THE PRIVY COUNCIL in the fall of 1929.

PETERSON, OSCAR EMANUEL (1925–), jazz pianist. Born in Montreal, Peterson was playing on Montreal radio by 1940. In 1949 he debuted, playing with his own trio, at Carnegie Hall and built an international reputation as an exponent of mainstream jazz.

PETRO-CANADA, federal CROWN CORPORATION established by the Liberal government of Prime Minister PIERRE TRUDEAU in 1975 to ensure a government presence in exploration, extraction, and marketing of petroleum products. The CROWN CORPORATION then acquired such privately owned companies as Petro-Fina, Pacific 66, and the retail operations of Gulf Canada. It is currently the largest gasoline retailer in Canada. The company is also engaged in exploration, particularly in frontier areas, and in extraction and refining.

PICKERSGILL, JOHN WHITNEY (1905–), public servant, politician. Born at Wyecombe, Ont., and educated at the univs. of Manitoba and Oxford, Pickersgill taught history at United College. He joined the Department of External Affairs in 1937, was assigned to the Prime Minister's Office and, clever and indefatigable, quickly became indispensable to MACKENZIE KING and then to LOUIS ST LAURENT. By 1952 he was clerk of the Privy Council. Two years later he entered the cabinet, then won election in Newfoundland, and, after the Liberal defeat in 1957, he played a key role in the opposition to JOHN DIEFENBAKER. He held two portfolios under Prime Minister LESTER PEARSON, retiring from politics in 1967 to become president of the CANADIAN TRANSPORT COMMISSION. His edited diaries of King and

his own two volumes of history-autobiography are important sources.

PIERCE, LORNE ALBERT (1890-1961), editor. Born at Delta, Ont., Pierce trained as a Methodist minister. He joined Ryerson Press in 1920 and, as a fervent cultural nationalist, quickly became a dominant figure in the small Canadian publishing industry. He started Ryerson's poetry chapbooks, launched a series of critical studies, and started prose and poetry text series. He wrote a biography himself and edited collections of poetry. His papers, now at Queen's Univ., are an important source of information on Canadian authors and publishing.

PIPELINE DEBATE, 1956 parliamentary debate that helped destroy the government of Prime Minister LOUIS ST LAURENT. In the early 1950s C.D. HOWE, the minister of trade and commerce, decided that a pipeline was needed to carry Alberta's natural gas to Ontario. In May 1956, he introduced a bill to authorize construction and loan Trans-Canada Pipelines, a private company, money so it could begin. The government ran into staunch opposition from the CO-OPERATIVE COMMONWEALTH FEDERATION, which wanted a public company used, and the PROGRESSIVE CONSERVATIVES, who felt there was too much American involvement in the project. Howe knew that construction had to start by June and invoked CLOSURE to cut off debate and ram the bill through the House of Commons. The Liberals succeeded and construction began, but the high-handed methods used shocked the country.

PITFIELD, PETER MICHAEL (1937–), public servant. Born in Montreal and educated at St Lawrence and McGill univs., he worked in Ottawa for DAVIE FULTON and for Governor General GEORGES VANIER. He joined the Privy Council Office in 1965, and became its deputy secretary in 1969 and clerk of the Privy Council in 1975. As such he became a key adviser to PIERRE TRUDEAU and arguably the most powerful civil servant in the land. Fired by JOE CLARK when he took power in 1979, Pitfield was brought back by Trudeau in 1980. He was named to the Senate in 1982.

PLAUNT, ALAN BUTTERWORTH (1904-41), broadcaster. Born at Ottawa to wealth, Plaunt was a nationalist reformer. One of the founders of the LEAGUE FOR SOCIAL RECONSTRUCTION, he helped draft the REGINA MANIFESTO. With GRAHAM SPRY, he founded the CANADIAN RADIO LEAGUE that campaigned successfully for the creation of state-owned radio, eventually the CANADIAN BROADCASTING CORP. He was named to the board of the CBC in 1936. *See also* CANADIAN RADIO BROADCASTING COMMISSION.

courtesy NFB-4/42, WR-521

Mackenzie King signing autographs on Plebiscite Day, 1942

PLEBISCITE, the vote on conscription, 27 April 1942. To secure release from its pledges against CONSCRIPTION for overseas service in WORLD WAR II, the MACKENZIE KING government asked the country to indicate its views in a non-binding ballot. Quebec voted 72.9 per cent against release, but English Canada voted heavily in favour, and the overall result was for release. The government response was to pass BILL 80 authorizing the use of NATIONAL RESOURCES MOBILIZATION ACT soldiers overseas, but King pledged to so use them only if it was necessary. *See also* CONSCRIPTION CRISIS.

POLANYI, JOHN CHARLES (1929–), chemist. Born in Berlin, Germany, in 1934 he and his family took refuge in England, where Polanyi was educated. He joined the faculty of Univ. of Toronto in 1959. Polanyi specializes in chemical transformation and had gained a wide reputation as a scientist before being awarded the Nobel Prize for Chemistry in 1986.

POPE, JAMES COLLEDGE (1826-85), premier of Prince Edward Island, federal politician.

Born at Bedeque, P.E.I., Pope was a shipowner and businessman when he went into politics in 1857 as a Tory. He served as premier three times, built a railway, and led his province into CONFEDERATION in 1873. Elected an MP, he became fisheries minister in SIR JOHN A. MACDONALD's government from 1878 to 1882.

courtesy National Archives of Canada/PA-110845

Sir Joseph Pope

POPE, SIR JOSEPH (1854-1926), public servant. Born at Charlottetown, P.E.I., he became private secretary to SIR JOHN A. MACDONALD in Ottawa. In 1896, he became under-secretary of state for external affairs, a post he held into the 1920s that gave him substantial power. Pope created the Department of External Affairs. He wrote and edited volumes on Macdonald.

POPE, MAURICE ARTHUR (1889-1978), soldier. Born at Rivière du Loup, Que., the son of Sir Joseph Pope, he enlisted in the CANADIAN EXPEDITIONARY FORCE in 1915 and served overseas. He stayed in the peacetime permanent force, and by 1941 was vice-chief of the general staff. He served on the PERMANENT JOINT BOARD ON DEFENCE, as head of Canada's joint staff mission in Washington, and as military adviser to the prime minister. From 1950 to 1956 he was ambassador, first in Belgium and then in Spain.

PORT HOPE CONFERENCE, 1942, CONSERVATIVE PARTY meeting on 4-6 Sept. that adopted progressive policies. With the party devastated in the 1935 and 1940 elections and threatened by the rise of the CO-OPERATIVE COMMONWEALTH FEDERATION during World War II, a few Conservatives organized the meeting. The result was a policy statement that, stressing social security and down-playing tariffs, moved the party firmly into the centre, a result that seemed to be confirmed in Dec. 1942 when JOHN BRACKEN was selected as leader and the party's name was changed to PROGRESSIVE CONSERVATIVE.

PORTER, JOHN ARTHUR (1921-79), sociologist. Born in Vancouver and educated at the London School of Economics and the Univ. of London, Porter taught at Carleton Univ. and the Univ. of Toronto. His book *The Vertical Mosaic,* an analysis of the disparities of class and power in Canada, established him as the leading sociologist in Canada.

courtesy O.B. Buell/National Archives of Canada/C-1875

Poundmaker

POUNDMAKER (1842-86), Cree chief. A Stoney but with family connections to the Cree, Poundmaker was adoped by CROWFOOT and became a powerful Cree chief in 1873. He tried to restrain his followers during the NORTH-WEST REBELLION of 1885, but did not succeed. He was tried for felony-treason and sentenced to three years. He served a year, was released, but died soon after.

POWER, CHARLES GAVAN, "CHUBBY" (1888-1968), politician. Born at Sillery, Que., and trained in law, Power served overseas in World War I and was both wounded and decorated. Elected to the House of Commons in 1917 as a Liberal, he held his seat until 1955 when he became a senator. Able and bibulous, Power was first appointed to cabinet in 1935. His most important role was as minister of national defence (air) from 1940 to 1944 when he directed the BRITISH COMMONWEALTH AIR TRAINING PLAN. He resigned during the CONSCRIPTION CRISIS of 1944. Power was a key strategist for the Liberals in Quebec. He ran for the Liberal leadership in 1948 as a reformer and was trounced. His memoirs are a delight.

PRAIRIE FARM REHABILITATION ADMINISTRATION, federal agency set up to battle the effects of drought and soil erosion in the PALLISER'S TRIANGLE AREA of the southern Prairies, and established under the Prairie Farm Rehabilitation Act of 1935. Using expertise provided by the DOMINION EXPERIMENTAL FARM, PFRA experts taught western grain farmers how to preserve moisture in the soil and regenerate dried-out land, while land that could not be saved for agriculture was returned to pasture. Among the techniques championed by the PFRA was STRIP FARMING, the planting of trees in shelter belts, the establishment of stock-watering dams on farms, and ploughing in such a manner as to preserve a stubble mulch. *See also* NOBLE BLADE.

PRATT, EDWIN JOHN (1882-1964), poet. Born at Western Bay, Nfld, Pratt studied for the ministry in St John's and Toronto, and was ordained in 1913. Joining the English department at Victoria College, Univ. of Toronto, in 1920, he taught there for 33 years. Pratt first drew attention when his book of poetry *Newfoundland Verse* (1923) appeared. A further dozen volumes followed, three of which won Governor General's Awards. Realistic, deeply affected by the sea and his Newfoundland youth, Pratt ranks as Canada's most important poet of the 20th century.

PRICE, SIR WILLIAM, (1867-1924), merchant, manufacturer. Price was born in Talca, Chile, and educated in Canada and Great Britain. He joined the Price Brothers lumber company in 1886 and three years later became president. He added a pulp and paper mill in the Saguenay, Que., area to the company, and it subsequently became the largest producer of newsprint in Canada. Price sat in the House of Commons as a Conservative, 1908-12.

PROGRESSIVE CONSERVATIVE PARTY, name adopted by the CONSERVATIVE PARTY at its 1942 convention. Fearing the rise of the CO-OPERATIVE COMMONWEALTH FEDERATION, Conservative sachems turned to Manitoba's Liberal-Progressive premier JOHN BRACKEN to be their leader. As a condition of leadership, Bracken insisted on the name change to indicate that the party's new direction, first shown at the PORT HOPE CONFERENCE, was genuine.

PROGRESSIVE PARTY, a loose organization of western and Ontario farmers and MPs led by T.A. CRERAR, a former UNION GOVERNMENT cabinet minister who had resigned over the government's budget in 1919. The party was endorsed by the CANADIAN COUNCIL OF AGRICULTURE in Dec. 1920, and it won 65 seats in the 1921 federal election, second only to the Liberals. For the first time a third party had the chance to form the opposition, but the Progressives refused it. The party had lost much of its appeal by 1926 and soon withered into obscurity, a victim of conflicting ideologies – GROUP GOVERNMENT versus "BROADENING OUT" – and strategies. Most Progressives were swallowed by MACKENZIE KING's Liberals, but enough of the protest tradition survived to lead to the creation of the CO-OPERATIVE COMMONWEALTH FEDERATION, SOCIAL CREDIT, and the insistence by JOHN BRACKEN on adding the word Progressive to the name of the Conservative Party as a condition of his accepting its leadership in 1942. *See also* ROBERT FORKE.

PROHIBITION, the prohibition by law of the sale, or import, or manufacture of alcoholic beverages. In Canada various temperance groups such as the WOMAN'S CHRISTIAN TEMPERANCE UNION lobbied for prohibition as early as the 1870s. The first legislative result was the Canada Temperance Act, also known as the Scott Act, passed in

F.S. Spence, a leader of the Prohibition crusade

1878, which introduced local option for counties or municipalities. In 1898 the government of Prime Minister WILFRID LAURIER held a national referendum on the introduction of prohibition. The "drys" won by a tiny majority but only about 44 per cent of the electorate voted. Laurier refused to pursue the matter and prohibitionists turned their attention to the provinces. By 1907 all provinces had enacted local option laws enabling municipalities, counties, etc., to ban the bar in their areas. During WORLD WAR I all the provinces except Quebec introduced prohibition as a measure to reform public morality and increase social efficiency during wartime. Prohibition proved to be impractical, however, and by the late 1920s provincial government ownership of retail liquor outlets and control of the sale of alcoholic beverages in bars, hotels, and restaurants had replaced total prohibition in most areas of Canada.

"PROPERTY AND CIVIL RIGHTS," words in section 92 of the BRITISH NORTH AMERICA ACT that gave the provinces exclusive right to make laws concerning "Property and Civil Rights in the

Province." Using this clause as a guide the JUDICIAL COMMITTEE OF THE PRIVY COUNCIL frequently struck down federal labour and social legislation as ULTRA VIRES because it was alleged to impinge on the exclusive right of the provinces to make laws respecting property and civil rights. In so doing, the JCPC denied that the federal government had a right to introduce such legislation for all of Canada under its power to legislate for "PEACE, ORDER AND GOOD GOVERNMENT." This effectively stripped the federal government of the ability to introduce laws aimed at social betterment until the 1960s when shared-cost programs such as MEDICARE were introduced.

"PROVE UP," term used to describe the process of improvement of the homestead required under the DOMINION LANDS ACT before a HOMESTEADER was given clear title to his farm.

PROVINCIAL WORKMEN'S ASSN, labour union formed in Nova Scotia in 1879. First called the Provincial Miners' Assn, the PWA was organized by coal-miners in 1879. It lobbied the Nova Scotia government for better mine safety legislation and functioned as a cooperative as well as a labour union. In the early years of the 20th century the PWA fought to keep the United Mine Workers out of the province, but it finally merged with the UMW in 1917 to form the AMALGAMATED MINE WORKERS OF NOVA SOCTIA.

PUBLIC SERVICE STAFF RELATIONS ACT, federal labour law passed by the liberal government of Prime Minister LESTER PEARSON in 1967. It gave most federal civil servants essentially the same collective bargaining rights as workers in the private sector. Under the act the Treasury Board became the federal government's overall employer and the Public Service Staff Relations Board was created with many of the functions exercised by the CANADA LABOUR RELATIONS BOARD.

PUTTEE, ARTHUR W. (1868-1957), labour journalist, politician. Born in Folkstone, Eng., Puttee was elected to the House of Commons under a labour banner for Winnipeg in 1900 and served four years. He was founder and editor of the Winnipeg VOICE, one of western Canada's most important labour papers. He lost the sup-

port of organized labour during World War I when he opposed labour's swing to radicalism.

QUARTER SECTION, the basic farm unit as laid out in the DOMINION LANDS ACT of 1872. The act provided for the surveying of the Canadian Prairies into square townships, measuring 10 km on each side. These townships were divided into 36 sections of 640 acres each, and each section was divided into 4 quarter sections.

QUEBEC CENTRAL RAILWAY, the railway incorporated in 1869 as the Sherbrooke, Eastern Townships, and Kennebec Railway. It became known as the Quebec Central in 1874 and was leased to the CANADIAN PACIFIC RAILWAY in 1913.

QUEBEC CONFERENCE, 1864, conference of the FATHERS OF CONFEDERATION held 10-27 Oct. that followed the CHARLOTTETOWN CONFERENCE. At Quebec, the outline of the BRITISH NORTH AMERICA ACT was embodied in 72 RESOLUTIONS, which were adopted in 1865 by the UNITED PROVINCE OF CANADA and broadly affirmed by New Brunswick and Nova Scotia in 1866, laying the groundwork for CONFEDERATION.

QUEBEC CONFERENCES, 1943, 1944, two British-American wartime conferences, the first held from 17-24 Aug. 1943 and the second 10-15 Sept. 1944. U.S. President Franklin Roosevelt and British Prime Minister Winston Churchill and their staffs met regularly to plan Allied strategy during World War II. Canada played host to two of the 1943 and 1944 conferences, and, although Prime Minister MACKENZIE KING, some of his ministers, and the Canadian chiefs of staff were on hand, they were not privy to the great secrets, much to Canadian chagrin.

QUEBEC RIOTS (1918), anti-CONSCRIPTION riots in Quebec City in the spring of 1918, climaxing on 1 April. Thousands of protesters rioted in Lower Town after enlistment officers became somewhat zealous in seeking draft evaders, and the government called out troops to maintain order. At least four civilians were killed and a number wounded by gunfire, but the exact casualty list was never determined.

QUEEN'S PLATE, thoroughbred horse race first run in Toronto in 1860. It is the oldest uninterrupted stakes race in North America.

QUIET REVOLUTION, term used to describe a period of rapid change in Quebec under the Liberal government of JEAN LESAGE from 1960 to 1966. The reforms the government introduced were wide ranging and represented a complete break with the society protected by MAURICE DUPLESSIS and the UNION NATIONALE since 1944. The hallmark of the Quiet Revolution was massive government intervention in the province's economic, political, and cultural affairs. The Liberals also launched an all-out attack on patronage and secret election funds. The voting age was lowered and electoral boundaries changed to provide better urban representation. There was a massive growth in governmental institutions, in educational development, labour reforms, social reforms, and publicly owned utilities. At the same time Lesage tested the limits of Confederation by demanding the right to operate Quebec's own programs in hospitalization, education, and social insurance. In part this was done using the OPTING OUT formula worked out by Lesage in conjunction with Liberal Prime Minister LESTER PEARSON after the latter's election victory in 1963. The most spectacular example of the Quiet Revolution was the nationalization of Quebec's privately owned electric power companies and their consolidation into HYDRO-QUÉBEC following the 1962 election, an operation led by RENÉ LÉVESQUE who was then minister of natural resources. The revolution greatly affected French Canada's perception of itself, creating great self-confidence. Although the Liberals were defeated by a renewed Union nationale in 1966, all Quebec governments have since acknowledged the importance of the Lesage era. *See also* ERIC KIERANS.

QUEBEC REFERENDUM, referendum held by the PARTI QUÉBÉCOIS government of Premier RENÉ LÉVESQUE in May 1980 which asked the people of Quebec to grant the government permission to negotiate "SOVEREIGNTY-ASSOCIATION" with the rest

of Canada. The referendum was organized as a first step towards the achievement of sovereignty-association. Instead of seeking a mandate to negotiate the outright separation of Quebec from Canada, Lévesque chose to seek the right to negotiate an agreement that would grant Quebec both sovereignty and economic association with the rest of Canada. The plan was foiled when 59.5 per cent voted no.

RALLIEMENT DES CRÉDITISTES, the SOCIAL CREDIT PARTY in Quebec. Formed in the 1940s as a right-wing populist movement, the Créditistes became a political party in 1958 under the leadership of RÉAL CAOUETTE. In the 1962 federal election, now joined with the Social Credit party under ROBERT THOMPSON, Caouette's group captured 26 seats in Quebec and held the balance of power in a minority House of Commons. The Créditistes split from the Social Credit party in 1963, entered a long decline, and disappeared after Caouette's demise in 1976.

Colonel J.L. Ralston meeting with troops in England, 1940

RALSTON, JAMES LAYTON (1881-1948), politician. Born at Amherst, N.S., and trained in law at Dalhousie Univ., he sat in the Nova Scotia legislature as a Liberal from 1911 to 1920. He served overseas in World War I, becoming a much decorated and admired battalion commander. Elected to Parliament in 1925, he was minister of national defence under MACKENZIE KING. He did not run in 1935, but King brought him back to Ottawa in 1939 to be minister of finance. In 1940, he became defence minister and presided over the huge expansion of the CANADIAN ARMY. He was a strong supporter of CONSCRIPTION in both 1942 and 1944, and King forced him out of the cabinet in Nov. 1944 in one of the epic struggles in our politics.

RAND, IVAN CLEVELAND (1884-1969), judge, labour arbitrator. Born in Moncton, N.B., Rand attended Harvard Law School and was inspired by the liberalism of U.S. Supreme Court judge Louis D. Brandeis. He spent a brief period (1924-5) as Liberal attorney general in the government of New Brunswick and was appointed to the SUPREME COURT of Canada in 1943. In 1946 Rand acted as mediator following a strike of the United Auto Workers against the Ford Motor Co. at Windsor and recommended what soon became known as the RAND FORMULA. In 1947 he was appointed Canada's representative on the United Nations Special Committee on Palestine and sided with those committee members recommending the partition of Palestine into two independent states, one Arab and the other Jewish. He served on the Supreme Court until 1959 when he retired to become the first dean of the Faculty of Law at the Univ. of Western Ontario. *See also* WINDSOR STRIKE.

RAND FORMULA, provision in collective agreements first recommended by IVAN RAND following a 1945 strike at the Ford Motor Co. in Windsor, Ont. The formula provides that employers must deduct union dues from all employees, union members or not, but that all employees are not obliged to join the union. It is based on the notion that workers should be free to stay outside the union if they wish, but that they must pay dues since they benefit from the union's presence in the plant. *See also* WINDSOR STRIKE.

RASMINSKY, LOUIS (1908–), central banker. Born in Montreal and educated at the Univ. of Toronto and the London School of Economics, Rasminsky worked for the LEAGUE OF NATIONS before joining the FOREIGN EXCHANGE CONTROL BOARD in 1940 and quickly winning a place among Ottawa's MANDARINS. After the war, Rasminsky rose

rapidly through the BANK OF CANADA, becoming governor after the COYNE AFFAIR of 1961. He restored relations with government and set down the rules that have since governed bank – government dealings. He stepped down as governor in 1973.

RASSEMBLEMENT POUR L'INDÉPEN-DANCE NATIONALE, a centre-left separatist movement formed in Quebec in the early 1960s. It was led by PIERRE BOURGAULT from 1964 until it merged with the PARTI QUÉBÉCOIS in 1968. The RIN captured 6 per cent of the popular vote in the 1966 provincial election.

RAYMOND, MAXIME (1883-1961), Quebec politician, nationalist. A graduate of Univ. Laval and a lawyer, he was first elected to Parliament as a Liberal in 1925. He won re-election continuously through the election of 1945. In Sept. 1942, Raymond broke away from the Liberals and founded the BLOC POPULAIRE CANADIEN, a nationalist party that emerged from the LIGUE POUR LA DÉFENSE DU CANADA. The Bloc ran candidates provincially in 1944 and federally in 1945, with little success.

RCMP, *see* ROYAL CANADIAN MOUNTED POLICE

The Liberals and Reciprocity, 1891

courtesy J.W. Bengough/National Archives of Canada/C-6541

RECIPROCITY, term used to refer to a trade agreement with the United States that allows a large number of trade items to pass back and forth across the Canada-U.S. border without duty. The first reciprocity agreement, concluded between the United States and the British American colonies in 1854, expired after 10 years. Canadians then made numerous efforts to reach another such agreement and came close on a number of occasions. The most notable was in 1910-11 when an agreement was actually negotiated by the Liberal government of SIR WILFRID LAURIER only to be rendered null and void by the victory of the anti-reciprocity Conservatives under ROBERT BORDEN in the 1911 election. In the 1930s a number of Canadian-American trade agreements were concluded and a full reciprocity or FREE TRADE agreement was discussed after World War II. *See also* CUSTOMS UNION.

RECONSTRUCTION, term used to describe the reconstruction of Canadian society after World Wars I and II. Towards the end of both wars the government began to prepare for peacetime and the change of society and the economy from a war to a peace footing. In WORLD WAR I these efforts were neither far-sighted nor extensive and were mainly concentrated on the reintegration of war veterans into society through the Department of Soldiers Civil Re-establishment, formed in Feb. 1918. Since the government had not intervened extensively in the Canadian economy during the war, Prime Minister ROBERT BORDEN did not think much more was required. During WORLD WAR II, however, government intervention was far more extensive and it was recognized that a far-reaching and well organized effort was necessary to convert Canadian society to peacetime. Measures included family allowances, changes to the National Housing Act, export credits, and major veterans benefits. In Oct. 1944 C.D. HOWE was named minister of reconstruction.

RECONSTRUCTION PARTY, political party created by H.H. STEVENS for the 1935 general election. Stevens broke with R.B. BENNETT, the Conservative prime minister, and set up his party to champion small business. He was the only MP elected, but his 174 candidates drew 384,095 votes and unquestionably cost the Conservatives many seats.

RED ENSIGN, unofficial flag of Canada, consisting of the ensign of the British Merchant Marine with the Canadian coat of arms added to the fly. The flag was approved for official use on government buildings in 1924 but was never made the official flag of Canada. In 1965 it was replaced by the Maple Leaf Flag.

RED FIFE, the dominant strain of wheat grown by western grain farmers until the development of MARQUIS WHEAT in the early 20th century.

RED RIVER REBELLION, uprising of MÉTIS in the Red River area led by LOUIS RIEL in 1869-70. The uprising was precipitated by Canada's annexation of Rupert's Land following its purchase from the HUDSON'S BAY CO. in 1868. According to the Rupert's Land Act, Canada was to take possession of all lands and territories on 1 Dec. 1869. The Métis objected to being transferred to Canadian jurisdiction. They feared that annexation to Canada would bring a flood of white settlers who would destroy their way of life. Led by Riel, they formed a National Committee of the Métis, stopped the Canadian governor-designate, WILLIAM MCDOUGALL, from entering the territory, seized the Hudson's Bay Co. post at Lower Fort Garry, imprisoned a number of Canadian settlers who had been agitating for annexation to Canada, and declared a provisional government. In a show of force, Riel ordered the execution of one of the Canadian prisoners, THOMAS SCOTT, following an unsuccessful escape attempt. Prime Minister JOHN A. MACDONALD suspended the transfer of Rupert's Land to Canada as soon as he heard of the troubles and asked Britain to send a military expedition to Red River. The British agreed on condition that Macdonald open negotiations with the Métis. Discussions proceeded while the military expedition was being readied. Those discussions produced the MANITOBA ACT, designed to add Manitoba to Canada while offering the Métis some protection for their culture and confirmation of their rights to land. In Aug. 1870, the military expedition under General GARNET WOLSELEY arrived, and Riel and his cohorts were forced to flee. The Métis, who had ostensibly won what they sought in the Manitoba Act, soon moved further west as settlers trickled in from the east. The NORTH-WEST REBELLION, 1885, again led by Riel, was the result.

RED RIVER SETTLEMENT, settlement in Manitoba located at the junction of the Red and Assiniboine rivers, on the site of present-day Winnipeg. It was on a large tract of land granted to Lord Selkirk in 1812 which was known both as the Selkirk Settlement and the Red River Colony. Although the original Selkirk settlers were Scottish, by the time the province of Manitoba was created in 1870 the Red River settlement had become a mixed settlement of whites and Métis.

RED RIVER TRANSPORTATION CO., company established in 1872 by JAMES J. HILL and NORMAN W. KITSON, which operated steamboats on the Red River between Red River (Winnipeg) and the United States border. The company later formed the basis for the partnership of Hill, Kitson, DONALD A. SMITH and GEORGE STEPHEN in the CANADIAN PACIFIC RAILWAY syndicate.

RED SCARE, term used to describe a period between the end of World War I and early 1922 in which many people feared that a revolution was about to take place in Canada and the United States. The fears were fuelled by the Bolshevik Revolution and other revolutionary activity in Europe and by the outbreak of major strikes such as the Seattle General Strike, the WINNIPEG GENERAL STRIKE, and the Boston Police Strike.

RED TORY, term coined by 1960s political thinkers such as GEORGE GRANT and Gad Horowitz to describe men and women who support the Conservative party but who also share certain assumptions with social democrats and liberals about the need for government to maintain basic social services and regulate parts of the marketplace. Other political thinkers deny that "red" Tories exist and claim that Conservative support for measures such as medicare stems from good old political opportunism.

REFUS GLOBAL, Quebec artists' manifesto drafted in 1948 by PAUL-ÉMILE BORDUAS and others. The manifesto challenged Quebec's traditional values and rejected any ideology that hindered creativity. Denounced for anarchism, the manifesto had genuine artistic importance in Quebec, pointing the way to the freedom engendered by the QUIET REVOLUTION.

REGAN, GERALD AUGUSTINE (1928–), premier of Nova Scotia, federal politician. Born at Windsor, N.S., and educated at St Mary's and Dalhousie univs., Regan was elected to the House of Commons in 1963 as a Liberal but left Ottawa to lead the Nova Scotia Liberal party in 1965. He won a minority victory in 1970 and a majority four years later. Defeated in 1978, he

returned to the House of Commons in 1980, holding two portfolios in the TRUDEAU government.

REGINA MANIFESTO, a program produced by the LEAGUE FOR SOCIAL RECONSTRUCTION and adopted by the CO-OPERATIVE COMMONWEALTH FEDERATION at its convention in 1933. It called for the replacement of the capitalist system by a social order which would eliminate class exploitation, establish a welfare state with pensions and unemployment insurance, provide socialized planning, and create a mixed economy through nationalization and public ownership of key industries. The manifesto was the CCF platform until it was replaced by the Winnipeg Declaration in 1956.

REGINA RIOT, labour and police riot that took place in Regina on 1 July 1935. The culminating event of the ON-TO-OTTAWA TREK, the riot began when Regina police and members of the ROYAL CANADIAN MOUNTED POLICE attempted to clear unemployed trekkers out of Regina after Prime Minister R.B. BENNETT had ordered the trek halted.

REGULATION 17, issued by Ontario's Conservative government in 1912 to restrict French as a language of instruction to the first two years of elementary school. The measure, at least partly aimed at improving francophone students' chances to compete in Ontario, caused an uproar in French Canada and was used to justify Quebec's lukewarm support for the World War I effort. The regulation was amended in 1913 to allow one hour of French a day for subsequent years, and it was eliminated by Premier G. HOWARD FERGUSON in 1927.

REID, ESCOTT MEREDITH (1905–), diplomat. Born in Campbellford, Ont., and a graduate of the univs. of Toronto and Oxford, Reid was one of the most innovative young political scientists in Canada in the 1930s. He joined the CANADIAN INSTITUTE OF INTERNATIONAL AFFAIRS as national secretary in 1932, simultaneously writing neutralist articles. In 1938 Reid went to the Department of External Affairs where his restless energy gave him quick advancement. He served in Washington and Ottawa, galvanized air transport policy, and helped create the UNITED NATIONS. By 1946 he was LESTER PEARSON's chief aide and one of the creators of NATO. He then served in New Delhi and Bonn, at the International Bank for Reconstruction and Development and, after his retirement from diplomacy, as principal of Glendon College, York Univ. Reid's books on NATO's origins, the UN's foundation, and his time in India are invaluable.

RELIEF CAMP, camps established for unemployed men during the GREAT DEPRESSION. Most were in the west and the majority in British Columbia; they were designed to keep unemployed men out of the cities. Conditions in the camps varied widely, but they were almost always strongly regimented, especially after they came under the direction of the Department of National Defence in 1933. *See also* ON-TO-OTTAWA TREK; REGINA RIOT; ROYAL TWENTY CENTERS.

RELIEF CAMP WORKERS' UNION, labour organization founded by the Communist-led WORKERS' UNITY LEAGUE. The RCWU attempted to organize RELIEF CAMP workers and led the ON-TO-OTTAWA TREK of June 1935.

REMEMBRANCE DAY, originally dedicated as the official memorial day for soldiers killed in action in WORLD WAR I. The armistice which ended that war went into effect at 11 a.m., 11 Nov. 1918. Thus Remembrance Day was set for Nov. 11 with a period of silence to be observed at 11 a.m. Remembrance Day was designated as the memorial day for Canadians killed in action in WORLD WAR II and Korea as well.

REMITTANCE MAN, English immigrant to Canada living on a remittance. The ne'er-do-well sons of wealthy English families were often sent to the colonies to make something of themselves. Their basic stipend was the remittance received from home. A large number who settled in southwestern Alberta went into ranching.

"REP-BY-POP," representation by population, the rallying cry of the GRIT party in CANADA WEST prior to CONFEDERATION. In the legislature of the UNITED PROVINCE OF CANADA, which preceded Confederation, CANADA WEST and CANADA EAST had been given an equal number of seats to give more weight to the less-populated, English-speaking section of Canada West. But by the late 1850s, it was French-speaking Canada East that

had less population. In Canada West, the Grit movement began to agitate for representation by population, and the demand was one of the factors leading to the Confederation movement. *See also* BRITISH NORTH AMERICA ACT; GEORGE BROWN.

RESOLUTION IX, a declaration of the IMPERIAL WAR CONFERENCE, London, passed on 16 April 1917, that left readjustment of imperial constitutional relations until the peace but proclaimed the dominions to be "autonomous nations" entitled to "an adequate voice in foreign policy" and "continuous consultation in all important matters of common Imperial concern." Prime Minister SIR ROBERT BORDEN had initiated this resolution which expressed his desire for Canada to function within the Empire. MACKENZIE KING, however, was the Canadian statesman of the future, and his route to autonomy admitted no desire for consultation which led inevitably to commitment.

RESOURCES FOR TOMORROW CONFERENCE, 1961, DIEFENBAKER government effort to coordinate federal and provincial policies on land, water, and resource use. Held in Montreal, the conference led to the creation of the Canadian Council of Resource Ministers.

RHINELAND, BATTLE OF, 1945, an important operation of the FIRST CANADIAN ARMY from 8 Feb. to 10 March directed at forcing the German army back to the Rhine River. Defending their own territory, the Germans resisted fiercely as the Canadians attacked in difficult weather conditions over flooded ground initially and then through the Hochwald forest. Canadian casualties were 5300 in the bitter struggle; German losses were over 90,000 with 52,000 taken prisoner.

RHINOCEROS PARTY, mock political party founded in 1963 by Jacques Ferron to jeer at the pomposities of the genuine parties. The group fielded candidates in 1964 by-elections and subsequent general elections, injecting levity into the campaigns and often putting up more credible candidates than the major parties.

RHODES, EDGAR NELSON (1877-1942), premier of Nova Scotia, federal politician. Born at Amherst, N.S., Rhodes was elected to Parliament in 1908, becoming speaker of the House in 1917. He went to Nova Scotia to head the provincial Conservative party and was premier from 1925 to 1930 when he returned to Ottawa to become minister of fisheries and then finance minister in Prime Minister R.B. BENNETT's government. He was made a senator in 1935.

courtesy Club de hockey canadien/Hockey Hall of Fame

Maurice Richard

RICHARD, JOSEPH-HENRI-MAURICE (1921–), hockey player. Born at Montreal, "Rocket" Richard joined the Montreal Canadiens in 1942-3. In 1944-5 he scored 50 goals in 50 games, one of many records he set until a severed tendon forced his retirement in 1960. He was a national hero among Québécois for his speed, goal-scoring, and fiery temper, and his suspension in 1955 following an incident with a Boston Bruins player and a linesman precipitated the worst sports riot in Canadian history. Richard had 544 career goals in regular season play and 82 goals in STANLEY CUP competition.

RICHARDSON, JAMES ARMSTRONG, SR. (1885-1939), financier. He entered the family grain-exporting business in 1906, becoming president in 1919. He served as director of many companies, including the Canadian Pacific Railway, the Canadian Bank of Commerce, International Nickel, the Great West Life Assurance Co., and as president of the Winnipeg Grain Exchange.

RICHARDSON, JAMES ARMSTRONG, JR. (1922–), grain merchant, politician. The son of JAMES A. RICHARDSON, SR, he was a bomber pilot during World War II before entering the family business in 1945. Elected to the House of Commons in 1968, he served as minister without portfolio until appointed minister of supply and services, 1969-72. Re-elected in 1972, he became defence minister but resigned over Prime Minister PIERRE TRUDEAU's language policy in 1976. He sat as an independent in 1978-9, and then left politics.

RICHLER, MORDECAI (1931–), writer. Born in Montreal, Richler grew up in the Jewish district of "the Main" and was educated at Sir George Williams College. He lived in France and Spain in 1951-2 and then in England until his return to Montreal in 1972. His fourth novel, *The Apprenticeship of Duddy Kravitz* (1959), won him critical acclaim (and became a spendid film in 1974) but a certain animosity in the Jewish community which thought itself cruelly satirized. The same criticism swirled around *St. Urbain's Horseman* (1971) and *Joshua Then and Now* (1980). All his work reveals his extraordinary gift for black humour and his ability to evoke the texture of Montreal. His non-fiction writing in magazines, often marked by his opposition to Canadian nationalism, has been less successful, but his children's books have won a high reputation.

RIDDELL INCIDENT, political embarrassment that occurred when, during the Italo-Ethiopian War of 1935, Dr Walter Riddell, Canada's permanent representative at the LEAGUE OF NATIONS, Geneva, proposed oil sanctions against the aggressor, Italy. Riddell had acted without instructions in the middle of the general election campaign in Canada, and he soon was repudiated by MACKENZIE KING's newly elected Liberal government. Quebec viewed Fascist Italy with some favour, the League was a weak reed, and commitments abroad, King believed, were divisive in Canada.

"RIDING THE RODS," term used to describe the way men moved about Canada in search of work during the GREAT DEPRESSION. They defied railway police and train crews to hop freight trains and "ride the rods" to wherever they needed to go.

RIEL, LOUIS DAVID (1844-85), MÉTIS leader, politician, founder of Manitoba. The central figure in the RED RIVER REBELLION and the NORTH-WEST REBELLION, Riel was born at St-Boniface, Assiniboia (Man.), educated there and for the priesthood in Montreal. He also studied law before returning to St-Boniface in 1868. In 1869 he became secretary of the Comité national des Métis and, following the seizure of Fort Garry in Nov. 1869, president of the provisional government of the North-West Territories. The MANITOBA ACT, 1870, gave provincial status to a small square of land around Fort Garry. But when an expeditionary force under GARNET WOLSELEY arrived in the summer of 1870, Riel fled, largely to avoid reprisals for the execution of THOMAS SCOTT. Nonetheless elected to the House of Commons in 1873, Riel was expelled from the House before he could take his seat. He was re-elected in 1874 but was unseated and declared an outlaw in 1875, a sentence commuted on the condition of a five-year banishment. Riel then suffered a nervous breakdown, spent time in mental hospitals (1876-8), moved to the United States, joined the Republican party, and became an American citizen in 1883. Convinced that he was on a divine mission when he returned to Canada in 1884 at the behest of Métis seeking legal rights in the North Saskatchewan valley, the self-proclaimed "Prophet of the New World" seized the parish church in the battle of BATOCHE in March 1885 and sought to raise the Indian tribes. The rebellion he led was a short-lived affair that saw Riel hamper the military tactics devised by his brilliant field general, GABRIEL DUMONT. He was captured by Canadian troops, tried for treason, and, after the cabinet of SIR JOHN A. MACDONALD failed to grant him clemency, hanged at Regina on 16 Nov. 1885. The storm raised by his hanging poisoned Canadian politics and helped turn Quebec against the Conservative party.

RIOPELLE, JEAN-PAUL (1923-), painter. Canada's most internationally acclaimed painter of the 20th century was born at Montreal and studied under PAUL-ÉMILE BORDUAS at the École du Meuble. An original member of the *Automatistes*, Riopelle exhibited in Montreal in 1946 before moving to Paris. He returned briefly to Canada in 1948 to sign the REFUS GLOBAL, the cover of which bears one of his ink drawings. Concerned with spontaneity in art, he experimented with many techniques, from supple brushstrokes to the drip method developed by Jackson Pollack to the palette knife, which he uses to create mosaic-like canvases.

RITCHIE, CHARLES STEWART ALMON (1906-), diplomat, author. Ritchie, born at Halifax and educated at Oxford, joined the Department of External Affairs in 1934. He served in London during the war, as assistant under-secretary from 1950 to 1954 and subsequently as ambassador to Germany (1954-8), the United Nations (1958-62), the United States (1962-6), to NATO and the European Community (1966-7), and HIGH COMMISSIONER in the United Kingdom (1967-71). He has published four volumes of his splendidly written personal diaries, including *The Siren Years* (1974), which won him the Governor General's Award, *An Appetite for Life* (1977), *Diplomatic Passport* (1981) and *Storm Signals* (1983). The volumes are less comments on public affairs than on Ritchie's aesthetics.

ROADS TO RESOURCES, scheme developed by ALVIN HAMILTON to build roads in remote areas to facilitate resource development. Hamilton sold the idea to Conservative leader JOHN DIEFENBAKER during the 1957 campaign and it was implemented in the first session of the new Parliament, Ottawa providing 50 per cent of the cost of roads that qualified.

ROBARTS, JOHN PARMENTER (1917-82), premier of Ontario. Born at Banff, Alta, Robarts graduated from the Univ. of Western Ontario. He served in the ROYAL CANADIAN NAVY during World War II, then practised law in London, Ont. He was elected to the provincial legislature in 1951, joined the cabinet in 1958, and succeeded LESLIE FROST as Conservative leader and premier three years later. In his nine years in office, Robarts continued the development of Ontario, played a central role in the constitutional debates of the decade, and was quite popular. After his resignation in 1970, he chaired a royal commission on Metro Toronto and co-chaired the Task Force on Canadian Unity.

ROBERTS, SIR CHARLES GEORGE DOUGLAS (1860-1943), poet, animal-story writer. Born at Douglas, N.B., and educated at the Univ. of New Brunswick, Roberts was a schoolteacher, editor of *The Week*, and a professor at King's College, Windsor, N.B., before moving to New York in 1897. He left for Europe in 1907, served in World War I, and returned to Canada in 1925. A member of the "poets of Confederation," Roberts wrote *Orion and Other Poems* (1880), and numerous animal stories, such as *Earth's Enigmas* (1896) and *Eyes of the Wilderness* (1933).

ROBERTSON, GIDEON D. (1874-1933), labour leader, politician. Born in Welland, Ont., he was a vice-president of the Order of Railway Telegraphers when appointed to the Senate in 1917. He served for a little over a year as a labour troubleshooter for the government of Prime Minister ROBERT BORDEN and was appointed minister of labour in 1918. He played a prominent role in bringing about the defeat of the WINNIPEG GENERAL STRIKE and the downfall of the ONE BIG UNION. In 1930 he was again appointed minister of labour in the government of R.B. BENNETT but resigned in Feb. 1932.

ROBERTSON, JOHN ROSS (1841-1918), newspaper publisher. Founder of the Toronto *Telegram*, Robertson was born at Toronto. Known as "the old lady of Melinda Street," his newspaper espoused the virtues and exemplified the defects of Conservative Orange Toronto and became a bitter rival of the Toronto *Star*. Robertson's interest in local history led to several volumes of *Landmarks of Toronto*. A philanthropist, he donated money to Toronto's Hospital for Sick Children. The *Telegram* was a family operation until the 1930s and publication ceased in 1971.

Norman A. Robertson

ROBERTSON, NORMAN ALEXANDER (1904-68), public servant, diplomat. One of Canada's most distinguished diplomats and MANDARINS, Robertson was born at Vancouver and educated at the univs. of British Columbia, Oxford, and the Brookings Institute before joining the Department of External Affairs in 1929. He attracted MACKENZIE KING's attention while working on trade policies during the 1930s and succeeded O.D. SKELTON as under-secretary in 1941. Robertson played a crucial role during WORLD WAR II, helping to give force to FUNCTIONALISM. In 1946 he went to London as HIGH COMMISSIONER, and then returned to Canada to be clerk of the Privy Council. He served in London once more, as ambassador in Washington, and as under-secretary in the DIEFENBAKER years when his opposition to nuclear weapons had critical importance as he provided his minister, HOWARD GREEN, with the arguments that so divided the cabinet. Introspective and brooding, Robertson gave the Department of External Affairs its reputation for intellectualism and devotion.

ROBERTSON, ROBERT GORDON (1917–), public servant. Born at Davidson, Sask., and educated at the univs. of Saskatchewan, Oxford, and Toronto, he joined the Department of External Affairs in 1941 but worked primarily in the

Prime Minister's Office and the Privy Council Office. He served as deputy minister of northern affairs and national resources (1953-63) before becoming clerk of the Privy Council and cabinet secretary (1963-75). From 1975 to 1979 he was secretary to the cabinet for federal-provincial relations and played a vital role in constitutional negotiations. Admired for his discretion, ability, and efficiency, he became president of the Institute for Research on Public Policy in Ottawa after retiring.

ROBICHAUD, LOUIS-JOSEPH (1925–), premier of New Brunswick. Born at St-Antoine, N.B., and educated at Sacré-Coeur and Laval, Robichaud was a lawyer. First elected to the New Brunswick legislature in 1952 as a Liberal, he became party leader six years later. He won power in 1960, becoming the first Acadian to lead the province. His reforming government tried to equalize economic opportunity and make the province more bilingual. His government was defeated in 1970 by the Conservatives under RICHARD HATFIELD. Robichaud resigned as leader the next year, became Canadian chair of the INTERNATIONAL JOINT COMMISSION, and a senator in 1973.

courtesy Manitoba Archives

Dufferin "Duff" Roblin

ROBLIN, DUFFERIN (1917–), premier of Manitoba. Grandson of SIR RODMOND ROBLIN, Duff Roblin was born at Winnipeg, attended the univs. of Manitoba and Chicago, and served in the ROYAL CANADIAN AIR FORCE. He became leader of the provincial Conservatives in 1954, defeated the Liberals in 1958, and was re-elected three times. His government, while conservative, was extraordinarily vigorous, effectively creating Manitoba as a modern province. In 1967, he left provincial politics and, after hesitating too long, lost the national PROGRESSIVE CONSERVATIVE PARTY leadership to ROBERT STANFIELD; the next year he failed to win a seat in the House of Commons. In 1978 he was named to the Senate and in 1984 he joined the BRIAN MULRONEY cabinet.

ROBLIN, SIR RODMOND PALEN (1853-1937), premier of Manitoba. Born at Sophiasburg, Canada West, he went to Winnipeg in 1877 and operated a number of businesses. He was elected to the legislature as an independent in 1888, but he nonetheless succeeded JOHN NORQUAY in 1889 as Conservative leader. Not until 1900 would Roblin become premier, but he then held power for 15 years. His government, notoriously effective on the patronage-machine side of politics, established a government-run telephone system and extended provincial boundaries. His government fell in a scandal surrounding the construction of the new legislative building in 1915.

ROBSON REPORT, popular name for the report of Mr Justice H.A. Robson on the causes of the WINNIPEG GENERAL STRIKE. The report, prepared for the Manitoba government, downplayed the role of revolutionaries in the strike and pointed to grievances such as low wages and employer opposition to unions as the real causes.

ROGERS, EDWARD SAMUEL (1900-39), broadcasting pioneer. Born at Toronto, Rogers at 13 won a provincial prize for the best amateur-built radio. At 21 he won an American competition for low-power broadcasts across the Atlantic and four years later he perfected an alternating-current radio tube that swept the home radio industry. He and his father founded the Rogers Majestic Co. as well as several broadcasting companies, including station 9RB, now CFRB, in Toronto.

ROGERS, NORMAN MCLEOD (1894-1940), politician, scholar. Rogers, born at Amherst,

N.S., was educated at Acadia and Oxford univs. He served in World War I before returning to Canada to become professor of history at Acadia from 1922 to 1927 and Prime Minister MACKENZIE KING's private secretary between 1927 and 1929. He returned to academe as professor of political science at Queen's (1929-35) but did not sever his political connections. Elected to the House of Commons in 1935, Rogers served as a progressive minister of labour (1935-9) and as minister of national defence from 1939 until his death in a plane crash in 1940.

ROGERS PASS, pass in the Selkirk Mountains, B.C., discovered by Major A.B. Rogers, an American surveyor working for the CANADIAN PACIFIC RAILWAY. Discovery of the pass made the CPR's projected southerly route through the mountains practicable.

ROMAN, STEPHEN B. (1921-88), mining executive. Roman was born in Velky Ruskov, Slovakia, and immigrated to Canada at age 16. He founded Denison Mines Ltd in the 1950s. Roman made headlines when he sued Prime Minister PIERRE TRUDEAU and J.J. Greene, Trudeau's minister of energy, mines and resources, over a government attempt to block the sale of his company to American interests.

RONCARELLI V. DUPLESSIS, legal case involving civil liberties questions. In 1946, Premier MAURICE DUPLESSIS of Quebec revoked the Montreal restaurant liquor licence of Frank Roncarelli, a provider of bail to Jehovah's Witnesses charged with distributing material attacking Roman Catholicism. After a lengthy battle through the courts led by F.R. SCOTT, representing Roncarelli, the SUPREME COURT of Canada in 1959 held that Duplessis had committed a civil wrong and ordered him to pay damages.

RONNING, CHESTER ALVIN (1894-1984), diplomat. Born at Fancheng, China, Ronning attended the univs. of Alberta and Minnesota and served during World War I before returning to China as a teacher, 1922-7. He went back to Alberta as principal of Camrose Lutheran College (1927-42). Elected as a UNITED FARMERS OF ALBERTA MLA in 1932, he soon became active in the CO-OPERATIVE COMMONWEALTH FEDERATION. He joined the Department of External Affairs after

wartime service in the air force, subsequently serving in China (1945-51), in Ottawa (1951-4), in Norway (1954-7), in India (1957-64), and as a delegation member at conferences on Korea (1954) and Laos (1961-2). In 1965 and 1966 PAUL MARTIN sent him to Hanoi in attempts to mediate the Vietnam War. He was a strong advocate of recognition of the People's Republic of China.

ROSE, FRED (1907-83), politician. Born in Lublin, Poland, Rose was a member of the COMMUNIST PARTY of Canada who won a by-election in the Montreal riding of Cartier in 1943 as a candidate of the LABOUR PROGRESSIVE PARTY. He was re-elected in the general election of 1945 but was forced to resign his seat when charged with espionage during the GOUZENKO AFFAIR in 1946. He eventually served six years in prison and, when released, left Canada to live out his life in Poland.

ROSE, SIR JOHN (1820-88), banker, politician. Rose came to Canada from Scotland in 1836, began to practise law in the 1840s, and soon became a prominent corporation lawyer with important connections in the business community and the Conservative party. He served in a number of posts in the government of the UNITED PROVINCE OF CANADA and, after CONFEDERATION, entered the ministry of Conservative Prime Minister JOHN A. MACDONALD as minister of finance. In 1869 he moved to London, Eng., to start his own investment banking firm. There he acted as unofficial representative of the Canadian government and was an important figure arranging the financing of the CANADIAN PACIFIC RAILWAY.

ROSENFELD, FANNY (1903-69), track and field athlete, sportswriter. Canada's female athlete of the half century, "Bobbie" Rosenfeld was born in Russia. She represented Canada at the 1928 Amsterdam Olympics, winning the silver medal in the 100 metre dash and leading the 4 x 100 metre relay team to a record victory. She held Canadian records for the running and standing broad jump and the discus and for a time shared the 100-yard world record.

ROSS, JAMES (1848-1913), financier. Born in Cromarty, Scot., he worked on the construction of the CANADIAN PACIFIC RAILWAY, as an engineer. Later he joined a number of investors in promoting and expanding electric railways in Canada and abroad. In 1901 Ross restructured the DOMINION COAL CO. and Dominion Steel.

ROSS, JAMES SINCLAIR (1908–), writer. Born at Shellbrook, Sask., he left school at 16 to join the ROYAL BANK OF CANADA, where he worked until 1968. He wrote in his spare time, publishing his acclaimed Prairie novel, *As for Me and My House* in 1941. This was followed by *The Well* (1959), *Whir of Gold* (1970), and the highly praised novella, *Sawbones Memorial* (1974).

ROSS, PHYLLIS GREGORY TURNER, (1903-88), civil servant. Born at Rossland, B.C., Phyllis Gregory was educated at the Univ. of Brithish Columbia and Bryn Mawr. She married Leonard Turner, had three children, including JOHN N. TURNER, was widowed at 29, and took a job at the Dominion Tariff Board in 1934, eventually becoming chief economist. During the war, she joined the WARTIMES PRICES AND TRADE BOARD, and became Oils and Fats Administrator, the most senior position in the public service held by a woman. In 1945, she married industrialist Frank Ross, subsequently Lieutenant-Governor of B.C., and in 1961 was named Chancellor of her alma mater.

ROSS RIFLE, a hunting rifle developed by Sir Charles Ross and manufactured in Quebec. The rifle was adopted for Canada by SIR FREDERICK BORDEN, militia minister in SIR WILFRID LAURIER's government in 1901. The British government objected, but the rifle, a fine target weapon, had many supporters, notably Colonel SAM HUGHES, the Tory MP who became militia minister in the BORDEN government. Hughes equipped the CANADIAN EXPEDITIONARY FORCE with the Ross in 1914, but the rifle failed at YPRES in 1915 when it jammed with British ammunition. The Ross also failed to work consistently in muddy trench conditions, and soldiers threw it away whenever they could acquire a Lee-Enfield rifle. By Sept. 1916, the CANADIAN CORPS had been re-equipped with Lee-Enfields.

ROSS, SIR GEORGE WILLIAM (1841-1914), premier of Ontario. Born at Nairn, Canada West, Ross was a teacher and journalist who sat in the House of Commons as a Liberal from 1872 to 1883. In 1883 he entered the provincial cabinet

of SIR OLIVER MOWAT as education minister. He became premier in 1899, lost the election of 1905, and after serving as opposition leader for two years, was named to the Senate.

ROUND TABLE MOVEMENT, an organization, founded in Britain in 1909, that proselytized for imperial union. The Round Table group, operating throughout the dominions and using *The Round Table* as its journal, played an important role through World War I in urging union as a way to enhance the strength of the Empire. Canadian members, notably Professor GEORGE WRONG, JOSEPH FLAVELLE, and VINCENT MASSEY, were mildly dubious about imperial union though fervent anglophiles. For some nationalist Canadians, the movement acquired a near-demonic status. *See also* IMPERIALISM.

ROWELL, NEWTON WESLEY (1867-1941), politician, jurist. Born in London Township, Ont., and educated at Osgoode Hall, Rowell practised law at Toronto. Sternly Methodist, he was elected to the Ontario legislature in 1911 and led the Liberal opposition in the direction of PROHIBITION until his support for CONSCRIPTION led him to resign in 1917 to run federally as a Unionist. A key adviser to SIR ROBERT BORDEN, he served as president of the Privy Council from 1917 to 1920 and as the first minister of health from 1919 to 1920. He left the government in 1921 and became chief justice of the Supreme Court of Ontario (1936-8). He is perhaps best remembered as chairman of the ROYAL COMMISSION ON DOMINION-PROVINCIAL RELATIONS.

ROY, GABRIELLE (1909-83), writer. Three times winner of the Governor General's Award, Roy was born at St-Boniface, Man. She lived and taught school in Manitoba until 1937, when she moved to Europe and began writing. The approach of war forced her return to Canada, and she settled in Montreal as a freelance journalist. In 1945 she published *Bonheur d'occasion (The Tin Flute)*, a superb study of the impact of depression and war on poor Quebecers. In 1947 she moved to France, where she wrote *La Petite Poule d'eau* (1950), a novel based on her memories of the Prairies. She returned to Canada and

Gabrielle Roy

settled in Quebec City, producing a number of works including *Alexandre Chenevert* (1954), *Un Jardin au bout du monde* (1975), and *De quoi t'ennuies-tu, Eveline?* (1982).

ROYAL BANK OF CANADA, established in 1864 as the Merchant Bank of Halifax. It was especially active in investing in Bermuda, the Caribbean area, and the United States. In 1901 it adopted its present name and in 1906 moved its head offices to Montreal. Through absorptions of other banks the Royal Bank eventually bypassed the older BANK OF MONTREAL to become Canada's largest bank.

ROYAL CANADIAN AIR FORCE, the Canadian air arm, 1924-68. The RCAF begun under that title on 1 April 1924, the inheritor of a tradition of Canadian military aviation. During WORLD WAR I, more than 20,000 Canadians served in the Royal Flying Corps, the Royal Naval Air Service, and the Royal Air Force. Pilots such as WILLIAM BISHOP, RAYMOND COLLISHAW, and WILLIAM BARKER had impressive "kill" records, and pressure developed in Canada for a distinctive Canadian force. At that time the government of SIR ROBERT BORDEN created the Canadian Naval Air Service for coastal defence against German U-boats and the Canadian Air Force of two squadrons for operations on the Western Front. Both were disbanded soon after the Armistice. In 1920, a small Canadian Air Force was established, and when the National Defence Act was

passed in 1922 the CAF became a permanent force. In 1923, the CAF was designated "Royal." Through the inter-war period, the RCAF, tiny, ill-equipped, and ill-trained, largely performed civil air operations, most notably air survey and mapping flights. By the outbreak of war in 1939, the air force had a strength of 4061 permanent force and reserves and 270 aircraft of which only 37 were modern.

WORLD WAR II changed all that. The RCAF took over operation of the BRITISH COMMONWEALTH AIR TRAINING PLAN that ultimately produced 131,553 aircrew, including some 73,000 Canadians. In all, a quarter million served in the RCAF, 94,000 going overseas, including substantial numbers of the Women's Division of the RCAF. Most airmen flew with the RAF, but there were 48 RCAF squadrons which served in every theatre, notably in Bomber Command, based in England, and in the Battle of the ATLANTIC, largely from east coast bases. Fatal casualties were over 17,000.

The return of peace saw the RCAF dwindle, but Canada's joining NATO and the rearmament occasioned by the KOREAN WAR caused the air force to grow. In 1951, Ottawa agreed to send an air division of 12 fighter squadrons to Europe, and in 1957, the RCAF and the U.S. Air Force joined in NORAD to coordinate the air defences of North America. The RCAF ceased to exist as a separate service when UNIFICATION took effect in 1968.

ROYAL CANADIAN LEGION, veterans' organization that originated from a number of WORLD WAR I veterans' organizations. In 1925, Field Marshal Earl Haig, the creator of the British Empire Service League, visited Canada to urge veterans to unite, and the Canadian Legion was formed the next year. In 1960, the Legion took the title "Royal." With some half million members from all of Canada's wars, it continues to press the veterans' case with government and to engage in public service work.

ROYAL CANADIAN MOUNTED POLICE, federal police force. The RCMP began in 1873 when the Conservative government of Prime Minister JOHN A. MACDONALD created the North-West Mounted Police, a small force of mounted riflemen with police and magistrate powers to enforce federal law in the North-West Territories. In the summer of 1874 the police, 318 officers and men, marched west from Manitoba, along the boundary with the United States, to the foothills of the Rocky Mountains, building a number of posts and forts as they went. After establishing their presence in the West, the mounties played an important role in policing the treaty and reserve system, and they fought in the NORTH-WEST REBELLION of 1885. Some NWMP detachments volunteered for service in the BOER WAR and the name of the force was changed to Royal North-West Mounted Police as a token of having participated. In 1919 the RNWMP was joined to the DOMINION POLICE to form the Royal Canadian Mounted Police, charged with enforcing federal law and policing federal property. In that role it was often involved in labour disputes in the first decades of the 20th century playing a predominantly anti-union part in maintaining public order during violent industrial disputes. Since the 1930s the RCMP has frequently acted as a provincial police force in provinces that have not established their own provincial police, and in small municipalities in provinces that chose not to have a municipal police force. Until the creation of the CANADIAN SECURITY AND INTELLIGENCE SERVICE, the RCMP was also responsible for all counter-intelligence, counter-espionage, and anti-terrorist operations inside Canada.

courtesy of G.A. Milne/DND/National Archives of Canada/PA-131506

RCN landing craft putting troops ashore on D-Day, 6 June 1944

ROYAL CANADIAN NAVY, the Canadian naval service, 1910-68, created by the NAVAL SERVICE ACT in 1910. Tiny, ill-equipped, and ill-trained, the Navy played a small but useful role in helping to counter the German U-boat threat in the western Atlantic in WORLD WAR I. In the inter-war

years, the Navy resisted attempts to eliminate it entirely. By 1939, thanks to budget increases in the late 1930s, the RCN had eight destroyers and five minesweepers with 191 officers and 1799 ratings. During WORLD WAR II, the Navy grew dramatically, reaching a strength of 100,000 and 365 ships in 1945, the third-largest Allied navy. There were also more than 6000 WRCN's or Wrens, the female members of the Navy. The RCN's main role in the war was the protection of convoys, and by May 1943 this complicated task was under control to such an extent that the British and Americans gave command of a new theatre, the Canadian Northwest Atlantic, to a Canadian officer, Admiral L.W. Murray. The RCN also served in virtually all theatres of war, played an important role in the NORMANDY INVASION, and had ships in the Pacific in 1945. Fatal casualties amounted to 2024. The cut-backs that followed the peace demoralized the Navy with three mutinies resulting in 1949, but Canada's participation in NATO and the KOREAN WAR increased the force once more. NATO service gave the force expertise in anti-submarine warfare, and the Navy in the 1950s operated a fleet of advanced Canadian-designed destroyer escorts. UNIFICATION in 1968 was bitterly opposed in the RCN, Admiral W.M. LANDYMORE leading the fight with such vigour that he was retired.

ROYAL COMMISSION ON BANKING AND FINANCE, commission appointed in 1961 to examine all aspects of banking, including the BANK OF CANADA. Chaired by Chief Justice Dana Porter of the Ontario Supreme Court, the commission recommended the abolition of the 6 per cent interest-rate ceiling on loans, entry of banks into conventional mortgages, and other changes incorporated into the BANK ACT, 1967. The report's key proposals concerned the Bank of Canada whose governor, JAMES COYNE, had run into difficulty with the DIEFENBAKER government. The commission maintained that the government had the responsibility for monetary policy and could override the governor by order in council.

ROYAL COMMISSION ON BILINGUALISM AND BICULTURALISM, established in 1963 to examine relations between French and English Canadians. Set up by Prime Minister LESTER PEARSON with co-chairs ANDRÉ LAURENDEAU and DAVIDSON DUNTON, the commission sought an "equal partnership" between French and English Canadians. The principal recommendation was that the federal public service become bilingual and employ more French-speaking Canadians. Other Canadians objected to their exclusion from the original make-up of the commission, and Pearson added ethnic representatives, one of the first gestures towards MULTICULTURALISM. *See also* BILINGUALISM AND BICULTURALISM; OFFICIAL LANGUAGES ACT.

ROYAL COMMISSION ON CANADA'S ECONOMIC PROSPECTS, commission appointed in 1955 and chaired by WALTER GORDON, to investigate the country's prospects for the next 25 years. The commission's final report, which appeared in 1958, was generally optimistic, but expressed concern about Canada's heavy dependence on foreign investment and the extent of foreign ownership. The Gordon report provided much of the basis for Gordon's policies as finance minister in the PEARSON government.

ROYAL COMMISSION ON DOMINION-PROVINCIAL RELATIONS, created in 1937, under NEWTON ROWELL as chair, to examine and make recommendations on constitutional and financial relations between the federal and provincial governments. The 1940 final report of the commission, usually called the Rowell-Sirois Commission after its first and second chairs, recommended that Ottawa take control of taxation from the provinces in return for annual provincial grants. The federal government was to be responsible for unemployment insurance, pensions, and provincial debts. The war and provincial opposition blocked implementation.

ROYAL COMMISSION ON THE ECONOMIC UNION AND DEVELOPMENT PROSPECTS FOR CANADA, federal inquiry into the economy. Led by Donald S. Macdonald, former Liberal cabinet minister, the royal commission was created on 5 Nov. 1982 and delivered its report in 1985. Among the Macdonald Commission's principal recommendations was a call for FREE TRADE with the United States and a major revision of social services. The royal commission also purchased a vast body of research and presented it in a massive array of volumes, the largest output of scholarly work to be published by the federal government since the ROYAL COMMISSION ON DOMINION-PROVINCIAL RELATIONS almost 45 years earlier.

ROYAL COMMISSION ON HEALTH SERVICES, created in 1961 and chaired by Mr Justice EMMETT HALL, to examine Canada's medical system. In June 1964 the commission recommended MEDICARE, a result that shocked organized medicine and that was not supported by Conservative leader JOHN DIEFENBAKER who had appointed it.

ROYAL COMMISSION OF INQUIRY ON CONSTITUTIONAL PROBLEMS, Quebec royal commission, appointed in 1953 and chaired by Quebec's chief justice, Thomas Tremblay, to examine fiscal relations between the federal and provincial governments. Appointed by the DUPLESSIS government to make the case that direct taxation rested with the provinces, the commission proposed restructuring of the country, argued that the federal government was the creation of the provinces, and called for all social programs to be run by the provinces. The report, released in 1954, was an important conservative-nationalist document.

ROYAL COMMISSION ON NATIONAL DEVELOPMENT IN THE ARTS, LETTERS, AND SCIENCES, commission appointed in 1949 under the chairmanship of VINCENT MASSEY to investigate the state of Canada's culture and cultural institutions. The commission's "Massey Report," released in 1951, was a mixture of lamentation for a passing age and excitement over future possibilities. It recommended the creation of a CANADA COUNCIL to encourage development in the arts, federal grants to universities, and the strengthening of agencies such as the CANADIAN BROADCASTING CORP. and the NATIONAL FILM BOARD.

ROYAL COMMISSION ON PRICE SPREADS AND MASS BUYING, commission established in 1934 to investigate the disparity between production costs and selling prices. Chaired by H.H. STEVENS, the Conservative minister of trade and commerce until his resignation from the cabinet, and then headed by W.W. Kennedy but still dominated by Stevens, the commission, reporting in 1935, collected a mass of evidence to document big business abuses, the existence of sweat shops, and the methods employed by large companies (and especially department stores) to force down their suppliers' prices.

ROYAL COMMISSION ON PUBLICATIONS, commission appointed in 1960 and chaired by GRATTON O'LEARY, to study the problems of Canadian magazines in the face of foreign competition. Its 1961 report called for an end to tax deductions for advertisers using foreign magazines (especially *Time*) targeted at the Canadian market.

ROYAL COMMISSION ON THE RELATIONS OF LABOUR AND CAPITAL, commission appointed by Prime Minister JOHN A. MACDONALD in 1887 to inquire into labour and capital in Canada. The commission heard extensive evidence on the living and working conditions of Canadian workers and the attitudes and practices of employers. Its report, issued in 1889, recommended a variety of measures such as the establishment of a bureau of labour statistics, but it was virtually ignored by the Macdonald government.

ROYAL COMMISSION ON THE STATUS OF WOMEN IN CANADA, commission appointed in 1967 and chaired by FLORENCE BIRD, to investigate all matters concerning the status of women in Canada. The 1970 report made 167 recommendations for improving the status of Canadian women, chief of which was the concept of equal pay for work of equal value; others covered such matters as maternity leave, day care, birth control, educational opportunity, and the role of women in managerial positions.

ROYAL COMMISSION ON TAXATION, appointed in 1962 and chaired by KENNETH CARTER, to examine the federal tax system. The 1967 report found the tax system unfair and proposed that each "buck" be taxed the same way no matter how it was earned.

ROYAL MILITARY COLLEGE OF CANADA, officer training institution founded at Kingston, Ont., in 1874 and opened in 1876. Most of its cadets initially turned to civilian pursuits on graduation, although substantial numbers joined the British forces and Canada's tiny regulars. In WORLD WAR I, the college's graduates showed their mettle, filling hundreds of officer billets in the CANADIAN CORPS and winning countless decorations. The same situation held true in WORLD WAR II, although the college closed its doors during the war. After the war, RMC reopened on a tri-service basis, and in 1959 received degree-granting status. Graduates since 1954 (except for a small number of reserve entry cadets) have been obliged to serve in the forces.

ROYAL TWENTY CENTERS, derisive name given to themselves by inmates of 1930s RELIEF CAMPS. Run by the Department of National Defence and located all across Canada, the camps paid their residents 20 cents a day and board, a pitiful wage even in the GREAT DEPRESSION.

RUPERT'S LAND, territories adjacent to Hudson Bay granted to the HUDSON'S BAY CO. in 1670 by King Charles II of England. Rupert's Land was defined as all lands drained by Hudson Bay – today's Prairie provinces, northern Ontario, northwestern Quebec, and portions of the Northwest Territories. Canada purchased Rupert's Land in 1869 and that acquisition helped spark off the RED RIVER REBELLION. *See also* LOUIS RIEL.

RUSSELL, ANNA (1913–), concert comedienne. Reputedly "the funniest woman in the world," Russell, born at London, Eng., immigrated to Canada in 1939 and performed often in Canada after 1944. Well known for her irreverent parodies of singers and German opera, she made appearances on Broadway and in London's West End.

RUSSELL, ROBERT BOYD (1888-1964), labour leader. Russell came to Canada from Scotland in 1911 and became active in the International Assn of Machinists and the SOCIALIST PARTY of Canada. During World War I, he became prominent in the Winnipeg metal trades unions. He was a key factor in the decision of the Winnipeg Trades and Labor Council to support the metal trades in May 1919 by conducting a general strike vote. Russell was charged with seditious conspiracy for his role in the WINNIPEG GENERAL STRIKE and served two years in prison. When he was freed he became secretary-treasurer of the ONE BIG UNION, a post he held until the OBU dissolved in 1964.

RUSSELL V. THE QUEEN, constitutional case. Russell, a tavern owner in New Brunswick, challenged the Canada Temperance Act because it interfered with provincial licensing. Ottawa claimed the power to regulate the liquor trade under the "PEACE, ORDER, AND GOOD GOVERNMENT" power in the BRITISH NORTH AMERICA ACT, and the JUDICIAL COMMITTEE OF THE PRIVY COUNCIL in 1882 upheld this argument.

RUTHERFORD, ALEXANDER CAMERON (1857-1941), premier of Alberta. Born at Osgoode, Canada West, and educated at McGill Univ., Rutherford was called to the bar in 1885. He went to the North-West Territories in the early 1890s, was elected to the territorial legislature in 1902, and when the province of Alberta was formed in 1905, the LAURIER administration arranged that he was called on to become Liberal premier. He was forced to resign as premier in 1910 on charges of conflict of interest, and he lost his seat in 1913.

RUTHERFORD, ERNEST, BARON RUTH-ERFORD OF NELSON (1871-1937), physicist. One of the greatest experimental physicists of the 20th century, Rutherford was born at Nelson, New Zealand, and educated at Canterbury College, Christchurch. He worked in the Cavendish Laboratory at Cambridge before moving to McGill Univ. in 1898 as Macdonald professor of physics. The results of his research at McGill were published in *Radio-Activity* (1904), his major contribution being the elaboration of the disintegration theory of the atom. Feeling isolated in Montreal, Rutherford accepted a position at Manchester in 1907. He won the Nobel Prize in chemistry a year later and became head of the Cavendish Laboratory in 1919. He was knighted in 1914 and created baron in 1931. McGill's physics laboratories are named in his honour.

RYAN, CLAUDE (1925–), journalist, politician. Ryan, born at Montreal, was national secretary of *Action catholique* from 1945 to 1962 and chaired the Quebec Ministry of Education's adult-education study committee from 1962 to 1963 before taking over editorship of *Le Devoir* in 1965. A prickly constitutionalist, he left the paper in 1978 after being chosen to lead the Quebec Liberal party. Elected to the assembly in 1979, he campaigned against SOVEREIGNTY-ASSOCIATION,

but his party was defeated in the 1981 election. He resigned the leadership in 1982 but remained a member of the assembly and served as a minister in ROBERT BOURASSA's government after 1985.

RYERSON, ADOLPHUS EGERTON (1803-82), Methodist minister, educator. A key figure in 19th-century Ontario education and politics, Ryerson was born in Norfolk County, Upper Canada, to an Anglican Loyalist family. Converted to the Methodist Episcopal Church and ordained a minister in 1827, he was president of the Methodist Church of Canada from 1874 to 1878. He helped found and edited the *Christian Guardian* in 1829, began Upper Canada Academy in 1836, and was the first principal of Victoria College in 1841. Appointed superintendent of education for Canada West in 1844, he held the position until retiring in 1876, establishing Ontario's school system on firm foundations. Ryerson believed education had to be religious and promoted denominational universities.

courtesy National Archives of Canada/C-21524

Louis S. St-Laurent

ST LAURENT, LOUIS STEPHEN (1882-1973), prime minister of Canada. Louis St Laurent, born at Compton, Que., and educated at the Univ. Laval, was a successful corporate lawyer. Although he held high positions in the Quebec bar and served a term as president of the Canadian Bar Assn, he was little known outside Quebec, even after service as counsel to the ROYAL

COMMISSION ON DOMINION-PROVINCIAL RELATIONS from 1937 to 1940. It came as a surprise when, after ERNEST LAPOINTE, Prime Minister MACKENZIE KING's Quebec lieutenant, died, St Laurent was named minister of justice to succeed him in Dec. 1941. A political novice but a man of great intelligence and integrity, St Laurent, quickly elected in a by-election, soon established himself as a force in Ottawa.

During the CONSCRIPTION CRISIS of 1942 and 1944, he supported King's policies, and he was one of the few ministers directly involved in the GOUZENKO AFFAIR in Sept. 1945 and after. In 1946, King named him secretary of state for external affairs in an attempt to keep a reluctant St Laurent in politics, and two years later, still somewhat reluctant, St Laurent entered – and easily won – the race to succeed King.

As prime minister from 15 Nov. 1948, St Laurent led Canada into NATO, the KOREAN WAR, and a program of rearmament; his government extended OLD AGE PENSIONS, created the CANADA COUNCIL, and, aided by St Laurent's friendly guise of a baby-kissing "Uncle Louis," handily won the elections of 1949 and 1953. But in 1957, after the SUEZ CRISIS and the PIPELINE DEBATE had provoked charges of Liberal arrogance largely directed at C.D. HOWE, St Laurent's tired government was narrowly defeated by JOHN DIEFENBAKER and the Conservatives. St Laurent announced his retirement and a party convention selected LESTER PEARSON as his successor in Jan. 1958.

ST LAWRENCE SEAWAY, usual name for the St Lawrence Seaway – Great Lakes Waterway, a system of waterways linking the Great Lakes to the Atlantic Ocean via the St Lawrence River. The crude system of canals in place by 1900 could not support modern shipping, and in 1941 Canada signed an agreement with the United States to enlarge the system. A deal was finally struck in 1954 to build a modern seaway capable of handling vessels up to 222.5 metres long and 23.1 metres wide with a draft of up to 7.9 metres. After a massive and expensive construction effort, the seaway was officially opened on 26 June 1959.

ST PAUL, MINNEAPOLIS AND MANITOBA RAILWAY CO., railway chartered to build a line from St Paul, Minn., to the Canadian border in 1857. After a portion of the line was com-

pleted, the company went into receivership. In 1873 a group of investors including J.J. HILL and GEORGE STEPHEN gained control of the company and completed the line to Winnipeg. Hill, Stephen and the other partners gained experience they used in their proposal to Prime Minister JOHN A. MACDONALD in 1880 to build the long-delayed Pacific railway. *See also* CANADIAN PACIFIC RAILWAY.

ST-PIERRE AND MIQUELON AFFAIR, 1941, the political crisis started by the seizure by Free French forces of the islands off the south coast of Newfoundland controlled by the Vichy government. On 24 Dec. 1941, forces under Admiral Muselier seized the islands, strategically located near convoy routes. The Canadian government had earlier made plans for such a coup but had backed off, and the United States government, apparently seeing collusion between Ottawa and Muselier, protested vigorously, ordering Ottawa to remove the Free French. NORMAN ROBERTSON of external affairs and J.W. PICKERSGILL of the Prime Minister's Office persuaded MACKENZIE KING not to do so, and the crisis cooled down quickly.

SASKATCHEWAN CO-OPERATIVE ELEVATOR CO., a farmer-owned elevator cooperative, established by the provincial government in Feb. 1911. It was created in response to farmers' complaints about weighing, grading, and pricing carried out by privately owned elevator companies which enjoyed monopolies at country railway sidings.

SASKATCHEWAN DOCTORS' STRIKE, 1962, withdrawal of medical services by doctors to protest MEDICARE. When the WOODROW LLOYD government passed legislation in Nov. 1961 to bring medicare into effect in the province on 1 July 1962, the response of the Saskatchewan College of Physicians and Surgeons was to go on strike that same day. The strike lasted until 23 July when it was ended as a result of the efforts of Lord Taylor, a British mediator, and minor concessions by the government.

SATURDAY NIGHT, magazine begun in Toronto in 1887 under the editorship of E.E. Sheppard as a weekly newspaper. By the 1930s, with B.K. Sandwell as editor, the magazine became the leading serious popular journal in Canada, giving good space to both national and world events and the arts. After Sandwell's departure, *Saturday Night* had its dark era, and not until 1968 when ROBERT FULFORD took over, did it flourish again. Fulford attracted able writers, gave ample space to the arts, and featured occasionally superb profiles of political, business, and cultural leaders. But the magazine was in frequent financial troubles. In 1987, Conrad Black purchased the magazine and Fulford resigned, to be succeeded by John Fraser as editor.

SAUNDERS, SIR CHARLES EDWARD (1867-1937), agronomist. Born at London, Ont., Saunders was appointed dominion cerealist at the Experimental Farms Branch in Ottawa in 1903. There he continued work on the crossbreeding of wheat strains that had been initiated by his father, WILLIAM SAUNDERS. Charles Saunders was responsible for the development and testing of MARQUIS WHEAT which became the standard spring wheat in the North American grain belt. *See also* DOMINION EXPERIMENTAL FARM.

SAUNDERS, WILLIAM (1836-1914), agronomist. Born in Crediton, Eng., he came to Canada in 1848 and pursued a variety of scientific interests while operating a drug store. In 1885 he wrote a report on experimental farms in the United States which was partly responsible for the establishment of the Experimental Farms Branch in Ottawa. Saunders, the first director of the farm, initiated the plant-breeding programs that eventually led to the development of MARQUIS WHEAT and other grains suitable for the Canadian environment and oversaw the establishment of the experimental stations at Indian Head, Sask., and four other locations across Canada. *See also* DOMINION EXPERIMENTAL FARM.

SAUVÉ, JEANNE-MATHILDE (1922–), politician, governor general of Canada. Jeanne Benoit was borne at Prud'homme, Sask., and educated at the Univ. of Ottawa. She worked as a journalist and broadcaster in Montreal, in 1948 married Maurice Sauvé, an economist and later Liberal MP and cabinet minister, and entered Liberal party politics herself by winning election to the House of Commons in 1972. She was quickly brought into the TRUDEAU cabinet where she held a number of portfolios. In 1980 she became speaker of the House of Commons, the first woman to hold that post, and four years later she became governor general, again the first woman to occupy the vice-regal office.

SAUVÉ, JOSEPH-MIGNAULT-PAUL (1907-60), premier of Quebec. Born at St-Benoit, Que., and educated at the Univ. de Montréal, Sauvé was elected to the provincial legislature in 1930 as a Conservative. Defeated in 1935, he was returned in 1936 under the UNION NATIONALE banner and became speaker. Overseas during World War II with the infantry, he returned to politics and became designated successor to MAURICE DUPLESSIS. When Le Chef died in 1959, Sauvé became premier, promising great change in a single word – *désormais* or henceforth. He began to carry out his promise by quickly resolving the longstanding dispute with Ottawa over university grants and hospital insurance, but he died on 2 Jan. 1960.

SAVARD, FÉLIX-ANTOINE (1896-1982), priest, writer, educator. Savard, born at Quebec City and raised in the Saguenay, was ordained a priest in 1922. He was active in colonizing the Abitibi region during the 1930s. Dean of Laval's faculty of arts for seven years, he taught literature and pursued research in folklore. His novel, *Menaud, maître-draveur*, a work that took years to complete, was published in 1937.

SAWCHUK, TERRANCE GORDON (1929-70), hockey player. An outstanding goalie, Sawchuck played junior hockey in Winnipeg and Galt and professionally with Omaha before joining the Detroit Red Wings in 1951. He won the Calder Trophy for best rookie and the VEZINA Trophy for fewest goals allowed three times. Plagued by physical and psychological problems in the early 1960s, he led the Toronto Maple Leafs to a 1967 STANLEY CUP victory during a comeback. His record of 103 shutouts remains unchallenged.

SCHREYER, EDWARD RICHARD (1935–), politician, premier of Manitoba, governor general of Canada, diplomat. Born at Beauséjour, Man., he studied at United College and the Univ. of Manitoba. He won election to the Manitoba legislature in 1958 at age 22 and served there until 1965 when he was elected to the House of Commons as a NEW DEMOCRATIC PARTY MP. He re-

Edward Schreyer being sworn in as Governor General

mained in Ottawa four years, then won the leadership of the Manitoba NDP in 1969, the same year his party won the provincial election. His moderate and liberal government lasted eight years. Prime Minister TRUDEAU surprised observers by picking Schreyer to be governor general in 1979, in part because his origins were neither French nor English. Like others before him, Schreyer tried to democratize Rideau Hall and, unlike recent incumbents, he found himself in political controversy for his delay in granting JOE CLARK a dissolution in 1979 and for his comment that he might have dissolved Parliament had Trudeau unilaterally imposed his constitutional proposals in 1981-2. At the conclusion of his term in 1984, Schreyer was appointed high commissioner to Australia.

SCOTT ACT, *see* PROHIBITION

SCOTT, BARBARA ANN (1929–), figure skater. Born in Ottawa, Scott won the Canadian senior crown each year from 1944 to 1948, the North American championship from 1945 to 1948, and the European and world titles in 1947 and 1948. She capped her career with the Olympic gold in 1948 and was greeted with extraordinary adulation across Canada.

SCOTT, DUNCAN CAMPBELL (1862-1947), poet. One of the "poets of Confederation," Scott was born at Ottawa and joined the Department of Indian Affairs in 1879, becoming deputy superintendent in 1913. Encouraged by ARCHIBALD LAMPMAN in the 1880s to write poetry, Scott became a regular contributor to *Scribner's Magazine* and in 1893 published his first volume,

The Magic House and Other Poems. This was followed by nine collections, including his acclaimed "Indian" poems. Scott also contributed to the Toronto *Globe* and wrote a biograpy of John Graves Simcoe for the *Makers of Canada* series (1905), which he helped direct.

SCOTT, FRANCIS REGINALD (1899-1985), poet, law professor, political figure. Born at Quebec City and educated at Bishop's College and Magdalen College, Oxford (Rhodes scholar), Scott returned to Canada in 1923. He enrolled in the McGill law faculty in 1924, later joining the faculty as professor. In the early 1930s, concerned with the economic causes and social consequences of the Great Depression, with historian FRANK UNDERHILL he founded the LEAGUE FOR SOCIAL RECONSTRUCTION. Scott helped to draft the CO-OPERATIVE COMMONWEALTH FEDERATION's famous REGINA MANIFESTO and to write *Social Planning For Canada* (1935). As a contributor to CANADIAN FORUM, he argued for Canadian neutrality in the face of the international chaos of the late 1930s. Scott served as national chairman of the CCF from 1942 to 1950, and he won two landmark cases before the Supreme Court in the mid-1950s (the PADLOCK LAW and RONCARELLI v. DUPLESSIS). He retired from partisan politics following the formation of the New Democratic Party, was appointed dean of law (1961-4), and named a member of the ROYAL COMMISSION ON BILINGUALISM AND BICULTURALISM. Scott also won Governor General's Awards for non-fiction and for poetry. His commitment to a better society and his profound influence on the development of Canada's artistic and political culture earned him a leading place among Canadian intellectuals of the 20th century.

SCOTT, FREDERICK GEORGE (1861-1944), Anglican clergyman. The father of F.R. SCOTT, Scott was born at Montreal and educated at Bishop's College. Ordained in the Anglican ministry in 1886, he was appointed canon of the Anglican Cathedral in Quebec in 1906 and archdeacon in 1925. During World War I, he was the much-loved senior chaplain of the 1st Canadian Division and published, in 1922, *The Great War as I Saw It.*

Thomas Scott's execution, 4 March 1870

SCOTT, THOMAS (1842-70), Red River agitator. Born at Clandeboye, Ireland, Scott immigrated to Canada in 1863 and drifted to the RED RIVER SETTLEMENT in 1869. A boisterous Protestant Orangeman who was particularly scornful of the MÉTIS, he was imprisoned after the Métis seized control of the Colony during the RED RIVER REBELLION. LOUIS RIEL approved his court-martial for treason against the provisional government and execution in 1870, largely as a demonstration of the provisional government's power. His execution brought a howl of protest from the ORANGE ORDER, and played a part in the continuing antipathy to Riel through the 1870s.

SCOTT, THOMAS WALTER (1867-1938), premier of Saskatchewan. Scott moved from Ontario to Portage La Prairie in 1885 and worked as a printer. He continued west to Regina the next year, worked as a journalist, and by 1896 owned newspapers in Regina and Moose Jaw. Elected to Parliament in 1900 and re-elected in 1904, he became leader of the Saskatchewan Liberal party on the formation of the province in 1905, and as such he was asked to form the first provincial government. He won three successive elections and remained as premier until forced to resign by ill-health in 1916.

SEABORN, JAMES BLAIR (1924–), public servant. Seaborn joined the Department of External Affairs in 1948. During the mid-1960s he was the Canadian head of the INTERNATIONAL CONTROL COMMISSION in Vietnam and, at the request of the United States and with the concurrence of his government, engaged in a controversial attempt to establish communications between the United States and North Vietnam. He served as assistant deputy minister of consumer and corporate affairs from 1970 to 1974 and as deputy minister of Environment Canada from 1975 to 1982. He became a senior adviser to the Privy Council Office on security and intelligence questions in 1985.

SEAGRAM, JOSEPH EMM (1841-1919), distiller, politician. Born at Fisher Mills, Canada West, Seagram purchased a Waterloo distillery in 1883 and began producing high-quality spirits for a world market. Success in distilling was followed by other endeavours, such as horse-racing and politics. Seagram was founder of the Canadian Racing Assn and president of the Ontario Jockey Club, and his stables owned or bred an unprecedented 15 QUEEN'S PLATE winners. Seagram was elected to the House of Commons for the Conservative party in 1896 and served until 1908.

SEAGRAM CO. LTD., company started in 1883 when JOSEPH E. SEAGRAM purchased a Waterloo distillery. The Bronfman family gained controlling interests in the company in 1928 and since that time the corporation has grown and diversified, changing its name to Seagram Co. Ltd in 1975. It is currently the world's largest distillery.

SECTION 98, section of the Criminal Code of Canada passed in 1919 that consolidated measures adopted by the Union Government of Prime Minister ROBERT BORDEN to deal with a threat of incipient revolution during the period of the RED SCARE. It abolished the right of those accused of trying to foment revolution of being regarded as innocent until proven guilty and gave the government the right to deport persons without trial. It was severely attacked by civil libertarians and was repealed by Prime Minister WILLIAM LYON MACKENZIE KING in 1936.

SELYE, HANS (1907-82), endocrinologist, stress expert. Born at Vienna and educated in Prague, Paris, and Rome, Selye came to McGill Univ. in 1932 and became director of the Univ. de Montréal's Institute of Experimental Medicine and Surgery in 1945. Selye argued that stress plays an important role in disease, and he popularized his views through books and speeches.

SENATE REFORM, a matter of discussion for Canadians since the issue was first raised at the Interprovincial Conference of 1887. A variety of schemes to reform the Senate have been advanced from election to compulsory early retirement. Prime ministers have been loathe to act on these suggestions because appointment to the Senate is a favourite plum handed out for faithful service by the governing party.

SENÉCAL, LOUIS-ADÉLARD (1829-87), businessman, politician. Born in Varennes, Lower Canada, he began as a grain merchant in the mid-1850s and then expanded his interests to other commercial and investment pursuits and emerged a wealthy man by the time of CONFEDERATION. A political opportunist, he entered political life as a Liberal, sitting in the Quebec legislature from 1867 to 1871 and the House of Commons from 1867 to 1872. But he jumped to the Conservatives when they came to power in Quebec City. He was named to the Senate in 1887.

SEPARATE SCHOOLS, religiously based, tax-supported schools. The term "separate school" may mean something different in each province because each one may define the term in its own way. Generally, the term applies to the tax-supported religious or religiously based schools of either a Catholic or Protestant minority. Separate schools originated before CONFEDERATION in a number of the British American colonies which had allowed them to be established because of the political strength of the religious minorities or, in the case of Quebec, guarantees to the French which dated back to the Quebec Act of 1774. Seven of the ten provinces, Newfoundland, Nova Scotia, Prince Edward Island, Quebec, Ontario, Saskatchewan, and Alberta, have some form of separate schools. Many major political crises in Canadian history such as the MANITOBA SCHOOLS QUESTION and the NORTH-WEST SCHOOLS QUESTION have revolved around the fight to eliminate or preserve separate schools. *See also* AUTONOMY BILLS; NEW BRUNSWICK SCHOOL QUESTION.

SEPARATISM, the desire to separate from Canada. In the 19th century separatism was strongest in Atlantic Canada, especially Nova Scotia, which tried to leave CONFEDERATION almost as soon as the DOMINION OF CANADA was created.

In 1886 the Nova Scotia legislature even passed a resolution favouring a repeal of the BRITISH NORTH AMERICA ACT. In the 20th century separatism has been more marked in Quebec. In this century it was first put forward by extreme right-wing Catholics such as J.P. TARDIVEL and was favoured by ABBÉ LIONEL GROULX who advanced the notion of a Catholic, agrarian society on the banks of the St Lawrence River which he called Laurentie. In the 1960s the campaign for Quebec separatism was taken up by movements such as the RASSEMBLEMENT POUR L'INDÉPENDENCE NATIONALE and finally by the PARTI QUÉBÉCOIS, led by RENÉ LÉVESQUE, which was formed in the fall of 1968. *See also* INDÉPENDANTISTE; QUEBEC REFERENDUM; SOVEREIGNTY-ASSOCIATION.

SERVICE, ROBERT WILLIAM (1874-1958), poet. The "Poet of the Yukon," Service came to Canada in 1894, joined the Bank of Commerce, and worked for it in British Columbia and in Whitehorse and Dawson City in the Yukon. Fascinated by the north and its legends, he won enormous popularity through his verse. *Song of a Sourdough* (1907) was followed by a number of other books. During World War I, he served as an ambulance driver and published a book of war poems. He lived in France for most of the rest of his life.

SETON, ERNEST THOMPSON (1860-1946), author, naturalist. Born at South Shields, Eng., Seton was educated at the Ontario College of Art and in London, Paris, and New York before moving to Manitoba to begin his lifelong study of animals. In 1891 he published *The Birds of Manitoba* and was appointed Manitoba government naturalist. Seton left Canada for the United States in 1896, eventually moving to New Mexico, where he established his institute of wildlife and woodcraft. His works include *Wild Animals I Have Known* (1898) and *The Arctic Prairies* (1911). His autobiography was published in 1940.

72 RESOLUTIONS, resolutions embodying the conclusions of the QUEBEC CONFERENCE of Oct. 1864, which formed the basis of the BRITISH NORTH AMERICA ACT. *See also* CHARLOTTETOWN CONFERENCE; CONFEDERATION; FATHERS OF CONFEDERATION.

SÉVIGNY, JOSEPH-PIERRE-ALBERT (1917-), politician. Sévigny was born at Quebec City and educated at Loyola College and Univ. Laval. He served during World War II, was grievously wounded, and emerged with the rank of lieutenant-colonel. A Conservative in a Liberal-dominated Quebec, he was finally elected to the House of Commons in 1958. Deputy speaker in 1958-9, he was associate minister of national defence from 1959 until resigning over Prime Minister DIEFENBAKER's defence policy in Feb. 1963. He was defeated in the 1963 election and last came to public attention when he was named as a central figure in the MUNSINGER AFFAIR.

SHADBOLT, JACK LEONARD (1909-), artist. Shadbolt immigrated from England to British Columbia, where he has lived since 1912. Educated in New York, London, and Paris, he taught art to children before joining the Vancouver School of Art. After serving in World War II, including as a Canadian war artist in 1944-5, he returned to the Vancouver school and taught until 1966. An extremely prolific artist, Shadbolt has exhibited in more than 50 solo shows and his reputation is international.

SHARP, MITCHELL WILLIAM (1911-), public servant, politician. Sharp, born at Winnipeg, joined the Department of Finance in 1942. In 1951 C.D. HOWE had him transferred to the Department of Trade and Commerce, where he became deputy minister. Sharp entered private business during the DIEFENBAKER era but returned to Ottawa in 1963 as Liberal MP for Toronto-Eglinton. He was Prime Minister PEARSON's minister of trade and commerce from 1963 to 1965 and a conservative minister of finance from 1965 to 1968. As Prime Minister TRUDEAU's external affairs minister from 1968 to 1974, he presided over reviews of Canadian foreign policy, 1968-72. He left politics in 1978 and became commissioner for the Northern Pipeline Agency. *See also* THIRD OPTION.

SHARED-COST PROGRAM, federal-provincial programs used frequently after World War II and designed as a solution to the problem that most social legislation falls within provincial jurisdiction while Ottawa has most of the taxing powers. The first such program, established in 1918, was designed to combat venereal disease.

Shared-cost programs are generally financed by Ottawa, which also establishes their basic guidelines, but are administered by the provinces on the basis of provincial legislation. MEDICARE is a shared-cost program. *See also* OPTING-OUT FORMULA.

SHATFORD, SIDNEY SMITH (1864-1956), businessman. Born in Hubbards, N.S., Shatford was the province's first oilman. He merged his distribution company, Shatford Brothers Ltd (founded 1885), with his major competition, Joseph Bullock Ltd, to form the Eastern Oil Co. in 1894. Four years later the company was taken over by IMPERIAL OIL. Shatford remained an executive of Imperial until 1930.

SHAUGHNESSY, THOMAS GEORGE, 1ST BARON SHAUGHNESSY (1853-1923), railway executive. Born in Milwaukee, Wis., Shaughnessy worked for WILLIAM VAN HORNE in the United States before joining CANADIAN PACIFIC RAILWAY in 1882. By 1891, Shaughnessy had risen to vice-president; eight years later he was named president. Shaughnessy presided over expansions of Canadian Pacific's railway and steamship operations in the period between 1900 and the outbreak of World War I and moved aggressively into mining and smelting on CP's properties near Trail, B.C. *See also* COMINCO.

SHAW, WALTER RUSSELL (1887-1981), premier of Prince Edward Island. An Island-born and bred farmer, Shaw became leader of the Conservative party in 1957 at age 70 and led the party to victory two years later. In power until 1966, Shaw tried to address the problems of rural P.E.I. and to attract manufacturing.

SHAWINIGAN WATER AND POWER CO., founded in 1898 by John Edward Aldred on the St-Maurice River in Quebec. The company grew in conjunction with the surrounding industries, supplying them with most of their power. It was taken over by HYDRO-QUÉBEC when the province's power companies were nationalized in 1963. *See also* QUIET REVOLUTION; RENÉ LÉVESQUE.

SHELL COMMITTEE, organization created in Sept. 1914 by minister of militia SAM HUGHES to handle British orders for munitions. The committee was a quick success, instantly securing orders for 200,000 shells and $170 million in contracts by May 1915. But the committee, as with most things Hughes touched, got bogged down in patronage, inefficiency, and politics, and deliveries fell far behind. By Nov. 1915, SIR ROBERT BORDEN had dumped the committee and Hughes's friends, replacing them with the IMPERIAL MUNITIONS BOARD which proved far more efficient.

SHERMAN, FRANK ALBERT (1887-1969), industrialist. Sherman was born in Crown Point, N.Y., and came to Hamilton in 1914 to join the DOMINION FOUNDRIES AND STEEL LTD (Dofasco). As president and later chairman of Dofasco, he is best remembered for keeping unions out of the company. Sherman was also president of the Hamilton Tiger-Cats Football Club.

SHINPLASTERS, 25-cent notes issued by the dominion government from the 1870s until the mid-1930s.

SHORTT, ADAM (1859-1931), economist, public servant. One of the founders of the social sciences in Canada, Shortt was born at Kilworth, Canada West, and educated at Queen's and the univs. of Glasgow and Edinburgh. He taught philosophy at Queen's until appointed to the Sir John A. Macdonald Chair of political science in 1891. Shortt was the first Canadian-born economist to bring a historical approach to a study of the Canadian economy. In 1908, he was appointed to the CIVIL SERVICE COMMISSION in Ottawa, a post that gave him a chance to cleanse the Augean stables of patronage, a truly herculean task. From 1918 until just before he died he was chairman of the Board of Historical Publications of the Public Archives of Canada. He was also co-editor of the 23-volume *Canada and Its Provinces* (1913-17).

SHOYAMA, THOMAS KUNITO (1916–), economist, public servant. Born at Kamloops, B.C., Shoyama was one of the leaders of second-generation Japanese Canadians in British Columbia. He edited the *New Canadian*, campaigned for full civil rights, and struggled successfully to be allowed to enlist in the army during World War II. After the war, he helped set up the new social programs in Saskatchewan under T.C. DOUGLAS, and became economic adviser to premier W.S. LLOYD. He left in 1964 to become senior economist for the ECONOMIC COUNCIL OF CANADA and

then held senior positions in the federal government as deputy minister of energy, mines, and resources, deputy minister of finance, and special adviser to the Privy Council Office on the Constitution. He was a member of the ROYAL COMMISSION ON THE ECONOMIC UNION AND DEVELOPMENT PROSPECTS FOR CANADA.

SHRUM, GORDON MERRITT (1896-1987), physicist. He was born at Smithville, Ont., and was educated at the Univ. of Toronto. He joined the Univ. of British Columbia in 1925, eventually becoming dean of graduate studies. An ardent supporter of research, he was a member of the NATIONAL RESEARCH COUNCIL and the Defence Research Board and a key figure in the establishment of the British Columbia Research Council in 1944. After retiring from the Univ. of B.C., he was chairman of B.C. Hydro for 12 years.

SIDBEC-DOSCO LTÉE, Quebec steel company organized by the Quebec government in 1964 as part of the QUIET REVOLUTION. It is an integrated steelmaking facility using the Midrex process to combine sponge iron with scrap steel to produce high-quality steel. Its present name was adopted in 1972.

SIFTON, ARTHUR LEWIS (1858-1921), premier of Alberta. Born at St Johns, Canada West, the brother of SIR CLIFFORD SIFTON, A.L. Sifton practised law in Brandon, Prince Albert, and Calgary. In 1889 he was elected to the legislature of the North-West Territories, quickly becoming a proponent of provincial status. In 1903, he became the territories' chief justice and in 1907 first chief justice of Alberta. He left the bench three years later to become Liberal premier, a post he filled with great effect until 1917. He then moved to Ottawa to join SIR ROBERT BORDEN'S UNION GOVERNMENT, serving in the war committee, as minister of customs, and later as minister of public works.

SIFTON, SIR CLIFFORD (1861-1929), politician, businessman. As Prime Minister WILFRID LAURIER's minister of the interior and superintendent general of Indian affairs from 1896 to 1905, he was responsible for the promotion of immigration to settle the Prairies. Born near Arva, Canada West, he moved to Manitoba in 1875 and was called to the Manitoba bar in 1882. He first

courtesy National Archives of Canada/C-1860

Sir Clifford Sifton

entered provincial politics as a Liberal in 1888, becoming attorney general and minister of education in the GREENWAY government in 1891. Elected to the House of Commons in 1896, he distinguished himself as an able negotiator and administrator in such issues as the CROW'S NEST PASS AGREEMENT, the administration of the Yukon during the gold rush, and as British agent before the Alaska Boundary Tribunal in 1903. He resigned in 1905 after breaking with the government's policy towards separate schools for Alberta and Saskatchewan and supported the Conservative stand against RECIPROCITY during the 1911 election but did not seek election. In 1917, he was a leading pro-conscriptionist. From 1909 to 1918 he was chairman of the COMMISSION OF CONSERVATION. Always secretive about his business dealings, Sifton left an estate valued at about $10 million. He was president of Atlantic Oil Co., managing director of Imperial Pulp Co., and owner of the *Manitoba Free Press* (now the Winnipeg *Free Press*), on which the Sifton newspaper empire is founded. *See also* AUTONOMY BILLS.

SIGNAL HILL, hill near St John's, Nfld, and the site chosen by Guglielmo Marconi to receive the first transatlantic radio signal, sent from England, on 12 Dec. 1901.

SILK TRAINS, special fast CANADIAN PACIFIC RAILWAY freight trains that travelled from Vancouver to the east with cargos of raw silk from the orient. The trains travelled at high speed because of the great value of the commodity.

courtesy DND/AH-100-1

At the controls of the Silver Dart

SILVER DART, the first airplane to fly in the British Empire. A product of the AERIAL EXPERIMENT ASSN founded by ALEXANDER GRAHAM BELL and others, the plane was piloted on its maiden flight in 1909 by J.A.D. MCCURDY.

SILVERHEELS, JAY (1919-80), actor. Silverheels, the stage name of Harold Jay Smith, was born on the Six Nations Reserve at Brantford, Ont. An outstanding lacrosse player and boxer, he was discovered by comedian Joe Brown in 1938. He landed roles in many films, including *Broken Arrow* (1950) and *Saskatchewan* (1954), but it was for his role as Tonto in the Lone Ranger films (1956, 1958) that Silverheels is best known.

SIMONDS, GUY GRANVILLE (1903-74), army officer. Simonds, born at Toronto and educated at the ROYAL MILITARY COLLEGE, commanded the 1st Canadian Division in SICILY and Italy before taking command of the II Canadian Corps in northwest Europe during WORLD WAR II. When General H.D.G. CRERAR became ill, he commanded the FIRST CANADIAN ARMY, leading it during the Scheldt battle of Oct.-Nov. 1944. Although unloved by his troops, he is generally credited with being the most brilliant Canadian commander of the war, a genuine tactical innovator. After 1945 General Simonds served as chief instructor at Britain's Imperial Defence College (1946-9) and as commandant of Canada's National Defence College (1949-51). As chief of the general staff from 1951 to 1955, he was outspokenly critical of closer military ties with the United States, advocating peacetime CONSCRIPTION and closer relations with Britain.

SIMPSON, ROBERT (1834-97), merchant. Founder of Robert Simpson Co., Simpson immigrated to Canada from Scotland in 1854. He opened a dry-goods store in Newmarket in 1855 and in 1872 he opened a small store in Toronto. By 1894 he had expanded the business to a six-storey Queen St location. Although a fire destroyed the business in 1895, within a year Simpson had built a new store employing nearly 500 people in 35 departments. The business was sold to three Toronto businessmen following his sudden death.

courtesy Cunard Steamship/National Archives of Canada/PA-117595

O.D. Skelton

SKELTON, OSCAR DOUGLAS (1878-1941), scholar, public servant. Skelton, born at Orangeville, Ont., was educated at Queen's and Chicago univs. before returning to Queen's as professor of political science and economics from 1909 to 1925 and dean of arts from 1919 to 1925. Brought to Ottawa by MACKENZIE KING in 1923 and appointed under-secretary of state for external affairs in 1925, a post he held until his death, Skelton was an ardent nationalist and in some ways an isola-

tionist who believed Canada had to take control of its own affairs. He worked assiduously towards this goal, creating the foundations of a superb diplomatic corps and recruiting able men for other departments of government. Although not a strong administrator himself, he was the founder of the modern public service. His publications include *Socialism: A Critical Analysis* (1911), *Life and Times of Sir Alexander Tilloch Galt* (1920), and *Life and Letters of Sir Wilfrid Laurier* (1921).

SKI-DOO, the Ski-doo is a small, motorcycle-sized snowmobile invented in 1959 by JOSEPH-ARMAND BOMBARDIER. It is used as a winter sports vehicle and has replaced the dog team as the principal means of northern ground transportation in winter.

SKY PILOT, term used by workers in western Canada in the early 20th century to refer to a preacher.

SMALLWOOD, JOSEPH ROBERTS (1900-), premier of Newfoundland. Born at Gambo, Nfld, Smallwood was a journalist, union organizer, farmer, broadcaster, and an advocate of union with Canada. He spearheaded the drive after World War II to end the rule of the COMMISSION OF GOVERNMENT and replace it with provincial status in the Canadian confederation, a task he carried out with great skill. After two referenda to decide Newfoundland's course, he was named the first premier, taking office 1 April 1949. A Liberal, he won the subsequent election – and all others until his government fell in early 1972. Smallwood integrated his province into the dominion, engaged in ambitious, but largely unsuccessful, development and resettlement schemes, and occasionally fought the trade unions. His popularity was enormous as a Father of Confederation and as a personality. After his final retirement from politics in 1977, he turned to the preparation of a multi-volume Newfoundland encyclopedia.

SMITH, ALBERT EDWARD (1871-1947), minister, labour leader, politician. Born in Guelph, Ont., Smith was ordained as a Methodist minister and served in western Canada prior to World War I. During the WINNIPEG GENERAL STRIKE he organized a People's Church in Brandon, Man. He resigned from the ministry in June 1919 and was elected to the Manitoba legislature as a Labour member in 1920. In 1925 he joined the COMMUNIST PARTY and became head of its CANADIAN LABOUR DEFENCE LEAGUE. In 1929 he became general secretary of the party, a post he held until 1940.

courtesy Notman/National Archives of Canada/C-17767

Donald A. Smith, 1st Baron Strathcona and Mount Royal

SMITH, DONALD ALEXANDER, 1ST BARON STRATHCONA AND MOUNT ROYAL (1820-1914), fur trader, railway financier. Born at Forres, Scot., Smith joined the HUDSON'S BAY CO. in 1838, eventually working his way to chief commissioner in 1871, director (and largest shareholder) by 1883, and governor in 1889. In 1869 he was dispatched to Fort Garry to assist negotiations between LOUIS RIEL's provisional government and Ottawa. He entered politics as a Conservative, sitting in the Manitoba legislature from 1870 to 1874 and in the House of Commons from 1871 to 1878. Defeated in 1880 but successful in 1887, he sat in the House until appointed HIGH COMMISSIONER for Canada in Britain in 1896, a post he held until his death. Enormously wealthy, his support enabled the completion of the CANADIAN PACIFIC RAILWAY and in 1885 he was invited to drive the LAST SPIKE. Smith was also president of the BANK OF MONTREAL (1887-1905), director of Paton Manufacturing Co., the New Brunswick Railway, and the DOMINION COAL CO., and vice-president and part-owner of the ST PAUL, MINNEAPOLIS AND MANI-

TOBA RAILWAY. As chancellor of McGill Univ. he founded Royal Victoria College for women in 1896. During the BOER WAR he personally financed Lord Strathcona's Horse, a cavalry regiment of 500 men. He was created Baron Strathcona in 1897.

SMITH, GOLDWIN (1823-1910), historian, journalist. Born at Reading, Eng., and educated at Eton and Oxford, Smith was Regius professor of modern history at Oxford before emigrating to the United States. He settled in Toronto in 1871 and became the leading intellectual in the dominion. A CONTINENTALIST, Smith advocated union with the United States on the grounds that Canada was not viable as a nation, a view put forth in his *Canada and the Canada Question* (1891). A prolific journalist, he wrote for British periodicals and for the *Weekly Sun* and the *Week*, which he helped found in 1883.

SMITH, SIDNEY EARLE (1897-1959), academic administrator, politician. Born at Port Hood, N.S., and educated at King's College, Dalhousie, and Harvard univs., he was dean of Dalhousie Law School before becoming president of the Univ. of Manitoba (1934-44) and the Univ. of Toronto (1944-57). Named in 1957 as Prime Minister JOHN DIEFENBAKER's secretary of state for external affairs, Smith was only beginning to gain respect in diplomatic affairs when he died suddenly.

SMITH-SHORTT, ELIZABETH (1859-1949), physician. Born at Winona, Canada West, Smith graduated in 1884 from the Women's Medical College at Kingston, Ont., and set up practice in Hamilton, one of the first female medical doctors in Canada. In 1886 she married ADAM SHORTT and moved to Kingston, where she lectured at the Women's Medical College. A champion of women's rights, she served as vice-president of the NATIONAL COUNCIL OF WOMEN.

SMYTHE, CONSTANTINE FALKLAND CARY (1895-1980), sports entrepreneur. Born at Toronto, Conn Smythe served in both world wars; his reports of reinforcement shortages in 1944 sparked the CONSCRIPTION CRISIS. He coached the Univ. of Toronto Varsity Grads before joining with others to buy the Toronto St Pats hockey team in 1927, changing its name to the Maple

Leafs. A key figure behind the construction of Maple Leaf Gardens in 1931, he sold controlling interest in the Gardens and the team in 1961. His autobiography, *Conn Smythe: If You Can't Beat 'em in the Alley*, appeared in 1981.

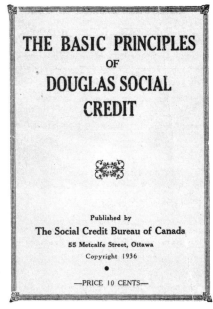

THE BASIC PRINCIPLES

OF

DOUGLAS SOCIAL CREDIT

Published by

The Social Credit Bureau of Canada

55 Metcalfe Street, Ottawa

Copyright 1936

●

—PRICE 10 CENTS—

Handbook explaining the worth and sensibility of the Social Credit philosophy

SOCIAL CREDIT, an economic doctrine developed by Major C.H. DOUGLAS, a Scottish engineer, which served as the basis for the SOCIAL CREDIT PARTY. The doctrine, roundly attacked by orthodox economists, was popularly known as the A+B theorem. It held that since people never had enough money to buy all the goods produced by modern industry, governments should issue money to everyone in the form of "social credits." Alberta evangelist WILLIAM ABERHART seized the idea in 1932, formed a party, and won the 1935 Alberta provincial election. *See also* W.A.C. BENNETT.

SOCIAL CREDIT PARTY, political party originally organized to follow the doctrine of SOCIAL CREDIT. Seized on by WILLIAM ABERHART in 1932 in Alberta, the doctrine and party swept Alberta in the 1935 election, and Aberhart and his successors, ERNEST MANNING and HARRY STROM, governed the province until 1971. The party also made headway in British Columbia under the leader-

ship of W.A.C. BENNETT, who governed from 1952 to 1972, and his successors, who ruled from 1975, though the economic doctrine was never embraced there. The federal party also enjoyed some success, taking 17 seats in the 1935 election, and, under ROBERT THOMPSON (allied with RÉAL CAOUETTE and the RALLIEMENT DES CRÉDITISTES), it managed to win 30 seats in the 1962 election. The federal party has largely disappeared since 1980. *See also* C.H. DOUGLAS.

SOCIAL DEMOCRATIC PARTY OF CANADA, labour party founded in 1911 by breakaway members of the SOCIALIST PARTY of Canada who rejected the SPC's doctrinaire approach to political and economic questions and who demanded a greater voice for immigrant radicals. The party was no less Marxist than the SPC but believed that social and political change could be brought about by electoral action, as well as by revolution.

SOCIAL GOSPEL, religious movement with roots in Britain and the United States which became strong in Canada in the early 20th century. Followers of the Social Gospel believed that the souls of men and women could not be saved until their physical welfare was provided for, and they embarked on extensive reform programs to improve living conditions in working class and immigrant neighbourhoods. Most Social Gospellers came from Methodist and Presbyterian backgrounds. Some, such as J.S. WOODSWORTH and A.E. SMITH ultimately abandoned the Social Gospel route to join reform and even radical political movements. By the mid-1920s the Social Gospel had virtually disappeared.

SOCIAL INSURANCE NUMBER, number issued by the government of Canada to Canadians enrolled in the CANADA PENSION PLAN as an indication of that enrolment and to keep track of premiums paid to the Unemployment Insurance Commission. The numbers were introduced in 1964 by the UIC.

SOCIALIST PARTY OF CANADA, a doctrinaire and Marxist labour party established in 1904 when the Socialist party of British Columbia joined with the Canadian Socialist League. By 1910, it had spread across Canada but gradually disappeared after the failure of the general strikes of 1919.

SOD SHACK, prairie homesteading farmhouse. To "PROVE UP" a homestead, a farmer was required to live on it for three years and make improvements on his QUARTER SECTION. Many started out by building small houses made of prairie sod cut into brick-like shapes and piled to form walls. Sod shacks were replaced with more permanent homes as soon as possible. *See also* HOMESTEADER.

SOLANDT, OMOND MCKILLOP (1909–), scientist, administrator. Solandt, born at Winnipeg, was educated at Toronto and England. During World War II, he resolved the problem of fainting tank crews (gases released by guns firing had to be directed outside) and became superintendent of the British Army's Operational Research Group. He returned to Canada to become founding chairman of the Defence Research Board in 1947. From 1956 to 1963 he was vice-president for research and development at CANADIAN NATIONAL RAILWAYS and from 1963 to 1966 worked at DE HAVILLAND AIRCRAFT of Canada. Chancellor of the Univ. of Toronto from 1965 to 1971, he was chairman of the Science Council of Canada from 1966 to 1972.

SOMERS, HARRY STEWART (1925–), composer. A founding member of the Canadian League of Composers in 1951, Somers, born at Toronto, studied piano and classical guitar at the Royal Conservatory in Toronto before going to study in Paris. As one of Canada's most prolific and original composers, he was involved in the John Adaskin Project (1963) to promote Canadian composers and in 1967 wrote the opera *Louis Riel*.

SOMME, BATTLE OF THE, 1916, the bloody battles of July to Nov. 1916 that became a byword for the futility of WORLD WAR I. The German defences north of the River Somme were attacked in a series of engagements by British, French, and dominion troops beginning 1 July when the Newfoundland Regiment was slaughtered at Beaumont Hamel. Under General SIR JULIAN BYNG, the CANADIAN CORPS joined in the battle on 30 Aug. and did well against German machine guns, barbed wire, and tenacity in attacks on Regina Trench, Courcelette, and elsewhere. By

Nov., the Allies had advanced 13 km and suffered approximately 624,000 casualties, of which 24,713 were Canadians or Newfoundlanders. Estimated German casualties were 660,000.

SOUTHAM, WILLIAM (1843-1932), newspaper publisher. Born near Montreal, Southam worked on the London *Free Press* before buying a half-interest in the Hamilton *Spectator* in 1877. With his six sons he expanded the operation into one of Canada's largest newspaper chains. Preferring to buy existing newspapers rather than start his own, the conservative Southam acquired the Ottawa *Citizen*, Calgary *Herald*, Edmonton *Journal*, Windsor *Star*, and the Montreal *Gazette*.

SOVEREIGNTY-ASSOCIATION, policy of the PARTI QUÉBÉCOIS for independence with an economic link to Canada. Initially developed by RENÉ LÉVESQUE's Mouvement souveraineté-association in the late 1960s and carried into the Parti Québécois, the idea involved a common currency with Canada, free trade and a common tariff policy, and freedom of movement for Québécois and Canadians. The object was to give Quebec independence and all the advantages of the federal union. This policy was rejected by 59.5 per cent of the voters in the May 1980 QUEBEC REFERENDUM and was dropped from the Parti Québécois program in 1985.

SPINKS, JOHN WILLIAM TRANTOR (1908–), chemist. Born in Norfolk Eng., Spinks joined the Univ. of Saskatchewan in 1930, and played a key role in bringing GERHARD HERZBERG to Canada from Germany in 1935. Specializing in radiation research, Spinks worked in both pure and applied areas. He was appointed president of the Univ. of Saskatchewan in 1959.

SPRINGHILL MINE DISASTER, mine explosion on 13 Oct. 1958 which killed 74 men at Springhill, N.S. The mines were shut down after the accident, only one in a long succession of mishaps which had plagued the Springhill mines for years.

SPRY, GRAHAM (1900-83), publicist, broadcasting enthusiast. Born at St Thomas, Ont., Spry, a Rhodes scholar, began his career as a reporter for the *Manitoba Free Press* from 1920 to 1922. In 1930 he founded the CANADIAN RADIO

LEAGUE with ALLAN B. PLAUNT to promote the use of radio in securing national unity. He served as chairman of the league from 1930 to 1934 and later of the Canadian Broadcasting League from 1968 to 1973. A political activist, he published the *Farmers' Sun* and served as chairman of the Ontario CO-OPERATIVE COMMONWEALTH FEDERATION from 1934 to 1936. Director of Standard Oil of California's British subsidiaries, 1940-6, he was Sir Stafford Cripps' personal assistant during World War II. From 1946 to 1968 he was agent-general for Saskatchewan in London. He spent his last years fighting critics of public broadcasting.

SQUIRES, SIR RICHARD ANDERSON (1880-1940), prime minister of Newfoundland, 1919-23 and 1928-32. Born at Grace Harbour, Nfld, he entered the assembly in 1909 and sat until defeated in 1913. Appointed to the Legislative Council and the cabinet, he lost his cabinet position in 1918. In 1919 he founded the Liberal Reform party and won election. Resigning in the face of charges of corruption (later proved true) in 1923, he came back to win the 1928 election but further charges of corruption brought his and his party's downfall in 1932.

courtesy DND/National Archives of Canada/PA-501024

Charles P. Stacey

STACEY, CHARLES PERRY (1906-), historian. Stacey, born at Toronto, was educated at Toronto, Oxford and Princeton univs. He taught at Princeton from 1934 to 1940, before serving as the Canadian Army's historian in London during World War II. In 1945 he became director of the historical section of the Canadian Army in Ottawa. Retiring in 1959, he was a professor at the Univ. of Toronto until 1976. A prolific writer, his books include *Canada and the British Army* (1936), *Six Years of War* (1955), *Quebec, 1759* (1959), *Arms, Men and Governments* (1970), *A Very Double Life* (1976), a controversial study of MACKENZIE KING, and *Canada and the Age of Conflict* (2 vols., 1977-81).

STANFIELD, ROBERT LORNE (1914-), premier of Nova Scotia, federal politician. Born at Truro, N.S., and educated at Dalhousie and Harvard univs., Stanfield became leader of the Nova Scotia Conservative party in 1948, reorganized it, and led it to victory in 1956. He governed effectively for 11 years despite a laconic style, seeking to create a self-reliant province. In 1967 he became national CONSERVATIVE PARTY leader, but his party was wracked by divisions (some promoted by JOHN DIEFENBAKER), and he was unable to overcome the charisma of PIERRE TRUDEAU, although in 1972 he came close. He was replaced by JOE CLARK in 1976.

STANLEY, FREDERICK ARTHUR, BARON STANLEY OF PRESTON, 16TH EARL OF DERBY (1841-1908), governor general of Canada. After sitting in the House of Commons and the House of Lords, Stanley came to Canada as governor general in 1888 and served for five years. Quiet and careful, he had little political impact and is best remembered as the donor in 1893 of hockey's STANLEY CUP.

STANLEY CUP, hockey trophy donated by LORD STANLEY in 1893. The Stanley Cup is now awarded to the team which wins the National Hockey League's final playoff series.

STATUTE OF WESTMINSTER, a 1931 act of the British Parliament that gave Canada (and the other dominions) autonomy in external relations to go with independence in domestic policy. The statute effectively created the modern Commonwealth. To satisfy provincial concerns, the statute permitted amendment to the BRITISH NORTH AMERICA ACT only at Westminster; this remained in force until the constitution was patriated in 1982.

STATUTORY RATES, *see* CROW'S NEST PASS AGREEMENT

STEACIE, EDGAR WILLIAM RICHARD (1900-62), chemist. Steacie, born at Ottawa, attended McGill Univ. and taught there until becoming director of the chemistry division of the NATIONAL RESEARCH COUNCIL in 1939. Appointed vice-president of NRC in 1950, he became president in 1952, a post he held until his death. Under his direction the council became an international centre for chemical research.

STEEL CO. OF CANADA, *see* STELCO INC.

STEEL WORKERS' ORGANIZING COM- MITTEE, labour group formed by the Congress of Industrial Organizations in the United States to organize the North American steel industry. The United Steel Workers of America succeeded SWOC.

STEELE, SIR SAMUEL BENFIELD (1849-1919), policeman, soldier. The epitome of the NORTH-WEST MOUNTED POLICE, "Sam" Steele was born at Purbrook, Canada West, and joined the militia in 1866. In 1871 he entered the Permanent Force Artillery and became a sergeant major in the newly created NWMP in 1873. Commissioned in 1878, he took command at Fort Qu'Appelle in 1879. Promoted superintendent in 1885, he subsequently helped establish law and order during the KLONDIKE GOLD RUSH. During the BOER WAR he commanded Lord Strathcona's Horse and was given command of the second Canadian contingent in WORLD WAR I. Appointed general officer commanding the Shorncliffe area in England in 1916, he held the post until retiring in 1918.

STEFANSSON, VILHJALMUR (1879-1962), Arctic explorer. Born at Arnes, Man., he was educated at North Dakota, Iowa, and Harvard univs. Between 1906 and 1918 he embarked on three Arctic expeditions. As commander of the 1913-18 Canadian Arctic Expedition he discovered a number of major land masses, including Lougheed, Borden, Meighen, and Brock islands. A firm believer that the north was more friendly than inhospitable, he saw many of his schemes for development end in disaster, and he spent much of his time embroiled in controversy. From the mid-1920s on he lived mostly in the United States. A shrewd publicist, Stefansson wrote many books, the best-known being *The Friendly Arctic* (1921). *See also* WRANGEL ISLAND.

STEINBERG, SAMUEL (1905-78), businessman. Born in Hungary, Steinberg moved to Canada prior to World War I. He and his brothers began working in their mother's small grocery store, and they used it as the basis of a small chain. Steinberg is credited with opening Canada's first self-serve retail food store, a harbinger of the modern supermarket.

STEINHAUER, RALPH GARVIN (1905-87), native leader, lieutenant governor of Alberta. The first native Canadian to become lieutenant governor, Steinhauer, born at Morley, Alta, was educated at Brandon Indian Residential School. He began farming at Saddle Lake, Alta, founded the Indian Assn of Alberta, and served as president of the Alberta Indian Development Corp. Sworn in as lieutenant governor in 1974, he served until 1979.

STELCO INC., iron and steel company, founded in 1910 as the Steel Co. of Canada, based in Hamilton, Ont., when Montreal Rolling Mills and several other metal producers amalgamated. ROSS H. MCMASTER became president of the company in 1926 and led it through a major expansion and modernization. By the end of World War II Stelco had become an important North American steel producer. The company was responsible in 1988 for a large part of Canada's iron and steel production.

STEPHEN, GEORGE, 1ST BARON MOUNT STEPHEN (1829-1921), banker, railway president. Stephen immigrated from Scotland to Canada in 1850 and soon became an active and successful member of the Montreal business community. In 1873 he became a director of the BANK OF MONTREAL and a partner with DONALD SMITH and J.J. HILL in the struggling ST PAUL, MINNEAPOLIS AND MANITOBA RAILWAY. He was president of the bank from 1876 to 1881 and became president of the railway in 1879. The experience he gained prepared him for the presidency of the CANADIAN PACIFIC RAILWAY (1880-88). He is given much of the credit for the survival of the CPR during con-

courtesy National Archives of Canada/C-16322

George Stephen, 1st Baron Mount Stephen

struction, at one point pledging his personal fortune to back CPR loans. Stephen moved to England in 1888.

STEPHENSON, SIR WILLIAM SAMUEL (1896–), businessman, intelligence coordinator. Born at Winnipeg and educated at the Univ. of Manitoba, Stephenson served as a fighter pilot in World War I before moving to England in 1921 to make a fortune from his various inventions. During WORLD WAR II, he led British Security Coordination, headquartered at the New York City cable address "Intrepid" (later said to be Stephenson's code name). Set up to conduct counter-espionage, BSC censored letters, forged documents, guarded against sabotage, and trained allied agents at the famed CAMP X near Whitby, Ont. After the war Stephenson moved to Bermuda. Many of Stephenson's wartime activities remained a mystery. In 1962 H. Montgomery Hyde published *The Quiet Canadian*, a sober account of Stephenson's career. Journalist William Stevenson's two accounts, *A Man Called Intrepid* (1977) and *Intrepid's Last Case* (1983), however, have been treated with much skepticism by historians.

STEVENS, HENRY HERBERT (1878-1973), politician. Born in Bristol, Eng., Stevens was an alderman in Vancouver in 1910-11. First elected to the House of Commons in 1911 as a Conserva-

tive, he served as Prime Minister MEIGHEN's minister of trade and commerce (1921) and minister of customs and excise (1926) and as Prime Minister BENNETT's minister of trade and commerce (1930-4). Resigning from the government in a well-publicized dispute with Bennett, who had demanded he curb his assaults on corporate abuses, he formed the small business-oriented RECONSTRUCTION PARTY to contest the 1935 election. Although his party took 10 per cent of the popular vote, he was the only candidate to be elected. In 1939 he rejoined the CONSERVATIVE PARTY, but after three defeats quit politics to return to business.

STOWE, EMILY HOWARD (1831-1903), physician. Born Emily Jennings at Norwich, Upper Canada, she taught school before seeking a career in medicine. Barred from male-only Canadian institutions, she entered the New York Medical College for Women, graduated in 1867 and set up practice in Toronto. The first woman to practise medicine in Canada, she organized the Women's Medical College in 1883 and founded the Toronto Women's Literary Club in 1876. A champion of women's rights, she was first president of the Dominion Women's Enfranchisement Assn, established in 1889.

STOWE-GULLEN, ANN AUGUSTA (1857-1943), physician. Daughter of EMILY STOWE, Stowe-Gullen was the first woman to earn a medical degree in Canada. She married Dr John B. Gullen, founder in 1896 of the Toronto Western Hospital, and taught at the Ontario Medical College for Women. From 1910 to 1922 she served on the Univ. of Toronto Senate. An advocate of WOMEN'S SUFFRAGE, she succeeded her mother as president of the Dominion Women's Enfranchisement Assn in 1903.

STRATAS, TERESA (1938–), soprano. Stratas was born at Toronto. She debuted at the Toronto Opera Festival in 1958 as Mimi in *La Bohème* and at the Metropolitan Opera in 1959, co-winning the Met auditions. Since then she has sung internationally at La Scala, the Bolshoi Opera, and elsewhere. She appeared at the 1960 Vancouver International Festival and sang Desdemona in *Otello* at EXPO 67. Her films and recordings include Franco Zeffirelli's *La Traviata* (1983).

STRATFORD STRIKE, strike of furniture workers and chicken pluckers in Stratford, Ont., from Sept. to Nov. 1933. The workers, led by the WORKERS' UNITY LEAGUE, were opposed by municipal and federal authorities. Prime Minister R.B. BENNETT ordered the militia into Stratford to suppress the strike, an act that became a symbol of his allegedly unsympathetic attitude to labour. He thenceforth became known as "iron heel Bennett."

STREIT, MARLENE STEWART (1934–), golfer. Streit played junior golf in Ontario. An extremely competitive player, she won the Canadian Ladies Open Amateur 11 times, the Ontario Ladies Amateur Championship 11 times, the Ladies British Open Amateur in 1953, the U.S. Women's Amateur in 1956, and the Australian Women's Amateur in 1963.

STRIP FARMING, technique promoted by the PRAIRIE FARM REHABILITATION ADMINISTRATION to fight DUST BOWL conditions in the 1930s. Farmers were instructed to alternate strips of cultivated and fallow land at right angles to the prevailing wind.

STROM, HARRY EDWIN (1914-84), premier of Alberta, Strom was elected to the Alberta Legislature for SOCIAL CREDIT in 1955 and served in the cabinet of Premier E.C. MANNING from 1967. When Manning retired in 1968, Strom became party leader and premier. He was defeated by Conservative PETER LOUGHEED in the 1971 provincial election and remained leader of the opposition until 1973.

STRONG, MAURICE FREDERICK (1929–), business administrator, environmentalist. Born at Oak Lake, Man., Strong began working for the HUDSON'S BAY CO. in the Arctic in 1944. He worked in business until 1966 when he became involved in international and environmental concerns. Head of the CANADIAN INTERNATIONAL DEVELOPMENT AGENCY until 1970, he was secretary-general of the United Nations Switzerland office from 1970 to 1972 and executive director of the UN Environment Program in Nairobi, Kenya, from 1973 to 1975. In 1976 he became head of PETRO-CANADA and then chairman of the International Energy Development Corp. (1980-4).

STUART, KENNETH (1891-1945), soldier. Born at Trois-Rivières, Que., Stuart attended the ROYAL MILITARY COLLEGE and served overseas with the Royal Canadian Engineers during WORLD WAR I. As a staff officer in Ottawa in the interwar years, Stuart edited the *Canadian Defence Quarterly*. He was made chief of the general staff in Dec. 1941 and chief of staff of Canadian military headquarters in London from Dec. 1943 to Nov. 1944. A very political general, Stuart had helped secure the ouster of General A.G.L. MCNAUGHTON from his command of the FIRST CANADIAN ARMY, and McNaughton, named defence minister in Nov. 1944, in turn removed Stuart from his post. Stuart's too-optimistic reports on reinforcement strength helped cause the CONSCRIPTION CRISIS of 1944.

STUDENT UNION FOR PEACE ACTION, 1960s radical student group. In the mid-1960s, the impact of the Vietnam War and the civil rights movement in the United States spread to Canada. SUPA adopted the rhetoric of the U.S. Students for a Democratic Society; it organized community groups and worked with the poor, as well as calling for peace and disarmament.

SUEZ CRISIS, 1956, political crisis provoked by the combined Israeli-British-French attack on Egypt in Oct. 1956. After Egypt's President Nasser nationalized the Suez Canal on 26 July 1956, Britain and France prepared military action and colluded with Israel in plans for attack. Israel launched its invasion on 29 Oct. and Paris and London ordered the combatants to withdraw from the Canal; Egypt refused and the two European powers, as planned, invaded.

Despite warnings from Ottawa that such action could split the Commonwealth, London proceeded, the invasion going slowly and the political costs mounting rapidly, notably in Washington. At the United Nations, secretary of state for external affairs LESTER PEARSON proposed the creation of the UNITED NATIONS EMERGENCY FORCE to separate the combatants; this was accepted on 4 Nov. and General E.L.M. BURNS was named commander. A ceasefire followed two days later. Pearson's brilliant diplomacy, rewarded with the Nobel Peace Prize, produced embarrassment in Ottawa when Nasser refused to permit the unfortunately named Queen's Own Rifles to be the Canadian contribution to UNEF.

SULLIVAN, JOHN ALLAN PATRICK, "PAT" (1893-1957?), labour leader. Born in Carrick-on-Shannon, Ireland, Sullivan was a founding member of the CANADIAN SEAMEN'S UNION and joined the COMMUNIST PARTY of Canada sometime in 1936. Guided by Sullivan, the CSU grew rapidly in the late 1930s and during World War II. He was interned by the Canadian government in June 1940 because of the Communist party's opposition to the war but was released in March 1942 after the Soviet Union had been attacked by Nazi Germany and the Communist party swung behind the war effort. He was elected vice-president of the TRADES AND LABOUR CONGRESS in 1942 and secretary-treasurer in 1943. In the spring of 1947 Sullivan suddenly revealed his long-time affiliation to the Communist party to the labour movement and denounced party influence in the CSU. Partially in response to this, anti-Communist unions and the federal government collaborated to bring HAL BANKS to Canada to destroy Communist influence among Canadian sailors.

SUPREME COURT OF CANADA, federal institution created by the Liberal government of Prime Minister ALEXANDER MACKENZIE in Sept. 1875 to operate as a court of last resort for Canada. The JUDICIAL COMMITTEE OF THE PRIVY COUNCIL, however, continued to fulfil that function until 1949.

SUZOR-COTÉ, MARC-AURÈLE DE FOY (1869-1937), artist. Suzor-Coté, born at Arthabaska, Que., displayed unusual talent in school and after study in France (1891-4 and 1897-1901) returned to Canada, eventually settling at the Arthabaska studio he built in 1895 and at Montreal. Involvement in various projects, including church decoration, sculpture, and commissions from WILFRID LAURIER, brought him wide fame, despite his being disabled by paralysis for the last ten years of his life.

TANNER, ELAINE (1951-), swimmer. Considered Canada's best female swimmer, "Mighty Mouse" Tanner, born at Vancouver, had a brief but illustrious career. A specialist in the backstroke, butterfly, and individual medley, she set world records in the 220-yard individual medley and the 220-yard butterfly in 1966. At the Commonwealth Games that year she won 4 gold and 3 silver medals. At age 15 the youngest person ever to receive the Lou Marsh Trophy as Canada's outstanding athlete, she went on to take 2 gold and 2 silver medals at the 1967 Pan-American Games and 2 bronze at the 1968 Mexico Olympics.

TARDIVEL, JULES-PAUL (1851-1905), journalist, novelist. Tardivel, born at Covington, Ky, came to Quebec in 1868. He worked for various newspapers, including *La Minerve* in Montreal, before founding his own weekly, *La Vérité*, in 1881. Obsessed with ULTRAMONTANISM and nationalism, he spent his life advocating a rural, agricultural, and hierarchical society dominated by the Roman Catholic Church. In later years he advocated SEPARATISM and wrote a futuristic novel, *Pour la patrie* (1895), outlining separatist thought.

TARTE, JOSEPH-ISRAËL (1848-1907), journalist, politician. Born at Lanoraie, Canada East, Tarte attended the Collège de l'Assomption and in 1871 became a notary public. A caustic journalist, he edited many newspapers, including *Le Canadien* (1874-93) and *La Patrie* (1897-1907). Elected to the Quebec assembly in 1877, he was an advocate of ULTRAMONTANISM but later moderated his stand. He entered the House of Commons as a Conservative in 1891, and exposed the McGreevy-Langevin scandal which discredited the Conservatives, forced the resignation of SIR HECTOR LANGEVIN and drove Tarte into the Liberal camp. He served as LAURIER's minister of public works from 1896 to 1902. He was always outspoken; his opposition to sending troops to fight in the BOER WAR, his speeches on Canadian independence, and his campaign for imperial economic unity and higher tariffs were too controversial, and Laurier dismissed him in 1902.

TASCHEREAU, ELZÉAR-ALEXANDRE (1820-98), first Canadian Roman Catholic cardinal. Born at Ste-Marie-de-la-Beauce, Lower Canada, Taschereau was educated at the Séminaire de Québec (1826-36, 1837-42) and at Rome. He taught at the Séminaire de Québec and helped found Univ. Laval in 1852, serving as rector, 1860-6 and 1869-71. As archbishop of Quebec from 1870, Taschereau opposed ULTRAMONTANISM and sought to avoid confrontation with the state during the great debates over clerical influence in politics, Catholic liberalism, and reform of the civil code. Pope Leo XIII named him cardinal in June 1886.

courtesy National Archives of Canada/C-19515

Louis Taschereau and his wife

TASCHEREAU, LOUIS-ALEXANDRE (1867-1952), premier of Quebec. Born at Quebec City into one of the leading families of the province, Taschereau studied law at Univ. Laval. He was first elected to the legislature as a Liberal in 1900, became a cabinet minister in 1907, and succeeded SIR LOMER GOUIN as premier in 1920. His government encouraged foreign investment but resisted depression pressures for social welfare and social security. Attacked from within by the ACTION LIBÉRAL NATIONALE and from without by the Conservative party, Taschereau's government fell in 1936 to MAURICE DUPLESSIS and the UNION NATIONALE that had united the opposition factions.

TASK FORCE ON FOREIGN OWNERSHIP AND THE STRUCTURE OF CANADIAN INDUSTRY (WATKINS REPORT), federal task force appointed in 1967 under Melville Watkins, to study the political and economic significance of foreign investment. Set up through the efforts of WALTER GORDON, the task force proposed a government agency to monitor foreign investment, establishment of a CANADA DEVELOPMENT CORP., and efforts to block the application of foreign laws to the activities of foreign-owned firms in Canada.

TASK FORCE ON FOREIGN OWNERSHIP (GRAY REPORT), report prepared for cabinet in 1970-1 under the minister of national revenue Herb Gray on the impact and effects of foreign ownership. The report suggested that, although foreign investment did benefit Canada, it also caused difficulties, but the report refused to advocate a strategy of buying back control. An early draft of the report was leaked to CANADIAN FORUM and published in Nov. 1971, causing a minor sensation.

TASK FORCE ON LABOUR RELATIONS, see WOODS' TASK FORCE

TAYLOR, EDWARD PLUNKETT, "E.P." (1901–), businessman. Taylor, born at Ottawa, made much of his fortune during the GREAT DEPRESSION. He joined the brokerage firm McLeod, Young, Weir and Co. in Ottawa in 1923, moved to Toronto and became a director in 1929. Following the 1929 crash, through a series of crafty mergers, Taylor formed Canadian Breweries. During World War II he served in various capacities, including president of the British Supply Council in North America, head of the British Purchasing Commission and as C.D. HOWE's deputy on the Combined Production and Resources Board. In 1945 Taylor and others formed the Argus Corp., an investment group he served as president until 1969 and chairman from 1969 to 1971. Interested in breeding and racing horses, he was a director of the Ontario Jockey Club and, through Windfields Farms, bred the champion thoroughbred NORTHERN DANCER.

TAYLOR, FREDERICK WELLINGTON (1883-1979), hockey player. Known as "Cyclone" because of his great speed, he played in Ontario and Manitoba before turning professional. He played for Ottawa in 1908, Renfrew Millionaires in 1910-11, and Vancouver Millionaires, 1913-21.

A colourful player who could attract large crowds, he scored 194 goals in 186 games and once scored a goal while skating backwards.

TELESAT CANADA, crown agency established by the TRANS-CANADA TELEPHONE SYSTEM and the federal government in 1969 to oversee the construction, launching and operation of communications satellites. The ANIK A-1, launched in 1972, was a product of this collaboration.

TEMPERANCE, *see* PROHIBITION

TERM 29, of the Terms of Union of Newfoundland and Canada, 1949. It called for a review of the financial position of Newfoundland within eight years. A royal commission reported on this subject in 1958 and recommended an additional federal payment of $6.6 million in 1957-8 rising to $8 million in 1962-3, much less than the amount sought by Premier JOSEPH SMALLWOOD. The DIEFENBAKER government offered only the recommended sums and cut off payments completely in 1962.

THATCHER, WILBERT ROSS (1917-71), premier of Saskatchewan. Born at Neville, Sask., Thatcher attended Queen's Univ. First elected to the House of Commons in 1945 for the CO-OPERATIVE COMMONWEALTH FEDERATION, he held his seat until in 1955 he broke with the party. After failing to buck the Conservative tide in the federal elections in 1957 and 1958, he turned to provincial politics, won the Liberal leadership in 1959, and captured the province in 1964 when he benefited from a backlash against the social-democratic government and MEDICARE. As premier, he fought viciously with his Liberal colleagues in Ottawa, stressed development, and scarcely tampered with medicare. He lost in 1971 to the NEW DEMOCRATIC PARTY.

THIRD OPTION, an abortive TRUDEAU government effort to lessen Canadian dependence on the United States. The culmination of the review of foreign policy begun in 1968, secretary of state for external affairs MITCHELL SHARP's paper, "Canada-U.S. Relations: Options for the Future" (1972) rejected the status quo and closer integration and proclaimed a third option that would, Sharp maintained, strengthen Canadian nationality and reduce the country's vulnerability by

trade diversification abroad, industrial specialization at home, and increased self-sufficiency. As a result Canada sought contractual links with the European Economic Community and Japan, but these ties failed to re-direct exports, and the proportion of Canadian trade with the United States continued to increase.

THODE, HENRY (1910–), scientist, educator. Born at Dundurn, Sask., Thode joined the faculty of McMaster Univ. in 1939. During World War II he did research on atomic energy under the auspices of the NATIONAL RESEARCH COUNCIL and he was a moving force behind the establishment of a nuclear research reactor at McMaster in 1957.

Sir John Thompson

courtesy National Archives of Canada/C-8650

THOMPSON, SIR JOHN SPARROW DAVID (1845-94), prime minister of Canada. Born at Halifax and trained as a lawyer, Thompson began his political career as a Halifax alderman in 1871. Six years later he entered provincial politics as a Conservative MLA and served as Attorney General from 1878 to 1882 and, briefly, as premier in 1882. When his government lost the election in that year, he was made a judge of the Nova Scotia Supreme Court.

With an able legal mind, Thompson suffered under the stigma of having converted from Methodism to Roman Catholicism, a major issue in that sectarian era. His wife Annie was a Catholic, and his conversion occurred shortly after their 1870 marriage. Nonetheless, a "pervert" (in the phrase of the day) or not, SIR JOHN A. MACDONALD persuaded him to enter the Conservative cabinet as minister of justice in 1885, and Thompson quickly became the right-hand man. Although he was the logical successor when the Old Chief died in 1891, Thompson yielded to Senator J.J.C. ABBOTT to avoid inflaming religious controversy. The next year, however, Thompson took over as prime minister on 24 Nov. Although the country was wracked by the MANITOBA SCHOOLS QUESTION, the affable and courteous Thompson kept his government under control and continued to win by-elections. Whether he could have defeated WILFRID LAURIER and the LIBERAL PARTY must remain moot for on 12 Dec. 1894, while at Windsor Castle to be sworn in as member of the imperial Privy Council, Thompson died of a heart attack. Without him, the Conservatives fell apart and Laurier won the 1896 election.

THOMPSON, ROBERT NORMAN (1914–), politician, teacher. Thompson, born at Duluth, Minn., came to Canada in 1918. Educated at the Univ. of British Columbia, he taught school and practised chiropractic before serving with the air force from 1941 to 1943. He then taught school in Ethiopia, became minister of education in the imperial Ethiopian government (1947-51) and director of the Sudan Interior Mission. Shortly after returning to Canada, he was elected leader of the Social Credit Assn of Canada and in 1961 leader of the SOCIAL CREDIT PARTY. Elected to the House of Commons in 1962, his party, with RÉAL CAOUETTE as deputy leader, held the balance of power in Parliament. Ineffective as leader, Thompson is best remembered for his marvellous malapropisms.

THOMPSON, THOMAS PHILLIPS (1843-1933), labour journalist and theoretician. Born in England, Thompson was based in Ontario in the latter decades of the 19th century. He supported the KNIGHTS OF LABOR in the 1880s and published *The Politics of Labor*, one of the few labour critiques of the capitalist system to emerge in Canada before the 20th century.

THOMSON, KENNETH (1923–), businessman. Born in Toronto, he is the son of ROY THOMSON

and succeeded his father as head of the Thomson media empire in 1976. In 1979 he engineered the acquisition of F.P. Publications and the HUDSON'S BAY CO.

THOMSON, ROY HERBERT, BARON THOMSON OF FLEET (1894-1976), newspaper publisher. From humble beginnings, Thomson built an enormous newspaper empire. He began buying small radio stations and newspapers in northern Ontario and eventually controlled hundreds of newspapers in Canada, the United States, and England, including the *The Times* of London. The tight-fisted tycoon was also involved in magazines, travel agencies, television, and later oil exploration. Elevated to the peerage in 1963, he died at London, Eng.

courtesy J. Thomas/National Archives of Canada/C-17399

Tom Thomson

THOMSON, THOMAS JOHN (1877-1917), painter. Largely self-taught, Tom Thomson drew his inspiration from the typical Ontarian scenes of Algonquin Park where his sketches and paintings of wind-swept pines, lakes, and rocks inspired the founders of the GROUP OF SEVEN. Born in Claremont, Ont., he worked as an engraver in Seattle and Toronto, finding his talent in the latter city where he established a small but growing reputation as a passionate artist. He drowned in 1917 in Algonquin Park.

THORNTON, SIR HENRY WORTH (1871-1933), railway executive. Born in Indiana, Thornton worked for the Pennsylvania Railroad until in 1914 he went to England to become general manager of the Great Eastern Railway. Prime Minister MACKENZIE KING named him president of the CANADIAN NATIONAL RAILWAYS in 1922, and Thornton helped establish the new government line on a firm footing. By the onset of the GREAT DEPRESSION, however, the CNR was in difficulty, and Thornton, under attack from the government of R.B. BENNETT, resigned in 1932.

courtesy Topley/National Archives of Canada/C-10436

Sir Samuel Tilley

TILLEY, SIR SAMUEL LEONARD (1818-96), politician. Born at Gagetown, N.B., Tilley entered politics at the beginning of the 1850s. Active in promoting both railways and CONFEDERATION, Tilley attended the CHARLOTTETOWN CONFERENCE and the QUEBEC CONFERENCE and was named customs minister in SIR JOHN A. MACDONALD's first government. In 1873 he became lieutenant governor of New Brunswick, a position he held only until Macdonald returned to power in 1878 when Tilley became, as finance minister, the man who introduced the NATIONAL POLICY. In 1885, Macdonald made him lieutenant governor once more, and he held that post until 1893. *See also* FATHERS OF CONFEDERATION.

TIMMINS, NOAH ANTHONY (1867-1936), mining executive. Born in Mattawa, Canada West, he was involved in developing a number of mining projects in Ontario. The town of Timmins was named after him to honour his service to the industry. His most notable accomplishments included the development of the La Rose silver mine and the giant Hollinger Gold Mines. He became president of Hollinger and was an avid promoter of the Noranda-Hollinger copper mine project in Quebec.

TOLMIE, SIMON FRASER (1867-1937), premier of British Columbia. Born at Victoria, B.C., Tolmie attended the Ontario Veterinary College and joined the federal public service, eventually becoming chief of livestock inspection. He first won election in 1917 as a supporter of UNION GOVERNMENT and served as agriculture minister under Prime Ministers BORDEN and MEIGHEN. In 1926 he became provincial Conservative leader in B.C. and won the 1928 election. His government was undistinguished in coping with the depression and was soundly thrashed by T.D. PATTULLO in 1933.

TORONTO-DOMINION BANK, created in 1955 with the merger of the Bank of Toronto and the Dominion Bank of Canada. The Bank of Toronto was chartered in 1853 by a group of Ontario millers, and for most of the 19th century it was dominated by the families of James Worts and William Gooderham, brothers-in-law and partners in the milling and distilling business. The Dominion Bank, chartered in 1869, took over the assets of a failed predecessor and tended to confine its activities to the Toronto area. By the mid-20th century the Toronto-Dominion had become one of Canada's five largest chartered banks.

TORONTO EIGHTEEN, prominent group of Toronto Liberal businessmen who opposed Prime Minister SIR WILFRID LAURIER's proposed RECIPROCITY treaty with the United States in 1911 because they feared that it was the first step towards annexation and a threat to their business interests. The eighteen issued a manifesto against reciprocity and one, SIR BYRON EDMUND WALKER, declared: "although a Liberal, I am an Imperialist."

TORONTO ELECTRIC COMMISSIONERS V. *SNIDER*, labour-related court case brought to the JUDICIAL COMMITTEE OF THE PRIVY COUNCIL in 1925 in which the JCPC decided that the INDUSTRIAL DISPUTES INVESTIGATION ACT of 1907 was unconstitutional because it impinged on provincial jurisdiction. The federal government then re-enacted the IDIA to apply only to workers directly under federal jurisdiction. It is a landmark case because it placed the primary responsibility for labour law on the provinces.

TORONTO PRINTERS' STRIKE, strike of Toronto printers in 1872 against a number of Toronto print shops and newspapers led by the *Globe*, owned by GEORGE BROWN. The strike began with a demand for increased pay by the Toronto Typographical Union in the form of a reduced work day but with wages unchanged. The TTU received strong support from organized labour in Toronto but the employers, spearheaded by Brown, instigated the arrest of the leaders for having formed a union illegally. Prime Minister JOHN A. MACDONALD saw a chance to embarrass Brown, a Liberal, and secure worker votes and introduced the TRADE UNIONS ACT which legalized unions.

TORONTO STOCK EXCHANGE, opened on 24 Oct. 1852, and reorganized in 1861 listing chartered bank, trading company, and Hudson's Bay Co. securities. The Ontario legislature granted it official recognition in 1878. Although it suffered from the 1929 stock market crash, it remained open for business throughout the GREAT DEPRESSION. In 1934 the exchange amalgamated with the Standard Stock and Mining Exchange and three years later opened for business at its famous though no longer current BAY STREET address. The Toronto Stock Exchange is the largest in Canada.

TORONTO TRADES ASSEMBLY, labour organization formed in 1871 when local unions banded together. The Assembly was active in the NINE-HOUR MOVEMENT which aimed to secure a maximum working day of nine hours for Canadian workers. The Trades Assembly supported the TORONTO PRINTERS' STRIKE in 1872 and twice tried to form national labour organizations, the CANADIAN LABOR UNION in 1873 and the CANADIAN LABOUR CONGRESS in 1883.

TORY, HENRY MARSHALL (1864-1947), educator. Born at Shoreham, N.S., he studied at McGill Univ. and taught mathematics there. In 1905, he went to British Columbia to examine McGill's affiliated colleges in Vancouver and Victoria, and his efforts helped lead to the establishment of the Univ. of British Columbia three years later. In 1908, he was named president of the Univ. of Alberta, and during World War I he ran the Khaki Univ. overseas. Named in 1923 to the NATIONAL RESEARCH COUNCIL which he had helped to create, Tory became its chair and in 1928 its president, a post he held until 1935. He was largely responsible for creating the NRC's vigorous laboratories. During World War II, he headed the drive to create Carleton College in Ottawa.

TORY, colloquial term for a member of the CONSERVATIVE PARTY. Of Irish origin, the term was widely used in British politics from the late 17th century and has continued to be applied to the British Conservative party. It began to be used for Canadian Conservatives in the 19th century.

TOWERS, GRAHAM FORD (1897-1975), banker, public servant. Born at Ottawa, he served in World War I and graduated from McGill Univ. in 1919. He joined the Royal Bank of Canada, becoming assistant general manager in 1933. Appointed first governor of the Bank of Canada by Prime Minister R.B. BENNETT in 1934, Towers wielded tremendous influence over the development of Canadian monetary and economic policy. He played a major role in the tangled federal-provincial scene and in the 1937 appointment of the ROYAL COMMISSION ON DOMINION-PROVINCIAL RELATIONS. During World War II, Towers was one of the key bureaucratic MANDARINS running Canada's vastly expanded economy and international dealings. He retired as governor in 1954.

TOWN, HAROLD BARLING (1924–), artist. Town, born at Toronto, was educated at the Ontario College of Art. He worked as an illustrator for various magazines before holding his first exhibition in Toronto in 1954. He was a member of the Painters Eleven, a group which exhibited from 1954 to 1960. An artist of many talents. Town has painted abstracts, murals and portraits, sculpted, produced collages and prints, and illustrated books. He has also written books on TOM THOMSON and ALBERT FRANCK.

TRADE UNIONS ACT, labour law passed by the federal parliament in 1872 following the TORONTO PRINTERS' STRIKE. The act legalized unions which had previously been considered illegal combinations in restraint of trade under the common law.

TRADES AND LABOUR CONGRESS OF CANADA, labour organization founded in 1883 as the Canadian Labour Congress; its name was changed to Trades and Labour Congress in 1886. Until 1902 the TLC aimed to be an all-inclusive union federation and invited both craft and non-craft unions to affiliate. Most of the latter were KNIGHTS OF LABOR affiliates. In 1902, at the BERLIN CONVENTION, the American-affiliated craft unions succeeded in forcing the TLC to become a branch of the American Federation of Labor. Resolutions passed at that meeting had the effect of expelling any Canadian unions that duplicated the efforts of United States unions affiliated to the AFL. The TLC was again wracked by internal divisions in the late 1930s when the AFL forced it to expel unions such as the United Auto Workers which were affiliated to the Committee (later Congress) of Industrial Organizations in the United States. When the rival AFL and CIO organizations began to discuss a merger in the early 1950s, the TLC and the CANADIAN CONGRESS OF LABOUR followed suit and in 1956 the CANADIAN LABOUR CONGRESS was established.

TRANS-ATLANTIC FERRY SERVICE, service bringing aircraft and aircrew to Great Britain from Canada during WORLD WAR II. First proposed by MAX AITKEN, it was operated by CANADIAN PACIFIC AIRLINES. The system proved to be fast and efficient and greatly aided the Allied war effort.

TRANS-CANADA AIRLINES, *see* AIR CANADA

TRANS-CANADA HIGHWAY, federally funded highway linking Canada from Atlantic to Pacific. Work on the highway began in the early 1950s and the project was formally opened in ROGERS PASS in 1957. It was not totally paved for at least another decade. Much of the highway is an obsolete, two-lane road, but several provinces have begun projects to create a divided highway.

TRANS-CANADA TELEPHONE SYSTEM, system formed by Canadian telephone companies in 1931 as the first all-Canadian long-distance service. Member telephone companies across Canada cooperated in this voluntary association to provide long-distance service and to coordinate long-distance policies. Member companies manage the system and cooperate with the CANADIAN RADIO-TELEVISION AND TELECOMMUNICATIONS COMMISSION. *See also* TELESAT CANADA; ANIK A-1.

TREASURY BRANCHES, provincial banks chartered by the government of Alberta. They were formed in the late 1930s by the SOCIAL CREDIT government of Premier WILLIAM ABERHART to carry out the SOCIAL CREDIT philosophy as espoused by Major C.H. DOUGLAS, but they have always operated strictly as provincially chartered banks.

courtesy National Archives of Canada/C-2422

Sir John A. Macdonald with British High Commissioners discussing the Treaty of Washington, 1871

TREATY OF WASHINGTON, 1871, treaty signed between Britain and the United States and designed to resolve issues arising out of the U.S. Civil War, including the ALABAMA AFFAIR. SIR JOHN A. MACDONALD was one of five British commissioners but Canadian aims were largely ignored. The United States refused to consider Canadian claims for losses caused by raids by the FENIANS, the Americans won the San Juan Islands in the Straits of Georgia in an arbitration, and the United States was given access to the Canadian east coast inshore fisheries for 12 years, Canada getting free access to the American market for its fish and $5.5 million in return. The unsatisfactory result led many Canadians to conclude that Britain would always sacrifice Canadian interests for the sake of U.S. friendship; the logic suggested that Canada had to handle its own foreign relations, an aim realized a half-century later when the HALIBUT TREATY was negotiated.

TREMBLAY, MICHEL (1942–), playwright. Born at Montreal, he attended the Institut des arts graphique and worked as a linotype operator from 1963 to 1966. His first play, *Le Train*, appeared in 1964 and won a Radio-Canada prize. Since then Tremblay has won many awards, including the 1972 CHALMERS Award for the play *A toi, pour toujours, ta Marie-Lou*, and France's Prix Victor-Morin in 1974. Although critics have placed him in the theatre of realism, he has often utilized anti-realism and comedy. His work is popular in both English and French Canada.

TRUDEAU, PIERRE ELLIOTT (1919–), prime minister of Canada. Born in Montreal into a wealthy family, he had the best of educations at Collège Jean de Brébeuf, the Univ. de Montréal, Harvard Univ., and the London School of Economics. As a youth, he was caught up in the nationalist and anti-conscriptionist fervor of the World War II years, but his education, globe-trotting travels, and deep intelligence gradually turned him into one who saw serious dangers in nationalism, and not only in Quebec. At the time the UNION NATIONALE government of MAURICE DUPLESSIS held Quebec in tight control, and in 1949 Trudeau played a major role in the ASBESTOS STRIKE that challenged the regime. After brief service in the Privy Council Office in Ottawa (1949-51), Trudeau returned to Montreal, helped found *CITÉ LIBRE*, an intellectual journal that challenged Duplessis and his authoritarianism, and worked to defeat the Union nationale. The victory of JEAN LESAGE and the Liberals in 1960 unleashed the QUIET REVOLUTION, and through television appearances and his writings Trudeau soon found himself resisting the nationalism and nascent SEPARATISM of former allies such as RENÉ LÉVESQUE.

In 1965, with his friends JEAN MARCHAND and GÉRARD PELLETIER, Trudeau ran for the federal Liberals, won, and was named parliamentary secretary to Prime Minister LESTER PEARSON. A new toughness towards Quebec quickly began to appear in the federal government's negotiating positions, something that was confirmed when Trudeau became minister of justice in 1967. Ottawa was defending the federal position with vigour. Trudeau also pushed through a major reform of the Criminal Code, and he won national attention with his remark that "the state has no place in the bedrooms of the nation."

When Pearson announced his retirement in Dec. 1967, Trudeau was persuaded to enter the race for the succession. His style, charm, and intelligence captivated the intellectuals, the media, and eventually the public, and he won the convention's accolade narrowly. In a quickly called election, he captured a comfortable majority. His government undertook a sweeping review of foreign policy and reduced the Canadian military contribution to NATO by half. It passed the OFFICIAL LANGUAGES ACT and began, among other efforts, to give Canada a truly bilingual public service. Trudeau acted with toughness in 1970 when James Cross, a British diplomat, and PIERRE LAPORTE, a Quebec cabinet minister, were kidnapped and the latter murdered by the FRONT DE LIBÉRATION DU QUEBEC in the OCTOBER CRISIS. He implemented the WAR MEASURES ACT and used troops to control the situation. The immediate public response was virtually unanimous in his support, although many soon were worried by the seeming disregard for civil rights. By the election of 1972, Trudeau was widely viewed as arrogant and uncaring, and he won only a minority victory.

From 1972 to 1974, Trudeau remained dependent on the support of the NEW DEMOCRATIC PARTY in the House, and his government, spending freely and passing popular legislation, rebounded in popular support. In 1974, he won another election, this time with a majority, although much of his renewed popularity was quickly forfeited when, in an effort to control soaring inflation, he imposed wage and price controls against which he had campaigned during the election. The economic crisis was compounded in Nov. 1976 when René Lévesque's PARTI QUÉBÉCOIS defeated the Quebec Liberals of ROBERT BOURASSA. An avowedly separatist government was in power, a direct challenge to Trudeau and his federal policies. At the same time, Trudeau's 1971 marriage to Margaret Sinclair was in the midst of an agonizing public break-up; separation came in 1977 and divorce in 1984, with Trudeau gaining custody of the couple's three boys.

In the 1979 election, Trudeau's government lost to JOE CLARK's Conservatives who formed a minority government. Trudeau himself announced his resignation from politics but, before a leadership convention could be organized, Clark's government was defeated in the House, and Trudeau was prevailed on by most of his colleagues to lead the Liberals in the election. Astonishingly, he won the election of 18 Feb. 1980 with a majority, completing an unprecedented comeback. In office once more, Trudeau intervened with crushing force in the QUEBEC REFERENDUM of May 1980, and contributed largely to the defeat of the Parti Québécois' SOV- EREIGNTY-ASSOCIATION proposals. Also decisive was the provincial consent he finally secured for the CANADIAN CHARTER OF RIGHTS AND FREEDOMS and the patriation of the CONSTITUTION in 1982, a victory achieved through a tough-minded policy. Trudeau's last government was also uncharacteristically nationalistic, as shown by the NATIONAL ENERGY PROGRAM, and internationalist, as demonstrated by his "peace mission" of late 1983 that sought to ease Soviet-American tensions. On 29 Feb. 1984, Trudeau announced his intention to retire, and in June a party convention chose JOHN TURNER as his successor.

Admired and hated, Trudeau remained an enigma to most Canadians and Québécois. His powerful intellect, however, was as much a rarity in Canadian politics as were his anti-nationalist convictions.

TRUDEAUMANIA, public hysteria generated by the appearance of PIERRE TRUDEAU. Although relatively unknown when he decided to seek the Liberal leadership in 1968, Trudeau was a marked change from previous Canadian politicians. Athletic, sexy, and clearly someone who enjoyed female company, Trudeau attracted the sort of squealing fans at the convention and during the subsequent election that had hitherto been confined to rock concerts. The phrase has subsequently come to suggest a collective lack of sense or a willing suspension of disbelief.

TUPPER, SIR CHARLES (1821-1915), prime minister of Canada. Born at Amherst, N.S., and educated in that province and in Scotland as a medical doctor, he first won election to the provincial assembly in 1855 as a Conservative.

Sir Charles Tupper

courtesy Lancefield Abell Co./National Archives of Canada/C-690

After twice serving in the cabinet, he became provincial premier in 1864 as a champion of CONFEDERATION, but he could not win the support of his legislature. Elected in 1867 to Parliament as Nova Scotia's solitary supporter of the new union, he helped negotiate "better terms" for his province in 1869. In 1870 he entered the cabinet of SIR JOHN A. MACDONALD and, as a capable administrator, served in a variety of posts until in 1884 he became HIGH COMMISSIONER to Great Britain, a post he gave up in 1887 to become minister of finance for a year. He then spent eight more years in London until, in 1896, with the Conservative party threatened with break-up over the MANITOBA SCHOOLS QUESTION and sectarian disputes, he returned to Ottawa and on 1 May became prime minister. Tupper introduced remedial legislation in an effort to protect the schooling rights of Manitoba's Catholics, but his effort went for naught when the bill was talked out in the House and Parliament dissolved. In the subsequent election, Tupper campaigned vigorously, but fell before WILFRID LAURIER and the Liberals. His term of office had lasted just 10 weeks. Tupper remained leader of the opposition until 1901 when he passed the reins to ROBERT BORDEN and retired to Vancouver.

TURNBULL, WALLACE (1870-1954), aeronautical engineer. Turnbull was born at Saint John,

N.B., and studied engineering in the United States and Germany. His interest in aeronautical research began early and he was awarded a medal from the Royal Aeronautical Society in 1909. His greatest contribution to aviation was his invention of the variable-pitch propeller in 1922.

TURNER, JOHN NAPIER (1929–), prime minister of Canada. Born in England, Turner came with his mother to Canada at the age of three. Educated in Ottawa, he moved to British Columbia at the end of World War II, and attended university in Vancouver, at Oxford as a Rhodes scholar, and at the Univ. de Paris. Turner joined a Montreal law firm in 1954 and was first elected to the House of Commons as a Liberal in 1962. LESTER PEARSON brought him into the cabinet in 1965, and, in the leadership convention of 1968, he ran well but lost to PIERRE TRUDEAU. Trudeau appointed him justice minister in 1968 and minister of finance in 1972. In the 1972-4 minority government, Trudeau and Turner catered to the NEW DEMOCRATIC PARTY and lowered taxes and increased spending. After the 1974 election, the screws were tightened, but Turner suddenly and without explanation resigned from the ministry in Sept. 1975 and the House six months later. Out of Parliament and in a Toronto law firm, he became a focus of Liberal opposition to Trudeau. In 1984 when Trudeau finally announced his resignation as party leader, Turner mounted a disorganized but nonetheless successful campaign for the succession. He became prime minister on 30 June, instantly plunged into a patronage morass, and dissolved Parliament on 9 July. In the election that followed, Turner's reputation as a speaker and organizer collapsed, as did the Liberal campaign after Turner's poor performance in nationally televised debates. BRIAN MULRONEY and the Progressive Conservative party scored a massive victory, and Turner, who won his own seat in Vancouver, was now opposition leader. Turner stayed on, defeated his opposition in the party, and saw his standing rise in the opinion polls as Mulroney's tumbled. But he seemed unable to get his fractious caucus and party to find new policies, he faced substantial criticism because of his support for the MEECH LAKE ACCORD and opposition to FREE TRADE, and his hold on the Liberal party by 1988 seemed tenuous.

TURNER VALLEY, located approximately 40 km southwest of Calgary, and the site of the Dingman well which opened Alberta's first oil boom in 1914. *See also* LEDUC.

TYRRELL, JOSEPH BURR (1858-1957), geologist. Born at Weston, Canada West, Tyrrell joined the GEOLOGICAL SURVEY OF CANADA in 1881. He explored much of what is now south central Alberta including the coal fields and fossil deposits around Drumheller. He edited the diaries of explorers Samuel Hearne and David Thompson.

UKRAINIAN LABOUR FARMER TEMPLE ASSN, leftist organization formed in 1925 from the Ukrainian Workers' Temple Assn. The ULFTA was a COMMUNIST PARTY front, the only Ukrainian-Canadian organization to condone the deliberately created famine in the Ukraine in the early 1930s. Rivalry with the Ukrainian Canadian Citizens' Committee, a nationalist and right-wing organization, was sharp. The ULFTA was banned by Ottawa under the DEFENCE OF CANADA REGULATIONS in June 1940, and many of its members were interned. The Ukrainian Canadian Committee, formed with government encouragement in Nov. 1940, united Canadian Ukrainian organizations behind the war effort; it still exists in 1988.

ULTRAMONTANISM, religious and political ideology that was originally a phenomenon of European church politics which pitted national Catholics against those who took their political cues from Rome. In Quebec, ultramontanists looked to the bishops for political as well as spiritual leadership. They allied themselves with the Conservative party, attacked Liberals for being anti-clerical and pro-republican, and advocated an active role for the church in Canadian and Quebec politics. They were opposed by Liberals such as WILFRID LAURIER who warned that a church-Conservative alliance would force the numerically superior Protestants to form an exclusive secular party of their own, thus permanently denying power to French Canada. *See also* CASTORS.

ULTRA VIRES, legal term to describe a law judged outside the constitutional jurisdiction of the body that passed it.

UNDERHILL, FRANK HAWKINS (1889-1971), historian. He was educated at the univs. of Toronto and Oxford. Service in World War I left him with an abiding distaste for war. He taught at the Univ. of Saskatchewan until moving to the Univ. of Toronto in 1927, where he became a great teacher and pursued many outside interests. He wrote often for CANADIAN FORUM, was the first president of the LEAGUE FOR SOCIAL RECONSTRUCTION, and wrote the first draft of the CO-OPERATIVE COMMONWEALTH FEDERATION'S REGINA MANIFESTO. In 1940 he was nearly dismissed from the university for stating the obvious truth that Canada's ties with the United States would grow stronger while those with Britain would weaken. A self-proclaimed enemy of the establishment, Underhill nevertheless supported the Cold War, and in 1955 became curator of Laurier House, the late MACKENZIE KING's Ottawa residence. His only book, *In Search of Canadian Liberalism*, was published in 1960.

UNEMPLOYMENT INSURANCE, federal program introduced by the Liberal government of Prime Minister MACKENZIE KING in 1940 following amendment of the BRITISH NORTH AMERICA ACT to give Ottawa the power to create such a scheme. There had been demands for one since early in the GREAT DEPRESSION but court decisions rendered in the 1920s indicated that Ottawa did not have the constitutional power. In 1935 Conservative Prime Minister R.B. BENNETT introduced the Employment and Social Insurance Act as part of his New Deal, but that act was struck down by the JUDICIAL COMMITTEE OF THE PRIVY COUNCIL. In 1940, unanimous consent was finally reached between Ottawa and the provinces on the introduction of the program. *See also* BENNETT NEW DEAL.

UNEMPLOYMENT INSURANCE COMMISSION, federal agency, established in 1941, to administer UNEMPLOYMENT INSURANCE. In 1976 UIC and the Department of Manpower and Immigration merged.

UNIFICATION, term used for the 1968 amalgamation of the three armed services into one force. The Canadian Forces Reorganization Act, proclaimed on 1 Feb. 1968, abolished the CANADIAN ARMY, ROYAL CANADIAN NAVY, and ROYAL CANADIAN AIR FORCE, creating a single CANADIAN ARMED FORCES. Canada was the only country to go this route and had done so on the insistence of defence minister PAUL HELLYER who was convinced that triplication led to waste and inefficiency.

UNION GOVERNMENT, term applied to the Conservative-Liberal coalition during WORLD WAR I created in autumn 1917. Prime Minister SIR ROBERT BORDEN announced in May 1917 that his government was going to introduce CONSCRIPTION and then approached Liberal leader SIR WILFRID LAURIER with a proposal to form a coalition government to get support for the measure. Laurier refused, but after the government passed the WARTIME ELECTIONS ACT and the MILITARY VOTERS' ACT many English-speaking Liberals broke with Laurier and joined a Union Government under Borden. The Union Government won the 1917 federal election, became extremely unpopular, and effectively died when Borden retired in 1920.

UNION NATIONALE, political party created when MAURICE DUPLESSIS and his Conservative party joined PAUL GOUIN and the ACTION LIBÉRALE NATIONALE to fight the 1935 Quebec provincial election. The party lost the election but returned, under Duplessis, to win the next year. It was again defeated in 1939 but won the 1944 election and governed Quebec until Duplessis died in 1959. He was succeeded by PAUL SAUVÉ who died in Jan. 1960. The UN lost the 1960 election to the Liberals under JEAN LESAGE and has held office only once since (1966-70).

UNITED FARMERS OF ALBERTA, farm organization formed in 1909 to promote measures to benefit farmers, such as the establishment of the UNITED GRAIN GROWERS, a cooperative elevator company. Although UFA leader HENRY WISE WOOD initially opposed taking independent political action, the organization entered the 1921 provincial election and won a sweeping victory. Wood refused to become premier, and HERBERT GREENFIELD was chosen instead and was succeeded by J.E. BROWNLEE (1925-34). Although the

UFA promised sweeping reforms, it was a conservative party inclined against government interventionism. For example, it refused to introduce the GROUP GOVERNMENT reforms that Wood championed. In 1935 it was defeated by the ALBERTA SOCIAL CREDIT LEAGUE, led by WILLIAM A. ABERHART. *See also* NON-PARTISAN LEAGUE.

UNITED FARMERS OF CANADA (SASKAT-CHEWAN SECTION), farm organization established in 1926 by the Saskatchewan Grain Growers' Assn and the Farmers' Union of Canada. The UFC (SS), the most militant of the prairie farm organizations, entered politics in 1931 and supported the formation of the CO-OPERATIVE COMMONWEALTH FEDERATION in 1932.

UNITED FARMERS OF MANITOBA, farm organization formed in 1920 to replace the Manitoba Grain Growers' Assn. The UFM supported farm candidates running under the PROGRESSIVE PARTY banner in the 1920 provincial election and the 1921 federal election. *See also* JOHN BRACKEN.

UNITED FARMERS OF ONTARIO, farm organization founded in 1914. The fears of the effects of rural depopulation in a period of urbanization were behind the UFO's move into provincial politics in 1919. The UFO was unprepared when it won most seats in the election that year, and offered the premiership first to SIR ADAM BECK, head of ONTARIO HYDRO. Eventually, E.C. DRURY was named premier and formed a coalition with the INDEPENDENT LABOUR PARTY OF ONTARIO but his government fell apart by 1923 owing to internal divisions.

UNITED GRAIN GROWERS LTD, a farmer-owned elevator cooperative formed in 1917 when two Alberta cooperative elevator companies amalgamated. The UGG soon expanded out of the province and, at one time, owned a lumber company in British Columbia.

UNITED NATIONS, world organization, founded at the end of WORLD WAR II. The United Nations initially embodied the hopes of a war-weary globe for peace. The Canadian government of MACKENZIE KING and its extraordinarily able crew of diplomats, led by NORMAN ROBERTSON, LESTER PEARSON, and HUME WRONG, played an important role in shaping the organization's charter

and in carving out a place for a MIDDLE POWER like Canada. The UN quickly got caught up in the Cold War (not least during the KOREAN WAR), ending the idealistic hopes it had engendered, though supporters still praise its role in PEACEKEEPING and in a variety of technical agencies.

UNITED NATIONS EMERGENCY FORCE, force set up to separate the Egyptian and Israeli-French-British forces after the 1956 war. Created by a UN resolution moved by LESTER PEARSON on 4 Nov. 1956, UNEF consisted of several national contingents, including a Canadian one, and was initially commanded by General E.L.M. BURNS. Just prior to the 1967 Arab-Israeli War, the Canadian contingent was unceremoniously ordered out of Egypt by President Nasser, action that hurt support for PEACEKEEPING in Canada.

UNITED PROVINCE OF CANADA, official name for the union of Upper and Lower Canada (Ontario and Quebec) that existed from 1841 to 1867. Partly as a result of the 1837-8 rebellions, UPPER CANADA and LOWER CANADA were united by Britain in the Act of Union, assented to in June 1840, which came into force in Feb. 1841. One government was created with equal representation from CANADA WEST (formerly Upper Canada) and CANADA EAST (Lower Canada) in the Legislative Assembly, despite the greater population of Canada East. The hope of the British government was that the French Canadians would eventually be assimilated. When the population of Canada West passed that of Canada East in the 1850s, politicians in Canada West, especially the CLEAR GRITS, began to demand "REP-BY-POP" or representation by population. This demand was one factor behind the move to CONFEDERATION.

UPPER CANADA, name of the British colony centred on present-day Ontario from 1791 to 1841. In 1841 the name was changed to CANADA WEST and in 1867 to Ontario. *See also* UNITED PROVINCE OF CANADA.

VALLIÈRES, PIERRE (1938–), writer, political activist. Born in the working-class district of Montreal, Vallières wrote for *Le Devoir* and *CITÉ LIBRE*, which he edited for a time. In 1966 he was arrested for demonstrating on behalf of the FRONT DE LIBÉRATION DU QUÉBEC, a terrorist organization, at the United Nations in New York. While serving time in the Manhattan House of Detention for Men he wrote much of *Nègres blancs d'Amérique*, published in 1968, and in English in 1971 as *White Niggers of America*. After spending another four years in jail for his FLQ activities, in 1971 he moved towards the PARTI QUÉBÉCOIS, the subject of *L'Urgence de choisir* (1971). Latterly, he has worked as a federal civil servant.

VANCOUVER ISLAND COAL STRIKE, 1913-14, *see* NANAIMO COAL STRIKE

VANCOUVER SIT-IN, demonstration by unemployed workers in Vancouver in June 1938. Demanding relief, they occupied the Vancouver post office and remained there until cleared out by police using tear gas and truncheons.

courtesy Notman Photographic Archives

Sir William Van Horne

VAN HORNE, SIR WILLIAM CORNELIUS (1843-1915), railway executive. Born in Chelsea, Ill., Van Horne gained his railway experience in the United States before accepting a position as general manager for the struggling CANADIAN PACIFIC RAILWAY in 1882. He was a driving force during the construction of the line and later, as

CPR president, he continued to provide leadership and direction. He was responsible for the formation of the CANADIAN PACIFIC STEAMSHIP CO. and Canadian Pacific Hotels, and he was involved in negotiation of the CROW'S NEST PASS AGREEMENT.

courtesy NFB

Georges Vanier

VANIER, GEORGES-PHILÉAS (1888-1967), soldier, diplomat, governor general of Canada. Born in Montreal, Vanier was educated at Loyola College and Univ. Laval and was called to the bar in 1911. He joined the Royal 22ᵉ Régiment in 1915 and served with great distinction in France and Flanders, winning the Military Cross and Distinguished Service Order and losing a leg. After post-war military service, he joined the Department of External Affairs, representing Canada at conferences and in London before becoming minister to France in 1943. During World War II, he served in the army once more and after 1943 as minister to the exiled governments sheltered in London. He returned to his Paris post after the liberation and served there until 1953.

In 1959, Prime Minister JOHN DIEFENBAKER made him governor general, a post he filled until his death. As a wartime comrade of General de Gaulle, Vanier was saddened by the general's exploitation of SEPARATISM in his home province. Gallant soldier that he was, he remained in office as an example of service and dedication, a role in which he was assisted by his wife Pauline.

VARLEY, FREDERICK HORSMAN (1881-1969), painter. A member of the GROUP OF SEVEN,

Varley immigrated to Canada from England in 1912 and began working as a commercial illustrator in Toronto. Commissioned as a war artist towards the end of World War I, he won acclaim for his portraits and war scenes. He taught at the Vancouver School of Decorative and Applied Art from 1926 until 1933, when he and J.W.G. Macdonald opened the B.C. College of Art. Returning east to teach near Kitchener in 1948-9, he thereafter travelled around Canada. Varley's paintings are renowned for their draftmanship, colour, unusual vantage points, and later for the use of form.

VAUGHAN, ROBERT CHARLES (1883-1966), railway executive. Born at Toronto, Vaughan began as a messenger. In 1902 he joined the CANADIAN NORTHERN RAILWAY, rising to vice-president and president of CANADIAN NATIONAL RAILWAYS (1941-50). During World War II he served as chairman of the Defence Purchasing Board.

VERIGIN, PETER VASILEVICH (1859-1924), DOUKHOBOR leader. He came to Canada in 1903 on the heels of 7000 followers admitted in 1898-9. They settled in the Kootenay region of British Columbia, where Verigin sought to create a self-supporting and self-governing commune dedicated to the doctrines of Leo Tolstoy, the Christian anarchist novelist. The Doukhobor community broke up after Verigin's death in a train explosion, but many small communities still practise his doctrines.

VÉZINA, GEORGES (1887-1926), hockey player. He played goal for the Montreal Canadiens from 1910 to 1925. Known as "The Chicoutimi Cucumber," he displayed remarkable coolness in the nets, once stopping 78 shots in a game. He collapsed during a game in 1925 and died of tuberculosis four months later. In 1926-7 the Canadiens donated the Vezina Trophy to honour the NHL goalkeeper with the lowest goals-against average.

VIA RAIL, crown corporation established by the Liberal government of Prime Minister PIERRE TRUDEAU in 1978 to take over most of the passenger-carrying responsibilities of CANADIAN NATIONAL RAILWAYS and CANADIAN PACIFIC RAILWAY. It operates inter-city passenger traffic in Canada using the rails and facilities of the two major railways. Via Rail was intended to revive rail passenger service by taking it out of the hands of companies clearly not interested in it because of the heavy losses it entailed.

VICTORIA CHARTER, constitutional changes agreed to by Ottawa and the premiers at Victoria, B.C., in June 1971. The charter contained a limited bill of rights, provision for French and English language rights, and an amending formula. After agreeing to the charter in Victoria, Quebec Premier ROBERT BOURASSA soon reversed himself, killing the agreement. *See also* PIERRE TRUDEAU.

VICTORIA DAY, national holiday established by Parliament in 1901 to be celebrated on Queen Victoria's birthday, 24 May. In 1952 it was fixed that it would be celebrated on the first Monday before 25 May. *See also* EMPIRE DAY.

Victory loan poster

VICTORY LOANS, loans floated by the federal government in World Wars I and II to help pay for the wars. The loans were designed to raise money from institutional investors and the general public and used a variety of approaches from the sale of Victory Bonds to War Savings Certificates and War Savings Stamps. Following World War II, many of the Victory Bonds were exchanged for Canada Savings Bonds, introduced by the government as another means of financing its debt.

VIGNEAULT, GILLES (1928–), singer-songwriter, poet. Well known at home and abroad, Vigneault, born at Natashquan, Que., attended Univ. Laval. In 1959 he founded and contributed to editions de l'arc and later formed his own record label, Le Nordet. As a singer, he has amazing rapport with his many audiences in Canada and throughout Europe. His 1965 hit "Mon Pays" became a Québécois and Canadian anthem, and there was widespread outrage when singer Patsy Gallant Americanized it.

VILLENEUVE, GILLES (1950-82), auto racer. Villeneuve, born at Berthierville, Que., began racing snowmobiles, winning the North American championship in 1971 and the Canadian title in 1973. He then entered Formula Ford racing, capturing the 1973 Quebec crown. After racing Formula Atlantic, he entered Can-Am and joined the Ferrari team on the world circuit. He won 6 of 67 races for Ferrari and in 1979 was second only to teammate Jody Scheckter as the world's best Grand Prix racer. He was killed while attempting to qualify for the Belgian Grand Prix.

VILLENEUVE, JEAN-MARIE-RODRIGUE (1883-1947), cardinal of the Roman Catholic Church. An Oblate priest, Villeneuve was born in Montreal and educated at the Univ. of Ottawa where he taught theology. In 1930, he was appointed bishop of Gravelbourg, Sask., in 1932 bishop of Quebec, and the next year cardinal. Although his sentiments were *nationaliste*, Villeneuve essentially supported the war effort of the MACKENZIE KING government, treading a delicate line as manpower pressures increased and CONSCRIPTION became a political issue during World War II.

VIMY RIDGE, BATTLE OF, captured by the CANADIAN CORPS, 9-14 April 1917. The long ridge was a key German defensive position, one that had resisted previous assaults. The Corps, commanded by General SIR JULIAN BYNG, trained for its assault with assiduity and, supported by a

courtesy National Archives of Canada/PA-1017

Machine gunners atop Vimy Ridge

massive artillery barrage, attacked with all four of its divisions on 9 April. The Germans were routed, suffering heavy losses. The victory cost the Canadians 10,602 casualties, but won them a reputation as shock troops.

VOICE, labour newspaper published in Winnipeg by Arthur W. Puttee. In 1918, the *Voice* was replaced as the city's labour newspaper by the *Western Labor News*, owned by the Winnipeg Trades and Labor Council.

VOLKOFF, BORIS VLADIMIROVICH (1900-74), dancer. The "Father of Canadian Ballet," Volkoff, a graduate of the Bolshoi dance school, immigrated to Toronto from Russia in 1929. In 1930 he founded the Boris Volkoff School of the Dance. His dancers represented Canada at the 1936 Berlin Olympiad, winning a Tanz-Spiele medal, and he choreographed skater BARBARA ANN SCOTT's routines. In 1951 he donated his studio and dancers to help the National Ballet of Canada.

WAFFLE, ironically named radical caucus within the NEW DEMOCRATIC PARTY. Led by Mel Watkins and James Laxer, the Waffle movement tried to press the NDP in the direction outlined in its Manifesto for an Independent Socialist Canada. Aggressively socialist and nationalistic, the Waffle ran Laxer as its leadership candidate in 1971 and placed him second to DAVID LEWIS. The NDP purged Waffle members, especially in Ontario, and the movement had largely disappeared by 1974.

WAGE AND PRICE CONTROLS, controls instituted by the federal government, generally during wartime. In Canada few such controls were introduced during WORLD WAR I owing to the government's inexperience with a total war effort and its ideological commitment to voluntarism during the first three years of the war. By 1918 Ottawa began to move closer to production quotas and price controls on consumer goods, but the war ended before a comprehensive program was put into place. During WORLD WAR II the government rapidly instituted comprehensive controls through the WARTIME PRICES AND TRADE BOARD and the NATIONAL WAR LABOUR BOARD. A limited wage and price control program was introduced by the Liberal government of Prime Minister PIERRE TRUDEAU between 1975 and 1978 to fight inflation. It was administered by the Anti-Inflation Board.

WAGNER, CLAUDE (1925-79), judge, politician. Born at Shawinigan, Que., Wagner served as a hard-line minister of justice in JEAN LESAGE's provincial Liberal government from 1964 to 1966. He became a judge of the Sessions Court in 1970 but returned to politics as a Conservative MP in 1972. He placed second to JOE CLARK at the 1976 Conservative federal leadership convention. In 1978 he became a senator.

WALKER, SIR BYRON EDMUND (1848-1924), banker. Born in Haldimand County, Canada West, Walker rose from clerk to president of the CANADIAN BANK OF COMMERCE. Though

a Liberal, Walker joined the TORONTO EIGHTEEN in opposing RECIPROCITY with the United States in the 1911 general election.

WALKER, HIRAM (1816-99), distiller, businessman. Walker immigrated to Canada from the United States in 1859 and stayed for only five years, during which he built a distillery, a town, and a railway. He began purchasing land around Walkerville (now Windsor, Ont.) in 1856 and established the Windsor Distillery and Flouring Mill in 1859. In 1884 he began producing Walker's Canadian Club Whiskey, one of the greatest Canadian whiskey exports.

WAR BABIES, *see* BABY BOOM

WAR LABOUR BOARD, *see* NATIONAL WAR LABOUR BOARD

WAR MEASURES ACT, legislation giving the federal government emergency powers during time of war, invasion, or insurrection. Passed in Aug. 1914, the act severely limited the freedoms of Canadians, including the suspension of habeas corpus and deportation without trial. The act was invoked during WORLD WAR I, WORLD WAR II, and the 1970 OCTOBER CRISIS. The government of BRIAN MULRONEY in 1987 proposed its replacement.

WAR SAVINGS CERTIFICATES, *see* VICTORY LOANS

WAR SAVINGS STAMPS, *see* VICTORY LOANS

WARD, MAXWELL WILLIAM (1921-), aviator, businessman. Born at Edmonton, Ward served in the air force during World War II as a flight instructor. A bush pilot after the war, he formed Polaris Charter Co. Ltd in 1946 and in 1953 founded Wardair Ltd, both based in Yellowknife. After obtaining a licence to run international air charters, the company became Wardair Canada with head offices in Edmonton. Wardair began operating regular scheduled flights within Canada in 1986.

WARE, JOHN (1845-1905), rancher. Ware was born a slave in South Carolina and became a cowboy in Texas following the United States Civil War. In 1882 he came to Canada on a cattle drive and nine years later started a small ranch west of Turner Valley in southern Alberta. He was one of the first black immigrants into the area and gained fame as a rodeo performer. In 1903, Ware expanded his operations by moving north of the Red Deer River into central Alberta. He was killed in a riding accident two years later.

WARTIME ELECTIONS ACT, 1917, legislation that removed the vote from citizens who had immigrated from enemy alien countries. Passed by SIR ROBERT BORDEN's government in Sept. 1917, the act took the vote away from all enemy-alien immigrants who came to Canada after 31 March 1902, as well as conscientious objectors. It gave the vote to all women who had immediate relatives serving in the Canadian army. The act was designed to increase Borden's chances at the polls, and, hence, to ensure the success of his CONSCRIPTION policy.

WARTIME INFORMATION BOARD, government information agency created in 1942 to succeed the Bureau of Public Information. The board produced a plethora of publications, conducted secret opinion polling, and had a network of correspondents to report on opinion across the country. The key figure on the board was documentary filmmaker JOHN GRIERSON.

WARTIME PRICES AND TRADE BOARD, federal agency established at the outbreak of WORLD WAR II to oversee the operation of the war economy and to regulate trade and commerce in such a way as to avoid the high rates of inflation that had occurred in Canada during World War I. At first the board was under the jurisdiction of the Department of Labour but it was transferred to the Department of Finance in 1941. Under the leadership of DONALD GORDON, the board had enormous powers. It most directly affected the lives of ordinary Canadians through its massive rationing and subsidy program. The board was successful in keeping inflation under 3 per cent from 1941 to 1945, well below World War I rates. *See also* NATIONAL WAR LABOUR BOARD.

WATKINS, JOHN B.C. (1903-64), diplomat. Watkins taught at the Univ. of Manitoba before joining the Department of External Affairs in 1946. Fluent in Russian, he was sent to Moscow as chargé d'affaires from 1948 to 1951 and, after

brief service as minister to Norway (1952-4), as ambassador from 1954 to 1956. He was also assistant under-secretary of state for external affairs and ambassador to Denmark. He died of a heart attack while under RCMP interrogation about his contacts in the Soviet Union. The circumstances of his death were hushed up for almost 20 years.

WATKINS REPORT, *see* TASK FORCE ON FOREIGN OWNERSHIP AND THE STRUCTURE OF CANADIAN INVESTMENT

WATTERS, JAMES C. (1869-1947), labour leader. He was founding president of the British Columbia Federation of Labor and was elected president of the TRADES AND LABOUR CONGRESS in 1911. Watters opposed CONSCRIPTION in 1917 and incurred the wrath of conservative eastern labour leaders who strongly supported the American Federation of Labor. He was defeated in his bid for re-election to the presidency in 1918 by TOM MOORE.

courtesy Ken Bell/National Archives of Canada/PA-132730

Wayne and Schuster with cast of Canadian Army show, 1944

WAYNE AND SHUSTER, comedy team. John Louis Wayne and Frank Shuster, who make up Canada's best-known comedy team, met at school in Toronto. During World War II they served in the infantry, but were soon performing for the

Army Show. They continued performing after the war, first on radio and then on television. Their comedy is a mixture of slapstick and pantomime, often corny and sometime ingenious, particularly in their use of the classics.

WESSON, JOHN HENRY (1887-1965), farm leader. Born near Sheffield, Eng., Wesson came to Canada in 1907 to farm in Saskatchewan. He soon joined the farmers' movement and was an early and active advocate of pooling. He helped organize the Saskatchewan Wheat Pool and was one of its first directors. *See also* WHEAT POOLS.

WESTERN ECONOMIC OPPORTUNITIES CONFERENCE, conference held in Calgary in the summer of 1973. The conference brought Liberal Prime Minister PIERRE TRUDEAU together with the premiers of the four western provinces to discuss western grievances and to explore means of stimulating economic development in the west. The conference followed a dramatic decline in western support for the Liberal party.

WESTERN FEDERATION OF MINERS, labour union that moved into Canada in the 1890s and attempted to organize miners in Alberta and British Columbia. It was strongly opposed by the federal government and the mine owners and was forced to abandon its efforts early in the 20th century.

WESTERN LABOR CONFERENCE, labour conference held in Calgary, Alta, in March 1919. The conference had been planned by militant western labour leaders, fed up with the conservative policies of the TRADES AND LABOUR CONGRESS. But radicals seized control of the conference and passed resolutions favouring the dismantling of capitalism and the TLC. The chief resolution called upon westerners to take the lead in forming a new, radical labour organization to be called the ONE BIG UNION.

WESTERN LABOR NEWS, labour newspaper founded in 1918 as the official organ of the Winnipeg Trades and Labor Council. The paper was first edited by William Ivens, a former Methodist minister and follower of the SOCIAL GOSPEL; it strongly supported the WINNIPEG GENERAL STRIKE.

WESTON, WILLARD GARFIELD (1893-1978), food merchant. He was born in Toronto, son of George Weston of George Weston Ltd. He took over his father's biscuit company and expanded the business into other countries and products. Although Weston moved to England in the 1930s, he maintained control of his Canadian-based multinational food company with the help of his sons.

WHEAT POOLS, grain-marketing cooperatives. The first of the three Prairie wheat pools, the Alberta Wheat Pool, was formed in 1923 by Aaron Sapiro, an American farm activist invited to Alberta by the UNITED FARMERS OF ALBERTA and the Calgary *Herald*. Sapiro convinced Alberta farm leaders, especially HENRY WISE WOOD, to organize a volunteer pool to market the 1923 grain crop. More than 80 per cent of the province's grain farmers joined the pool by the end of the growing season. Grain farmers in Saskatchewan and Manitoba quickly followed suit and established wheat pools in those two provinces. In 1924 the three prairie pools set up CANADIAN CO-OPERATIVE WHEAT PRODUCERS LTD to act as their central selling agency. The pool system was virtually wiped out by the drastic fall in world grain prices that followed the GREAT DEPRESSION, and the pools were only saved through massive government aid. Their function as central selling agencies was taken over by the CANADIAN WHEAT BOARD after 1935.

WHEELER, LUCILE (1935–), skier. The winner of Canada's first Olympic ski medal in 1956, Wheeler was one of the first North Americans to break the European monopoly on world ski championships, capturing the downhill and giant slalom titles in 1958.

WHITE, ROBERT (1935–), labour leader. Born in Upper Lands, Northern Ireland, White became active in union affairs in the late 1950s and first attracted attention as president of United Auto Workers local 636 in 1959. He became director of the UAW in Canada in 1978. Under his direction the Canadian UAW seceded from its parent union in the United States in 1986 to form the Canadian Auto Workers Union.

WHITE, SIR WILLIAM THOMAS (1866-1955) politician, banker. Successful as a lawyer and financier, he became director and chairman of the Bank of Commerce (1938-44), director of Canadian Life Assurance Co. and the Steel Company of Canada, and general manager of the National Trust Co. (1900-10). A Liberal until the RECIPROCITY issue turned his allegiance, he was elected to the House of Commons as a Conservative in 1911. As Prime Minister BORDEN's minister of finance from 1911 to 1919, he was responsible for policies that saw Canada emerge from World War I in sound financial shape. He left politics in 1921.

WHITE EMPRESS FLEET, *see* CANADIAN PACIFIC STEAMSHIP CO.

WHITE PAPER ON EMPLOYMENT AND INCOME, 1945, federal government paper on the economy, issued in April 1945 by C.D. HOWE. Drafted by W.A. MACKINTOSH, the white paper for the first time declared full employment to be a priority and pledged to use deficit financing if necessary to achieve it. The policy reflected the new orientation towards the theories of British economist John Maynard Keynes. Briefly, Keynes had advocated that governments balance their budgets over the business cycle, instead of annually, and that they spend more than they took in during bad economic times while taking in more than they spent during good times. This, he thought, would ease the impact of economic recessions and allow the government to save for a rainy day during periods of prosperity.

WHITE PAPER ON FOREIGN POLICY, 1970, the product of the TRUDEAU government's review of foreign policy. The white paper appeared in six pamphlets emphasizing sovereignty and independence, peace and security, social justice, quality of life, a harmonious natural environment, and economic growth. The relations of Canada and the United States were not directly discussed, a deficiency remedied two years later by secretary of state for external affairs MITCHELL SHARP when he proposed a THIRD OPTION for Canada.

WHITE PASS AND YUKON RAILWAY, railway connecting Skagway, Alaska, with Whitehorse, Yukon Territory, begun during the KLONDIKE GOLD RUSH to provide a reliable overland route from the Pacific Coast to the goldfields.

The railway was completed in 1900, after the gold rush was over. It survived for several decades, but collapsed in 1982 after many of the major mines in the territory had been shut down.

WHITNEY, SIR JAMES PLINY (1843-1914), premier of Ontario. Born at Williamsburg Township, Canada West, he first won election to the Ontario legislature in 1888. He became Conservative leader in 1896, and his party captured the province in 1905. His government began publicly owned hydro, salvaged the Univ. of Toronto, implemented REGULATION 17 (which was popular except with francophones) and passed new liquor legislation.

WHITTON, CHARLOTTE (1896-1975), social worker, municipal politician. Canada's first female mayor, Whitton, born at Renfrew, Ont., taught at Queen's before becoming director of the Canadian Council on Child Welfare (later the Canadian Council on Social Development) from 1920 to 1941. She resigned in 1941 and devoted her time to furthering women's equality. Elected mayor of Ottawa in 1951, she was re-elected four times until defeated by property developers in 1964. Conservative in her politics and her thinking, Whitton espoused apparently contradictory views by demonstrating genuine concern for the underprivileged while denouncing the welfare state in *The Dawn of Ampler Life* (1943) and fighting for women's rights but opposing liberal divorce laws.

WIELAND, JOYCE (1931-), artist, filmmaker. She held her first exhibition at the Isaacs Gallery in Toronto in 1960. She moved to New York in 1962 and began making experimental films, such as the award winning *Rat Life and Diet in North America* (1968) and *Raison avant la passion* (1967-9). Her early work fell generally in the abstract expressionist genre, and in 1971 she was honoured with the first retrospective of a living Canadian female artist at the National Gallery of Canada. Her recent work, still popular, is representational.

WILGRESS, LEOLYN DANA (1892-1969), public servant. Wilgress, born at Vancouver, entered the Trade Commissioner Service in 1914, becoming director of the Commercial Intelligence Service in Ottawa and deputy minister of trade and commerce. During World War II he served as minister (1942-4) and then ambassador (1944-6) to the Soviet Union. Untarnished by Cold War hysteria, he remained a moderate. He was a key figure in the framing of the GENERAL AGREEMENT ON TARIFFS AND TRADE. Other positions he held include high commissioner to the United Kingdom (1949-52), under-secretary of state for external affairs (1952-3), and permanent representative to NATO. His anodyne memoirs appeared in 1967.

WILLIAM DAVIES CO., meatpacking company founded in Toronto by William Davies who began shipping cured pork products to England in the late 1850s. Davies built the company into one of the largest pork packers in the Toronto area even before JOSEPH W. FLAVELLE joined it in 1887. Flavelle expanded exports to Britain and made the company the largest packing house in the British Empire.

WILLINGDON, FREEMAN FREEMAN-THOMAS, 1ST MARQUESS OF (1866-1941), governor general of Canada. He had sat at Westminster as a Liberal MP, 1900–10 and done two tours as governor of Indian provinces, before serving as vice-regal representative in Ottawa from 1926 to 1931. Although the British government had been cool to his inclusion on the list of suitable candidates, George V intervened on his behalf, and MACKENZIE KING selected him, his Liberal credentials outweighing all else. His tenure, which followed the stormy term of VISCOUNT BYNG during the KING-BYNG AFFAIR, was placid and uneventful.

WILLISON, SIR JOHN STEPHEN (1856-1927), journalist. A prominent imperialist and member of the ROUND TABLE MOVEMENT, Willison began editing the Toronto *Globe* in 1890, moving to the *News* from 1903 to 1917, after a break with SIR WILFRID LAURIER and the Liberals, and then to *Willison's Monthly* from 1925 to 1927. A staunch upholder of the Empire, he wrote for *The Times* from 1909 to 1927. He was an unofficial but important adviser to Prime Ministers LAURIER and BORDEN.

WILSON, CAIRINE REAY (1885-1962), senator. Born Cairine Mackay at Montreal, she helped organize women's LIBERAL PARTY organizations in the 1920s. Mackenzie King named her to the Senate in 1930, Canada's first woman senator. She played a major role in urging a more tolerant policy towards pre-war refugees from Naziism.

WILSON, SIR DANIEL (1816-92), scientist, educator. Born at Edinburgh, Scot., Wilson was appointed in 1853 professor of history and English at the as-yet-unbuilt University College, Univ. of Toronto. He became president of the college in 1880, president of the Royal Society of Canada two years later, and first president of the Univ. of Toronto in 1887. As a scientist, Wilson worked on ethnology, accepted the Darwinian idea of evolution, but sharply opposed the idea of natural selection, primarily on religious grounds.

WINDSOR STRIKE, 1945, strike of 17,000 members of the United Auto Workers against the Ford Motor Co. The strike began 12 Sept. 1945 after the company refused union demands for a union shop (closed shop) and a compulsory check-off. It was marked by mass demonstrations and ended on 29 Dec. 1945. It was followed by mediation conducted by Justice IVAN C. RAND. *See also* RAND FORMULA.

WINNIPEG COMMODITY EXCHANGE, financial institution, established in 1887 as a central marketplace for prairie grain and originally known as the Winnipeg Grain Exchange. In 1904 trading in grain futures began. Although the exchange was the only agricultural commodities market in Canada, its prices closely followed those set in Chicago and Britain, prompting farmers to complain about grain price instability. Organizational efforts of prairie grain farmers in the early 20th century were directed towards achieving higher and more stable prices by bypassing the exchange.

WINNIPEG GENERAL STRIKE, strike of Winnipeg workers from 15 May to 26 June 1919. It involved virtually all the organized workers in Winnipeg and many thousands of non-unionized workers, approximately 30,000 in all, and began when the Winnipeg Trades and Labor Council ordered a strike in support of striking metal and construction workers. The strikers were opposed by employers, the CITIZENS COMMITTEE OF 1000, and eventually by all three levels of government.

Winnipeg General Strike, 1919

Many World War I veterans and the city's non–Anglo Saxon immigrants supported them. As the strike progressed, the city hired "special police" and the federal government increased the militia in the city. Strike leaders were arrested on 17 June and a pro-strike demonstration by veterans was crushed on BLOODY SATURDAY, 21 June 1919. The strike collapsed on 26 June.

WINNIPEG GRAIN EXCHANGE, *see* WINNIPEG COMMODITY EXCHANGE

WINTERS, ROBERT HENRY (1910-69), politician, businessman. Winters became an engineer in his hometown of Lunenburg, N.S. In 1934 he joined Northern Electric in Montreal, one of many corporations he worked for. He entered the House of Commons as a Liberal in 1945, following service in World War II, and became successively minister of transport (1948), reconstruction and supply (1948-50), resources and development (1950-3), and public works (1953-7). Defeated in the 1957 election, he returned in the 1965 election to become Prime Minister PEARSON's very conservative minister of trade and commerce and a warm supporter of American investment in Canada. Narrowly defeated by PIERRE TRUDEAU in the 1968 Liberal leadership convention, he retired from politics and became president of Brazilian Light and Power Ltd.

WITNESS AGAINST WAR, pacifist manifesto, 1939. At the outbreak of WORLD WAR II a substantial group of United Church ministers decided their church was about to support the war effort, a repudiation of pacifist positions adopted earlier. Initially 68 clergy, most from Toronto and Montreal, signed the manifesto and a further 64, lay

and clerical, later endorsed it. The attorney general of Ontario decided it contravened the DEFENCE OF CANADA REGULATIONS, but no action was taken.

Viscount Wolseley

WOLSELEY, GARNET JOSEPH WOLSELEY, 1ST VISCOUNT (1833-1913), soldier. He served with the British army in India, the Crimea, and China before coming to Canada in 1861 as assistant quartermaster general. He commanded the 1870 expedition to the Red River to quell the RED RIVER REBELLION. From 1895 to 1900 he served as commander-in-chief of the British army.

WOMAN'S CHRISTIAN TEMPERANCE UNION, prohibition organization founded in 1875. The WCTU, which saw alcohol as responsible for most social ills, began in Ontario and spread its campaign for PROHIBITION across the country within a decade. The union, which still exists in an attenuated form, also played a conservative role as a women's rights movement.

WOMEN'S INTERNATIONAL LEAGUE FOR PEACE AND FREEDOM, pacifist movement. Begun in WORLD WAR I as the Canadian Women's Peace Party, the league was essentially a stop-the-war movement, its leaders advocating a unilateral Canadian withdrawal from the conflict. After the Armistice, the league continued its operations, calling for an end to cadet training, the "pacification" of textbooks, disarmament, and assistance to refugees.

WOMEN'S LABOUR LEAGUES, modelled after the Women's Labour Leagues in Britain, and originally affiliated to and auxiliaries of labour parties prior to 1918.

WOMEN'S PARLIAMENT, mock parliament, organized by the Manitoba Political Equality League, and held by women reformers in Winnipeg in 1914. NELLIE MCCLUNG acted as the "premier" and the "parliament" voted down a male "request" to be granted the vote. *See also* E. CORA HIND.

A view of women's suffrage

courtesy Glenbow Archives, Calgary/NA-369

WOMEN'S SUFFRAGE, term used to describe women's struggle to win the right to vote. Although women of property voted in LOWER CANADA and CANADA EAST between 1809 and 1849, male suffrage only was legislated in 1849. Propertied women in CANADA WEST, however, could vote for school trustees after 1850 and by 1900 women could vote in municipal elections across most of Canada. But the situation was different at the provincial and federal levels. Led initially by members of the Toronto Women's Literary Club, the women's suffrage movement began in 1876. In 1883 the club became the Toronto Women's Suffrage Assn and six years later the Dominion Women's Enfranchisement Assn. Whatever its name, success was limited for years as politicians – who clearly had public support behind them – blocked women's suffrage. Many believed that once women got the vote male-created social ills

like drunkenness and prostitution would disappear, as would war. Ironically, it was WORLD WAR I that brought women the vote, Manitoba becoming the first province to enact it in 1916. Saskatchewan, Alberta, B.C., and Ontario followed by 1917, and the other provinces, except Quebec, followed by 1922. Women did not get the vote in Quebec until 1940. Federally, women relatives of soldiers received the vote under the WARTIME ELECTIONS ACT of 1917; the next year, the UNION GOVERNMENT gave women citizens over 21 the right to vote in federal elections.

WOOD, EDWARD ROGERS (1866-1941), businessman. Born in Toronto, Wood went to work for the Central Canada Loan and Savings company (later Dominion Securities) in the mid-1880s, and eventually became president. Wood served on numerous corporate boards of directors and was the vice-president of a number of major companies including Brazilian Traction.

WOOD, HENRY WISE (1860-1941), farm leader. Wood was born near Munroe City, Missouri, where he took up farming before emigrating to near Calgary, Alta, in 1905. He soon became active in the farm movement and in 1916 was elected president of the UNITED FARMERS OF ALBERTA, a post he kept until 1931. Wood opposed the entry of the UFA into active politics but, under pressure, dropped his opposition in 1921. He refused to become premier after the UFA election victory that year, but he played an active role in the UFA parent organization throughout the 1920s and was instrumental in the establishment of the Alberta Wheat Pool in 1923. Wood favoured reform of the legislative system through the introduction of GROUP GOVERNMENT, a system in which occupation groups, not constituencies, sent representatives to the legislature. But although the UFA government was nominally responsible to the UFA parent organization which Wood headed, it never seriously considered introducing group government to Alberta. Wood strongly opposed the efforts of moderate farm leaders such as T.A. CRERAR and ROBERT FORKE to form a broad alliance of farmers and liberal progressives inside the PROGRESSIVE PARTY and insisted that farmers should support only pure farm parties. His attitude helped to split the party and cause its rapid decline.

WOODCOCK, GEORGE (1912–), author, polymath. Born at Winnipeg, Woodcock spent his first 37 years in England where he was trained in literary journalism and embraced anarchism. Returning to Canada in 1949, he began a long and prolific career writing history and literary criticism. He founded *Canadian Literature* in 1959 and edited it until 1977. Some of his huge collection of works on disparate subjects include *The Centre Cannot Hold* (1943), a collection of poems; with Ivan Avakumovic, *The Anarchist Prince: A Biographical Study of Peter Kropotkin* (1950) and *The Doukhobors* (1960); *The Crystal Spirit* (1966), a study of George Orwell; and *The Canadians* (1979). The first volume of his autobiography, *Letters to the Past*, appeared in 1982.

WOODS' TASK FORCE, the Task Force on Labour Relations appointed by the federal government in 1966 under H.D. Woods of McGill Univ. to enquire into the increase in labour unrest. The task force reported in 1969 and strongly supported the existing adversarial system of labour relations as the best available.

courtesy National Archives of Canada/C-3940

James S. Woodsworth

WOODSWORTH, JAMES SHAVER (1874-1942), minister, labour leader, politician. Woodsworth was ordained as a Methodist minister in 1896 and after the turn of the century began to work with All People's Mission in the immigrant and working class neighbourhoods of Winnipeg's North End. His experiences converted him to the SOCIAL GOSPEL, and he became one of its best-known practitioners in Canada. Much of his philosophy in this period was contained in his two books, *Strangers within Our Gates* and *My Neighbour*. A strong pacifist, he opposed CONSCRIPTION during WORLD WAR I, and resigned the ministry in 1918 because of the Methodist Church's support for the war. He was caught up in the WINNIPEG GENERAL STRIKE when he succeeded WILLIAM IVENS as editor of the *WESTERN LABOR NEWS* after Ivens had been arrested. Woodsworth was himself arrested several days later but never brought to trial. In 1921 he was elected to the House of Commons on the INDEPENDENT LABOUR PARTY OF MANITOBA ticket. In the Commons he worked closely with WILLIAM IRVINE, a labour member for Calgary, and members of the PROGRESSIVE PARTY, forming a loose GINGER GROUP of farm and labour radicals. He was a leading figure behind the creation of the CO-OPERATIVE COMMONWEALTH FEDERATION and became the CCF's first leader. He broke with the CCF in Sept. 1939, when he opposed Canada's declaration of war on Germany, and although he was not formally replaced as CCF leader, he was shunted aside in favour of M.J. COLDWELL. Despite his opposition to the war, he was re-elected in 1940, but with a reduced majority, and died shortly after.

WORKERS' COMPENSATION, provincial legislation designed to provide compensation, without concern as to fault, to workers injured on the job. Prior to the introduction of workers' compensation (Ontario was the first province to introduce it in 1914), injured employees usually had to sue employers and prove that injuries were due to employer negligence. Compensation laws established an insurance fund financed by employer contributions which paid a proportion of the injured worker's wages (generally up to 75 per cent) without regard as to the cause of the accident.

WORKERS' PARTY OF CANADA, *see* COMMUNIST PARTY OF CANADA

WORKERS' UNITY LEAGUE, labour federation founded by the COMMUNIST PARTY of Canada in 1929. The WUL championed labour militancy and national and industrial unionism. Many of its constituent unions had formerly been connected to the ALL-CANADIAN CONGRESS OF LABOUR. It was formed when the Communist International ordered Communist party members around the world to concentrate in Communist-led labour organizations instead of remaining inside non-Communist ones and was ended in 1936 when the Communist International reversed itself. The WUL made special efforts to organize the unemployed. *See also* RELIEF CAMP WORKERS' UNION; ON-TO-OTTAWA TREK; JAMES B. McLACHLAN.

WORLD BANK, international agency, originally called the International Bank for Reconstruction and Development, that emerged from the Bretton Woods Conference of 1944, along with the INTERNATIONAL MONETARY FUND. The bank is supposed to regulate the world's currencies and help to redistribute wealth to the poorer nations by way of loans and expert advice. *See also* LOUIS RASMINSKY.

WORLD WAR I, 1914-18, the Great War. Canada went to war when Britain did on 4 Aug. 1914. The conflict initially united Canadians, but there was a telling sign of trouble ahead when the first contingent of the CANADIAN EXPEDITIONARY FORCE contained few French-speaking Canadians and, other than in the officer ranks, relatively few of the Canadian-born. This contingent, called the 1st Canadian Division, set sail for Britain in Oct. 1914 and, after training there, reached France and Flanders in March 1915, just in time to participate on the receiving end of the first German gas attack at YPRES. The Canadians held their ground despite high casualties, and the reputation established was never tarnished. By 1917, the CANADIAN CORPS of four divisions was a formidable force, as shown by its capture of the hitherto impregnable VIMY RIDGE. Because of the conditions on the front and the uninspired generalship of the day, however, casualties were terrible. The first Canadian to command the Corps, General SIR ARTHUR CURRIE, was an exception to that criticism, believing as he did in the necessity for planning, reconnaissance, training, and use of all technical aids. The high casualties nonetheless caused the difficult CONSCRIPTION CRISIS of 1917 that led Prime Minister SIR ROBERT BORDEN to create a UNION GOVERNMENT to enforce it

on a reluctant Quebec and rural Canada. Even though conscription did little to resolve the Corps' manpower needs, the Canadians continued their victorious efforts through the "Hundred Days" that began with their smashing success on 8 Aug. 1918, the "black day of the German Army." By the Armistice on 11 Nov. 1918, the Canadians had reached Mons, Belgium. The Corps' success is widely believed to have created the Canadian nationality. The price paid, however, was 60,000 dead.

Canadians also played a distinguished role in the air war with more than 20,000 serving in the Royal Flying Corps, Royal Naval Air Service, and Royal Air Force. Such pilots as WILLIAM BISHOP, ROY BROWN, and RAY COLLISHAW earned formidable reputations. At sea, the ROYAL CANADIAN NAVY contribution was useful in convoy protection in the Western Atlantic.

WORLD WAR II, 1939-45, Canada declared war on Germany on 10 Sept. 1939. There was little enthusiasm for the struggle, Canadians recalling too well the casualties of WORLD WAR I and the CONSCRIPTION CRISIS that had so divided the country. Thus Prime Minister MACKENZIE KING's policy was one of "limited liability," and Canada's commitment initially was declared to be one division of infantry, the BRITISH COMMONWEALTH AIR TRAINING PLAN, and such support as the tiny ROYAL CANADIAN NAVY could offer. Events did not permit this wish to be fulfilled. After the Anglo-French defeat on the Continent in May-June 1940, the attitude in Ottawa changed. Production increased greatly, both in factory and farm, and reached unheard-of peaks. By 1942 Canada was giving its allies billions of dollars worth of goods. Although conscription for home defence was imposed under the NATIONAL RESOURCES MOBILIZATION ACT of 1940, opinion in Quebec remained strongly against any compulsory overseas service. In the summer of 1942, after a plebiscite on conscription, overseas service for conscripts was authorized, but it was not enforced. By Nov. 1944, with infantry reinforcements in short supply thanks to heavy fighting, the King government agreed to send 16,000 home defence conscripts overseas. Few arrived at units in time to participate in the fighting.

Overseas, the army expanded greatly, reaching five divisions with another three at home; the ROYAL CANADIAN AIR FORCE raised a quarter million men and women and sent 94,000 overseas, and the ROYAL CANADIAN NAVY ended the war with almost 100,000 in navy blue and operating a 365-ship fleet. Canadian soldiers suffered heavy losses when HONG KONG fell to the Japanese in Dec. 1941 and in the abortive raid on DIEPPE in 1942. More successfully, they fought in SICILY, Italy, and northwest Europe. One division participated in the NORMANDY INVASION of June 1944, and, before the month was out, the FIRST CANADIAN ARMY, the largest force ever commanded by a Canadian, was in the field under General H.D.G. CRERAR. In the Italian fighting, 5764 Canadian soldiers died; in northwest Europe the toll was 11,336. The RCAF sent 48 squadrons overseas and tens of thousands of its officers and men served with Royal Air Force squadrons, all over the world but most notably in Bomber Command; 17,101 lost their lives. The RCN played a massive role in convoy escorts, by 1943 taking responsibility for the Canadian Northwest Atlantic Theatre, but also sending ships to the Pacific fighting. Twenty-four ships were lost to enemy action and 2024 sailors were killed. The overall Canadian war effort was massive, one million men and women serving in the forces.

WRANGEL ISLAND, island located 225 km north of Siberia, sought by Canada. First sighted in 1849, Wrangel Island was initially "occupied" by shipwrecked Canadian sailors from an Arctic expedition. Explorer VILHJALMUR STEFANSSON began to press for Canada to exert sovereignty over Wrangel, supposedly rich in resources and strategically located. He sent four settlers to the island in 1921, all of whom died, and a second group two years later. The MACKENZIE KING government showed little interest and, at a British-Soviet conference in 1924, Soviet sovereignty over Wrangel Island was recognized.

WRIGHT, CECIL AUGUSTUS (1904-67), educator. A key figure in the development of legal education in Ontario, "Caesar" Wright, born at London, Ont., taught at Osgoode Hall Law School from 1927 to 1949. When the Law Society of Upper Canada rejected proposed changes in legal education, he and many of the staff resigned. With BORA LASKIN and John Willis, Wright turned the undergraduate law department at the Univ. of Toronto into Ontario's first professional university law school. He served as dean from 1949 to 1967.

WRIGHT, JOSEPH, SR (1864-1950), oarsman. Wright took a Toronto Argonaut crew to victory at the 1885 U.S. nationals, a feat he repeated 20 years later at the Royal Canadian Henley Regatta. He won 137 national titles during his career and from 1916 to 1926 coached Univ. of Pennsylvania crews. An all-round athlete, he also won the Canadian amateur heavyweight wrestling championship.

WRONG, GEORGE MACKINNON (1869-1948), historian. With ADAM SHORTT a founder of modern Canadian history, Wrong was born and educated at Toronto. Ordained an Anglican priest in 1883, he taught at Wycliffe College from 1883 to 1892 and at the Univ. of Toronto from 1892 to 1927, becoming head of the history department in 1894. He founded the *Review of Historical Publications Relating to Canada* in 1896-7 (from 1920 the *Canadian Historical Review*) and the Champlain Society in 1905. Wrong viewed history as a moral teacher, a theme which runs through his books on imperial history and French Canada. His best-known work, *A Canadian Manor and Its Seigneurs*, was published in 1908.

WRONG, HUMPHREY HUME (1894-1954), diplomat. Son of GEORGE WRONG and one of Canada's ablest diplomats, he grew up in Toronto. Educated at the univs. of Toronto and Oxford, he taught history in his father's department from 1921 to 1928. In 1928 he went to Washington as VINCENT MASSEY's first secretary. After serving unhappily in various capacities at the League of Nations, London, again in Washington, and Ottawa, he devised the theory of FUNCTIONALISM designed to give Canada as much weight as the great powers in those areas where it functioned as such, that is, food and mineral production and air policy. He was ambassador to Washington from 1946 to 1953, a post he filled with great distinction in a difficult period.

WYLE, FLORENCE (1881-1968), sculptor. One of Canada's little known sculptors, Wyle was born at Trenton, Ill., and immigrated to Canada in 1913. She and her fellow sculptor Frances Loring lived and worked in Toronto. Her genre was the human figure, such as the memorial to nurse Edith Cavell at Toronto General Hospital, and animals. A founding member of the Sculptors' Society of Canada (1928), she was the first female sculptor granted full membership in the Royal Canadian Academy of Arts.

YELLOWHEAD PASS, pass linking Alberta and British Columbia through the Rocky Mountains, approximately 340 km west of Edmonton. The pass had been well known since fur trade days and it was thought that the CANADIAN PACIFIC RAILWAY would use it until the discovery of ROGERS PASS further south. The Yellowhead was used by the CANADIAN NORTHERN and the GRAND TRUNK PACIFIC railways.

YOUNG, NEIL PERCIVAL (1945–), rock singer, songwriter. Born at Toronto, he worked as a milkman before becoming a force in rock music. After playing with Canadian bands The Squires and Mynah Birds, he became a founding member of Buffalo Springfield, a Los Angeles folk-rock band (1966-8). He then pursued a solo career but was a fourth member of Crosby, Stills and Nash from 1969 to 1974. Young has released some 15 albums, including *After the Goldrush, Harvest, Reactor* and *Rust Never Sleeps*.

YUKON FIELD FORCE, permanent force contingent sent to the Yukon in 1898. The KLONDIKE GOLD RUSH had flooded the territory, and there was building tension with the United States, its territory of Alaska adjoining. The force, numbering 203 all ranks, was at once an expression of sovereignty and a peacekeeping force. Half withdrew in 1899; the remainder left in 1900.

YPRES, BATTLE OF, battle in Belgium during April 1915 and the first major battle fought by Canadian soldiers in WORLD WAR I. At Ypres, men of the First Canadian Division stopped a German advance in the face of a gas attack. The battle established the division's reputation as a first-class

fighting force. More than 6000 Canadians were killed, wounded, or taken prisoner during the bloodbath.

ZOMBIES, derisive name for home defence conscripts in WORLD WAR II. Under the NATIONAL RESOURCES MOBILIZATION ACT, conscripts for home defence could not be sent overseas unless they volunteered. Called "soulless" and "living dead," as in popular movies of the day, Zombies were scorned. The sobriquet was widely employed, and likely helped build up resistance against volunteering among the NRMA soldiers.

ZOUAVES, French Canadian recruits for the Papal army, 1868-70. When Italian forces tried to seize the Papal state as part of the movement for Italian unification, some 390 men from across Quebec went to the Pope's support, raised by an organizational committee headed by Bishop BOURGET.

Directory of Appendices

Governors General of Canada

Viscount Monck of Ballytrammon—July 1, 1867
Baron Lisgar of Lisgar and Baileborough—Feb. 2, 1869
Earl of Dufferin—June 25, 1872
Marquis of Lorne—Nov. 25, 1878
Marquis of Lansdowne—Oct. 23, 1883
Baron Stanley of Preston—June 11, 1888
Earl of Aberdeen—Sept. 18, 1893
Earl of Minto—Nov. 12, 1898
Earl Grey—Dec. 10, 1904
Duke of Connaught—Oct. 13, 1911
Duke of Devonshire—Nov. 11, 1916
Baron Byng of Vimy—Aug. 11, 1921
Viscount Willingdon of Ratton—Oct. 2, 1926
Earl of Bessborough—April 4, 1931
Baron Tweedsmuir of Elsfield—Nov. 2, 1935
Earl of Athlone—June 21, 1940
Viscount Alexander of Tunis—April 12, 1946
Vincent Massey—Feb. 28, 1952
Georges P. Vanier—Sept. 15, 1959
Roland Michener—April 17, 1967
Jules Léger—Jan. 14, 1974
Edward Schreyer—Jan. 21, 1979
Jeanne Sauvé—May 14, 1984

Prime Ministers of Canada

Sir John A. Macdonald—Conservative—July 1, 1867-Nov. 5, 1873
Alexander Mackenzie—Liberal—Nov. 7, 1873-Oct. 8, 1878
Sir John A. Macdonald—Conservative—Oct. 17, 1878-June 6, 1891
Sir John Abbott—Conservative—June 16, 1891-Nov. 24, 1892
Sir John Thompson—Conservative—Dec. 5, 1892-Dec. 12, 1894
Sir Mackenzie Bowell—Conservative—Dec. 21, 1894-April 27, 1896
Sir Charles Tupper—Conservative—May 1, 1896-July 8, 1896
Sir Wilfrid Laurier—Liberal—July 11, 1896-Oct. 6, 1911
Sir Robert Borden—Conservative—Oct. 10, 1911-Oct. 12, 1917
Sir Robert Borden—Unionist—Oct. 12, 1917-July 10, 1920
Arthur Meighen—Unionist-National Liberal and Conservative—
July 10, 1920-Dec. 29, 1921
William Lyon Mackenzie King—Liberal—Dec. 29, 1921-June 28, 1926
Arthur Meighen—Conservative—June 29, 1926-Sept. 25, 1926
William Lyon Mackenzie King—Liberal—Sept. 25, 1926-Aug. 7, 1930
Richard Bennett—Conservative—Aug. 7, 1930-Oct. 23, 1935
William Lyon Mackenzie King—Liberal—Oct. 23, 1935-Nov. 15, 1948
Louis St Laurent—Liberal—Nov. 15, 1948-June 21, 1957
John Diefenbaker—Progressive Conservative—June 21, 1957-April 22, 1963
Lester Bowles Pearson—Liberal—April 22, 1963-April 20, 1968
Pierre Elliott Trudeau—Liberal—April 20, 1968-June 3, 1979
Joe Clark—Progressive Conservative—June 4, 1979-March 2, 1980
Pierre Elliott Trudeau—Liberal—March 3, 1980-June 30, 1984
John Turner—Liberal—June 30, 1984-Sept. 17, 1984
Brian Mulroney—Progressive Conservative—Sept. 17, 1984-

Provincial Premiers

British Columbia
John Foster McCreight—1871-2
Amor De Cosmos—1872-4
George Anthony Walkem—1874-6
Andrew Charles Elliott—1876-8
George Anthony Walkem—1878-82
Robert Beaven—1882-3
William Smithe—1883-7
Alexander Davie—Conservative—1887-9
John Robson—Liberal—1889-92
Theodore Davie—1892-5
John Herbert Turner—1895-8
Charles Augustin Semlin—Conservative—1898-1900
Joseph Martin—Liberal—1900
James Dunsmuir—Conservative—1900-2
Edward Gawler Prior—Conservative—1902-3
Sir Richard McBride—Conservative—1903-15
William John Bowser—Conservative—1915-16
Harlan Carey Brewster—Liberal—1916-18
John Oliver—Liberal—1918-27
John Duncan MacLean—Liberal—1927-8
Simon Fraser Tolmie—Conservative—1928-33
Thomas Dufferin Pattullo—Liberal—1933-41
John Hart—Coalition Government—1941-7
Byron Ingemar Johnson—Coalition Government—1947-52
W.A.C. Bennett—Social Credit—1952-72
David Barrett—New Democratic Party—1972-5
William Richards Bennett—Social Credit—1975-86
William Vander Zalm—Social Credit—1986-

Alberta
Alexander Cameron Rutherford—Liberal—1905-10
Arthur Lewis Sifton—Liberal—1910-17
Charles Stewart—Liberal—1917-21
Herbert Greenfield—United Farmers of Alberta—1921-5
John Edward Brownlee—United Farmers of Alberta—1925-34
Richard Gavin Reid—United Farmers of Alberta—1934-5
William Aberhart—Social Credit—1935-43
Ernest Charles Manning—Social Credit—1943-68
Harry Edwin Strom—Social Credit—1968-71
Peter Lougheed—Progressive Conservative—1971-86
Don Getty—Progressive Conservative—1986-

Saskatchewan
T. Walter Scott—Liberal—1905-16
William M. Martin—Liberal—1916-22
Charles A. Dunning—Liberal—1922-6
James G. Gardiner—Liberal—1926-9
James T. M. Anderson—Conservative—1929-34
James G. Gardiner —Liberal—1934-5
William J. Patterson—Liberal—1935-44
Thomas C. Douglas—Co-operative Commonwealth Federation—1944-61
Woodrow S. Lloyd—Co-operative Commonwealth Federation-New Democratic
Party—1961-4
W. Ross Thatcher—Liberal—1964-71
Allan E. Blakeney—New Democratic Party—1971-82
D. Grant Devine—Progressive Conservative—1982-

Manitoba
Alfred Boyd—1870-1
Marc A. Girard—1871-2
Henry J. Clarke—1872-4
Marc A. Girard—1874
Robert A. Davis—1874-8
John Norquay—1878-87
David H. Harrison—1887-8
Thomas Greenway—Liberal—1888-1900
Hugh John Macdonald—Conservative—1900
Rodmond P. Roblin—Conservative—1900-15
Tobias C. Norris—Liberal—1915-22
John Bracken—United Farmers of Manitoba—1922-8
John Bracken—Coalition—1928-42
Stuart S. Garson—Coalition—1942-8
Douglas L. Campbell—Coalition—1948-58
Dufferin Roblin—Progressive Conservative—1958-67
Walter C. Weir—Progressive Conservative—1967-9
Edward R. Schreyer—New Democratic Party—1969-77
Sterling Lyon—Progressive Conservative—1977-81
Howard Pawley—New DemocraticParty—1981-88
Gary Filmon—Progressive Conservative—1988-

Ontario

John Sandfield Macdonald—Liberal-Conservative—1867-71
Edward Blake—Liberal—1871-2
Oliver Mowat—Liberal—1872-96
Arthur Sturgis Hardy—Liberal—1896-9
George William Ross—Liberal—1899-1905
James Pliny Whitney—Conservative—1905-14
William Howard Hearst—Conservative—1914-19
Ernest Charles Drury—United Farmers of Ontario—1919-23
George Howard Ferguson—Conservative—1923-30
George Stewart Henry—Conservative—1930-4
Mitchell Frederick Hepburn—Liberal—1934-42
Gordon Daniel Conant—Liberal—1942-3
Harry Corwin Nixon—Liberal—1943
George Alexander Drew—Progressive Conservative—1943-8
Thomas Laird Kennedy—Progressive Conservative—1948-9
Leslie Miscampbell Frost—Progressive Conservative—1949-61
John Parmenter Robarts—Progressive Conservative—1961-71
William Grenville Davis—Progressive Conservative—1971-85
Frank Miller—Progressive Conservative—1985
David Peterson—Liberal—1985-

Quebec

Pierre-Joseph-Olivier Chauveau—Conservative—1867-73
Gédéon Ouimet—Conservative—1873-4
Charles-Eugène Boucher de Boucherville—Conservative—1874-8
Henri-Gustave Joly de Lotbinière—Liberal—1878-9
Joseph-Adolphe Chapleau—Conservative—1879-82
Joseph-Alfred Mousseau—Conservative—1882-4
John Jones Ross—Conservative—1884-7
Louis-Oliver Taillon—Conservative—1887
Honoré Mercier—Liberal—1887-91
Charles-Eugène Boucher de Boucherville—Conservative—1891-2
Louis-Oliver Taillon—Conservative—1892-6
Edmund James Flynn—Conservative—1896-7
Félix-Gabriel Marchand—Liberal—1897-1900
Simon-Napoléon Parent—Liberal—1900-5
Jean-Lomer Gouin—Liberal—1905-20
Louis-Alexandre Taschereau—Liberal—1920-36
Joseph-Adélard Godbout—Liberal—1936
Maurice Duplessis—Union Nationale—1936-9
Joseph-Adélard Godbout-Liberal—1939-44
Maurice Duplessis—Union Nationale—1944-59
Paul Sauvé—Union Nationale—1959-60
J. Antonio Barrette—Union Nationale—1960
Jean Lesage—Liberal—1960-6
Daniel Johnson—Union Nationale—1966-8
Jean-Jacques Bertrand—Union Nationale—1968-70
Robert Bourassa—Liberal—1970-6
René Lévesque—Parti Québécois—1976-85
Pierre-Marc Johnson—Parti Québécois—1985
Robert Bourassa—Liberal—1985-

New Brunswick
Peter Mitchell—1866-7
Andrew Rainsford Wetmore—1867-70
George Luther Hatheway—1871-2
George Edwin King—1872-8
John James Fraser—1878-82
Daniel Lionel Hanington—1882-3
Andrew George Blair—Liberal—1883-96
James Mitchell—Liberal—1896-7
Henry Robert Emmerson—Liberal—1897-1900
Lemuel John Tweedie—Liberal—1900-7
William Pugsley—Liberal—1907
Clifford William Robinson—Liberal—1907-8
John Douglas Hazen—Conservative—1908-11
James Kidd Flemming—Conservative—1911-14
George Johnson Clarke—Conservative—1914-17
James Alexander Murray—Conservative—1917
Walter Edward Foster—Liberal—1917-23
Peter John Veniot—Liberal—1923-5
John Baxter—Conservative—1925-31
Charles Dow Richards—Conservative—1931-3
Leonard Tilley—Conservative—1933-5
A. Allison Dysart—Liberal—1935-40
John Babbitt McNair—Liberal—1940-52
Hugh John Fleming—Progressive Conservative—1952-60
Louis J. Robichaud—Liberal—1960-70
Richard B. Hatfield—Progressive Conservative—1970-87
Frank McKenna—Liberal—1987-

Nova Scotia
Hiram Blanchard—Liberal—1867
William Annand—Anti-Confederation—1867-75
Philip Carteret Hill—Liberal—1875-8
Simon Hugh Holmes—Conservative—1878-82
John Thompson—Conservative—1882
William Thomas Pipes—Liberal—1882-4
William Stevens Fielding—Liberal—1884-96
George Henry Murray—Liberal—1896-1923
Ernest Howard Armstrong—Liberal—1923-5
Edgar Nelson Rhodes—Conservative—1925-30
Gordon Sidney Harrington—Conservative—1930-3
Angus Lewis Macdonald—Liberal—1933-40
Alexander Stirling MacMillan—Liberal—1940-5
Angus Lewis Macdonald—Liberal—1945-54
Harold Joseph Connolly—Liberal—1954
Henry Davies Hicks—Liberal—1954-6
Robert Lorne Stanfield—Progressive Conservative—1956-67
George Isaac Smith—Progressive Conservative—1967-70
Gerald A. Regan—Liberal—1970-78
John MacLennan Buchanan—Progressive Conservative—1978-

Prince Edward Island
J. C. Pope—Conservative—1873
L. C. Owen—Conservative—1873-6
L. H. Davies—Liberal—1876-9
W. W. Sullivan—Conservative—1879-89
N. McLeod—Conservative—1889-91
F. Peters—Liberal—1891-7
A. B. Warburton—Liberal—1897-8
D. Farquharson—Liberal—1898-1901
A. Peters—Liberal—1901-8
F. L. Haszard—Liberal—1908-11
H. James Palmer—Liberal—1911
John A. Mathieson—Conservative—1911-17
Aubin E. Arsenault—Conservative—1917-19
J. H. Bell—Liberal—1919-23
James D. Stewart—Conservative—1923-7
Albert C. Saunders—Liberal—1927-30
Walter M. Lea—Liberal—1930-1
James D. Stewart—Conservative—1931-3
William J. P. MacMillan—Conservative—1933-5
Walter M. Lea—Liberal—1935-6
Thane A. Campbell—Liberal—1936-43
J. Walter Jones—Liberal—1943-53
Alexander W. Matheson—Liberal—1953-9
Walter R. Shaw—Progressive Conservative—1959-66
Alexander B. Campbell—Liberal—1966-78
W. Bennett Campbell—Liberal—1978-9
J. Angus McLean—Progressive Conservative—1979-81
James M. Lee—Progressive Conservative—1981-6
Joe Ghiz—Liberal—1986-

Newfoundland
Joseph R. Smallwood—Liberal—1949-72
Frank D. Moores—Progressive Conservative—1972-9
A. Brian Peckford—Progressive Conservative—1979-

The Government of Canada in 1867

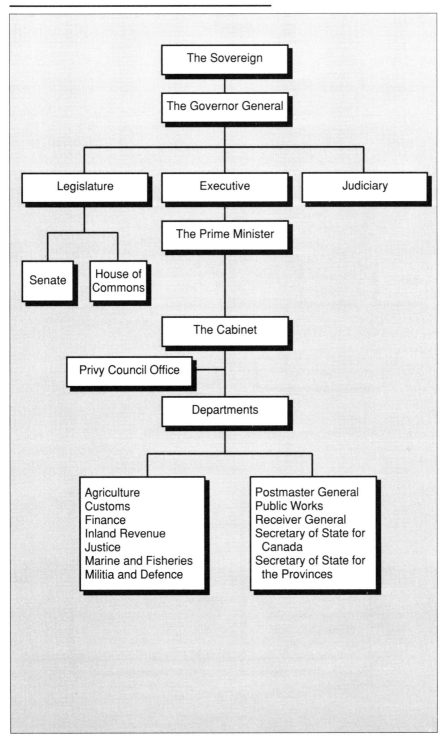

The Government of Canada in 1946

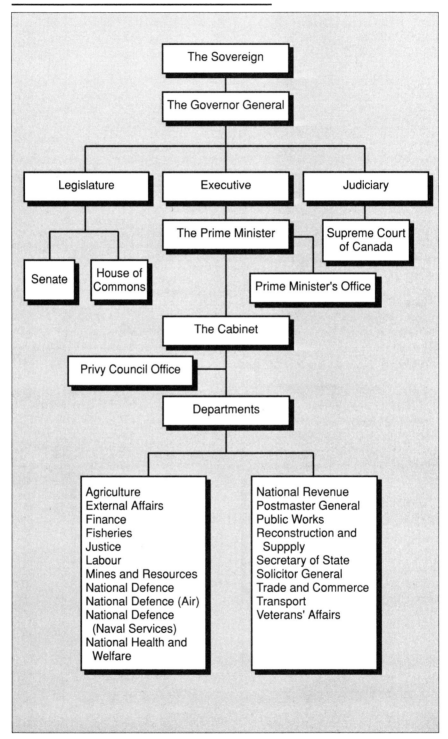

The Government of Canada in 1980

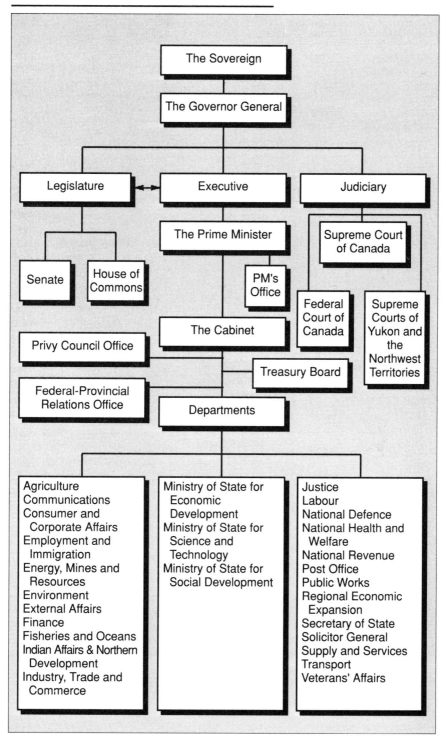

Federal Election Results

Date	Conserv-ative	Liberal	Social Credit	CCF/ NDP	Other
1867-7 Aug.-20Sept.	108	72			
1872-20 July-12 Oct.	104	96			
1874-22 Jan.	67	138			1
1878-17 Sept.	142	64			
1882-20 June	139	71			1
1887-22 Feb.	126	89			
1891-5 March	121	94			
1896-23 June	88	118			7
1900-7 Nov.	80	133			
1904-3 Nov.	75	138			1
1908-26 Oct.	85	135			1
1911-21 Sept.	134	87			
1917-17 Dec.		82			Unionist 153
1921-6 Dec.	50	116			5 (Progressive 64)
1925-29 Oct.	116	99			6 (Progressive 24)
1926-14 Sept.	91	128			6 (Progressive 20)
1930-28 July	137	91			5 (Progressive 12)
1935-14 Oct.	40	173	17	7	8
1940-26 March	40	181	10	8	6
1945-11June	67	125	13	28	12
1949-27 June	41	193	10	13	5
1953-10 Aug.	51	171	15	23	5
1957-10 June	112	105	19	25	4
1958-31 March	208	49		8	
1962-18 June	116	100	30	19	
1963-18 April	95	129	24	17	
1965-8 Nov.	97	131	5	21	2 (Créditiste 9)
1968-25 June	72	155		22	1 (Créditiste 14)
1972-30 Oct.	107	109	15	31	2
1974-8 July	95	141	11	16	1
1979-22 May	136	114	6	26	
1980-18 Feb.	103	146		32	
1984	211	40		30	1

Political Evolution of Canada

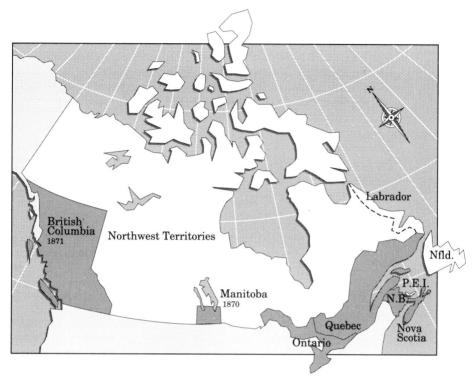

Canada in 1871

Source: D.G.G. Kerr, A Historical Atlas of Canada (1966)

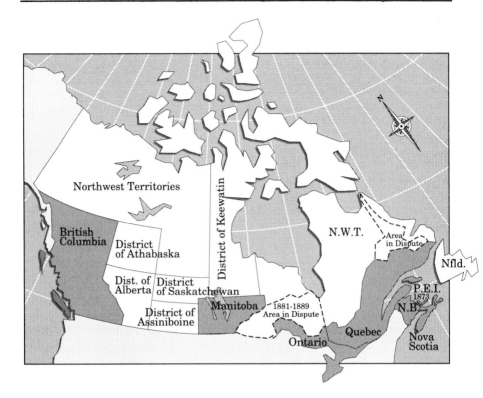

Canada in 1882

Source: D.G.G. Kerr, A Historical Atlas of Canada (1966)

Canada in 1898

Source: D.G.G. Kerr, A Historical Atlas of Canada (1966)

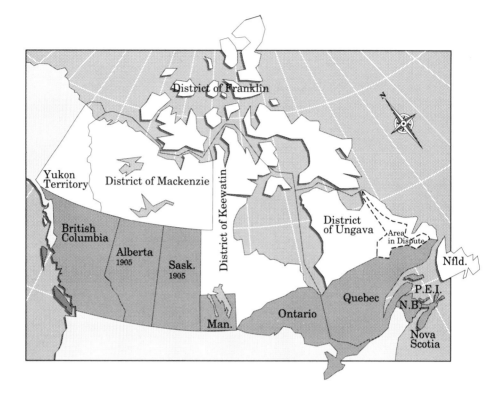

Canada in 1905

Source: D.G.G. Kerr, A Historical Atlas of Canada (1966)

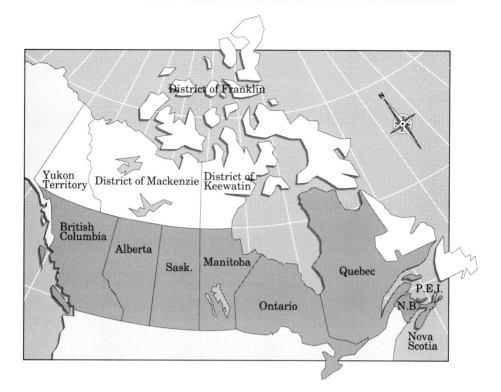

Canada in 1931

Source: D.G.G. Kerr, A Historical Atlas of Canada (1966)

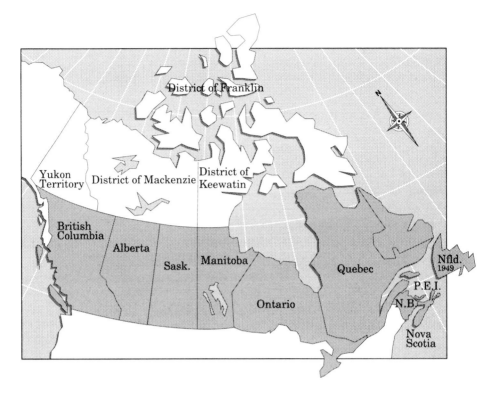

Canada in 1949

Source: D.G.G. Kerr, A Historical Atlas of Canada (1966)

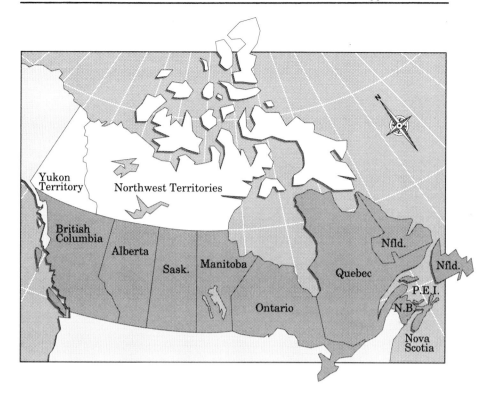

Canada in 1987

Source: Energy, Mines and Resources, National Atlas of Canada, 5th ed.

Distances Between Major Canadian Cities

(Distance by Highway and Ferry in km)

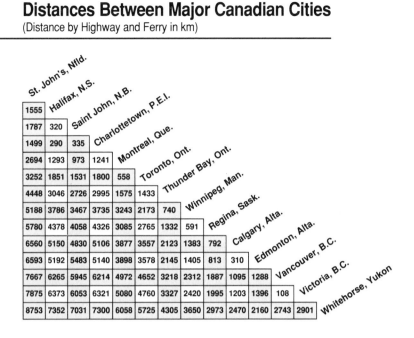

St. John's, Nfld.	Halifax, N.S.	Saint John, N.B.	Charlottetown, P.E.I.	Montreal, Que.	Toronto, Ont.	Thunder Bay, Ont.	Winnipeg, Man.	Regina, Sask.	Calgary, Alta.	Edmonton, Alta.	Vancouver, B.C.	Victoria, B.C.	Whitehorse, Yukon
1555													
1787	320												
1499	290	335											
2694	1293	973	1241										
3252	1851	1531	1800	558									
4448	3046	2726	2995	1575	1433								
5188	3786	3467	3735	3243	2173	740							
5780	4378	4058	4326	3085	2765	1332	591						
6560	5150	4830	5106	3877	3557	2123	1383	792					
6593	5192	5483	5140	3898	3578	2145	1405	813	310				
7667	6265	5945	6214	4972	4652	3218	2312	1887	1095	1288			
7875	6373	6053	6321	5080	4760	3327	2420	1995	1203	1396	108		
8753	7352	7031	7300	6058	5725	4305	3650	2973	2470	2160	2743	2901	

Source: The Canadian Pocket Encyclopedia, 32nd ed. (author's calculations)

Land Area Comparisons

(Canada and the World, Total Area in Thousands of km²)

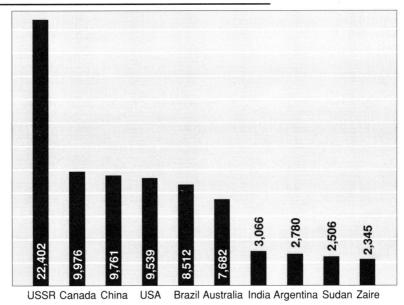

USSR	Canada	China	USA	Brazil	Australia	India	Argentina	Sudan	Zaire
22,402	9,976	9,761	9,539	8,512	7,682	3,066	2,780	2,506	2,345

Source: Victor Showers, World Facts and Figures (New York, 1979) p. 187

Land Area Comparison by Province

(Total Area in km²)

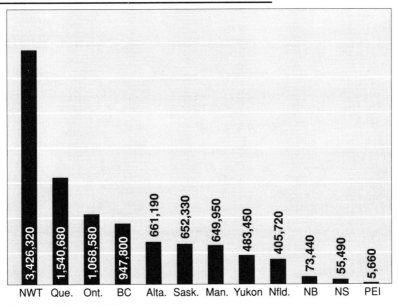

NWT	Que.	Ont.	BC	Alta.	Sask.	Man.	Yukon	Nfld.	NB	NS	PEI
3,426,320	1,540,680	1,068,580	947,800	661,190	652,330	649,950	483,450	405,720	73,440	55,490	5,660

Source: Canada Year Book, 1985

Geographic Distribution of Industry by Output
(Percentages of Canadian Output of Manufactured Goods by Provinces-1968)

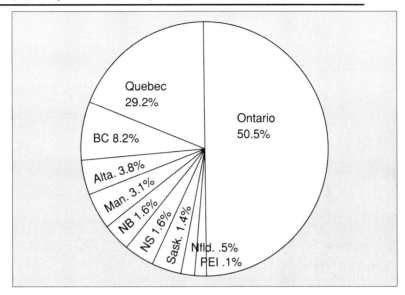

Source: James Peters, A Guide to Understanding Canada (1968), p. 42.

Immigration to Canada

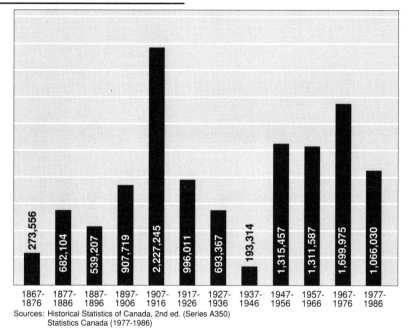

273,556	682,104	539,207	907,719	2,227,245	996,011	693,367	193,314	1,315,457	1,311,587	1,699,975	1,066,030
1867-1876	1877-1886	1887-1896	1897-1906	1907-1916	1917-1926	1927-1936	1937-1946	1947-1956	1957-1966	1967-1976	1977-1986

Sources: Historical Statistics of Canada, 2nd ed. (Series A350)
Statistics Canada (1977-1986)

Rural-Urban Population
(Thousands)

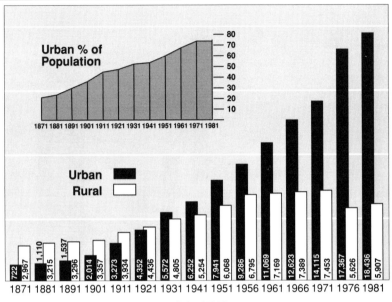

Sources: Historical Statistics of Canada, 2nd ed. (Series A67-69)
1981 Census of Canada, Cat. 92-901;
Inset from 1981 Census of Canada, Urban Growth in Canada, Cat. 99-942

Union Membership in Canada
(Total Union Membership in Thousands)

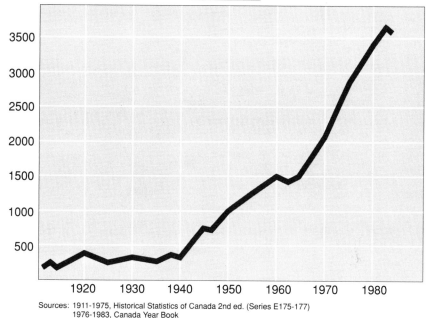

Sources: 1911-1975, Historical Statistics of Canada 2nd ed. (Series E175-177)
1976-1983, Canada Year Book

Strikes and Lockouts
(A: Number of Strikes and Lockouts; B: Average Days Lost per Worker)

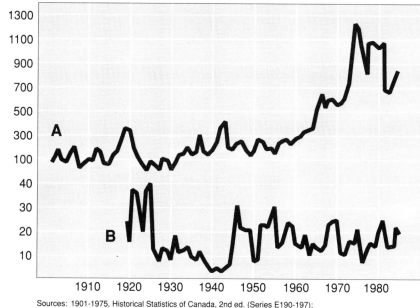

Sources: 1901-1975, Historical Statistics of Canada, 2nd ed. (Series E190-197);
1975-1985, Labour Canada, Strikes and Lockouts in Canada (author's calculations)

The Development of Major Labour Federations

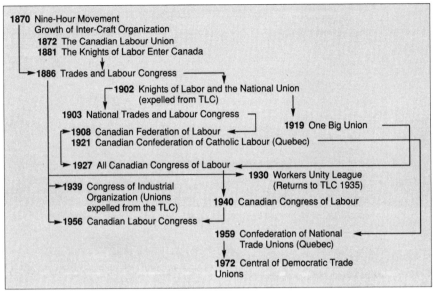

Source: Joseph Smucker, Industrialization in Canada, Scarborough, Prentice-Hall, 1980, p. 211

The Canadian Labour Force

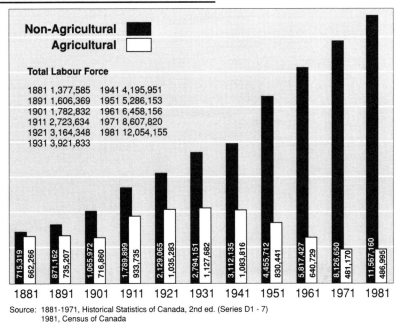

Total Labour Force			
1881	1,377,585	1941	4,195,951
1891	1,606,369	1951	5,286,153
1901	1,782,832	1961	6,458,156
1911	2,723,634	1971	8,607,820
1921	3,164,348	1981	12,054,155
1931	3,921,833		

Source: 1881-1971, Historical Statistics of Canada, 2nd ed. (Series D1 - 7)
1981, Census of Canada

The Canadian Labour Force

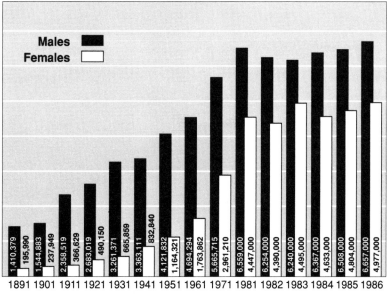

Sources: 1891-1901, Canada Year Book; 1911-1971, Historical Statistics of Canada, 2nd ed. (Series D8 - 85);
1981, Canada Year Book; 1982-1986, Statistics Canada

Female Labour Force Participation Rate 1959 - 1984
(Percentage)

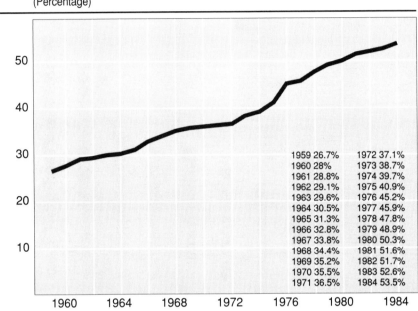

1959 26.7%	1972 37.1%
1960 28%	1973 38.7%
1961 28.8%	1974 39.7%
1962 29.1%	1975 40.9%
1963 29.6%	1976 45.2%
1964 30.5%	1977 45.9%
1965 31.3%	1978 47.8%
1966 32.8%	1979 48.9%
1967 33.8%	1980 50.3%
1968 34.4%	1981 51.6%
1969 35.2%	1982 51.7%
1970 35.5%	1983 52.6%
1971 36.5%	1984 53.5%

Sources: 1959-1975, Historical Statistics of Canada 2nd ed. (Series D431 - 448);
1975-1984, Labour Canada, Women in the Labour Force

Federal Civil Service Growth

(Thousands of Employees)

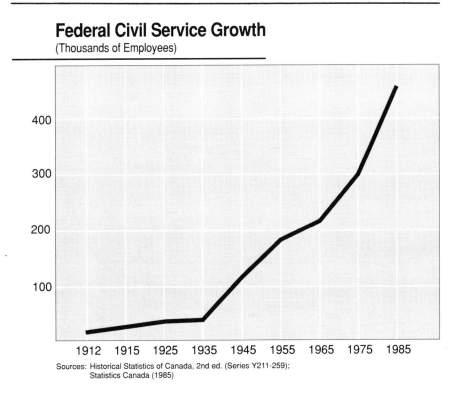

Sources: Historical Statistics of Canada, 2nd ed. (Series Y211-259);
Statistics Canada (1985)

Federal Government Revenues by Source

(percentage)

Year	Personal Income Tax	Corporate Income Tax	Excise & Customs Duties	Other
1867	—	—	85.7	14.3
1891	—	—	75.7	24.3
1911	—	—	76.5	23.5
1918	.25	.003	56.5	33.25
1929	5.9	9.2	53.9	34
1945	22.8	7.2	10.5	59.3
1960	31.2	22.2	13.6	33
1975	42.4	19.1	9	29.5
1985	41	13	26	20

The Cost of Living
(The Consumer Price Index for Canada 1971=100)

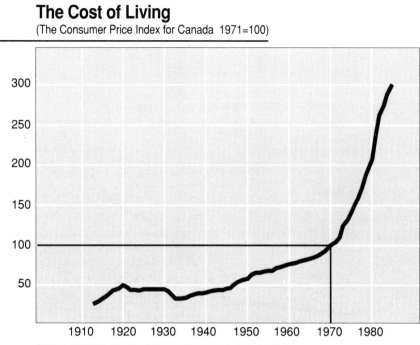

Sources: 1913-1975, Historical Statistics of Canada 2nd ed. (Series K8-18)
        1975-1985, The Consumer Price Index for Canada (author's calculations)

Distribution of Wealth

(1941, 1961, 1981)

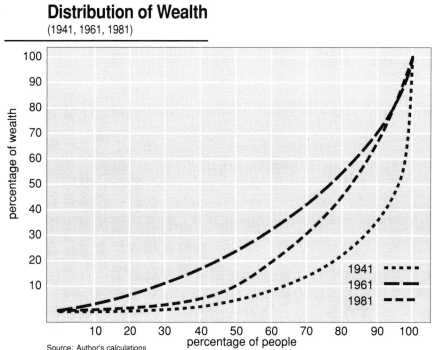

Source: Author's calculations

Gross Domestic Product
(Millions of Dollars)

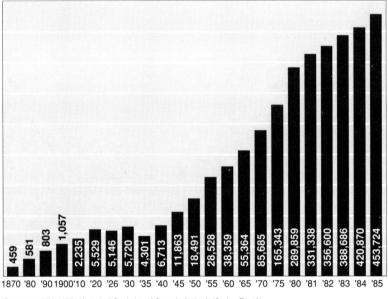

1870	459
'80	581
'90	803
1900	1,057
'10	2,235
'20	5,529
'26	5,146
'30	5,720
'35	4,301
'40	6,713
'45	11,863
'50	18,491
'55	28,528
'60	38,359
'65	55,364
'70	85,685
'75	165,343
'80	289,859
'81	331,338
'82	356,600
'83	388,686
'84	420,870
'85	453,724

Sources: 1870-1975, Historical Statistics of Canada 2nd ed. (Series F1-13)
1975-1985, Statistics Canada

Exports and Imports
(Millions of Dollars)

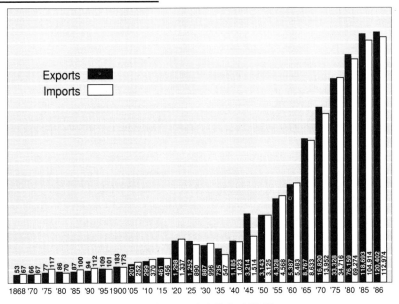

1868 '70 '75 '80 '85 '90 '95 1900 '05 '10 '15 '20 '25 '30 '35 '40 '45 '50 '55 '60 '65 '70 '75 '80 '85 '86

Source: 1868-1965, Historical Statistics of Canada, 2nd ed. (Series G381-85)
1970-1985, Dept. of Regional Industrial Expansion, Commodity Trade by Industrial Sector
1986, Statistical Survey of Canada

Exports and Imports of Principal Products

Year	Imports: $000	Exports: $000
1890	Woollen Goods 10,901 Coal 8,013 Sugar 6,453 Rolling-Mill Products 5,646 Cotton Goods 3,793 Raw Cotton 3,539 Tea 3,074 Grain & Grain Products 3,034 Fruits 2,401 Machinery (except farm) 1,878	Planks & Boards 17,637 Cheese 9,372 Fish 8,100 Cattle 6,949 Barley 4,600 Square Timber 4,354 Coal 2,448 Raw Furs 1,847 Fruits 1,074 Hay 1,069
1920	Sugar 73,618 Coal 60,073 Cotton Goods 49, 088 Woollen Goods 45,545 Rolling-Mill Products 39,986 Machinery (except farm) 36,717 Raw Cotton 33,854 Fruits 33,463 Hides and Skins 22,654 Crude Petroleum 20,307	Wheat 185,045 Meats 96,161 Wheat Flour 94,263 Planks & Boards 75,216 Newsprint 53,640 Cattle 46,065 Wood Pulp 41,383 Fish 40,687 Cheese 36,337 Sugar and Products 30,695 Furs 20,628
1950	Petroleum and Products 307,963 Machinery (except farm) 226,249 Coal 174,764 Farm Implements and Machinery 161,642 Automobile Parts 158,405 Rolling-Mill Products 93,639 Fruits 90,986 Raw Cotton 90,561 Sugar 86,945 Automobiles 85,917	Newsprint 485,746 Wheat 325,614 Planks and Boards 290,847 Wood Pulp 208,556 Fish 112,718 Aluminium & Products 106,867 Nickel 105,300 Wheat Flour 93,839 Farm Implements and Machinery 87,811 Copper 87,587 Cattle 79,126

Year	Imports: $000	Exports: $000
1980	Machinery 8,952,608 Motor Vehicle Parts 7,868,322 Crude Petroleum 6,919,053 Electronic Products 6,083,200 Motor Vehicles 5,617,092 Primary Metal 3,889,407 Food 3,315,470 Chemicals 3,586,975 Mining 3,003,462 Fabricated Metal Products 2,392,646	Motor Vehicles 7,368,422 Metal Smelting and Refining 4,762,207 Wood Products 4,071,139 Natural Gas 3,983,850 Wood Pulp 3,872,994 Wheat 3,861,718 Newsprint 3,694,402 Motor Vehicle Parts 3,646,427 Machinery 3,271,845 Chemicals 3,169,621 Crude Petroleum 2,899,099
1985	Motor Vehicle Parts 18,220,852 Motor Vehicles 14,023,728 Electronic Products 11,626,864 Machinery 9,948,568 Chemicals 5,578,437 Primary Metal 4,512,515 Food 3,869,418 Crude Petroleum 3,700,365 Fabricated Metal Products 3,196,834 Mining 2,517,471	Motor Vehicles 22,333,648 Motor Vehicle Parts 11,271,419 Crude Petroleum 5,916,516 Electronic Products 5,775,059 Wood Products 5,699,462 Newsprint 5,444,724 Chemicals 4,507,674 Food 4,246,147 Natural Gas 3,912,250 Wheat 3,778,603 Pulp 3,399,129

Sources: 1890, 1920, 1950, Canada Year Book;
      1980, 1985, Department of Regional Industrial Expansion, Commodity Trade by Industrial Sector

Principal Products of Canada in 1885

(Figures are 1885 Exports in $000)

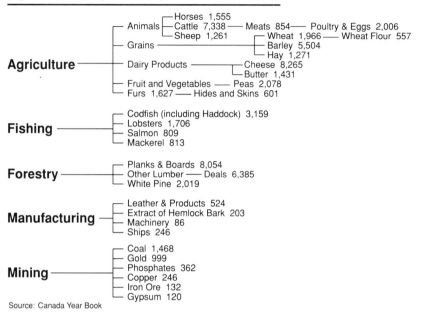

Agriculture
- Animals
  - Horses 1,555
  - Cattle 7,338 —— Meats 854 —— Poultry & Eggs 2,006
  - Sheep 1,261
- Grains
  - Wheat 1,966 —— Wheat Flour 557
  - Barley 5,504
  - Hay 1,271
- Dairy Products
  - Cheese 8,265
  - Butter 1,431
- Fruit and Vegetables —— Peas 2,078
- Furs 1,627 —— Hides and Skins 601

Fishing
- Codfish (including Haddock) 3,159
- Lobsters 1,706
- Salmon 809
- Mackerel 813

Forestry
- Planks & Boards 8,054
- Other Lumber —— Deals 6,385
- White Pine 2,019

Manufacturing
- Leather & Products 524
- Extract of Hemlock Bark 203
- Machinery 86
- Ships 246

Mining
- Coal 1,468
- Gold 999
- Phosphates 362
- Copper 246
- Iron Ore 132
- Gypsum 120

Source: Canada Year Book

Principal Products of Canada in 1920

(Figures are 1920 Exports in $000)

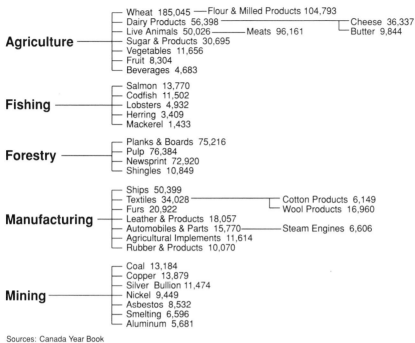

Agriculture
- Wheat 185,045 — Flour & Milled Products 104,793
- Dairy Products 56,398 ——— Cheese 36,337 / Butter 9,844
- Live Animals 50,026 ——— Meats 96,161
- Sugar & Products 30,695
- Vegetables 11,656
- Fruit 8,304
- Beverages 4,683

Fishing
- Salmon 13,770
- Codfish 11,502
- Lobsters 4,932
- Herring 3,409
- Mackerel 1,433

Forestry
- Planks & Boards 75,216
- Pulp 76,384
- Newsprint 72,920
- Shingles 10,849

Manufacturing
- Ships 50,399
- Textiles 34,028 ——— Cotton Products 6,149 / Wool Products 16,960
- Furs 20,922
- Leather & Products 18,057
- Automobiles & Parts 15,770 ——— Steam Engines 6,606
- Agricultural Implements 11,614
- Rubber & Products 10,070

Mining
- Coal 13,184
- Copper 13,879
- Silver Bullion 11,474
- Nickel 9,449
- Asbestos 8,532
- Smelting 6,596
- Aluminum 5,681

Sources: Canada Year Book
Historical Statistics of Canada, 2nd ed.

Principal Products of Canada in 1950

(Figures are 1950 Exports in $000)

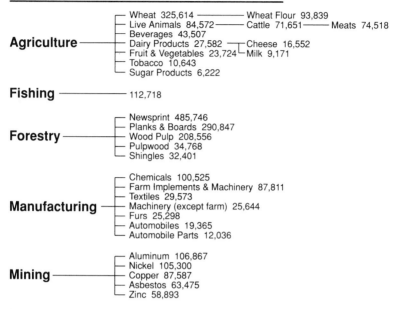

Agriculture
- Wheat 325,614 ———— Wheat Flour 93,839
- Live Animals 84,572 ———— Cattle 71,651 ———— Meats 74,518
- Beverages 43,507
- Dairy Products 27,582 ┬ Cheese 16,552
- Fruit & Vegetables 23,724 └ Milk 9,171
- Tobacco 10,643
- Sugar Products 6,222

Fishing ———— 112,718

Forestry
- Newsprint 485,746
- Planks & Boards 290,847
- Wood Pulp 208,556
- Pulpwood 34,768
- Shingles 32,401

Manufacturing
- Chemicals 100,525
- Farm Implements & Machinery 87,811
- Textiles 29,573
- Machinery (except farm) 25,644
- Furs 25,298
- Automobiles 19,365
- Automobile Parts 12,036

Mining
- Aluminum 106,867
- Nickel 105,300
- Copper 87,587
- Asbestos 63,475
- Zinc 58,893

Source: Canada Year Book

Principal Products of Canada in 1985

(Figures are 1985 Exports in $000)

Agriculture
- Wheat 3,778,603
- Live Animals 444,137 —— Meat 1,124,946
- Beverages 541,892
- Dairy Products 218,061
- Fruit & Vegetables 300,271
- Oilseeds 849,021
- Vegetable Oil 274,995

Fishing —————— 1,876,168

Forestry
- Wood Products 5,699,462
- Newsprint 5,444,724
- Pulp 3,399,129

Manufacturing
- Motor Vehicles 22,333,648
- Motor Vehicle Parts 11,271,419
- Electronic Products 5,775,059
- Chemicals 4,507,674
- Machinery 3,920,251

Mining
- Crude Petroleum 5,916,516
- Natural Gas 3,912,250
- Coal 1,996,459
- Iron 1,172,888
- Potash 946,375
- Aluminum 1,088,753

Sources: Department of Regional Industrial Expansion
Commodity Trade by Industrial Sector

Gross Value of Production
in the Manufacturing Industries
(Millions of Dollars)

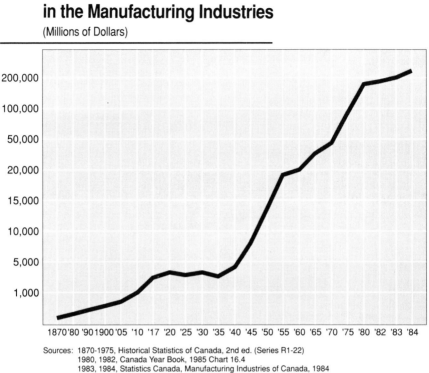

200,000	
100,000	
50,000	
20,000	
15,000	
10,000	
5,000	
1,000	

1870 '80 '90 1900 '05 '10 '17 '20 '25 '30 '35 '40 '45 '50 '55 '60 '65 '70 '75 '80 '82 '83 '84

Sources: 1870-1975, Historical Statistics of Canada, 2nd ed. (Series R1-22)
1980, 1982, Canada Year Book, 1985 Chart 16.4
1983, 1984, Statistics Canada, Manufacturing Industries of Canada, 1984

Annual Earnings of Production Workers in the Manufacturing Industries
(Thousands of Dollars)

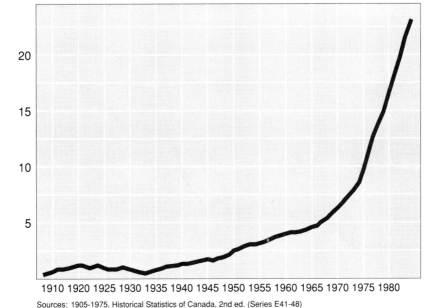

Sources: 1905-1975, Historical Statistics of Canada, 2nd ed. (Series E41-48)
1975-1984, Manufacturing Industries of Canada, National and Provincial Areas

Production and Related Workers in the Manufacturing Industries
(Thousands)

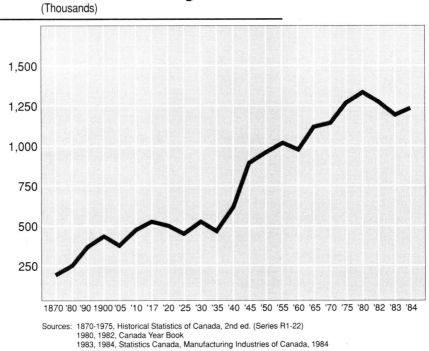

1870 '80 '90 1900 '05 '10 '17 '20 '25 '30 '35 '40 '45 '50 '55 '60 '65 '70 '75 '80 '82 '83 '84

Sources: 1870-1975, Historical Statistics of Canada, 2nd ed. (Series R1-22)
1980, 1982, Canada Year Book
1983, 1984, Statistics Canada, Manufacturing Industries of Canada, 1984

Number of Establishments in the Manufacturing Industries
(Thousands)

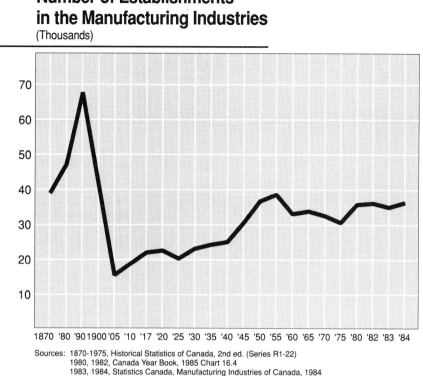

Sources: 1870-1975, Historical Statistics of Canada, 2nd ed. (Series R1-22)
1980, 1982, Canada Year Book, 1985 Chart 16.4
1983, 1984, Statistics Canada, Manufacturing Industries of Canada, 1984

Wartime Enlistments and Casualties

War	Enlisted	Killed	Wounded	POW
Boer War	7,368	89+135**	252	—
World War I				
Navy	7,000 (approx.)	225 (approx.)	?	?
Army	619,636	59,544*	172,950	2,084
World War II				
Navy	106,522	1,533+491**	319	87
Army	730,159	17,682+5,235**	52,679	6,433
Air	249,662	13,498+3,603**	1,416	2,475
Korean War				
Navy	3,621	3+6**	9	—
Army	21,940	311	1,143	30
Air	22 (operational, attached to US Air Force)			

* 1,563 airmen were killed while serving in the Royal Flying Corps
** Deaths from other than enemy action

Source: Directorate of History, Department of National Defence

Women's Enlistments and Casualties

War	Enlisted	Killed
World War I		
Nursing Sisters	2,854	21
World War II		
Navy (Wrens)	7,126	—
Army (CWACs)	21,624	—
Air (WDs)	17,467	4+3*
Nursing Sisters	4,439	1

* Deaths from other than enemy action

Source: Directorate of History, Department of National Defence
Ruth Pierson, "They're Still Women After All" (Toronto, 1986).

Sources

We have consulted hundreds of books in preparing the *Collins Dictionary of Canadian History*, and it is impossible to cite them all. Here we list only the main reference sources.

Beck, J.M. *Pendulum of Power: Canada's Federal Elections*. Toronto: Prentice-Hall, 1968.

Campbell, Colin. *Canadian Political Facts, 1945-1976*. Toronto: Methuen, 1977.

The Canadian Annual Review of Politics and Public Affairs. Edited by John Saywell. Toronto: University of Toronto Press, 1960-.

The Canadian Encyclopedia. Edited by James H. Marsh et al. Edmonton: Hurtig Publishers, 1985.

Canadian Who's Who. Toronto: University of Toronto Press. Annual volumes.

Colombo, J.R. *Colombo's Canadian References*. Toronto: Oxford University Press, 1976.

Crane, David. *A Dictionary of Canadian Economics*. Edmonton: Hurtig Publishers, 1980.

Dictionary of Canadian Biography. Edited by G.W. Brown et al. 10 vols. to date. Toronto: University of Toronto Press, 1965-.

Dictionary of Hamilton Biography. Edited by T.M. Bailey et al. 1 vol. to date. Hamilton: Dictionary of Hamilton Biography, 1981-.

Encyclopedia of Music in Canada. Edited by Hellmut Kallman et al. Toronto: University of Toronto Press, 1981.

Guide to Canadian Ministries Since Confederation, July 1, 1867-February 1, 1982. Ottawa: Supply and Services Canada, 1982.

Hopkins, J. Castel. *The Canadian Annual Review*. Toronto. Annual from 1902 to 1937-8.

Johnson, J.K., ed. *The Canadian Directory of Parliament, 1867-1967*. Ottawa: Public Archives of Canada, 1968.

Klinck, Carl F., gen. ed. *Literary History of Canada*. 3 vols. Toronto: University of Toronto Press, 1976.

Lazarus, Morden. *Up From the Ranks: Trade Union VIPs Past and Present*. Don Mills: Cooperative Press Associates, 1977.

Morgan, Henry J., ed. *The Canadian Men and Women of the Time. . . .* 2nd ed. Toronto, 1912.

Story, Norah. *The Oxford Companion to Canadian History and Literature*. Toronto: Oxford University Press, 1967.

Toye, William, gen. ed. *The Oxford Companion to Canadian Literature*. Toronto: Oxford University Press, 1983.

Toye, William, gen. ed. *Supplement to the Oxford Companion to Canadian History and Literature*. Toronto: Oxford University Press, 1973.

Wallace, W. Stewart. *The Macmillan Dictionary of Canadian Biography.* Edited by W.A. McKay. Toronto: Macmillan, 1978.

Who's Who in Canada. Toronto: International Press. Annual or biennial vols.

The Writers' Union of Canada: A Directory of Members. Edited by Ted Whittaker. Toronto: The Writers' Union of Canada, 1981.